The Gallipoli campaign of 1915 was the ill-fated brainchild of Winston Churchill, then First Lord of the Admiralty. In an attempt to unlock the stalemate of trench warfare on the Western Front of France and Belgium, he persuaded the British Government to support an attack against Turkey, whose defeat might weaken the German alliance and which could open up the Dardanelles waterway for use by Russia. Hastily planned and inadequately resourced, this was a chapter of military failure in which 50,000 British and colonial troops were killed.

The South Wales Borderers took part in this campaign and fought with great distinction in the most appalling conditions. This is their story, which is based on Regimental records and personal diaries, a number of which have never been published before. The author – a former Army officer - has weaved together a fascinating and compelling account which follows the highs and lows, as well as the hopes and fears, of an infantry battalion on active service. Meticulously researched, this journey across the battlefields of Gallipoli adds a new and different dimension to the traditional style of books written on one of the most dramatic campaigns in British military history.

Having grown up in East Africa and Mauritius, Lieutenant Colonel Rodney Ashwood was educated in Kenya and at the Royal Military Academy Sandhurst. Commissioned into the Welch Regiment in 1964, he served in the UK, Hong Kong, Canada, Cyprus, and Germany as well as active service in Northern Ireland. During his career he studied the history of his regimental predecessors who took part in such dramatic conflicts as the Zulu War of 1879 and the Gallipoli campaign of 1915. He took early retirement from the Army in 1993 to become the curator of his regimental museum where he developed his interest in military history further. In 2005 his first book *For Queen and Country, the Zulu War Diary of Lieutenant Wilfred Heaton the 24th Regiment of Foot* was published. Now retired, he lectures regularly on military subjects and he is a member of the Gallipoli Association. He has toured the battlefields of Gallipoli in preparation for this book. He lives with his wife in Brecon and has a son and daughter. His other interests include running a bed and breakfast business, ex-Servicemen's welfare, following equestrian three-day events and supporting Welsh rugby football.

Author photo © 2015 Jason Ashwood

DUTY NOBLY DONE

In my view, some of the best, toughest and most generous soldiers in the British Army come from Wales. It has been my privilege, and that of my family, to have served with them.

Major General Lennox Napier
Colonel of the Regiment 1983–1989

This book is dedicated to their memory

DUTY NOBLY DONE

The South Wales Borderers at Gallipoli 1915

Rodney Ashwood

Helion & Company

By the same author: *For Queen and Country – the Zulu War Diary of Lieutenant Wilfred Heaton 24th Regiment of Foot 1879*

Helion & Company Limited
26 Willow Road
Solihull
West Midlands
B91 1UE
England
Tel. 0121 705 3393
Fax 0121 711 4075
Email: info@helion.co.uk
Website: www.helion.co.uk
Twitter: @helionbooks
Visit our blog http://blog.helion.co.uk/

Published by Helion & Company 2017
Designed and typeset by Mary Woolley, Battlefield Design (www.battlefield-design.co.uk)
Cover designed by Paul Hewitt, Battlefield Design (www.battlefield-design.co.uk)
Printed by Short Run Press, Exeter, Devon

Text © Rodney Ashwood 2017
Images and maps © as individually credited
Material in appendices © Regimental Museum of the Royal Welsh 2015

Front cover: Casualty evacuation through the trenches at Gallipoli (IWM Q13325).
Rear cover: The grave of Private Llewellyn Jenkins SWB at Skew Bridge Cemetery, Gallipoli (Author's photo).

ISBN 978-1-911512-17-2

British Library Cataloguing-in-Publication Data.
A catalogue record for this book is available from the British Library.

For details of other military history titles published by Helion & Company Limited contact the above address, or visit our website: http://www.helion.co.uk.

We always welcome receiving book proposals from prospective authors.

Contents

List of Photographs — viii

List of Maps — x

List of Abbreviations — xi

Order of Battle — xiv

Chronology of Main Events — xviii

Foreword by Major General L A H Napier CB OStJ OBE MC DL — xxiv

Introduction — xxvii

1. The Road to Gallipoli — 31
2. Men of Harlech — 41
3. Battle Plans — 54
4. The First Invasion — 66
5. Krithia — 85
6. Gully Ravine — 112
7. The Fourth Battalion — 132
8. Suvla Bay — 148
9. Autumn Stalemate — 184
10. The Final Decision — 206
11. Evacuation — 227
12. Regimental Comrades — 256

Epilogue — 270

Appendix I: Officers of the 2nd Bn South Wales Borderers who served at Gallipoli 25 April 1915–8 January 1916 — 282

Appendix II: Officers and Soldiers of the 2nd Bn South Wales Borderers who were killed, or died of their wounds, during the Gallipoli campaign — 299

Appendix III: Officers of the 4th Bn South Wales Borderers who served at Gallipoli 11 July 1915–8 January 1916 — 313

SWB Officers on the staff of HQ 40 Infantry Brigade at Gallipoli — 321

Appendix IV: Officers and Soldiers of the 4th Bn South Wales Borderers who were killed, or died of their wounds, during the Gallipoli campaign — 323

Postscript — 329

Select Bibliography — 330

Index — 332

List of Photographs

Image 1. An infantry battalion in 1915 (Author). xv
Image 2. Officers of the 4th Battalion SWB – May 1915 (R Welsh Museum). xxv
Image 3. Ernest as a Lance Corporal (Mrs F Voelcker). 49
Image 4. On promotion to Colour Sergeant (Mrs F Voelcker). 49
Image 5. On promotion to Company Sergeant Major (WO2) (Mrs F Voelcker). 51
Image 6. Ernest as the Regimental Sergeant Major at a battalion sports day (Mrs F Voelcker). 51
Image 7. RSM Laman with the Colours of 1 SWB in India 1909 (Royal Welsh Museum). 53
Image 8. The approach to S Beach across Morto Bay (Author). 67
Image 9. S Beach and the slopes up to de Totts Battery – now marked by the Turkish War Memorial (Author). 68
Image 10. Lieutenant Colonel (later Brigadier General) Hugh Casson, CO 2 SWB at the start of the campaign (R Welsh Museum). 69
Image 11. Major Edward Margesson, 2 SWB, killed at S Beach on 25 April 1915 (Major H Margesson). 71
Image 12. Captain Desmond Somerville 2 SWB, who was awarded the MC for his actions on 25 April 1915 (Sir Nicholas Somerville). 71
Image 13. V Beach from the Helles Memorial. The SS *River Clyde* was beached close to the small headland in the middle distance (Author). 79
Image 14. V Beach close to the location where the troops came ashore from the SS *River Clyde* (Author). 80
Image 15. Lieutenant Rupert Inglis 2 SWB who died from his wounds on 29 June 1915 (R Welsh Museum). 113
Image 16. Captain Hugh Fowler 2 SWB who was awarded the DSO for his outstanding bravery on the night of 18 June 1915 (Mrs J Copping). 118
Image 17. The view north to Suvla Bay from the heights of Chunuk Bair. Damakjelik Spur is in the lower middle foreground (Author). 149
Image 18. Anzac Cove (Author). 152
Image 19. Lieutenant Colonel Franklin Gillespie CO 4 SWB who was killed at Damakjelik Spur on 9 August 1915 (R Welsh Museum). 159
Image 20. Major Sir William Napier 4 SWB who was killed on 13 August 1915 (Major General LAH Napier). 161
Image 21. The grave of Major Sir William Napier at 7 Field Ambulance Cemetery. The stone shows his original rank prior to re-enlistment for the Gallipoli campaign (Major MJ Everett). 163
Image 22. The Helles Memorial which commemorates the 19,000 British servicemen who have no known grave at Gallipoli, 423 of whom are South Wales Borderers (Author). 216
Image 23. The memorial to Colonel Mustafa Kemal at Chunuk Bair in honour of the Turkish war dead (Author). 216

Image 24. Casualty evacuation through a communications trench on the peninsula (IWM Q 3225).   219

Image 25. Taking a break – life in the trenches (V Godrich).   224

Image 26. Captain Charles Kitchin 4 SWB, who was awarded the DSO for exemplary service throughout the Gallipoli campaign (Mrs A Payne).   225

Image 27. The lineage of the Royal Welsh since 1689 (R Welsh Museum).   259

Image 28. 5th Battalion Welsh Regiment at Suvla Bay in August 1915 (R Welsh Museum).   262

Image 29. Presentation of medals at the Barracks Brecon in July 1919. Note the contingent of Womens Army Auxiliary Corps (WAAC) also on parade (Mrs J Copping).   265

Image 30. Battalion soldiers and ex servicemen falling in for the Brecon peace festivities in July 1919 (Mrs J Copping).   266

Image 31. 4 SWB on parade in Woking prior to embarking for Gallipoli in 1915 (R Welsh Museum).   267

Image 32. 4 SWB parade through Brecon in 1919 prior to disbandment after Gallipoli (R Welsh Museum).   268

Image 33. Ernest with his wife Sybil and their two sons Freddie and Bertie (Mrs F Voelcker).   274

Image 34. Ernest as a member of the Army Revolver XXX at Bisley in 1913 – fifth from left, centre row (Mrs F Voelcker).   274

Image 35. Captain Ernest Laman at the Depot in Brecon in 1928 – third from the right, front row (R Welsh Museum).   276

Image 36. Ernest admiring the garden at home in Dinas Powis South Wales (Mrs F Voelcker).   276

Image 37. Ernest with family and friends at Dinas Powis (Mrs F Voelcker).   277

Image 38. Ernest in pensive mood, recalling duty nobly done (Mrs F Voelcker).   278

List of Maps

Map 1.   The area of the Gallipoli operations (Cassell and Coy Ltd).   xx

Map 2.   The Gallipoli Peninsula (RWF Museum).   xxi

Map 3.   The Anzac sector (RWF Museum).   xxii

Map 4.   Suvla Bay (RWF Museum).   xxiii

Map 5.   A sketch map of Cape Helles by Captain Desmond Somerville (Sir Nicholas
Somerville).   74

Map 6.   The advance on Krithia April–May 1915 (Medici Society Ltd).   75

Map 7.   Gully Ravine – the Boomerang June 1915 (Medici Society Ltd).   126

Map 8.   Gully Ravine – British trench layout (Medici Society Ltd).   127

Map 9.   4 SWB at Damakjelik Bair – August 1915 (Medici Society Ltd).   156

Map 10. 4 SWB at Hill 60 on 21–22 August 1915 (Medici Society Ltd).   157

Map 11. The front line at Suvla Bay August – December 1915 (Medici Society Ltd).   164

Map 12. Sketch Map by Captain Kitchin of the Sari Bair operations August 1915 (Mrs A
Payne).   165

Map 13. Sketch Map by Captain Kitchin showing the dispositions of C Company 4 SWB
on 9 August 1915 (Mrs A Payne).   170

Map 14. Sketch Map by Captain Kitchin of Suvla Bay August 1915 (Mrs A Payne).   171

Map 15. Sketch Map by Captain Kitchin of the four sections of IX Corps at Suvla Bay
(Mrs A Payne).   178

Map 16. Sketch Map by Captain Kitchin of the Suvla front – B section trench plan (Mrs
A Payne).   179

Map 17. Sketch Map by Captain Kitchin of VIII Army Corps forward area at Cape Helles
(Mrs A Payne).   210

Map 18. Sketch Map by Captain Kitchin of the VIII Army Corps rear area at Cape Helles
(Mrs A Payne).   211

Map 19. Sketch Map by Captain Kitchin of the Helles front trench plan – January 1916
(Mrs A Payne).   244

Map 20. The final position at Cape Helles January 1916 (Medici Society Ltd).   245

List of Abbreviations

AA	Anti-Aircraft
AAA	Telegraphic abbreviation for a full stop
AG	Adjutant General
AAG	Assistant Adjutant General
Ack	Acknowledge
Adjt	Adjutant
ADOS	Assistant Director of Ordnance Services
Ammo	Ammunition
ANZAC	Australian and New Zealand Army Corps
AOD	Advance Ordnance Depot
Arty	Artillery
Asst Adjt	Assistant Adjutant
ASC	Army Service Corps
Bde	Brigade
Bks	Barracks
BM	Brigade Major
Bn	Battalion
Brig	Brigadier
Brig Gen	Brigadier General
Bty	Battery
Capt	Captain
CGS	Chief of the General Staff
CO	Commanding Officer
Col	Colonel
Comm(s)	Communication(s)
COS	Chief of Staff
Coy	Company
Cpl	Corporal
CQMS	Company Quarter Master Sergeant
CRE	Commander Royal Engineers
CSgt	Colour Sergeant
CSM	Company Sergeant Major
DADOS	Deputy Assistant Director of Ordnance Services
DAQMG	Deputy Assistant Quarter Master General
DAAQMG	Deputy Assistant Adjutant & Quarter Master General
DCM	Distinguished Conduct Medal

Div	Division
DSO	Distinguished Service Order
Engr(s)	Engineer(s)
Fd	Field
FM	Field Marshal
FUP	Forming Up Place
Gen	General
GHQ	General Headquarters
GOC	General Officer Commanding
Gren	Grenade
HE	High Explosive
HMS	His Majesty's Ship
Hosp	Hospital
HQ	Headquarter
Inf	Infantry
JNCO	Junior Non Commissioned Officer
KOSB	Kings Own Scottish Borderers
LCpl	Lance Corporal
Lt/Lieut	Lieutenant
Lt Col	Lieutenant Colonel
Lt Gen	Lieutenant General
Maj	Major
MC	Military Cross
Medic	Medical Orderly
MG	Machine Gun
MID	Mentioned in Despatches
MM	Military Medal
MO	Medical Officer
Mor	Mortar
NCO	Non Commissioned Officer
OC	Officer Commanding
Offr	Officer
Ord	Ordnance
ORQMS	Orderly Room Quarter Master Sergeant
OR	Other Rank

Pte	Private
QM	Quartermaster
RAMC	Royal Army Medical Corps
RE	Royal Engineer
Regt	Regiment
RFC	Royal Flying Corps
RMLI	Royal Marine Light Infantry
RN	Royal Navy
RND	Royal Naval Division
RQMS	Regimental Quarter Master Sergeant
RSM	Regimental Sergeant Major
R&F	Rank and File
RV	Rendezvous
RWF	Royal Welsh Fusiliers
SAA	Small Arms Ammunition
Sect	Section
Sgt	Sergeant
SNCO	Senior Non Commissioned Officer
Sp	Support
SWB	South Wales Borderers
TA	Territorial Army
TF	Territorial Force
VC	Victoria Cross
WAAC	Womens Army Auxilliary Corps
WELSH	The Welsh Regiment
WO1	Warrant Officer Class 1
WO2	Warrant Officer Class 2
Z Hour	Zulu Hour
2IC	Second in Command
2Lt	Second Lieutenant

Order of Battle

Order of Battle (Orbat) is military terminology for a group of combat units and personnel put together for a specific operational purpose. The shape, size and structure of the orbat will depend upon the task to be undertaken, but its main component will nearly always be the infantry, for it is the infantry who ultimately win wars. To carry out its task in battle, the infantry will normally be supported by armour (but not at Gallipoli in 1915), artillery, engineers and with a logistic backup. In addition, support may also come from units of the Royal Air Force (or the Royal Flying Corps as it was known during the First World War) and the Royal Navy. As this book is based primarily upon the exploits of the South Wales Borderers, which was an infantry battalion, a brief explanation of its structure in 1915 may assist the reader who might not have a military background.

The bedrock of an infantry battalion is the rifle section. This was made up of 10 private soldiers, and was commanded by a corporal who wore two chevrons on the upper sleeve of his uniform. His second in command was a lance corporal who wore one chevron. These ranks were known as junior non-commissioned officers. Four sections were grouped together into a rifle platoon. This was commanded by a junior officer, either a second lieutenant or a lieutenant and their badges of rank were one star or two stars respectively, worn in 1915 by all officers on the lower forearm of their service dress jacket, just above the cuff. The second in command of a platoon was a sergeant, who was a senior non commissioned officer, wearing three chevrons. In addition there would be a signaller and a runner, and the platoon commander would have a batman. Of the four sections in a platoon, two would be made up of riflemen while the other two might be a machine gun section and a bomber section.

Four platoons were then grouped together into a rifle company under the command of a major whose badge of rank was a crown. His second in command was a captain wearing three stars. In addition there was another senior non commissioned officer who was the colour sergeant, who wore three chevrons surmounted by a crown and who was responsible for administration within the company; he was also known as the Company Quartermaster Sergeant. Then there was a Warrant Officer Class 2 known as the Company Sergeant Major. Responsible for discipline and as the right hand man of the company commander, he was very much the backbone of the company. His badge of rank was a large crown, worn on the forearm of his uniform.

The four companies, each almost 200 strong, made up the battalion of which a lieutenant colonel was the commanding officer. Wearing a crown and a star as his badge of rank, he had a senior major as his second in command and an adjutant, in the rank of captain, who was responsible for daily administration. Then there was a Warrant Officer Class 1. Known as the Regimental Sergeant Major he was the most senior warrant officer (but not commissioned) in the battalion, and was responsible to the commanding officer for the overall discipline of the soldiers in the battalion. His badge of rank was a Royal coat of arms worn on the forearm of his uniform. Within a battalion, majors and lieutenant colonels were known as field officers, while captains and below were company officers.

Unlike today, where an infantry battalion has a separate administrative organisation known as headquarters company, in 1915 the battalion's administration was managed by battalion

An Infantry Battalion in 1915

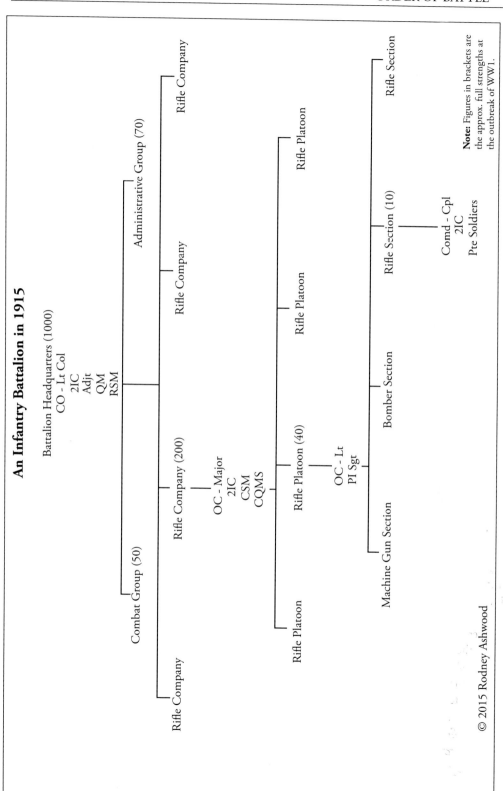

Battalion Headquarters (1000)
CO - Lt Col
2IC
Adjt
QM
RSM

Combat Group (50)

Administrative Group (70)

Rifle Company

Rifle Company (200)
OC - Major
2IC
CSM
CQMS

Rifle Company

Rifle Company

Rifle Platoon

Rifle Platoon (40)
OC - Lt
Pl Sgt

Rifle Platoon

Rifle Platoon

Machine Gun Section

Bomber Section

Rifle Section (10)
Comd - Cpl
2IC
Pte Soldiers

Rifle Section

Note: Figures in brackets are the approx. full strengths at the outbreak of WW1.

© 2015 Rodney Ashwood

Image 1. An infantry battalion in 1915 (Author).

headquarters which was divided into two rather unwieldy groups; the combat group responsible for training and operations and a logistic group which looked after all the administrative matters of the battalion. The key figure in this latter group was the quartermaster who was usually a very experienced officer, in the rank of lieutenant or captain, who had been commissioned from the ranks and about whom much more will be said in the main chapters of the book. These two groups totalled some 130 men, giving a battalion an all-up establishment of about 1,000 men. This was the theory, but the reality was quite different. In peacetime, the governmental war office could not afford to maintain battalions of this strength, so they were kept at about half this figure, but on the outbreak of war in 1914 they were built up to their full strength. Battle casualties soon reduced most battalions to at least half their size, as did sickness and disease, and the heavy toll on the lives of officers on the field of battle meant that other more junior ranks were often commanding platoons, companies and battalions way above their expected rank, until replacements became available.

A word about the connection between a regiment and a battalion. As far as the infantry is concerned the term regiment is the all embracing historical title given to a body of soldiers who wear the same cap badge – the Welch Regiment or the Royal Regiment of Wales for example. The word regiment does not have to appear in the title, as was the case with the Royal Welch Fusiliers or the South Wales Borderers. All of these former regiments are now amalgamated into the Royal Welsh; again a regiment without the actual word in its title. A regiment is then made up of a number of battalions, usually one or two regular battalions, for example the 1st Battalion the Royal Welsh and perhaps one reserve battalion, such as the 3rd Battalion the Royal Welsh. The number of battalions and their size will depend upon the manning constraints imposed by the Ministry of Defence and the operational circumstances at the time. A regiment as such does not form part of an orbat, but its battalions do and they are deployed outside their parent regiment to operate either on their own or more usually with other infantry battalions as part of a brigade as will become clear later.

There is also frequent mention throughout the coming pages of 'the staff' and 'staff officers,' the meaning of which may also benefit from some explanation. For example, at Gallipoli the 2nd Bn South Wales Borderers (2 SWB) was grouped together with three other battalions and some supporting units to form 87 Brigade. Up to 5,000 in strength – depending upon the rate of battle casualties at any given time – it was commanded by a brigadier-general, (later shortened in title to brigadier) and to assist him in the control and administration of such a large force, he had a small team, known as staff officers. Broadly speaking, in 1915 the staff officers were divided into three groups; the General Staff Branch (G Branch), responsible for operational planning, training and intelligence; the Adjutant General's Branch (A Branch), who looked after manpower and administrative matters; and the Quartermaster General's Branch (Q Branch), who co-ordinated the provision of ammunition, rations, transport, clothing and equipment. At this level, the senior staff officer was called the Brigade Major and the other branches were usually managed by captains, known as the Deputy Assistant Adjutant General (DAAG) and the Deputy Assistant Quartermaster General (DAQMG) respectively. On occasions these two posts were combined under one officer, known as the Deputy Assistant Adjutant and Quartermaster General (DAAQMG). These posts were replicated at divisional level (a grouping of brigades, commanded by a major general) and here the staff appointments would be held by officers in the rank of major or lieutenant colonel, the senior officer being called the chief of staff. The function of the staff officer was to collate information, provide advice and to draw up draft plans and directives on behalf of his commander. He did not take precedence over a regimental commanding officer, but as he often spoke on behalf of the brigade or divisional commander, his directions carried weight and influence. The orbat of 29 Division at the start of the campaign was as follows:

GOC – Major General A G Hunter-Weston CB

86 Brigade
2nd Bn Royal Fusiliers
1st Bn Lancashire Fusiliers
1st Bn Munster Fusiliers
1st Bn Dublin Fusiliers

87 Brigade
2nd Bn South Wales Borderers
1st Bn Kings Own Scottish Borderers
1st Bn Royal Inniskilling Fusiliers
1st Bn Border Regiment

88 Brigade
4th Bn Worcestershire Regiment
2nd Bn Hampshire Regiment
1st Bn Essex Regiment
5th Bn Royal Scots (Territorial Force)

Artillery
15 Brigade, Royal Horse Artillery (B, L and Y Batteries)
17 Brigade, Royal Field Artillery (13, 26 and 92 Batteries)
147 Brigade, Royal Field Artillery (10, 97 and 368 Batteries)
460 (Howitzer) Battery, Royal Field Artillery
4 (Highland) Mountain Brigade, Royal Garrison Artillery (TF) (Argyllshire Battery and Ross and Cromarty Battery)
90 Heavy Battery, Royal Garrison Artillery
14 Siege Battery, Royal Garrison Artillery

Engineers
1/2 London, 1/2 Lowland and 1/1 West Riding Field Coys Royal Engineers (TF)
Divisional Cyclist Coy

Today, all army officers undergo formal staff training and alternate between appointments in a staff headquarters and then at what is known as regimental duty (perhaps with a battalion or at a training unit) as part of their career progression. This was not the case in 1915; some officers remained at regimental duty throughout their whole career and avoided staff work wherever possible, while others followed a staff career for as long as they could. If there was one benefit emanating from the Great War, it was that the heavy toll on the lives of officers necessitated the need for them all to have staff experience, so that they were readily inter-changeable, which was to lead to a much better trained officer corps and a more professional career structure.

Chronology of Main Events

1689

28 March – Sir Edward Dering raises a Regiment of Foot, later to become the South Wales Borderers (SWB)

1875

4 December – Ernest Kirkland Laman (EKL) was born at Shoeburyness, Essex

1891

11 September – EKL joins 1 SWB as a junior soldier

1909

9 May – EKL becomes RSM of 1 SWB

1914

3 January – EKL commissioned as a lieutenant in 2 SWB to become the Quartermaster
4 August – Great Britain declares war on Germany
21 August – 4 SWB raised as a service battalion
2 September – 7 November – 2 SWB takes part in the Battle of Tsingtao, China

1915

12 January – 2 SWB arrives back in Great Britain and moves to Coventry to join 29 Division
13 January – Winston Churchill's plan for a naval operation to force the Dardanelles is approved by the British War Council
12 March – General Sir Ian Hamilton is appointed commander of the Mediterranean Expeditionary Force by the Secretary of State for War, Field Marshal Lord Kitchener
17 March – 2 SWB sails from Avonmouth for Gallipoli. Lieutenant Colonel H G Casson in command
18 March – Turkey defeats the final attempt by the British and French fleet to force the Dardanelles.
22 March – Decision taken to make an amphibious landing on the Gallipoli peninsula.
11 April – 2 SWB arrives at Lemnos
25 April – British Empire and French forces make amphibious landings on the Gallipoli peninsula.
- Landing at Cape Helles made by the British 29 Division and elements of the Royal Naval Division.
- Landing at Anzac Cove made by the Australian and New Zealand Army Corps (ANZAC).
- Diversionary landing at Kum Kale on the Asian shore by French forces.
- 2 SWB successfully captures S Beach

28 April – First Battle of Krithia

6 – 8 May – Second Battle of Krithia

4 – 8 June - Third Battle of Krithia

28 June to 5 July – Battle of Gully Ravine

29 June – 4 SWB sails from Avonmouth for Gallipoli. Lieutenant Colonel F M Gillespie in command

11 July – 4 SWB arrives at Lemnos

19 July – Major J Going takes over command of 2 SWB from Lieutenant Colonel H G Casson

3 August – 4 SWB deploys to the Anzac sector for the August offensive

6 August – IX Corps begins landing at Suvla Bay
- Under cover of darkness, two columns of Anzac, British & Indian troops (including 4 SWB) break out to the north, heading for the heights of Chunuk Bair and Hill 971.

7 August - Battle of the Nek. 8 RWF in support

8 – 10 August - Battle of Chunuk Bair. 8 Welsh in support

9 August – Lieutenant Colonel F M Gillespie CO 4 SWB killed by a sniper. Major M Beresford takes over command

12 August – Major Sir William Lennox Napier, OC A Coy 4 SWB killed by a sniper

13 August – On its way between Alexandria and Gallipoli, RMS *Royal Edward* is sunk by a German submarine. 56 soldiers of 2 SWB drowned

15 August – General Sir Frederick Stopford is sacked as commander of IX Corps.

21 – 30 August - Final British offensive of the campaign, launched to try and consolidate the Anzac and Suvla landings.
- Battle of Scimitar Hill
- Battle of Hill 60

26 September – Captain A E Williams takes over command of 2 SWB from Major J Going

15 October – General Sir Ian Hamilton is replaced as commander of the Mediterranean Expeditionary Force.

28 October – General Sir Charles Monro arrives to assume command of the Mediterranean Expeditionary Force.

9 - 15 November – Field Marshal Lord Kitchener visits Gallipoli.

22 November – Kitchener recommends evacuation of Anzac and Suvla.

27 November – A fierce storm and blizzard, lasting three days, strikes the peninsula.

7 December – The British Cabinet orders the evacuation of Anzac and Suvla.

18 December – Start of evacuation of Anzac and Suvla.

20 December – Evacuation of Anzac and Suvla completed

28 December
- The British Cabinet orders the evacuation of Helles.
- Major C E Kitchin takes over command of 4 SWB from Major Beresford

29 December – 4 SWB deploys to Cape Helles with 40 Brigade to assist in the evacuation

1916

7 January – British garrison reduced to 19,000. Turkish assault launched along Gully Spur.

9 January – Last British troops depart the Gallipoli peninsula.

Map 1. The area of the Gallipoli operations (Cassell and Coy Ltd).

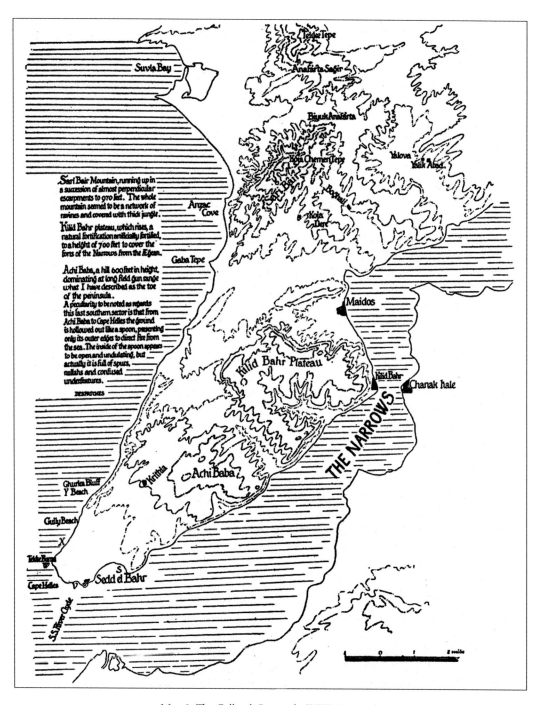

Map 2. The Gallipoli Peninsula (RWF Museum).

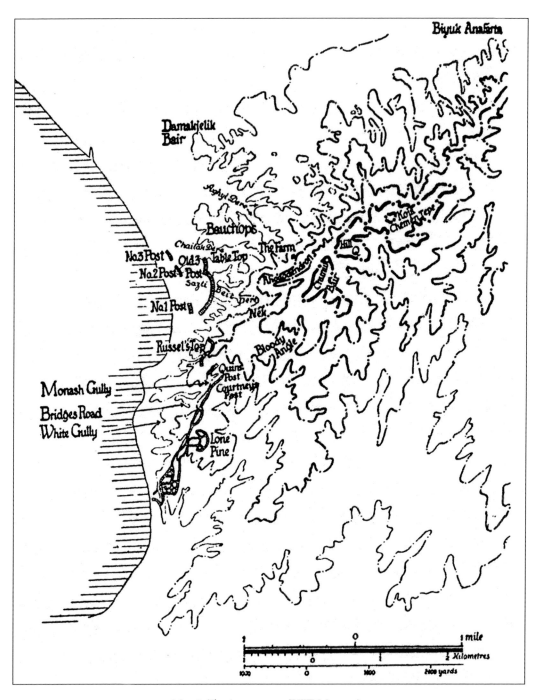

Map 3. The Anzac sector (RWF Museum).

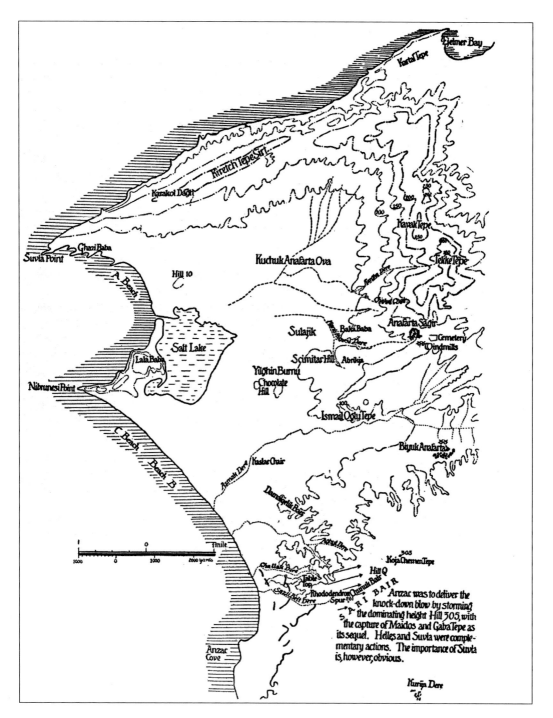

Map 4. Suvla Bay (RWF Museum).

Foreword

by Major General L A H Napier CB OStJ OBE MC DL

The South Wales Borderers, in which five generations of my family have served, is a source of considerable pride and inspiration to me. The Battle honours emblazoned on the Colours are etched in the regimental records as icons of bravery and courage, stretching back to 1689, when the regiment was first raised. Such valour does not come without a price however, and the centenary of the First World War reminds us that 5,777 officers and soldiers of the South Wales Borderers gave their lives for our King and country. While the main emphasis of the Great War was on the Western Front of France and Belgium, two battalions of the regiment took part in what was a lesser known conflict, but one of equal intensity and drama. This was at Gallipoli, on the shores of Turkey, between April 1915 and January 1916.

By December 1914, the war on the Western Front had ground to a halt in a stalemate of trench warfare, and Winston Churchill, then First Lord of the Admiralty, proposed a strategy to take Turkey, a German ally, out of the war. This could force Germany to fight on two fronts and could free up the Dardanelles waterway at Gallipoli. While the concept was sound, its execution was not, as it was hastily planned, and inadequately resourced. The 2nd Battalion the South Wales Borderers was present throughout the campaign. It was the only Welsh battalion to take part in the amphibious assault on 25 April 1915 (a distinction to be repeated almost 30 years later, when it went ashore at Normandy on D Day in 1944.) The 4th Battalion landed at Gallipoli a few months later, to take part in the second main offensive, at Suvla Bay, in August 1915. I have a personal connection with the 4th Battalion, as my grandfather, Major Sir William Lennox Napier, was killed by a sniper on 13 August 1915. His son, my uncle, was with him at the time. As well as fighting a demanding war against the Turkish army, the campaign took part amidst the most appalling conditions, such as the unrelenting heat of a mediterranean summer, a lack of water, poor food, inadequate equipment and without proper sanitation. Sickness and disease were rife, and at the height of the war there were up to 5,000 cases of dysentery a week. Both battalions of our regiment endured the privations of the campaign with great stoicism, courage and dignity and were amongst the last soldiers to leave the peninsula during the final evacuation in January 1916.

The story of their endeavours, recorded in a collection of diaries, reports and letters in the archives of the regimental museum in Brecon and elsewhere, deserves to be told and I am most grateful to Lieutenant Colonel Rodney Ashwood for taking the time to put all these sources together in this excellent book. This will serve as yet another chapter in our illustrious regimental history. Meticulously researched and written, the book takes us through the background to the war first of all, and includes a brief regimental history. Then, by a clever weave of official records and personal anecdotes, we journey through the highs and lows, as well as the poignant hopes and fears, of life on active service. The end result is a warm and personal account of the South Wales Borderers during the Gallipoli campaign (often known by the soldiers who took part as "Galley-Poley"), which adds an important social dimension to the traditional style of books already written

Image 2. Officers of the 4th Battalion SWB – May 1915 (R Welsh Museum).

on one of the most dramatic campaigns in British military history. The Turkish soldiers also fought well, and were held in much respect by the British and their allies.

The Great War was eventually won on the Western Front, while Gallipoli was for many years afterwards side-lined as a forgotten war. This book will ensure that this is no longer the case and it serves as a tribute to our magnificent soldiers. In my view, some of the best, toughest and most generous soldiers in the British army come from Wales. It has been my privilege, and that of my family, to have served with them.

I have enjoyed reading this book. I know that you will do so, too.

Major General Lennox Napier
Colonel of the Regiment 1983 - 1989
Monmouth
2016

Introduction

Having served most of my military career with the Royal Regiment of Wales, I grew up on the history of my illustrious forebears, the Welch Regiment and the South Wales Borderers. In particular, my imagination was fired by the Anglo-Zulu War of 1879, which seemed to take centre stage regimentally and it was a campaign I studied avidly. The advent of the centenary of the First World War, however, altered my focus considerably. I found the horror, privation and the incompetence of this conflict too shocking to fully comprehend and I experienced a growing feeling that I should do something to express my admiration and respect for the members of those Welsh regiments who fought and died during "the war to end all wars." The South Wales Borderers alone lost 5,777 officers and men between 1914 and 1918 and it occurred to me that an account of their experiences and achievements might serve as a tribute to their duty, nobly done. Various regimental histories have of course been written already, but with new and hitherto unpublished material coming to light, I felt that this was an appropriate time to offer another dimension in honour of their name and I have chosen the Gallipoli campaign of 1915 as the centre of my attention. The Royal Welch Fusiliers and the Welch Regiment also fought at Gallipoli with great distinction and although I have concentrated upon the South Wales Borderers, my book pays tribute to the sacrifices made by these regiments as well.

Much of the First World War took place on the battle fields of France and Belgium, known as the Western Front, which, like my perspective of the Zulu War, seemed to take precedence in the national consciousness, with Gallipoli often described as a side show. Most of the Welsh infantry battalions, raised as part of Lord Kitchener's new army, served on the Western Front, but some saw active service elsewhere, especially at Gallipoli, on the shores of Turkey. This begs the question – why were we there? Great Britain declared war on the central powers of Germany and Austria-Hungary on 4 August 1914, in a conflict which was popularly assumed would be over by Christmas. However, by December 1914, the war had ground to a halt in a stalemate of trench warfare. Anxious to find a way out of this impasse, Winston Churchill, then First Lord of the Admiralty, proposed a campaign to take Turkey, a German ally, out of the war, which would force Germany to fight on two fronts and would free up the Dardanelles waterway at Gallipoli for use by beleaguered Russian forces. While the concept was sound, its execution was not, as it was hastily planned, and poorly resourced. The campaign also took part amidst the most appalling conditions, such as the unrelenting heat of a mediterranean summer, a lack of water, poor food, insufficient equipment and without proper sanitation. With an incessant plague of flies throughout the summer, sickness and disease were rife and at the height of the war there were up to 5,000 cases of dysentery a week. Over half a million allied personnel took part, of whom 420,000 were British and empire troops, 80,000 French, 50,000 Australians and 9,000 New Zealanders. The cost in human terms was an appalling tragedy. The allies suffered 250,000 casualties, of whom approximately 58,000 were killed with only 11,000 having known graves, while the Turkish forces suffered similar appalling losses.

This labour of love has been several years in the making. In good military fashion, the plan to achieve my aim of writing a book on the subject was in four phases. First of all, there was plenty of background reading to be done, to gain an understanding of the subject matter and the books which have given me inspiration have been listed in the bibliography. During this time I transcribed the whole of Lieutenant Ernest Kirkland Laman's Gallipoli diary which I then put into a chart alongside the war diary of the 2nd Battalion so that I could compare the contents of the two documents day by day. I then conducted a similar exercise with the records of the 4th Battalion, all of which was a long but worthwhile project. Then, on the basis that a picture paints a thousand words, phase two was to undertake an immensely valuable and rewarding tour of the battlefields of the Gallipoli peninsula, which was well organised by Holt's Tours and expertly guided by John Dunlop. With the uniquely moving and evocative atmosphere of such places as Cape Helles, S Beach, Gully Ravine, Anzac Cove and Suvla Bay irrevocably etched into my mind I was then ready to begin the third phase, which was a detailed study of the archive material, much of which is held in the museum of the Royal Welsh in Brecon. From this followed phase four – the hardest part – which was to put pen to paper and develop the chapters which make up the framework of the book. Rather than just a list of diary entries, my intention was to weave together the factual accounts of the battalion war diaries with the various personal diaries, narrative reports, letters, newspaper cuttings, maps and diagrams which I had at my disposal.

In this respect I must, from the outset, record my grateful thanks to the trustees of the Museum who granted me full and unrestricted access to these records, without which I could never have undertaken this commitment. In addition the generosity, assistance and patience of the curator, Richard Davies and his team of Steve Farish, Lucy Jones and Sylvia Davies, has been very much appreciated.

The underlying core of the book is based on the official battalion war diaries of both the 2nd and 4th Battalions of the South Wales Borderers, which have been transcribed into a more digestible narrative. I have then added the reminiscences of a number of regimental personnel of all ranks, to add a personal dimension and to capture the atmosphere of life on active service. My main source has been the excellent diaries of Lieutenant Ernest Kirkland Laman, who was Quartermaster of the 2nd Battalion throughout the whole of the Great War and his diary for the Gallipoli campaign includes all entries verbatim. Never published in full before, I believe that it adds colour, depth and a sense of humour to the otherwise terse entries in the official diaries and his comments help considerably in describing to the general reader the various battles in which his battalion was involved. In this regard I must express my deep appreciation to Mrs Frances Voelcker, Ernest's granddaughter, for her considerable help in a number of ways. Not only did Frances give Ernest's original diaries to the museum, but she gave me access to a large number of photographs and other family papers and was also a great help in proof reading my drafts and providing valuable literary comment from an entirely different perspective.

Much of my material about the 4th Battalion comes from a summary of service held, once again, by the regimental museum. It is a lengthy document, written in narrative style rather than traditional diary format and was probably put together shortly after the war. It has no obvious author and for many years it was thought to have been written by Captain Charles Kitchin, the Adjutant in the early stages of the campaign, or possibly Major Marcus Beresford, the second in command, but a closer study of the document indicates that this was unlikely for a number of reasons, which come out in the text. In my considered opinion and by a process of elimination, this record was probably written by the Quartermaster of the 4th Battalion, Lieutenant John Mellsop, who, like his counterpart in the 2nd Battalion, would have had a better oversight of all the battalion's activities and who also would have had more time to put such a record together. In any event, whoever wrote it gave us an excellent account of that battalion's activities at Gallipoli and for that reason I have included the text, which has not been published before, in its entirety with little or no alteration.

I have added extracts from the diaries and letters of other officers in the battalion and if my book is guilty of being "officer heavy" as it were, it is because these people had a better oversight of the campaign and whose writing, by virtue of their more substantial education at the beginning of the 20th century, was understandably more eloquent.

This book does not aspire to any lofty academic status, nor, I must stress, have I attempted to write yet another account of the Gallipoli campaign. For this reason, I have not dwelt in detail on the exploits of the Anzac Corps, nor the French Division; likewise I have not covered to any great extent the vital role played by the other British arms and services, such as the Royal Navy, the Royal Flying Corps, the Royal Artillery, the Royal Engineers or the various logistic units, without whom little could have been achieved. This is not to demean their very important contribution; only that my focus has been on the South Wales Borderers. Similarly, I have not covered at any length the Turkish side of the war. I have the greatest respect for everything that was achieved at Gallipoli, by both units and individuals but I had to draw the line somewhere and their significant involvement has been covered by other historians who were better placed to do so. That said I have included an overview of the causes of the Great War and the build-up to the invasion on 25 April 1915 by way of introduction. Then, each chapter covers the main aspects of the campaign in general outline, so as to set the regimental involvement into context. I have also included a chapter on the regiment's history which hopefully will be of interest to the general reader as well as providing a back drop to the regiment's involvement in this campaign. Then there are lists of all those regimental officers who served at Gallipoli and a roll of honour giving the names of all those officers and soldiers who made the ultimate sacrifice in service of King and country. The end product is hopefully a tribute to the South Wales Borderers who fought with such distinction throughout this short but dramatic campaign.

A word about sources, notes and references. Having read the introductions to a good number of books, I am comforted to find that I am not alone in doubting the need to include numerous *op cits* and *ibids* on almost every page. Unless the book has been written for a specific academic purpose, which this one has not, they often distract the general reader who finds them of limited value, especially if the other books to which they refer are not readily available. For these reasons I have decided not to use them and to let the book tell its own story, but I have used citations and foot notes to acknowledge particular sources which might otherwise not be apparent, or to expand upon a point of detail. A select bibliography has been added at the end for those who wish to follow this absorbing subject further.

A book of this nature would not be possible without the assistance of a large number of people and I offer my sincere thanks to them all. In addition to those who I have already mentioned, I have appreciated having the interest and encouragement of Major General Lennox Napier, who kindly wrote the foreword. I am also most grateful to Brigadier Sir Nicholas Somerville for kindly giving me access to his family records about Gallipoli. Sir Nicholas told me that he had always felt that the 2nd Battalion's landing at S Beach was treated historically as a bit of a diversion. I agree with his assertion as a number of accounts I have read give little or no credit to what was one of the most successful beach landings on the day of the first invasion. I hope that I have been able to put the record straight in this respect.

Martin Everett, a former curator of the regimental museum, deserves special mention for letting me dip into his encyclopaedic knowledge of facts and figures about regimental personalities, dates and places, all of which he has willingly given me permission to publish. Of considerable help, he assembled the comprehensive lists of officers and regimental casualties at the rear of the book and he has met my incessant requests with patience and good humour. I also appreciate the assistance

I have received from Stephen Chambers, webmaster and historian of the Gallipoli Association for his professional advice and permission to quote from his own books on the subject. Mrs Bridget Hickey has most graciously agreed to my use of her late husband Michael's book on Gallipoli, which in many ways was the inspiration behind this literary journey. Then there has been Bill Cainan, another former curator of the Regimental Museum, for his enthusiastic support when I started out; Paul Johnson and Judy Nokes at the National Archives for permission to re-use crown copyright text material; Steven Greer of the Medici Society Ltd for permission to copy illustrations and text from Captain C T Atkinson's *History of the South Wales Borderers 1914 – 1918*; Jack Kemp for the use of his own history of the regiment at Gallipoli; Victor Godrich for the use of photographs from his book *The Mountains of Moab*; Mrs Jo Copping for the use of material regarding her grandfather Captain Hugh Fowler DSO; David Crampin and Jack Carlson for permission to use their article about the HMT *Royal Edward* disaster in the Journal of the Gallipoli Association number 136; Mrs Ann Payne for the use of the diary and maps of her grandfather Captain (later Lieutenant Colonel) Charles Kitchin DSO; the trustees of the RWF museum for permission to use material from *The Official History of the Royal Welch Fusiliers*; Katy Lawn of John Murray Publishers for advice on the use of the late Michael Hickey's book *Gallipoli*; Duncan Law and Richard Tuffney for their help in designing the back cover; Sophy Moynagh of the Imperial War Museum for her guidance on the provision of licences to publish images from their archives and to Irene Bristow and the staff of Freestyle Printers of Brecon for their willing assistance during the draft stages of this book. I would also like to acknowledge the advice and guidance of my publishers, Duncan Rogers, Michael LoCicero and Charles Singleton of Helion & Company as well as the expertise of Mary Woolley and Paul Hewitt of Battlefield Design. They have all contributed immensely to converting my dream into reality.

When I attended the Gallipoli Association conference in 2014, I met John Shephard who had served briefly with the South Wales Borderers some years ago. In no time at all he became as enthusiastic about my book as I am and he has been a font of knowledge and research for which I am extremely grateful. He has also been one of my valued proof readers. Along with Frances Voelcker, a group of long standing friends have given their time willingly in that painstaking task of checking and revising the text - Richard Peters, whose knowledge of the Great War seems to know no bounds, Peter Jenkins, who has a sharp eye for detail and the written word, Peter Davies, with whom I shared a military career, Peter Knox and Mike Lewis, both formerly of the Royal Welch Fusiliers - all of whom have offered invaluable advice from their own varied military and non-military perspectives. Any errors or omissions are mine entirely, as are views, opinions and possible infelicities of judgement about some of the major events of the campaign.

I have also had the greatest support and encouragement, as always, from my wife Jackie who has walked the battlefields of Gallipoli with me, acted as both sounding board and helpful critic as the text unfolded and who has been enthusiastic and patient in equal measure. Thank you.

Finally, every effort has been made to obtain the necessary permissions with reference to copyright material, both illustrative and quoted. I apologise for any omissions in this respect and will be pleased to make the appropriate acknowledgements in any future editions.

Rodney Ashwood
Brecon
2016

1

The Road to Gallipoli

are there not other alternatives than sending
our armies to chew barbed wire in Flanders?

Winston Churchill
to Prime Minister Asquith
29 December 1914

The month of August 1914 saw a conflagration ignite across the face of Europe, the nature of which had never been witnessed before. Sometimes called the Great War, this conflict which was to last four years changed the political landscape and social order of its protagonists forever. Within four months Great Britain and France were locked into static trench warfare with their adversaries, Germany and Austria-Hungary, across French and Belgian territory known as the Western Front.[1] Looking for a way out of this stalemate, in early 1915 Great Britain decided to launch a campaign against Turkey, another part of Germany's war alliance, on the Gallipoli peninsula. For the next ten months the best part of 500,000 troops from Britain and its Empire, along with a French contingent, were involved in this conflict with almost half becoming casualties – killed, maimed or struck down by illness and disease - in what was seen as an alternative strategy to alleviate the pressure of the main war effort on the Western Front. By defeating Turkey, Germany could lose one of its allies and the waterway of the Dardanelles could be opened up as far as the Black Sea, giving Russia access to the Mediterranean and countering the threat of a Muslim advance to the Indian sub continent. However, beset by a shortage of material resources, poor planning, indecision and weak leadership at the senior level, this campaign was doomed almost from the outset. It was to end in an ignominious evacuation, its saving grace being the outstanding courage and determination, as ever, of the individual soldier. To appreciate the road to Gallipoli, on which the South Wales Borderers were about to embark, let us turn the clock back a little to examine the genesis of this conflict.

The beginning of the First World War in 1914 is often popularly attributed to the assassination of the Archduke Franz Ferdinand of Austria-Hungary, but this is only partially correct. The causes of the war are more deeply rooted in a lethal cocktail of colonial acquisitions, the growth of nationalism, a naval arms race and a number of uneasy political alliances. As a consequence, the dawn of the 20th century over the continent of Europe was anything but peaceful as instability and tensions simmered amongst the more powerful countries. The major protagonists in this cauldron of dissent – for the actions of one would almost certainly cause a reaction from another – were Great Britain, France, Germany, Austria-Hungary and Russia. Also, the Balkan states and the Ottoman Empire, now Turkey, were to become significant pawns in the inevitable political meltdown, while

---

1   Also referred to as Austro-Hungary and sometimes as the Dual Monarchy, it is felt that Austria-Hungary more accurately describes this Alliance, so is therefore used throughout.

on the other side of the world Japan was also to have a part to play. For the time being, the United States of America remained neutral.

At this time, one of Great Britain's pre-occupations was the control and maintenance of her worldwide colonial interests. Britain needed a strong navy to police this vast empire and a merchant fleet to keep vital trade routes open. The Royal Navy ruled the high seas and the British army had garrisons across the globe, especially in India. Britain was heavily committed to the Boer War in South Africa between 1899 and 1902, but had no territorial aspirations on the European continent. Germany on the other hand viewed things differently. Since the defeat of France in the Franco-Prussian war of 1870 to 1871, the formal unification of Germany saw the rise of nationalism in a politically and administratively integrated nation state, which was particularly strengthened by the dual alliance with Austria-Hungary in 1879. Coming late to the "scramble for Africa" Germany's colonial acquisitions in central and southern Africa were relatively small, which created a feeling of inferiority. Consequently, the Kaiser embarked on a programme of naval expansion in an attempt to equal that of Britain and the ensuing arms race between the two countries only exacerbated the perception of instability on both sides.

France too had a colonial empire, particularly in north-west Africa and the Far East, but was particularly bitter about the loss of the provinces of Alsace-Lorraine along her border with Germany after the Franco-Prussian war of 1870 and any opportunity to recover this land by way of revenge would no doubt be seized upon. In similar vein, Russia had been humiliated in her war with Japan in 1905 and the Tsar was looking for ways and means to restore national prestige and to dampen down the stirrings of an internal proletariat revolution. There had been a Franco-Russian alliance in place since 1894 to defend themselves against the burgeoning German state and now Germany saw this alliance on two of her borders as yet another potential threat to her nationalistic aspirations. Meanwhile, Great Britain was waking up from her policy of "splendid isolation" to the realities of German expansion and in 1904 entered into an informal alliance with France known as the entente cordiale. By 1907 this had been extended to a triple entente, to include Russia, to counter the increasing nationalist and military threat from Germany.

While the major European powers were slowly but surely coalescing into distinct opposing groups, there were a number of other alliances and groupings taking place, particularly in the Balkans. Since 1878, the Austria-Hungary empire had occupied and administered the provinces of Bosnia and Herzegovina and in 1908 they were formally annexed from Turkey, exacerbating international tensions in the area further. This was not well received by Russia who not only had Slav cultural sympathies, but who also wanted to ensure that there was no threat to her trade routes south through the Black Sea and the eastern Balkans. The Balkan Wars of 1912-1913 led to increased tension between Russia and Austria-Hungary, as well as a strengthening of Serbia. It was also the hand of a Serbian dissident who lit the touch paper of the fireball which was about to engulf the whole of Europe and, by association, many other countries across the globe.

On 28 June 1914 the Archduke Franz Ferdinand, heir to the throne of the Austro-Hungarian Empire, and his wife the Countess Sofia were visiting Sarajevo, the capital of Bosnia-Herzegovina. The earlier annexation of these states was a cause of considerable dissent and a secret society known as the Black Hand was dedicated to liberating the Slav people from their oppressors. This visit was seen as an opportunity for an assassination by way of protest and that morning a bomb was thrown at the royal car. This attempt failed but as the vehicle drew up at the town hall, Gavrilo Princip, a 19 year old member of the dissident gang, stepped out of the crowd and fired his pistol into the open car killing the royal couple. He was immediately arrested and at his subsequent trial was surprisingly spared the death penalty due to his age, but he died in prison four years later from tuberculosis.

Austria-Hungary assumed Serbian complicity in the assassination and saw this as a chance to crush Slav opposition once and for all. An ultimatum was issued to the Serbian government (which was described as a declaration of war) and which would have emasculated their sovereignty. Serbia was not prepared to accept this, so on 28 July, Austria-Hungary declared war upon Serbia and the European stack of dominoes began to collapse quickly. Russia, who supported Slavic aspirations and who also saw this as a moment to flex her own political and military muscle, began to mobilize in support of Serbia, whereupon Germany declared war on Russia on 1 August. In accordance with the obligations of her alliance, France declared her support for Russia and she too began mobilisation. Germany, aware of the threat to both her borders, wanted to neutralize the French military machine before Russia was up and running, so declared war on France on 3 August and began to advance through Belgium. That Germany was able to effect this so rapidly was the result of the Schlieffen plan, a blueprint for such an invasion drawn up almost 20 years previously, evidence enough of her war-like intentions. Great Britain was not willing to accept any violation of Belgium's neutrality, contained in an obscure treaty in 1839, and as an ally of France declared war on Germany on 4 August. Thus the central powers of Germany and Austria-Hungary stood poised against the alliance of Russia, France and Great Britain – and by association the armies of her major colonies – for a war which was about to change the face of Europe and indeed the old world order for ever.

* * *

For centuries, the Ottoman Empire had influenced the culture, politics and religion of much of what is known as the Middle East with the capital city of Constantinople (now Istanbul) being the gateway between Europe and Asia and the scene of much dispute and conflict. Indeed it was the emperor Napoleon who is quoted as having said as long ago as 1808 "who is to have Constantinople? That is always the crux of the problem."[2] Likewise, the waterway between the Black Sea to the north, through the Bosphorus and the Dardanelles Straits to the Aegean Sea in the south was critical for the safe passage of ships, especially from Russia, importing and exporting goods vital to its economy. However, Turkey was now in serious decline. Often referred to as "the sick man of Europe" the country was ripe for revolution and political change and this was to come in 1908 through the committee of union and progress. Dominated by a group known as the "young Turks," led by Enver Pasha, (a 35 year old revolutionary who, having usurped the autocratic power of the Sultan, became de facto leader of Turkey), this revolution coincided with a downturn in Turkey's fortunes. The Balkan Wars of 1912-1913 saw Turkey deprived of much of her territory in Europe and while there were still at this stage many strong Anglo-Turkish links, Germany saw rich pickings in a floundering state which was also looking for outside assistance to restore her national pride. Consequently a German military mission was established in Turkey under the leadership of General Otto Liman von Sanders, which set about bringing some structure and order to an otherwise poorly trained conscript army. Germany also saw this as an opportunity to develop a railway line through Turkey from Berlin to Baghdad, a vital link in its aspiration to dominate the Middle East.

At the same time, Britain was making use of its naval mission, led by Rear Admiral Arthur Henry Limpus, to modernise the Turkish fleet. British shipyards were building two battleships for Turkey – the *Sultan Osman I* and the *Reshadieh* – at a cost of some £7.5 million which Turkey had raised by public subscription, money the country could ill-afford. Then, with war about to break out in Europe, Britain made the inept and fateful decision to impound both of these ships for her own fleet in the interests of security. The inevitable outrage felt by Turkey tipped the balance

2   Basil Henry Liddell Hart *Lawrence of Arabia* (New York: Halcyon House, 1937), p.24.

and played right into German hands. Germany sent two ships to Turkey by way of replacement, the *Goeben* and the *Breslau,* which, after a dramatic chase across the Mediterranean by the Royal Navy, arrived triumphantly in Constantinople to bolster the Turkish fleet. Turkey's neutrality was now compromised and in September 1914 the country closed the Dardanelles straits to all other shipping. Her navy was now effectively under the command of the German Admiral Wilhem Souchon who, for reasons that can only be regarded as a move to precipitate a war between Turkey and Russia, used this additional fire power to bombard Russia's Black Sea ports at the end of October 1914, an act which left Turkey's allegiance in no doubt at all. On 3 November 1914 a British squadron in the Aegean Sea opened fire on the outer defences of the Dardanelles at Sedd-el-Bahr (later to figure in the allied landings) with spectacular results and on 5 November Britain, France and Russia declared war on Turkey.

Britain's main priority at this stage was the Western Front in France and Belgium. After four months of bitter fighting with little progress, the Government's peace time Cabinet was subsumed into a War Council in November 1914. The key figures were the Prime Minister Herbert Asquith, Foreign Secretary Sir Edward Grey, Chancellor of the Exchequer David Lloyd George, Secretary of State for War Field Marshal Lord Horatio Kitchener, Chief of the Imperial General Staff General Sir Archibald Wolfe Murray, First Lord of the Admiralty Winston Churchill and the First Sea Lord Admiral 'Jacky' Fisher. The secretary was Lieutenant Colonel Sir Maurice Hankey. These were well established men of some standing but it was Churchill – controversial, impetuous, and fired with a vivid imagination – who was to influence the manner in which the road to Gallipoli unfolded. Just 40 years old, he represented the Admiralty and as such the whole of the Royal Navy on the War Council and he brought out of retirement the 73 year old Admiral Fisher to be his First Sea Lord and primary adviser on all naval matters. This was to become a tempestuous relationship which did little to enhance the role the Royal Navy was about to play in the forthcoming conflict.

By the end of 1914, operations on the Western Front had ground to a halt in the stalemate of trench warfare. Turkey's entry into the war on the side of Germany changed the balance of power to the extent that it closed the vital waterway from the Black Sea to the Mediterranean and was a threat to the security of Egypt and the Suez Canal – a key trade route for British colonial interests in the far east. Of maritime significance, this led Churchill in particular to consider an alternative offensive in the middle east to counter this threat. The concept did not meet with universal approval, but the seed had been sown and Churchill took every opportunity to persuade and cajole the war council into supporting his grand scheme. Both Lord Kitchener and David Lloyd George accepted that decisive action was necessary to break the deadlock on the Western Front, raise morale and to convince neutral states of the strength of the entente powers. The War Council secretary put together a paper, subsequently known as "The Boxing Day Memorandum" which proposed an attack on Turkey with the purpose of removing one of Germany's important allies, opening up a vital sea route to Russia and drawing the wavering neutral Balkan states – particularly Greece, Romania and Bulgaria – into the entente.

On Saturday 2 January 1915 came the opening that Churchill had been looking for in the shape of a message from the Grand Duke Nicholas of Russia, urgently requesting a "demonstration" against the Turks to divert attention away from the Caucasus so that Russia could concentrate on their war effort against the central powers of Germany and Austria-Hungary. What shape this demonstration should take was never made clear, but Kitchener was concerned about the non-availability of troops while Admiral Fisher initially supported the request by urging a totally impractical immediate joint naval and military attack on Turkey. Churchill quickly seized upon this as the opportunity to put his alternative strategy into place and his vivid imagination saw the Royal Navy forcing its way unaided through the defences of the Dardanelles (after all, Vice Admiral Sir John Duckworth had managed it in 1806) arriving at Constantinople, whereupon Turkey would immediately capitulate. The first move on the chess board was to coerce the naval commander in the Aegean, Vice Admiral Sir Sackville Carden, into backing his plan by sending him a somewhat loaded telegram on Sunday 3 January 1915:

> do you consider the forcing of the Dardanelles by ships alone a practical operation? It is assumed older battleships fitted with mine-bumpers would be used, preceded by colliers or other merchant craft as mine-bumpers and sweepers. Importance of results would justify severe loss. Let me know your views.

Two days later, Carden replied. His tone was cautious but in the manner which no doubt he believed was expected of him:

> with reference to your telegram of 3rd instant, I do not consider Dardanelles can be rushed. They might be forced by extended operations with large number of ships.[3]

This guarded reply was not exactly an enthusiastic endorsement of the proposal and ironically the defeat of the Turks in Armenia by the Russians on 4 January took the urgency out of the Grand Duke's plea for help, but this was conveniently ignored. What is also inexplicable is the manner in which previous intelligence appreciations were also overlooked. Less than 10 years earlier in 1906 the Director of Naval Intelligence and the British General Staff had drawn up a report on the Dardanelles defences which came to the conclusion that:

> Success must be certain. A mere naval raid into the Sea of Marmara being a dangerous and ineffective operation, the work will have to be undertaken by a joint naval and military expedition having for its objective the capture of the Gallipoli peninsula and the destruction of the forts which at present deny entrance to and exit from these waters.[4]

Churchill was not to be distracted from his grand scheme where he saw the Royal Navy, of which he was First Lord, being the lynchpin of an alternative strategy to alter the outcome of the war. As far as he was concerned the die had been cast and the road to Gallipoli was about to become a reality.

As Secretary of State for War, and in response to the situation overall, Lord Kitchener's priority was the provision of manpower and equipment for what he rightly predicted was going to be a long, bitter and costly conflict. In August 1914 the regular army was just under 250,000 strong with a reserve (men who had recently completed their regular service) of about 145,000. In addition there was a special reserve of some 64,000 in a lower category of readiness which could be trained up quickly to supplement the active service battalions. This was nowhere near enough however and on 4 August 1914 the territorial force (volunteer soldiers re-organised from the former militia and yeomanry units under the Haldane reforms of 1908) was mobilised. This category was not obliged to serve overseas, having been established as part time local home defence units, but in the event most volunteered to do so. These units were categorised into first line (overseas) and second line (home only) and every territorial battalion of infantry was affiliated to a regular army regiment. The territorial force was, in theory, capable of unlimited expansion but its weakness was the fact that it

3   Alan Moorehead, *Gallipoli* (London: Hamish Hamilton, 1956), pp.38–39.
4   Michael Hickey, *Gallipoli* (London: John Murray, 1995), p.28.

could not properly reinforce the regular army, as it lacked modern equipment, particularly artillery. In addition, it took time to form first line units composed only of men who had volunteered for overseas service.

Kitchener decided to go one step further and introduce a novel concept of "service" battalions, based entirely on new volunteers (hence also the title of "new army" units) recruited on a local and county basis, becoming an offspring of the existing regular county regiments. Due to the huge numbers of men wishing to sign up, in some places queues outside recruitment offices were up to a mile long. There were many problems in equipping and providing accommodation for the new recruits. The government quickly added many new recruitment centres, which eased the admissions burden, and began a programme of temporary construction at the main training camps. Almost two and a half million men volunteered for Kitchener's new army and by the end of 1914, the South Wales Borderers had eight such service battalions, numbered from the 4th to the 11th Battalions. The pressing problem was the provision of experienced officers and senior non commissioned officers to lead and train these totally inexperienced new recruits, so regular or reserve battalions had to provide valuable manpower (and did not always give up their best) and numerous officers were called out of retirement, which accounts for some of the ages seen on gravestones in battlefield cemeteries.[5]

The immediate concern was the availability of regular units to send to the Western Front, and a programme was set in place to recall various battalions, both at home and overseas, replacing them with territorial units. Of these was the 1st Battalion the South Wales Borderers (1 SWB), which was serving at Bordon in Hampshire, and the 2nd Battalion of the Regiment (2 SWB), which was in the far east at Tientsin in China. Much more will be said about this particular battalion in the next chapter, but no sooner had it disengaged from fighting the German contingent at Tsingtao in November 1914, than it was recalled to the United Kingdom. The 2nd Battalion sailed from China in December and by January 1915 had arrived home in England to join 29 Division, which at this point was still earmarked for service in France. Assigned to 87 Brigade, which was commanded by Brigadier General W G Marshall, the other units were the 1st Battalion the Kings Own Scottish Borderers, the 1st Battalion the Royal Inniskilling Fusiliers and the 1st Border Regiment. It is also a happy coincidence that these battalions of the Brigade (in total about 4,000 men with its supporting units) represented each of the four countries of the United Kingdom.

* * *

The next two months were a period of rather disjointed activity as the war council deliberated over the manner in which the Gallipoli campaign should be executed. There were a number of personality clashes, chief amongst these being between Churchill and Admiral Fisher, who vacillated between support for the Dardanelles and other naval actions in the North Sea in support of the Western Front, which was an unwanted distraction as far as Churchill was concerned. Prevarication by Lord Kitchener did not help either. While he supported the concept, he was not willing at first to commit ground troops in any number and he was under pressure from Sir John French, commander in chief on the Western Front, not to divert valuable resources elsewhere.

On Tuesday 19 January 1915 the war council eventually agreed in principle to capture the Dardanelles with the intention of knocking Turkey out of the war, but by means of the Royal Navy only. At the same time, the French agreed to provide a naval squadron in support, which gave much needed credence to the overall planning. A Royal Naval Division (RND), made up mainly of Royal

Marines and surplus naval manpower, was cobbled together for tactical landings to finish off the Turkish shore batteries and guns after bombardment of the defences by the allied fleet.[6] Churchill remained supremely confident that the British naval squadron beefed up by the addition of the latest battleship HMS *Queen Elizabeth* and supported by the French was up to the task and on 19 February the naval battle for the Dardanelles began in the form of a coastal bombardment.

Back in London, Lord Kitchener was still under pressure to provide ground troops in support of the navy and on Tuesday 16 February provisionally agreed to release 29 Division, which was originally earmarked for the Western Front, in a supporting role only. It was not intended that they should actually land on the peninsula and if the naval operation was not a success then all forces could be withdrawn. Just three days later Kitchener changed his mind as he did not believe that he had the resources or ships to commit such a force on operations, so he withdrew 29 Division, but he did signal General Sir John Maxwell, Commander in Chief in Egypt, to be prepared to make use of the Australian and New Zealand forces staging through there on their way to the Western Front, should the need arise. Meanwhile, Admiral Carden's initial bombardment of the outer defences of the Dardanelles was going well and during the last week of February the RND went ashore several times to put some 50 guns out of action. However, bombardment of the inner defences up to the area known as the Narrows at Chanakale had little effect and in early March the initiative was losing headway.[7] It was becoming clear, as it should have been from the outset, that this campaign would not succeed without full military support and by Thursday 11 March Kitchener had made the decision to commit 29 Division to the Dardanelles. A senior officer was needed to take overall command of the operation and so on the next day, Friday 12 March 1915, while His Majesty King George V inspected the division in all its glory at Dunsmore Heath in the Midlands, at the War Office in London Lord Kitchener was about to send his selected officer, General Sir Ian Hamilton, to Gallipoli with these words ringing in his ears:

> if the Fleet gets through, Constantinople will fall of itself and you will have won, not a battle, but the war.[8]

* * *

Ian Standish Monteith Hamilton was born in 1853 in Corfu, of Scottish ancestry. After school at Wellington College he was commissioned into the army in 1873 at the age of 20, first of all into the 12th Foot (the Suffolk Regiment) for just a year and then into the 92nd Foot (the Gordon Highlanders), his original choice. He soon saw active service in the Second Afghan War of 1878 to 1880 and then went to South Africa for the First Boer War of 1880. At the Battle of Majuba on 26 February 1880 he was shot in the left forearm which shattered his wrist and crippled him for life, but this did not hold back his military career in any way. In fact his rise through the ranks was almost meteoric. By 1882 he was a captain and then just three years later he was a brevet major before being promoted to acting lieutenant colonel in 1887.[9] An academic by inclination, he was recognised as an outstanding staff officer and a military reformer who wrote a number of books covering new developments in military technology. He had some radical views, particularly on

---

6   The original concept was that the RND would be able to defend naval bases, which was why it was deployed to Belgium in 1914.
7   Vice Admiral Sir Sackville Carden was the senior naval officer in command of the Dardanelles Squadron at the beginning of the campaign.
8   General Sir Ian Hamilton, *Gallipoli Diary*, 2 volumes (London: Edward Arnold, 1920). See diary entry for the 15th March 1915.
9   Brevet rank indicates promotion to the next higher rank, but without the corresponding pay. It is also known as local rank.

the future of the cavalry but he was well accepted in senior military circles, having been ADC to General Sir Frederick Roberts VC and chief of staff to General Kitchener during the Second Boer War of 1899 to 1901.

By 1891 he was the youngest colonel in the British army and just 10 years later he was a major general, having already held the local rank for a year. In 1905 he reached the rank of full general and then held such senior appointments as GOC Southern Command, Adjutant General (responsible for all manning and administrative matters in the army) and Inspector General of Overseas Training, travelling extensively in Australia and New Zealand. By the outbreak of the First World War he was commander in chief of all home forces in the United Kingdom, having been a very close contender to command the British expeditionary force to France, so it is no surprise that Lord Kitchener should have chosen him to lead the campaign to Gallipoli. However as events were to show, despite being an experienced senior officer who was intellectually bright and socially charming, he lacked that single minded ruthlessness necessary to influence the outcome of battle, preferring to leave tactical control to his field officers on the ground, a number of whom were clearly not up to the task in hand. Kitchener's brief to Hamilton on 12 March 1915 about such a major undertaking was terse and to the point "we are sending a military force to support the fleet now at the Dardanelles and you are to have command" but he did follow this up the next day with a written directive, if not a formal military operational order. He was keen to point out that:

> the employment of military forces on any large scale for land operations at this juncture is only contemplated in the event of the Fleet failing to get through after every effort has been exhausted, having entered on the project of forcing the straits there can be no idea of abandoning the scheme.

Lord Kitchener was also adamant that no occupation of the Asiatic side of the Dardanelles should occur and that all communications regarding the operation should be sent directly to him so that he was fully informed of the operations and Sir Ian's anticipations as to future developments.

The unfortunate general now had to cobble together a plan restricted by a shortage of time and limited resources due to the demands of the Western Front. Only four months before, an offensive on the Gallipoli peninsula had not been an option, so no prior operational staff work had taken place to guide the general. Even though the Chief of the Imperial General Staff was a member of the war cabinet, little or no pro-active planning had been set in motion and in any event most of the key staff officers were engaged on the Western Front, so those left behind in Whitehall were not exactly the best of the bunch. At Churchill's insistence Sir Ian Hamilton left London for France by train the next day, then on to Marseille for a ship to the Aegean island of Tenedos. He had woefully inadequate staff to support him apart from his newly appointed chief of staff, Major General Walter Braithwaite. They arrived at Tenedos on the afternoon of Wednesday 17 March, just one day before the next major allied naval assault against the Dardanelles defences was about to begin.[10]

* * *

In the preceding months, the strain of continual naval offensives against the Dardanelles had proved too much for Vice Admiral Carden and he was now on the verge of a nervous breakdown. At the last moment he was replaced by Vice Admiral Sir John Michael de Robek who was about to command one of the largest allied naval fleets in living memory, with General Hamilton as

---

10   John Lee, *A Soldier's Life – Gen Sir Ian Hamilton 1853-1947* (London: Macmillan, 2000).

a spectator, on an offensive to breach the minefield defences of the Dardanelles Narrows, thus clearing the way to Constantinople via the Sea of Marmara. The piecemeal bombardment of the coastal defences over the last month was losing its impact and momentum so on the morning of Thursday 18 March 1915, a major naval offensive in the shape of a fleet of 14 British and four French capital ships, preceded by an array of minesweepers, sailed into the Dardanelles with the British battleships leading. At first the assault made good progress with only the French battleship the *Gaulois* taking any serious damage, but in the early afternoon disaster struck. While the position of the main minefields across the Narrows were known, another smaller lane of mines had been secretly laid by the Turks a few days earlier along the southern side of the Dardanelles in Eren Keui Bay. As a number of allied ships turned to starboard as part of their battle drill they ran into these mines and by the end of the day the British had lost HMS *Irresistible* and HMS *Ocean* sunk, with HMS *Inflexible* being badly damaged but making it back to Tenedos, while the French lost the *Bouvet* sunk, the *Gaulois* beached and their Flagship the *Suffren* badly damaged.[11]

Despite this disastrous setback and blow to naval morale, Admiral de Roebek, encouraged by Commodore Roger Keyes his chief of staff, initially considered that he still had the resources to resume the next day, but General Hamilton, who had witnessed the whole spectacle, felt otherwise. His assessment was that the navy was not in a position to go it alone, and that if the army was needed, as had been the view of several members of the war council from the outset, then it should be there in more than just a supporting capacity. As General Hamilton recorded in his diary:

> there must be a deliberate and progressive military operation carried out at full strength so as to open a passage for the navy.

This view was telegraphed to the war council in London who concurred with Hamilton's appreciation; indeed, Lord Kitchener replied in no uncertain manner:

> You know my views, that the passage of the Dardanelles must be forced and that if large military operations are necessary to clear the way, they must be undertaken, and must be carried through.

With this unequivocal directive, the dynamics of the campaign shifted in favour of a military operation to seize the Gallipoli peninsula, so that the defences of the Dardanelles waterway could be neutralised. The original and overall concept – the fall of Constantinople and the removal of Turkey from the war – had not changed, but the manner in which this was to be achieved had altered markedly.

With little or no contingency planning having been made for such an eventuality, General Hamilton had to start virtually from scratch. His initial briefing by Lord Kitchener had been very thin to say the least and he did not have the correct balance of staff officers to support and advise him. Moreover 29 Division, which was on its way but would not arrive until early April, had been resourced for an unopposed move over-land to the Western Front, rather than for an operational beach assault against well prepared defences, so all their supplies and equipment had been packed on the transport ships in the wrong order. Consequently, the division had to be diverted to Alexandria in Egypt so that the ships could be re-organised accordingly, all of which would take valuable time. Of critical significance was the fact that no proper assessment had been made of the quantity of ammunition, especially artillery, needed for the campaign and with no medical staff officers on

11   Dan Van Der Vat, *The Dardanelles Disaster* (London and New York: Duckworth Overlook, 2009).

hand, the estimate of battle casualties and field hospital support needed was woefully inadequate.

Add to this the poor security measures adopted in Egypt while the campaign was being planned and the months of naval bombardment beforehand, the Turks were in no doubt as to allied intentions. They knew an attack would be forthcoming and every effort was put into making sure that the defence of the Gallipoli peninsula was as strong as it could be. General Liman von Sanders had the gift of time on his side – all he needed to know was where and when General Hamilton would launch his assault. The road to Gallipoli had reached its destination, but the journey was far from over.

2

Men of Harlech

Men of Harlech on to glory,
this will ever be your story

From 'Men of Harlech'
an ancient Welsh battle hymn
and Regimental March of The Royal Welsh

Although many British infantry regiments took part in the Gallipoli conflict of 1915, this account is based primarily on some of the personal diaries and official records of The South Wales Borderers, which became the Royal Regiment of Wales in 1969 and which since 2006, in yet another round of defence cuts and amalgamations, has been entitled the Royal Welsh. Involved in the majority of campaigns which make up the bold tapestry of British military history over the last 325 years, an introduction to the history of this famous regiment is not only of interest, but it is also an appropriate backdrop to all that was to happen to the South Wales Borderers during their campaign on the shores of Turkey.[1]

While the heritage of this regiment is now an inextricable part of Wales, its origins were very much elsewhere. In 1689, King William III of England signed a proclamation for the raising of 10 regiments of foot to serve in Ireland and in March 1689 Sir Edward Dering, a Kentish baronet who owned the manor of Surrenden near Ashford, raised one of these regiments. A commemorative stone at Pluckley Church in Kent records the event and by 28 March 1689, Dering's Regiment, as it was then known, took its place in the infantry of the line. At the time, an infantry regiment was the personal preserve of its colonel who was at liberty to determine its style of uniforms and other accoutrements and the expenditure of government funds for the clothing, quartering and the pay of his unit was left entirely in his hands. Until the mid 18th century the colonel of the regiment was the de facto commanding officer, with all the training and administrative responsibilities of that appointment, including active command in the field. It would be customary for him to appoint a lieutenant colonel as his second in command. Today the colonel of the regiment is more often than not a senior officer acting as the regimental figurehead in an honorary capacity, while the battalions are commanded by lieutenant colonels.

Less than five months after the first muster parade, Colonel Dering's Regiment found itself on active service. In August 1689 King William despatched a large expeditionary force to Northern Ireland to counter the catholic uprising there and on 13 August the Regiment landed at Bangor. Sir Edward Dering's tenure was short lived as he died of fever at Dundalk in September 1689 and his brother Daniel succeeded him, thus perpetuating the family name embodied in the regiment.

---

1   John Brereton, *A History of the Royal Regiment of Wales* (24th/41st Foot) 1689-1989 (Cardiff: RHQ RRW, 1989).

This was to be the custom for the next 50 years as the regiment's title changed with each new colonel, who was then at liberty to alter the colour and style of its uniforms and any other domestic paraphernalia. Returning from Northern Ireland in 1691, the regiment was stationed briefly in Somerset but soon moved to the south coast of England following threats of French invasion. For the next five years it saw service on the European continent until returning to Ireland once again, this time to Dublin, having been transferred to what was called the Irish establishment as a result of recently imposed cuts in strength.

In 1702 the colonel of the regiment changed once more, this time to the illustrious John Churchill, 1st Duke of Marlborough, who was colonel of the regiment from 1702 to 1704. At this time, the regiment was involved in the War of the Spanish Succession and such famous battles as Blenheim, Ramilies, Oudenarde and Malplaquet became enshrined in the annals of its military history. Another notable figure was Colonel Thomas Howard who was colonel from 1717 to 1737 and whose name gave rise to the regimental nickname of "Howard's Greens" from the green colour of the uniform facings and a colour which remains associated with the regiment to this day. The practice of name changes on succession of each new colonel ceased in 1751 when a Royal Warrant directed that henceforth all regiments were to be designated by a number according to their seniority in the line; that is the date on which the regiment was first raised. Thus Colonel Ancram's Regiment, as it was then known, became the 24th Regiment of Foot. Old habits die hard of course but before long this became the accepted practice and the new nomenclature of the 24th became synonymous with the Regiment and is still part of its title today, even after a number of reforms and amalgamations.

During this period other events of significance in the regiment's history took place. With the Seven Years' War with France looming, in 1756 the government ordered the raising of a further 15 battalions, one of which was the 2nd Battalion the 24th Regiment of Foot. Recruited mainly from the Midlands, this battalion assumed its own identity in 1758 when it took the title of the 69th Regiment of Foot. Later on, in 1881 as part of the Cardwell reforms, it changed names yet again to become the 2nd Battalion of the Welsh Regiment (the spelling of *Welch* in its name was not adopted until 1920) but that is another story.

Towards the latter part of the 18th century the regimental colonel was rarely the actual commanding officer, as he had been in Marlborough's day and before. By now nearly always an officer in the rank of general, he was usually found some staff appointment (that is, a more desk bound post in an administrative headquarters either in England or abroad) which supplemented his pay as colonel of the regiment; without such an appointment he received no pay of general's rank. From this stage onwards therefore, the active command of the regiment devolved to the lieutenant colonel as it has been ever since. At about the same time infantry regiments were allotted specific recruiting areas and the counties of Devon, Cornwall and Somerset were assigned to the 24th Foot. However, the regiment spent little or no time in this area and was in fact otherwise serving in such places as Cartagena in Spain, Minorca, Gibraltar, the war on the continent against the French and eventually in the American War of Independence from 1775 to 1781. Here the regiment fought with great distinction but sustained heavy casualties during its six years in North America, either in action or through disease and sickness.[2]

The 24th Foot returned home to a major change in the Army's recruiting policy, which was to have a significant bearing on its title for the next century. A Royal Warrant of 31 August 1782 conferred county titles on all regiments which did not have a Royal designation already

---

2   It was accepted that more lives would be lost through sickness and disease than enemy action in war, until the First World War.

and the 24th Foot was arbitrarily assigned to Warwickshire. It was apparently intended that regiments should cultivate a recruiting connection with counties whose name they took and the 24th Foot, who became the 2nd Battalion the Warwickshire Regiment (the 6th Foot being the 1st Warwickshires) were ordered to send a recruiting party to Tamworth. However, no special link with the county militia was established, nor were any depots or permanent recruiting centres set up. This county link was to remain in the regimental title for virtually 100 years, but as most infantry regiments continued to use their numerical title in preference anyway, it is fair to say that Warwickshire itself did not play a significant part in its regimental history. As we will see later, the regiment established a more lasting affiliation with the borders of South Wales where its depot was to be established in 1873.

The beginning of the 19th century saw an addition to the regiment when the Additional Forces Act of 1803 raised, once again, the 2nd Battalion the 24th of Foot. As was customary practice extra battalions would be raised in time of need only to be disbanded when the crisis was over and the government could no longer afford to maintain them. This was the fate of the 2nd Battalion, which was disbanded in 1814 after the Peninsular Wars only to be raised again in 1858 when commitments in India and elsewhere demanded a larger army once more. While these two battalions had links in title, their fortunes took them in different directions around the globe. Of particular interest is the 1st Battalion's service in India during the second Sikh war and the Battle of Chillianwallah in January 1849. While the outcome of the battle was eventually a success, the 24th Foot took severe casualties including the loss of its Colours. Flags, banners and standards have long been rallying points on the field of battle and over the centuries they have come to embody the honour, pride and spirit of a regiment. Each infantry battalion would have two such flags, or Colours as they are correctly called; one being the Queen's (or King's) Colour bearing the Union flag, the other being the regimental Colour which is unique to that battalion. Battle honours awarded by the Sovereign would be emblazoned on the Colours and until the time of the Boer War they were carried into battle, closely guarded by two officers and three senior non commissioned officers (known as the Colour party, so giving rise to the rank of colour sergeant) as it was a disgrace for the Colours to fall into the hands of the enemy. At Chillianwallah, the Queen's Colour disappeared completely, allegedly wrapped under the tunic and around the chest of an officer whose body was lost under the mud of the battlefield; at least it was not captured. When Ensign Collis fell during this battle carrying the regimental Colour, this was bravely rescued by Private Perry who was awarded a gallantry medal for his courageous action. This Colour continued in service until 1868, when it and the missing Queen's Colour were replaced by new ones which were to become immortalised 11 years later in 1879.

The Chillianwallah Colour, as it became known, was laid up in the Beauchamp Chapel of St Mary's Church in Warwick where it remained for the next 60 years until the regiment (by now the South Wales Borderers) requested its transfer in 1925 to its newly appointed chapel in Brecon Cathedral. There followed an 11 year struggle with the church authorities in Warwick for its release until the Chillianwallah Colour eventually returned to the spiritual home of the regiment in 1936. This was not the first time the regiment had lost its Colours, however – nor was it to be the last. During hostilities against the French in 1810, the 1st Battalion 24th Foot were en route to India by sea when their ships were engaged in the Mozambique Channel. With HMS *Ceylon* about to be taken captive, the commanding officer had the Colours with regimental books and records thrown overboard rather than surrender them to the enemy.

Meanwhile the 2nd Battalion had moved to Mauritius and then to Burma from 1865 to 1873 where the Regiment gained the first of its 23 Victoria Crosses, the nation's highest possible accolade for valour. Investigating a report that the crew of a British ship had been massacred by natives on one of the Andaman Islands, a company of the battalion became trapped on the beach, unable to get back to their own ship anchored offshore because of bad weather. In high running seas, the battalion doctor, Assistant Surgeon Douglas and four men ran a gig, or small boat, back and forth through the heavy surf from ship to shore, saving almost 100 soldiers of the battalion from being massacred, putting their own lives at risk in the process. All five men were awarded the VC for their undoubted courage and while this incident may not have met the prime requirement of conspicuous bravery in the face of the enemy in combat, it must be remembered that the carefully selective procedures which now determine the award of this medal had not then been introduced.

In 1873, the 2nd Battalion 24th Foot returned home to Aldershot at the same time as the brigade depot at Brecon was set up in the town barracks as part of the Cardwell reforms. Recruiting in the counties of Brecon, Radnor, Cardigan and Monmouth, the regiment began the development of its Welsh identity. However, the two battalions were not to serve together until early 1878, when the frontier wars of the Cape Colony (or the Kaffir Wars as they were also referred to) required more infantry battalions to be posted to South Africa. By 1874, the 1st Battalion 24th Foot was stationed in Gibraltar, but there was not a lot of time to enjoy the delights of a Mediterranean posting, as energies were taken up preparing the battalion for its forthcoming move to South Africa. By the autumn, more drafts had arrived and at the end of November 1874 the battalion set sail for South Africa in the troopships *Simoon* and *Himalaya*, arriving in Cape Town on New Year's Day 1875. The 2nd Battalion deployed to South Africa from England in 1878, arriving at East London, Cape Colony in March of that year.

During this time, the 1st Battalion helped the authorities in the Cape Colony defuse the confrontation known as the ninth frontier war. This was the culmination of a long period of territorial dispute between white settlers and the tribes of the indigenous Xhosa people around the Great Kei river along the eastern boundary of the Cape Colony, stretching back 100 years to the first frontier war in 1779. Most of these engagements were inconclusive but the pattern of cattle raid, destruction, reprisal and atrocity was to repeat itself regularly. On this occasion the war varied between such actions as native attacks on British and Mfengu entrenched positions in the Amathole Mountains and skirmishing tactics against the Ngicka army in the Perie Bush. As this particular war was drawing to its successful conclusion, events to the north in the colony of Natal were leading to an inevitable confrontation, this time with a much more aggressive and disciplined army – the Zulus of King Cetshwayo. The 24th Foot were highly praised for their professionalism during this frontier war, but their success was to create a false illusion. The ninth frontier war was won by a relatively small number of troops and at a low cost in white lives. The battle at Quintana (or Centane) was hailed as a model action against numerically superior but poorly armed forces. It resulted in a euphoric overestimation of the potency of disciplined infantry armed with the Martini-Henry rifle, an error which played a part in the terrible disaster a year later at Isandlwana.

For their own political and economic ends, the colonial authorities in South Africa instigated a quite unjustified war against the Zulu nation. Having issued the King with an ultimatum which was impossible to accept, on 11 January 1879, the invasion of Zululand began as the Imperial forces crossed the border from Natal at a river crossing called Rorke's Drift and some 10 days later they arrived at a small hill feature named Isandlwana, whose sphinx-like shape bore an uncanny resemblance to the collar badges of the 24th Regiment of Foot. Then, during the night of 21 January, Lord Chelmsford, commander in chief of all British and colonial forces in South Africa made the fatal tactical error of splitting his force in the face of an unknown enemy as he took the 2nd / 24th Foot to follow up what he thought was the main Zulu column, leaving the 1st / 24th

Foot, with some native auxiliaries, to guard the camp site. Tragically, he had been misled, for on the morning of 22 January, 20,000 warriors from the mighty army of King Cetshwayo swept down upon the unsuspecting camp site and in a few hours they had annihilated all but six soldiers of the battalion, out of a strength of over 600, from young drummer boys still in their teens to veterans such as 38 year old private William Griffiths who already held the Victoria Cross for outstanding bravery at the Andaman Islands in 1867. While many of the colonial forces broke ranks and fled from such an onslaught, the 24th of Foot stood its ground. The regiment does not seek to glorify the horror of war, but the bravery, self discipline and military pride must have shone out like a beacon of light as every officer and soldier stood side by side, unflinching in the face of totally overwhelming odds. The regiment remembers too, with great pride and humility, the selfless act of Lieutenants Coghill and Melvill who gave their lives in a gallant attempt to save the Queen's Colour of the battalion from falling into the enemy's hands. Tribute must also be paid to the 20,000 brave Zulu warriors who took such heavy casualties during a conflict which was not of their choosing. They were led into battle by the 60 year old chieftain, Ntshingwayo kaMahole Khosa and when their attack seemed to be faltering at one stage, another senior Zulu warrior, Mkhosana chief of the Biyela tribe, ran to the front, and in full view of the British, urged them on to victory. He paid with his life for such bravery, but he too was an inspiring example to his own army.

Flushed with success, the reserve force of 4,000 Zulus, led by Prince Dabulamanzi swept on to the little mission station some 15 miles away at Rorke's Drift where about 100 men of B Company 2nd Battalion the 24th Regiment of Foot were guarding a makeshift hospital and stores depot. Having been warned of the Zulu approach, the soldiers were able to put up a hurried defence of biscuit boxes and mealie bags, but even so it was impossible to believe that anything but a similar fate awaited this position as well. However, what happened that night defied all logic and has gone down in the annals of British military history as the Immortal Defence of Rorke's Drift. The Victoria Cross was awarded a total of 11 times and while there were those who attempted to deride such a high number as an effort by the authorities to obfuscate the disaster at Isandlwana the previous day, no-one can deny the incredible acts of individual heroism which took place that night. The citations of such men as Privates Henry Hook, Fred Hitch, Robert Jones, William Jones and John Williams, Corporal William Allen, and the outstanding leadership of Lieutenant Gonville Bromhead bear witness to unflinching courage and an unshakeable determination to stand by their colleagues at all costs, nurtured by the regimental system which is still cherished today. Forget the myth of an overage Lieutenant who was hard of hearing and who had been put out to grass on a quiet backwater duty. Gonville Bromhead epitomised the high degree of courage which has come to be associated with British soldiers, witnessed recently in Iraq and Afghanistan. Also, let there be no doubt that the success of that battle had as much to do with the bravery of the Welsh soldiers who were there that night as it did with the firepower of the .45 calibre Martini Henry rifle.

After the war, Her Majesty Queen Victoria asked to see the Colours of the 24th Regiment of Foot at Osborne House on the Isle of Wight, on their return to the United Kingdom. On 28 July 1880 she placed a floral wreath of immortelles upon the Colours, and decreed that this should be carried for evermore by the regiment, in honour of all those who had given their lives during the Zulu wars, and to commemorate the Immortal Defence of Rorke's Drift. The Queen's Colour now carries a permanent silver wreath at the top of its pike, this distinction being unique throughout the British army, and a privilege of which the regiment has every right to be most proud.

The following year was to see a significant change in the regimental title as part of the Cardwell reforms. On 1 July 1881, the regiment received orders that the time honoured numerical titles of the infantry of the line were to be discontinued officially and that all regiments were to be known henceforth by territorial titles only. Battalions were to be amalgamated by pairs, some into forced marriages with a strange partner, but fortunately the 24th Foot already had two battalions and so they became the 1st and 2nd Battalions of the South Wales Borderers, the title coming from one of the militia battalions under command of the brigade depot since 1873. However, by common practice and precedent, the regiment still continued to use the familiar title of the 24th, but all links with Warwickshire were finally abandoned, save for a musical regimental march, "The Warwickshire Lads," which continues to be played on ceremonial occasions.

Having stayed on in South Africa for a while after the Zulu Wars, primarily because of transportation problems, the 2nd Battalion eventually made their way to their next posting of Gibraltar. On 6 August 1880, the 2nd Battalion was presented with new Colours to replace those lost at Isandlwana. The Queen had intended to present them herself, but it was not possible to send a Colour party back to England for this purpose. On her behalf the Governor of Gibraltar, Lord Napier of Magdala, made the presentation with the Colours proudly bearing its new silver wreath of immortelles at the head of the pike. During this time, the battalion was under orders for its next period of active service and soon set sail for the East Indies, arriving at Bombay in September 1880. Initially intended for the Afghan frontier, there was a change in the operational situation and the battalion was diverted to Secunderabad, where they stayed until December 1883. In February 1884, the battalion moved to Madras. While there, a detachment of 150 men was sent for duty on the Andaman Islands, where the 2nd/24th Foot had been awarded five Victoria Crosses in 1867, while another company was detached to Malliapuram on the Malabar coast, where it was involved in suppressing an uprising among the Moplahs, a tribe of Mahomedan fanatics.

By the summer of 1886, 2 SWB was back on active service again, this time in Upper Burma. Since the accession of King Theebaw in 1878, relations between England and Burma had grown strained. With an uncanny similarity to the situation in South Africa prior to the Zulu wars, the King was issued an ultimatum, which he rejected and an invasion followed. The invasion was a success, but with the King overthrown and the country annexed, it now had to be conquered. When 2 SWB reached Rangoon in May 1886, the insurrection was in full swing. For the next two and a half years, the Battalion was involved in low level terrorist warfare, during which they lost one officer and nearly 60 NCOs and men. The battalion was not sorry to quit Burma for Calcutta, where it landed on 14 November 1888 prior to proceeding up country to Bareilly.

At the end of 1890, the battalion moved to Allahabad, and it was here that Gonville Bromhead, who was serving with the battalion, died of typhoid fever on 7 February 1891 at the age of 46. The following telegraph was received from the commander in chief on this sad occasion:

> Please let all ranks of the South Wales Borderers know how much the Chief sympathises with them in the loss of Maj Bromhead VC, who behaved with such conspicuous gallantry at Rorke's Drift and so well supported the reputation of his distinguished Regiment.

The 2nd Battalion remained in India until October 1892 when it moved to Aden for a year before it returned to Portsmouth, and then to Badajoz Barracks, Aldershot in August 1895.

Meanwhile, the 1st Battalion spent a period of frequent moves at home and abroad. At the end of 1880 it moved from Gosport to Colchester and then two years later in August 1882 was posted to Manchester, followed by a move to Kilkenny, Ireland, in September of the following year. Staying there until 1885 it then found itself at the Curragh, Dublin, but a year later went out to Birr in India until September 1887 when once again it returned to Dublin before going back to Aldershot in 1889. Some three years later in December of 1892 it then moved by troopship to Egypt where it appreciated another three years of stability before moving to Gibraltar in April 1895. Two years later, in 1897 the 1st Battalion went back to India where it was to remain in various stations for the next 10 years.

As its sister battalion moved to India, the 2nd Battalion found itself on home ground at Pembroke Dock in South Wales. Two years later it went to Dublin for less than a year before going back to its former barracks in Aldershot at the end of 1899, in preparation for its deployment to South Africa to take part in the Boer War. As part of 15 Brigade in 7 Division, the battalion fought in a number of the notable battles, such as the Relief of Kimberley and at Modder River, suffering some 220 casualties and by the end of the war in 1902 was on garrison duties in Johannesburg. On 20 May 1904 they were on their way home again, arriving at Bulford a month later where they remained for two years before transferring to Aldershot. 1909 found them in Chatham and a year later in December 1910 it was back to Pretoria in South Africa once more, just as the 1st Battalion returned to England, where it was to remain for the next four years, after its long sojourn in India. At about this time, in 1908, the Haldane reforms established the territorial force, under which a number of volunteer battalions of the regiment came into being and which were to figure in the Great War of 1914, more of which later.

After two years in South Africa, the 2nd Battalion moved to Tientsin, northern China in 1912 for what became an interesting and significant posting. For some years, Germany had had colonial interests in the Far East and had established the port of Tsingtao on the north eastern Chinese coast as a base for their Asiatic fleet. To redress the political balance within the region, an Anglo-Japanese alliance had been set up in 1902 which necessitated a British military presence in the area. Each delegation co-existed in harmony until the outbreak of the First World War on 4 August 1914, at which point the Germans were issued with an ultimatum to transfer control of the port to Japan. This ultimatum expired without answer on 23 August, at which stage Japan declared war on Germany and determined to seize Tsingtao. Under the terms of the 1902 agreement, Britain was required to support Japan and the 2nd Battalion found themselves in an unlikely alliance with this country.[3] The blockade of the port began on 27 August and the 2nd Battalion landed in Laoshan Bay a month later in preparation for an advance from the north towards Tsingtao. By 27 September, after a week's difficult marching, they were in position on the outskirts of Tsingtao for what in effect became a siege of the port with the Japanese. There were a number of indeterminate attacks over the next month in which the battalion took some casualties and by 7 November the Germans, heavily outnumbered, agreed to surrender. The allied forces took possession of the port on 16 November and a composite company, made up from a platoon from each company in the battalion, along with 36 Sikh Regiment who had also taken part in the siege, represented the British army at the formal entry into Tsingtao. Casualties of 12 killed and 53 wounded were thankfully light and the regiment is unique throughout the British army today in having the name *"Tsingtao"* as a battle honour on its Colours.[4]

The battalion left China three days later for Hong Kong, where they collected their families and then on 4 December sailed for home, arriving on 12 January 1915. There was no time for any leave however; the army was heavily embroiled in trench warfare on the Western Front and they set off for Coventry to join their new formation, 87 Brigade, which was part of 29 Division. Initially

---

3   At this time the Germans had a lease on the territories from China. The British, French, Italians and the Japanese all had concessions at Tientsin as part of their imperial interests in the region. The Japanese, as allies of Britain since 1902, were asked by the British to support them in the war against Germany. When the Japanese demanded that the Germans surrender the port of Tsingtao, and they did not, the British were obliged to assist the Japanese in besieging them.

4   C T Atkinson, *History of the 24th Foot.*

earmarked to serve in France, there was a change of plan at the last moment and on 12 March the division was inspected by His Majesty King George V at Dunsmore Heath in the West Midlands prior to embarking for the Dardanelles five days later. It is interesting to surmise that if the conflict at Tsingtao had continued for a longer period then the battalion may not have returned in time to take up its place in 29 Division and its role in the ensuing war would have been quite different. Of significance however is the fact that this battalion had just seen active service and its team of officers and non commissioned officers were battle trained with combat experience which would stand them in good stead for the unimaginable bloodshed, deprivation, disease and disillusionment which the Gallipoli campaign was about to unleash upon them.

* * *

In the same way as ships at sea are required to maintain a log book of their daily activity and movement, so do battalions keep a war diary on active service. The daily entries contain a record of operational activities, locations of units, lists of reinforcements and casualties and any other key events at the time. Officers and soldiers were discouraged from keeping personal diaries, as their contents could compromise security if they fell into the wrong hands. According to one account, they were certainly not allowed to mention casualties or units in any diaries or notes, nor were they allowed to make any sketches. After 14 May 1915 they were forbidden to keep diaries of any description. Fortunately, Lieutenant Ernest Laman, the Quartermaster of 2 SWB, (and as such, responsible for unit logistics) quietly ignored this instruction, as did many other officers as a matter of interest, leaving for posterity a unique personal perspective of the battalion's activities throughout the whole campaign.

Ernest Kirkland Laman was born on 4 December 1875 at Shoeburyness in Essex. His father was Thomas John Laman, born in 1841, who married Diana Kirkland from Londonderry Ireland, in 1870 at Pembroke, Bermuda. Her maiden name is significant as it eventually became a prefix to the family surname with later generations becoming known as Kirkland-Laman. Ernest was the youngest of three brothers, the eldest being Thomas Alexander who was born in 1872 and then William Edmund in 1874. Their father served as a sergeant in the Royal Engineers, but died at the age of 45 in 1886, five years after leaving the army when Ernest was just 11 years old. Two years later in January 1888 Ernest went to the Duke of York's Royal Military School. Founded in 1769, the school's primary purpose was to educate the orphans of British servicemen killed in the Napoleonic Wars of 1793-1815, but was later opened up to all servicemen's children. Originally established in London, the school moved to Dover in 1909, from where it continues to operate.

As well as providing Ernest with a sound military grounding, the school also gave him a comprehensive education over the next two and a half years and it soon became clear that he was a very bright young boy, with a strong clerical aptitude which was to stand him in good stead in later years. In the short time that he was there he reached the rank of colour-corporal, which was not an official army rank, but which, at the school, equated to being a sergeant. When he left the school at the age of 15½ he received a coveted certificate, which stated that he was of "good conduct being one of the two best boys who left the school during the year ending 30th June 1890." This was accompanied by a financial gratuity of 2 pounds, 7 shillings and 10 pence; a healthy sum at the time (approximately £200 in 2015) and indicative of his ability and potential.[5] As the son of a serviceman and with a military education behind him, it is not surprising that Ernest decided to

---

5   Pre-decimal currency. 12 pence = 1 shilling; 20 shillings = 1 pound. Compare this gratuity with a British private soldier who was paid 1 shilling a day at the time.

Image 3. Ernest as a Lance Corporal (Mrs F Voelcker).

Image 4. On promotion to Colour Sergeant (Mrs F Voelcker).

join the army and one year later on 11 September 1891 he joined up as a boy soldier at the tender age of 16½. His first choice was to follow his father into the Royal Engineers but he was turned down, not because of any educational deficiency, but because he was allegedly not tall enough; as a young teenager he stood just five feet tall and weighed only six stone. Not to be deterred he joined the 1st Battalion the South Wales Borderers as a boy soldier in the regimental band, having learnt to play the French horn while at school.

What made him choose a Welsh regiment is not clear as there were no family connections with Wales. However, the battalion was stationed in Aldershot at the time where his mother, Diana Kirkland, was, at one time, the housekeeper at the Royal Pavilion, Ascot and it is possible that he may have wanted to be based near her, at least when in UK. In any event, it was a turning point in his life and the beginning of a long and distinguished career. Within the space of a year he had passed his certificate of education at the top level of first class. This was a military educational requirement for promotion purposes and it is no surprise, after his achievements at the Duke of York's School, that he passed this so soon; many is the soldier who has struggled with this requirement for years and their career held back as a consequence. Five years later in 1896, at the age of 21, he was promoted to lance corporal while the battalion was in Gibraltar. Clearly destined for greater things and having moved to India in 1897, where he was to spend a lengthy part of his soldiering, he became a corporal in 1900 and then a lance sergeant in 1902. After 12 years' service, a soldier's record of service would be reviewed to see whether he had the potential for further promotion or whether he should be discharged. In Ernest's case there was no doubting his ability and he was re-engaged to complete the standard career of 21 years with the Colours, a military term denoting full and regular service. Promotion to sergeant soon followed in 1903 and then colour sergeant in 1905. During this year he returned to the UK for a few months to attend a weapon handling instructor's course at the School of Musketry at Hythe, Kent. Established in 1853 this military school became the benchmark for the army's standards of marksmanship and weapon training and Ernest passed out near the top of his course with a distinguished grading. With this skill behind him he represented the battalion on numerous occasions in shooting competitions.

The next few years were to be auspicious ones for Ernest, both militarily and personally. In March 1905, as a colour sergeant in Peshawar and coming up 30 years old, he had met a lovely young lady called Edith Sybil Johns. Twelve years younger than Ernest, Edith was the daughter of Frederick William Johns, the civilian manager of the local army commissariat, responsible for the provision of food supplies and other commodities for resident British battalions. Of Welsh origin, Edith was born in Brecon in 1887, but her parents had lived abroad for some time, first of all in Gibraltar and then in India where she went to St Dennis's School in West Pakistan. This was a whirlwind romance, despite Ernest having been back in England on his musketry course for some time and on Saint Valentine's Day, 14 February 1906 they were married in the Church of the Holy Trinity at Karachi. They were to be blessed with three children, all of whom were to follow their father into one service or another. First of all, Frederick Ernest was born on New Year's Eve 1906 at Karachi and eventually joined the army on the North West Frontier, being awarded the MC for action in Waziristan. He was to be posted as missing, presumed dead, at Singapore in 1942 during the Second World War while only 38. Then Albert Cyril was born at Quetta on 15 November 1908 and joined the Royal Navy, to become a commander and was awarded the OBE. Their third son, Eric Graham, was born in Brecon on 11 September 1915 while Ernest was at Gallipoli, and was commissioned into the South Wales Borderers, reaching the rank of major. He died in 2003 in Dorset at the age of 88.

Image 5. On promotion to Company Sergeant Major (WO2) (Mrs F Voelcker).

Image 6. Ernest as the Regimental Sergeant Major at a battalion sports day (Mrs F Voelcker).

On 9 May 1909, Ernest was promoted to the rank of Warrant Officer Class 1 and became the Regimental Sergeant Major (RSM).[6] This is the most senior rank in the army for any non commissioned officer and is a coveted and most highly sought-after position. The right hand man of the commanding officer and respected by all ranks, he is responsible for standards of discipline, bearing, ethos and morale and his word carries much weight throughout the battalion. To many an RSM, this would be the pinnacle of his career before retirement, but in the case of Ernest he was only 31 with the potential for further advancement. He reached the 21 year point in his career in September 1912, at which stage he would normally have been obliged to retire, but by exception he was granted a further two years extension. True to form, his star continued to rise and on 3 January 1914, at the age of 39 and after just 23 year's service he was commissioned into the rank of lieutenant and quartermaster. Not every RSM is automatically commissioned and selection is very demanding, the individual having to demonstrate the ability and potential to serve in an officer's post, possibly up to the age of 55. A contemporary as a lieutenant would probably be some 30 years younger at the age of 25 or thereabouts, so clearly he would not be expected to take on a similar appointment, such as a platoon commander. Being commissioned from the ranks – known as a quartermaster commission or in more recent years as a late entry commission – it would be usual to take on the role of quartermaster which involves the administration and logistics of a battalion. Having come up through the ranks he would be very familiar with these disciplines and his age and experience would be well suited to such a role. It is also common practice to cross post a newly appointed quartermaster to another battalion, so that he can make a clean break from his previous non commissioned appointment and to enable him to make a fresh start in his new role as an officer. This was the case with Ernest, who transferred to the 2nd Battalion South Wales Borderers, stationed by now on the other side of the world at Tientsin in China. As this was a sister battalion, Ernest would have known quite a few of the personalities there and of course would be at home in an equally Welsh environment, so he had no difficulty in settling in. More to the point, he was about to be thrown in at the deep end with the advent of the First World War and the Battle of Tsingtao later in that year.

Ernest Laman is owed a debt of gratitude in keeping a personal diary throughout the whole of the First World War. He wrote in a down to earth manner, without glossing over the uncertainties of war and as a consequence he has provided a most illuminating account of the conflict at Gallipoli. The pages of his diary follow the fortunes of his battalion, providing a unique opportunity to see the campaign from a new and fascinating angle.

---

6   Technically, he was the 'Sergeant Major' (Warrant Officer). The appointment of RSM and WO1 were introduced at the start of the Great War, along with CSM (WO2). However, as the title of RSM is more commonly understood, it is used here for convenience.

Image 7. RSM Laman with the Colours of 1 SWB in India 1909 (Royal Welsh Museum).

3

Battle Plans

to embark upon the most difficult of all military
operations – a descent on a hostile beach – before
every detail has been carefully weighed,
is to court, and to deserve, disaster

Brig C F Aspinall-Oglander
Official Military History of the Campaign

Despite a lack of overall strategic direction from the War Cabinet, a paucity of resources (particularly man power),and an incomplete staff headquarters, especially administrative and logistics officers, General Sir Ian Hamilton set about drawing up his battle plan soon after his arrival at Gallipoli. He had no detailed knowledge of the ground over which the forthcoming conflict was to be fought and the map coverage was poor to say the least, so he was limited to what he could see from the bridge of his ship as he sailed up and down the coast line of the Gallipoli peninsula, as discreetly as he could. There is no doubt that the Turkish force opposing him was aware of British intentions; indeed, security had been very lax for some time and the invading army was known initially as the Constantinople Field Force which left very little to the imagination. It was eventually changed to the Mediterranean Field Force, a classic example of locking the stable door after the horse had bolted. The best intelligence available put the Turkish ground troops at up to 70,000, with the opportunity of further reinforcements moving overland from mainland Turkey without hindrance. General Hamilton had a similar number of troops available to him, but based on the principle that an invading force should be three times the strength of a defending adversary, this was not nearly enough. Given the demands of the Western Front, reinforcements were going to be in short supply for the general, so he had to make do with what was immediately available to him. The Australian and New Zealand Army Corps (to become known famously by its initials ANZAC), originally bound for the Western Front, was being held in Egypt for the impending conflict and the port of Alexandria was a hive of activity as 29 Division had to unload and repack the stores on its ships so that they were more readily available for a campaign that the division had not expected to be involved in. The third component of General Hamilton's force was a contingent offered up by France as part of its alliance obligations. This was the Corps Expeditionnaire D'Orient (CEO), a force of almost 17,000 troops made up from the French Foreign Legion, Zouaves and Senegalese soldiers and commanded initially by General d'Amade. Finally, the general was supplemented by the Royal Naval Division (RND), an initiative of Winston Churchill as First Lord of the Admiralty, which was an amalgam of Royal Marine Light Infantry (RMLI) and battalions of naval reservists who were surplus to requirement in their primary role, or for whom no ships were available. There were eight such battalions, named after famous admirals – the Nelson Battalion for example – and they had been trained, albeit briefly, in the infantry role.

In making his appreciation, General Hamilton held fast to the primary objective of the campaign, which was the removal of the enemy batteries from the shores of the Dardanelles Narrows, so that the fleet could make its way along the waterway to capture Constantinople. To facilitate this, Hamilton could either land on the Asiatic side of the Dardanelles, or invade the Gallipoli peninsula. As far as the Asiatic option was concerned, this would lay the right flank of his force open to attack from mainland Turkey by a force which might be larger than his own. It would also change the nature of any ensuing conflict to a continental battle (that is, a conventional battle fought over a large land mass, rather than expeditionary warfare with a limited objective) for which he had neither the troops nor the resources. Finally he had been directed by Lord Kitchener from the outset, not to invade from the Asiatic side. While he was to set up a diversionary landing on Asiatic soil at Kum Kale by the French expeditionary force a little later on, General Hamilton therefore restricted his planning to an invasion of the peninsula itself.

The Gallipoli peninsula is about 40 miles (60kms) in length from the Gulf of Saros in the north to Cape Helles in the south and is only some 15 miles (25kms) across at its widest point. Typical of most Aegean islands, the landscape is a variety of open rocky expanse and dense, low growing mediterranean shrubs covered in spikes and barbs which can impede movement, particularly by large numbers of troops in tactical formations. As the ground rises, and mainly in the centre of the peninsula, the terrain gives way to numerous sharp backed ridges of limestone cliffs, intersected by a maze of valleys running down to the sea on either side of the peninsula. In the summer, the climate is insufferably hot, dry and dusty, and there were few, if any, flowing rivers and streams; ground water was, however, available in places. There is a large salt lake at Suvla Bay, the level of which is seasonal; in the summer of 1915 it was completely dry. There are a number of hills dominating the centre of the peninsula which were key factors in General Hamilton's planning. In the south is Achi Baba at about 700 feet (218m) with views across the lower reaches of the peninsula, control of which would dominate the Narrows; further to the north is the Kilid Bahr Plateau, looking down upon the Narrows to the east and then in the centre of the peninsula is the Sari Bair feature and the high point of Koja Chemin Tepe at 971 feet (308m), the capture of which would be the key to success by the invading forces. Along most of the western coastline and on the southern tip of the peninsula at Cape Helles, the beaches are very narrow in both width and length, and are faced by either rising ground or steep ridges in many areas, so the opportunity to land an invading force in strength at any one point was very limited indeed.

With this in mind, General Hamilton looked at a number of possible locations to commit his forces. Starting at the north of the peninsula, the first option was the Gulf of Saros, in the area known as the Bulair Lines, so called from three defensive lines across the narrow neck, built during the Crimean War of 1853 to 1856 by the British and the French, then strengthened later by the Turks. Here the peninsula was only a few miles wide and the lie of the land could cope with a large scale invasion. Success would effectively strangle the whole of the peninsula but it was some distance from the primary objective of the Dardanelles Narrows and both flanks of the invading force would be open to counter attack by the defending force. It was also an obvious place for an invasion and was therefore likely to be heavily defended. The next possibility was Suvla Bay on the western coast of the peninsula mid way between north and south. However, while more strategically located and a good position from which to strike at the heights of Sari Bair, the condition of the shallows approaching the beach were unknown and the large salt lake would present a significant obstacle to assaulting troops if filled with water at the time. Also, his flanks would still be exposed to the enemy, whose positions and strengths were not well known at this stage, and any enemy artillery fire from the heights of Sari Bair would inflict serious casualties on allied troops on the open and uncovered plain.

General Hamilton then considered the beaches to the north and south of Gaba Tepe. Opposite the Narrows on the other side of the peninsula to Chanakale, a rapid advance across the Kalid Bahr plateau would achieve the objective of taking out the Turkish defensive batteries, (a strategy applied during the Falklands campaign of 1982, when the British forces marched across the island from west to east to capture the airport at Port Stanley) but his northern flank would be exposed to any enemy positions on the high ground and the beaches did not lend themselves to a large concentration of troops. However, this area did have potential when considered in conjunction with the general's final option at the southern end of the peninsula – Cape Helles. There was no single beach large enough to support a *coup de main*, apart from Morto Bay, but this would be exposed to artillery fire from Kum Kale on the Asiatic side across the entrance to the Dardanelles. On the other hand an invading force at the base of the Cape would have its flanks secured by the Royal Navy on both sides and its advance northwards would sweep the peninsula clear of Turkish troops, thus laying bare the defences along the western approaches to the Dardanelles. With all this in mind, the general drew up his plan, which he would reveal to his divisional commanders in due course.

* * *

While General Hamilton was considering his options, Turkish hands were not idle. That an invasion was imminent was not in doubt, but the defences of the peninsula lacked cohesion, so on 24 March 1915, Enver Pasha, the Turkish war minister decided to combine his forces into one unified command under General Liman von Sanders, former head of the German military mission to Turkey. Like his opposite number, General von Sanders made an appreciation of likely landing places and came to similar conclusions, but from a different perspective. He believed that an invasion of the Asiatic coast was a high priority for the British commander and he also considered the Gulf of Saros to be most suitable for an offensive landing. Indeed, up to the day of the invasion he was almost certain that this is where the assaulting troops would land. Alternative locations might be the Gaba Tepe beaches and Cape Helles, just as General Hamilton had decided, but without firm intelligence he had to cover all options. On arriving at Gallipoli from Constantinople, General von Sanders was dismayed at what he found:

quite contrary to my principles, the troops were scattered all along the coast like the frontier detachments of days gone by. Everywhere the enemy would meet with a certain amount of opposition, but the absence of any reserves precluded the possibility of a sustained and vigorous defence.[1]

His general outline of defence was to concentrate his forces into small garrisons at likely invasion points but with strong mobile reserves at strategic locations, ready to deploy as required once the enemy intentions became known. In principle, this was sensible planning, but there was a considerable element of risk involved, as the actual number of defending troops in any one location was very thin. Had General Hamilton but known, there was only one company of infantry, with one more in close support, covering the beaches at Gaba Tepe, where the ANZAC forces were to

---

1   Gen Liman von Sanders, *Five Years in Turkey* (Annapolis MD: US Naval Academy, 1927).

land, and there was but one Turkish regiment, in total some four companies including engineers for beach defences, in the immediate area of the southern tip of the peninsula. In favour of General von Sanders however, were the obstacles he was able to put in place on the beaches he considered most likely to be used for the British assault. As well as a network of defensive trenches, barbed wire entanglements were spread across these beaches extending into the shallow waters, which would seriously impede assaulting troops embarking from their boats, and the enemy's weapons were cleverly sited to rake murderous fire across the expanse of the beaches, bringing down in the open those who had made it through the barbed wire. These two obstacles alone would, it was hoped, either stop the invaders in their tracks, or at least buy sufficient time for Turkish reserves to be rushed to the critical areas so as to launch a strong counter-attack, thus driving the assaulting forces back to the beaches and even in to the sea. It was going to be touch and go, but the Turks had more than a month since the great sea battle of 18 March, with no further offensive activity by the British, to strengthen their defences. As General von Sanders remarked in his memoirs:

> the English allowed us four good weeks of respite for all this work before their great disembarkation. This respite just sufficed for the most indispensable measures to be taken… a month earlier might have been fatal to the defenders.

* * *

Returning to activities at home in England, the 2nd Battalion the South Wales Borderers prepared for the reality of war, beginning with the journey by sea to the Dardanelles. With the initial embarkation having been delayed by 24 hours the battalion, commanded by Lieutenant Colonel H G Casson left Rugby station in the Midlands on Tuesday 16 March 1915 in two trains. Leaving at about 3:00 p.m. first to travel were 13 officers and 492 other ranks of A and B Companies as well as Battalion Headquarters, with 45 horses and mules plus 12 vehicles. In the second train two hours later were 14 Officers with 516 NCOs and men of C and D Companies with their machine gunners, along with 45 horses and mules with 13 vehicles. By late evening they had all arrived at Avonmouth Docks, where the River Severn opens out into the Bristol Channel, with a total of 28 Officers (they had now been joined by their medical officer, Lieutenant Blake RAMC) and 1008 other ranks, ready to embark on the SS *Canada*. One officer, Lieutenant Rawle and 70 soldiers (transport men and grooms) embarked separately, with the horses and mules, on the *City of Edinburgh*. The next day, on Wednesday 17 March, they set sail at about 5:00 p.m. but had to travel without lights due to the threat of enemy submarines. However, the journey was uneventful and on Sunday 21 March they passed Gibraltar, arriving in harbour at Malta on Wednesday 24 March for refuelling. While this was being done, the men had to remain on board while the officers and warrant officers had the privilege and pleasure of going ashore for some relaxation. As troop ships were the only means of travelling to the far corners of the British empire at this time, soldiers often grew attached to the vessels in which they spent many weeks or months at sea and personal diaries regularly contain affectionate reminiscences of various ships. While still in Malta, one account records that the HMT *Soudan*, the ship on which the battalion had sailed for South Africa in 1910 and which also took them to China in 1912, came into harbour, looking quite smart now that she had been converted into a hospital ship. What horror its crew was to witness in the coming months.

Two days later the battalion was on its way across the mediterranean for the port of Alexandria on the northern coast of Egypt. They arrived on Monday 29 March and moved into a temporary camp.

It would have been the responsibility of the quartermaster to make the necessary arrangements to set up such a camp and with a workforce from each of the rifle companies he would have gone on ahead to the new location with what is called the advance party. In his stores he would have sufficient tentage to house the battalion and his cooks would then set about preparing a meal, either from tinned food that was already held, or from whatever fresh produce he could procure locally.

Early the next day the battalion began to unload its stores which went by train to the transit area, known as Mex Camp. Some lucky soldiers accompanied the baggage while the remainder had to march from the port to the camp as was the custom – hence the expression today of "marching in" or "marching out" when taking over or leaving military accommodation – a distance of some six miles. In the heat of the afternoon and after 10 days at sea, it was a travel weary battalion that eventually arrived at their new destination, but at least they would have appreciated their tents being set up already and a basic but hot meal to welcome them. Two days later the horses arrived and the battalion was now complete.

An early entry in Ernest's diary reads:

Monday 29 March 1915

Arrived at Alexandria. Disembarked following day and proceeded to Camp Mex about 6 miles out. Messes and tentage set up. Owing to scanty preparations the ration question especially as regards bread was pretty serious and although water had been laid on the pressure was insufficient. These little inconveniences however were expected and eventually overcome. The glare was rather trying to the eyes.[2]

As the word Mess, or the Officers' Mess, will appear regularly in Ernest's diary, a brief explanation of its meaning and significance will be of assistance. Class distinction had long been part of the fabric of British society at the time and it was particularly noticeable throughout the army where men from all walks of life lived and worked much closer together than they would normally have done in civilian society. Officers came primarily from the upper classes, especially when commissions could be purchased and quite often social background meant more than military ability. From 1870 this started to change, when the purchase of commissions was abolished. The Cardwell reforms introduced a more progressive career structure and by 1914 officers had to demonstrate a level of professional competence, irrespective of their personal status. However, officers still remained predominantly young men from public schools and the aristocracy. While no longer the case today, there was also a social hierarchy within regiments at the time, with cavalry and infantry of the line being of perceived higher standing than, say, artillery, engineers or logistic support units. Those officers from the landed gentry took staff and servants for granted and on active service they would usually be allocated soldiers as a man-servant, or orderly, to look after their personal equipment and a groom to tend to their horse if they had one. Soldiers, on the other hand, were very much working class men and under normal circumstances the two groups would seldom mix or spend protracted periods of time together. The officers were responsible for the command of their soldiers, especially in battle, but the daily administrative routine was invariably left to the senior non commissioned officers.

While soldiers' living conditions in the field were very rudimentary, the officers of each regiment would, where possible and certainly during peacetime, live far more comfortably in a facility similar

2   Royal Welsh Museum, BRCRM: 2013.176 The Diary of Lieutenant (QM) EK Laman 1915 Vol 1. All subsequent extracts are from the same diary.

to a small country club, known as the Officers' Mess. This would range from a permanent building in a garrison town at home, or abroad in such places as India, to a makeshift building or series of tents on active service, but the concept was nearly always the same. There would be a dining room with as much regimental silver, crockery and cutlery as the regiment had been able to take with them. There would be an anteroom, or lounge, which was as well furnished as possible and each officer would then have his own room or tent as his bedroom. Soldiers would be employed as the cooks and servants and quite formal codes of behaviour and protocol were expected. Meals would usually be taken together by all mess members and they would, where practical and certainly during peacetime, dress formally for dinner. The regimental Colours would be housed in the mess and be on display each day, although by 1915 this custom was becoming restricted to home stations only. While in contact with the enemy such niceties did not apply of course, but away from the battlefield there would be an Officers' Mess somewhere and on this occasion it was in Mex Camp at Alexandria. Officers contributed to the upkeep of the Mess from their own pockets and received a mess bill at the end of each month for additional items purchased, such as drinks. Once the battalion was deployed on the Gallipoli peninsula then none of this would be practical but even in a makeshift rest area away from the front line, officers would try to re-create some semblance of normality if they could.

Over the next week, the battalion took part in some rigorous training with particular emphasis being placed on disembarking from boats in readiness for inevitable beach landings at Gallipoli. At this stage they did not know where and they did not know when such a landing might take place, but these were experienced regular soldiers who had seen combat at Tsingtao only six months previously and their preparation would have been meticulous. The fact that it was the Easter weekend saw no let-up in training and on Friday 2 April (Good Friday) the officers of the battalion attended a brigade demonstration, practising a forced beach landing from rowing boats, while the soldiers paraded at 9:00 a.m. for half an hour of rifle exercises for upper body strength, followed by half an hour of company drill under company sergeant majors, in preparation for an hour of battalion drill under the regimental sergeant major. Drill has always been – and still is today – a fundamental part of a soldiers training and military ethos. It instils personal and corporate discipline, team spirit, obedience to orders, bearing, pride and a deep seated esprit de corps of which all self respecting officers and soldiers are extremely proud.

On Easter Saturday, there was a five mile route march to a deserted beach where the battalion practised landing from rowing boats. Easter Sunday saw the traditional church parade and then on Easter Monday there was an early start at 2:40 a.m. for a brigade level operation, again centred on a beach landing at dawn, returning to camp by 7:00 a.m. Then on Tuesday 6 April they mustered for inspection by the commander in chief, General Sir Ian Hamilton. There were 25 officers and 871 other ranks on parade; perhaps the last time that so many of them would ever be assembled together during the campaign. The parade started at 11.30 a.m. during which they had to contend with a severe sandstorm for most of the inspection, but they had the satisfaction of being declared fit for purpose. The following day they received orders to embark within the next 24 hours and at mid-day on Thursday 8 April, with all stores and tentage having been packed away, they marched out of camp once more, this time much fitter than when they had arrived, reaching the quay side by 3:00 p.m. There they embarked on the SS *Alaunia*, along with 86 Brigade Headquarters and elements of the 2nd Royal Fusiliers, the Royal Naval Division and the 2nd London Field Company Royal Engineers – a total of over 60 officers and 2,000 soldiers.

On the morning of Sunday 11 April the battalion arrived at Lemnos which is a Greek island some 60 miles to the west of the Turkish coast so it was seen to be a secure administrative base for the invading force. Though the island itself had little to commend it, there was more than enough space to house units in transit (or for rest periods from battle later on) and Mudros Bay provided a large natural harbour. While the main body of the battalion had arrived without incident, the SS *Manitou* with about 600 men and the battalion's horses and transport on board was not so fortunate. Sailing without escort, it was apprehended on the Alexandria–Mudros transport route by a Turkish torpedo boat, the *Demir Hissar* and its German commander gave the captain of the *Manitou* just three minutes, then extended to 10, for all to abandon ship. Lifeboats were launched but in the ensuing chaos 51 soldiers were drowned, two of whom were thought to be from 2 SWB. Private Hogg of B Company was a casualty, but Lance Corporal Frost from A Company, assumed drowned, was discovered later in hospital in Malta having been plucked out of the sea by a tug. Ironically, all three torpedoes fired by the *Demir Hissar* missed their target and the Turkish boat was driven off by approaching destroyers, serving only to confirm the low opinion already held of the enemy's offensive capabilities. The *Manitou* then limped into Mudros Bay five days later, but with its cargo still intact.

In an attempt to keep the overall plan as secret as possible, not a great deal of information about the battle plan had been released, even at this late stage, so many of the soldiers did not know their final destination yet. However, some of the officers had a good idea of what was happening and as Ernest's diary tells us:

Sunday 11 April 1915

Arrived at Lemnos. Found the harbour full of shipping. It was understood that as soon as the Division was complete here, that we should be launched in the attack on the various beaches in the Gallipoli peninsula. We stayed 13 days at Lemnos practicing disembarkation, rowing, ladder scaling etc to keep men fit. Went out for a row myself a couple of times but didn't have an opportunity of going ashore. Something always had to be done just as the chance presented itself.

Sergeant (later CSM) Bean of D Company also kept a diary for the early part of the campaign and his entries capture the atmosphere of training for the next few days:

Monday 12 April 1915.

Lowered all ship's boats today so that troops can practice rowing. 16 men of each platoon to be instructed and trained in rowing. Took 16 men of the platoon out at 2pm and made fairly good progress as most of them knew something about rowing. Pte Carty, an ex fisherman, made a first class stroke. Crew of 2nd Bn Royal Fusiliers got out and could not row back so the Queen Elizabeth's steam pinnace went to the rescue and took them in tow. Practised descending rope ladders over the side into ship's boats – not quite as easy as from one deck to the other.

Tuesday 13 April 1915

Moved from original anchorage and tied up to SS Andania, sister ship to Alaunia. Rope ladder and rowing practice.

Wednesday 14 April 1915

Fire broke out in Gymnasium of Andania about 3pm and did considerable damage before it was under control. 4pm went out with platoon oarsmen who are now fairly proficient, rowed around the Queen Elizabeth. Returned to ship at 6.30pm. Rope ladder drill 8.30pm.

Thursday 15 April 1915

TS Ribble came in this morning with despatches. The Ribble was with us on the Tsingtao Expedition so several of our old friends came aboard as usual loaded with tobacco. They informed us that the Triumph and Usk are also here, both of which were on the same expedition so we shall probably be seeing some more of our Chinese friends. Rope ladder drill twice today.

Friday 16 April 1915

Still at anchor at Lemnos and no sign of a move. Rowing practice 2.30pm. Rope ladder drill 8pm. Troops getting fairly agile, all down in 12 minutes.

Saturday 17 April 1915

Coy paraded 9.15am in FSMO (Field Service Marching Order) and 200 rounds of small arms ammunition to practice the landing. Went down ordinary gangway into three ship's boats which were taken in tow by a Picquet Boat as far as possible then our oarsmen had to row ashore which they did in a very businesslike manner. Troops were very slow getting ashore through trying to keep dry feet. Returned to ship at 1.30pm. The Manitou came in last night (our regimental transport, Lt Rawle in charge, on board). She has lost all her boats and reports having been held up by a Turkish Torpedo Boat which fired three torpedoes at her, two of which passed under her amidships and one under the stern. The Torpedo Boat was probably too near, between 50 and 100 yards. Two of our men reported missing owing to breaking of a Davitt. Lemnos appears to be a very fertile island but there is hardly a tree to be seen. The Greeks appear to be mobilising the natives of the island as we saw several squads all in mufti[3] being drilled by Greek NCOs. First mail arrived today, latest letters dated up to 31 March. Rope ladder drill as usual.

In the meantime, General Hamilton was putting the finishing touches to his order of battle, which he had formulated in close conjunction with Lieutenant General Sir William Birdwood, commander of the ANZAC forces and Vice Admiral J de Robeck, who had taken over as the senior naval officer from Admiral Carden just before the main sea battle of 18 March. It has been put forward that the lack of joint planning and co-operation between the army and the navy was one of the major weaknesses of the Gallipoli campaign, but the initial invasion could not have taken place without the two services working closely together. It is true to say that the Royal Navy still favoured another assault upon the Narrows, as was the original concept of the campaign, but once General Hamilton had decided upon a beach landing as the priority, endorsed by Lord Kitchener back home, then the navy gave its full support.

---

3   A slang expression for civilian clothes, or casual non-military attire.

On 13 April Major General William Braithwaite, General Hamilton's chief of staff, issued Force Order Number 1 to the senior field officers on behalf of his commander in chief. Conscious of the fact that there was no one single location from which to launch a *coup de main* and as he was not fully aware of his enemy's dispositions, General Hamilton decided upon a number of simultaneous assaults in an attempt to confuse the Turkish commander and to unbalance the distribution of any reserves they might wish to deploy. First of all, in the north at the Bulair Lines there was to be a feint attack by the Royal Naval Division from the Gulf of Saros. There would be no actual landing as such, but it was hoped that sufficient naval activity off the coast would deceive the enemy into believing that this was a likely assault position, thus tying down defensive forces. As will be seen, this proved to be a success.

Then, at the other end of the peninsula, there was to be a diversionary landing by the French CEO at Kum Kale on the Asiatic side of the entrance to the Dardanelles. Here the purpose was two-fold. First of all, it was intended once again to confuse the enemy into believing that this was also a main attack force and secondly, and perhaps more to the point, it would prevent the Turkish artillery bombarding what was to be the primary effort just across the water way at the southern end of the peninsula. This assault by the French was intended to cause as much disruption as possible, but would be called off and the troops redeployed once the primary assault on the peninsula had achieved its first objectives. The main offensive was to be in two separate areas. First of all, an ANZAC covering force of some 1,500 troops was to land on the western coast of Gallipoli to the north of Gaba Tepe. Its aim was to secure the southern spurs of the Sari Bair ridge, to prevent any enemy reinforcement of the southern end of the peninsula and to clear the way for the main ANZAC body. At the same time, 29 Division, commanded by Major General Aylmer Hunter-Weston would land on five separate beaches at Cape Helles in the extreme south. The first troops ashore were to be the covering force with the task of securing the beaches, so that the remainder of the division could be landed without hindrance in preparation for an assault on Achi Baba as its immediate objective and the Kilid Bahr plateau for its ultimate goal.

All of these beaches were designated in reverse alphabetical order. Starting in the north, the ANZAC landing place, approximately mid way between Gaba Tepe and Ari Burnu was to be known as Z Beach. Moving south, the next location was the western (or left) attack position, between Gully Beach and Sari Tepe, known as Y Beach, with a force of 2,000 made up from 1 KOSB, an RMLI battalion and one company from 2 SWB. In similar vein to the French attack at Kum Kale, this force had the task of diverting enemy resources away from the main assault further south. Lower down the peninsula in an area to the north of Tekke Burnu was X Beach, where 2nd Battalion the Royal Fusiliers were to come ashore in what was perceived to be a lightly defended area to secure Hill 114.

The main effort was to be at the toe of the peninsula, but as there was no single beach large enough, the assault was in two locations, fairly close together. First of all and to the south of Tekke Burnu was W Beach, the landing place of 1st Battalion the Lancashire Fusiliers. Adjacent to this was V Beach, opposite the Sedd-el-Bahr Fort, where a covering force of 1st Battalion the Dublin Fusiliers, 1st Battalion the Munster Fusiliers and 2nd Battalion the Royal Hampshires were to come ashore. However, there were insufficient small boats, known as tows, to bring the troops close in to the beaches, so an ingenious plan of an amphibious Trojan horse (no doubt inspired by the close proximity of the historic town of Troy just across the water on the Asiatic shore) in the form of a converted collier ship – the SS *River Clyde* – was devised to beach itself close in to the shore and then rapidly disgorge its cargo of some 2,000 troops upon an unsuspecting enemy.

The final part of the plan was the eastern (or right) attack position, across Morto Bay towards

Eski Hissarlik Point, above which on the cliffs stood the old ruins of De Tott's Battery, named after Baron Francois de Tott, a French military officer who had been employed by the Ottoman government for the task of defending the Dardanelles with artillery fortifications during the Russo–Turkish War of 1768 to 1774. This area should have been designated as T Beach, but it was felt that the letter could be confused in the heat of battle with V Beach, so it was called S Beach instead. Just one battalion was allocated to this role, the task being given to 2 SWB, but as there were insufficient resources to land a full battalion, the force was reduced to three companies (B, C and D Companies) and the fourth company (A Company) was redeployed to the attack at Y Beach. The battalion's task was to cover the right flank of the main assault at V Beach and to divert enemy forces from that area. With the whole of 29 Division committed to this assault there was little if anything available as a reserve, apart from the RND and the French Division, once they had completed their respective tasks.

There is no doubt that this was a very ambitious plan, which entailed a significant amount of intricate staff planning, not least of which was the allocation of troops to tasks and the separate battle instructions for each unit involved, the co-ordination of the movement of naval vessels to transport the assaulting units to their respective beaches, close support artillery as the covering forces landed, plans to follow up with the subsequent landing of the main body, the logistic provision of ammunition, food and water for every individual soldier to carry and the inevitable evacuation of casualties as the battle unfolded. As far as the main divisions are concerned, such detail is outside the scope of this book, but this in no way diminishes its importance and the strengths and weaknesses of the administrative plan had a significant bearing on 2 SWB throughout the campaign, as will be seen.

Anticipation was running high throughout the allied forces and there was an air of optimism that the forthcoming battle against an army which was not held in any high regard would be swift and successful. On Wednesday 21 April, the commander in chief released the following Special Force Order:

Soldiers of France and the King, before us lies an adventure unprecedented in modern warfare. Together with our comrades of the Fleet we are about to force a landing on an open beach in face of positions which have been vaunted by our enemies as impregnable. The landing will be made good by the help of God and the Navy and the positions will be stormed and the war brought one step nearer to a glorious end. Remember, said Lord Kitchener, when bidding adieu to your comrades, remember once you set foot on the Gallipoli Peninsula you must fight this through to a finish. The whole world will be watching your progress and it is for us to prove ourselves worthy of the feat of arms entrusted to us.

(Signed) Ian Hamilton, General

* * *

Lieutenant Colonel Hugh Gilbert Casson, commanding officer of 2 SWB was no stranger to active service. Commissioned in 1886, he served as a captain in South Africa throughout the whole of the Boer War of 1899 to 1901 where he was mentioned in despatches for his exemplary service. Promoted to lieutenant colonel in 1911, he took the battalion to China and commanded during the Tsingtao conflict, so he was able to take preparation for the forthcoming Gallipoli campaign in his stride. Given the task of providing the covering force at S Beach he drew up a straightforward, but comprehensive plan to force a landing on the beach below De Tott's Battery. Not being privy to the Turkish plan of defence, he would have been unaware that this beach had surprisingly not been considered as a likely point of invasion and the Turks had made scant preparation to defend it. The beach had not been wired and there was only one platoon allocated to its actual defence with a second platoon in support about half a mile inland. What he did know was the fact that Morto Bay could be seen from the Asiatic side of the Dardanelles at Kum Kale and that he would be at the mercy of any Turkish artillery from there as his flotilla crossed the open water. It was hoped however that the French assault on that position would neutralise any such bombardment.

Lieutenant Colonel Casson had at his disposal just over 800 men, made up of three companies of his battalion, a detachment of engineers, an artillery liaison officer and signallers, medical support, and a party of Royal Marines and blue jackets from his support ship HMS *Cornwallis*, commanded by Captain A P Davidson. The outline plan was for B and C Companies to assault the enemy trenches on the beach to secure a bridgehead, while D Company, under Major E C Margesson would scale the cliff to take out any enemy in the battery ruins at the top. For this purpose they would be lightly armed and dressed, the remainder of their equipment being wrapped in waterproof sheets and stowed in their boats, ready to be brought up to them afterwards. Once the battle had begun, the three companies and their supporting detachments would disembark from the *Cornwallis* as it entered Morto Bay into four steam trawlers, each of which towed six large cutters, or rowing boats. Each company was about 200 strong and the number in each boat was 36, while the commanding officer also made up a boat with his escort, medical orderlies, signallers and artillery observation party. A number of soldiers were designated as the oarsmen and spare rowers were detailed, by name, to replace possible casualties and they were to be seated near the rowers to take their places immediately if required, all of which had been practised regularly in the days preceding the invasion. Each boat was pre-loaded with four boxes of ammunition and six cases of water and there was also to be a naval rating included who would secure the boat after the troops had landed. The trawlers would get the soldiers to within about 100 yards of the beach, whereupon the men would rapidly disgorge into these boats and row as fast as they could to the beach itself. It was not until later in the campaign that powered assault craft became available for beach landings, and it almost defies belief that the men should have to row themselves ashore, some therefore with their backs to the enemy, at the most critical moment of the assault. One can only wonder at the courage and resolve of the men in those boats, which provided no cover from enemy fire, as they rowed ashore to an unknown fate.

All battle preparation was to be ready by 20 April with an invasion date of 23 April, but bad weather set in so the start date had to be delayed. As the whole of 29 Division, ANZAC and the French Division were embarked on their ships by this stage, it would be a difficult task to resupply them all with fresh provisions to cover any lengthy delay, so any postponement could not realistically be more than 48 hours, giving a revised start date of Sunday 25 April. Fortunately, the bad weather was short lived and on 23 April the order was given to move to battle stations. The first move was that evening as A Company 2 SWB departed on the SS *Southend* to join up with 1 KOSB for its assault on Y Beach, while the remainder of the battalion steamed out of Mudros harbour at Lemnos on the *SS Alaunia*, bound for its start point on the island of Tenedos. There was an air of excited anticipation, as the regimental history records:

as the Alaunia passed the Triumph, the battalion's old friend on the China station and recently at Tsingtao, that battleship's band struck up "Men of Harlech." Her crew crowded the deck and cheered themselves hoarse, the SWB responding with equal vigour.

On the morning of 24 April, the battalion arrived at Tenedos, which was about 30 miles to the south of Morto Bay. As the *Alaunia* was only a transport ship, it was necessary for the battalion to transfer to the battleship HMS *Cornwallis* which was able to support them for the invasion. This was complete by about 9:00 p.m. and the battalion was given a good meal onboard, the last decent meal for some time as it transpired, before a final check of equipment. Each man was in FSMO (field service marching order) which consisted of canvas webbing – belt, pouches and pack held together by shoulder straps - with 250 rounds of ammunition in the front pouches and a small pack on their back containing some spare clothing and a waterproof sheet. They also carried two days worth of iron rations, a term used to describe the basic food of tins of meat, biscuits and water, so that they could at least survive independently until resupply was available. His uniform consisted of a khaki serge jacket and trousers and a thick flannel shirt, with puttees and heavy boots – all quite unsuitable in the scorching heat of the Mediterranean. Interestingly they did not wear a steel helmet, but a cap made of similar material to their jackets, or perhaps a solar sun hat. Officers continued to wear their service dress, shirt, collar and tie, leather Sam-Browne belt and service dress hat. Badges of rank were clearly displayed and apart from being totally impractical for the job in hand it made them obvious targets for Turkish snipers, which accounted for the high number of officer casualties in the early days of the campaign. With his rifle and the clothing he stood up in, each man was carrying over 60lbs (37kgs) which would seem even heavier as he got soaked wading through the sea to get onto the beaches the next day.

The atmosphere was still quite calm and Ernest, usually one of the busiest of men at a time like this, found time for *"a bit of dinner and a smoke"* before turning in. Myriad thoughts go through the mind of an individual soldier on the eve of battle and each man, despite the overall sense of anticipation, would have prepared for the coming conflict in a different manner. Interestingly enough, not every soldier is pre-occupied by the thought of being killed, but more concerned perhaps by the possibility of being badly wounded with life-changing consequences. Also a soldier does not want to let down his comrades or his unit in the heat of battle and once combat has begun, training kicks in and battle drills take over to the exclusion of personal thoughts or concerns. On a lighter note, the odd battle scar does not go amiss and is looked upon as an active service souvenir. A story recounted by a Second World War veteran of D Day in 1944, tells how he was shot through a finger as he landed on the beaches of Normandy. It was only a flesh wound and he was quietly pleased that he would have something to show once the war was over, but to his disappointment the scar quickly healed and by the time he returned home in 1945 there was nothing to see.[4]

---

4   A story recounted to the author by Major Joe Humphreys, a former Royal Marine soldier.

4

The First Invasion

*It is the first step of landing under fire which is
the most critical as well as the most vital*

General Sir Ian Hamilton
diary entry 22 March 1915

The coming of dawn on Sunday 25 April 1915 was quiet and tranquil with not a hint of the maelstrom which was about to be unleashed. 60,000 troops of General Sir Ian Hamilton's invading force were primed ready to go and on the preceding evening had set sail from Lemnos in their constituent parts for their allotted landing places. The Royal Naval Division had the furthest to go for they were the deception plan hoping to mislead the Turks into believing that the invasion would come from the Gulf of Saros well to the north. Next was the ANZAC force, steaming slowly towards the western coast of the peninsula with the intention of coming ashore between Gaba Tepe and Ari Burnu as dawn broke. Further south, 29 Division was poised to invade Cape Helles, landing at V, W and X Beaches with two flanking attacks at S and Y Beach. Finally the French division was ready to create a diversion by assaulting the Asiatic coast across the Dardanelles waterway at Kum Kale, with a view to drawing off enemy reinforcements and silencing the Turkish guns which threatened the landing of 29 Division. It had been advocated by GOC 29 Division, Major General Aylmer Hunter-Weston, that the invasion should take place in broad daylight so that the naval gunners could mark their targets and the troops could see their objectives; however, the disadvantage would be a lack of any surprise and the enemy having full view of the assaulting forces. An attack under the cover of darkness would enable the invasion to get as close as possible without detection, but artillery support would be extremely limited and control of the infantry on the beaches would be very difficult. The compromise decided upon therefore was an approach in darkness with the battle beginning at first light. [1]

After the storms of the last few days, the sea was flat and calm and there was a mist hanging across Morto Bay, where 2 SWB were to land, which the scorching sun would quickly disperse as it began its ascent across the Aegean sky. The Turks were soon alerted to the fact that the invasion, which had been long expected, had begun and their guns at Kum Kale on the other side of the Dardanelles water-way opened up on the vessels in Morto Bay and part of the southern end of the peninsula. At this stage, the mist in the Bay limited the effect of the shelling, but it was a wake-up call to the fact that the battalion was now irrevocably committed to battle. The *Cornwallis* had steamed slowly overnight from Tenedos and by 4:30 a.m. was just off the entrance to the Bay. The battalion had risen early and by now was ready to transfer into the trawlers which had

---

1   Brig Gen C F Aspinall-Oglander, *Official History of the Great War – Gallipoli* (Originally published London 1931) Vol 1 Chapter VII.

come alongside with their rowing boats in tow. By 5:00 a.m. everyone was in place and the flotilla steamed slowly forward under the cover of the naval bombardment which began at the same time.

Image 8. The approach to S Beach across Morto Bay (Author).

Sergeant Sidney Bean was the platoon sergeant of 13 Platoon, D Company. After the war he was asked by Major V Ferguson, a retired officer of the regiment and military historian, who was helping Captain C T Atkinson compile a regimental history, to write about his experiences at Gallipoli. Here, in his own words, is an account of the battalion's landing at S Beach:

Reveille 3.30am. Breakfast 4am. Battalion less A Coy paraded 4.30am FSMO with two days iron rations. D Coy under Major E C Margesson on Quarter Deck. Day breaking but very thick mist prevailing. Orders explained by OC Coys to NCOs and men whilst we are still slowly steaming towards Sedd el Bahir. The three Coys are to land at Morto Bay, D Coy on the extreme right. Trawlers will take us as far as possible then we are to take to rowing boats and row ashore. As soon as we get ashore (if circumstances permit) reorganise by platoons under cover and advance as quickly as possible to the summit of Hill 236 (de Tot's Battery) make good there and get into communication at once with the troops landed from the *River Clyde* on our left. They in turn to connect up with the troops on their left and so form a line right across the Peninsula as quickly as possible and then to push on at once.

5.30am lovely sunrise and mist gradually lifting. *HMS Cornwallis* had now got as near as was considered safe to the peninsula as we were ordered into the trawlers, D Coy into trawler No 362. As soon as everything was ready and reserve water (sealed in empty SAA boxes) and reserve ammunition on board the trawlers we stood off from the *Cornwallis* just long

Image 9. S Beach and the slopes up to de Tott's Battery – now marked by the Turkish War Memorial (Author).

enough to make fast a tow of three ordinary ship's boats on either side of the trawler in such a way that we could jump into them while still going at full speed, each boat party being already told off (sic) and every man detailed for his particular job and waiting men detailed to replace casualties. The Band of the *Cornwallis* in the meantime playing the regimental march "Men of Harlech" on deck. As soon as the tows were fast the trawlers went full steam ahead towards Morto Bay. We had only just left the *Cornwallis* when the bombardment by the Fleet commenced. It is a fine sight – the mist has now completely cleared and we can see the shells bursting on the peninsula but so far none are coming our way. Our men are now busily putting reserve water and ammunition into the rowing boats, four boxes of water and two of ammunition to each. The Russian "Packet of Woodbines" is cruising up and down close in the Asiatic side and firing broadsides for all she is worth, the Turkish shells falling all round here but none seeming to take effect.

We now seem to be getting within range for a shell has just landed in the water close to starboard and we can see them bursting in the water in front of us. We are now quite ready to take to the boats and shells are dropping in the water all around us, but we keep straight ahead, a Coy naval rating taking a semaphore message from the *Cornwallis* has his cap blown off by a bursting shell but continued reading as though quite used to it. We can see the *River Clyde* steaming in on our left and she is getting a warm reception from guns on the cliff above the beach. These guns must be in very good positions for although the shells from the Fleet are simply peppering the cliff there is no sign so far of them slackening their fire. At about 800 yards from shore we get the order to take to the boats which is done very quickly and quietly. My platoon, No 13, is detailed for the leading boat on the starboard side. A naval seaman has been detailed as Cox to each boat and is the first man in; the platoon officer follows and takes the bow. The oarsmen are next, tossing their oars as soon as they are seated. Then follows the remainder of the platoon, every man knows his place and gets to it without noise or confusion. As the last man gets in the boats are cut away and the oars are plied with a will. Shells are falling all around and rifle bullets are whistling harmlessly past. Lt Somerville's boat (15 Platoon) is the first away but we soon catch it up and our boat is the first to beach and without a casualty so far.

Image 10. Lieutenant Colonel (later Brigadier General) Hugh Casson, CO 2 SWB at the start of the campaign (R Welsh Museum).

Sergeant Bean does not mention the fact that the battalion's assault was running late and should have been launched an hour earlier. The delay was due to the constant three knots current flowing out of the Dardanelles and then northwards along the western side of the peninsula, which the Royal Navy would surely been aware of. There were also a number of French minesweepers in the Bay which were causing an obstruction. That apart, to Sergeant Bean the objective of the assault was quite straightforward. All the landings across Cape Helles were to be simultaneous with the aim of forming a line from shore to shore across the peninsula then pushing forward to the main objective of Achi Baba.

The fact that the ship's band paraded on deck in the early morning to play the battalion's regimental march as they prepared for battle is indicative of the sense of adventure and exhilaration which preceded this war. Preparation and training had been as thorough as it could be, for these were professional soldiers, most of whom had seen active service already, but insufficient respect had been given to the enemy about to face them. The Turkish forces in Morto Bay turned out to be far fewer in number than had been anticipated, but as the invading forces were soon to find out, their tenacity and determination came as a very unpleasant surprise. The "Packet of Woodbines" was the nickname given to the Russian battle cruiser *Askold*, so called because of its five thin upright funnels. Likewise, the French cruiser *Henry IV* became "The Angry Cat" because most British soldiers could not pronounce "Henri Quatre"!

Sergeant Bean's account continues:-

The cliff in front of us rises almost straight out of the sea to a height of about 200 feet and after wading thigh deep through the water for about 30 yards we make for the top. This is a difficult job, for our putties and trousers are wet through and although we are under cover from enemy fire the shells from the Fleet are still bursting on the top of the cliff, the falling stones etc, causing several minor casualties. As we near the top the guns lengthen their range very slightly and we get the men together ready for the final rush over the top. In the meantime glancing over the top of the cliff we can see the ruins of the outer walls of de Tot's Fort or Battery, one a few yards to the right of and at right angles to our right flank running north for about 100 yards varying from 8 to 12 feet in height. The other, varying from 2 to 12 feet in height, 100 yards in front of us runs west towards Morto Bay and forms two sides of a square with the first. No 15 Platoon, who are now up on our left make for the latter and our platoon the former which we soon fix up into loop holes etc for firing. No 15 Platoon are able from their position to enfilade[2] the Turkish trenches facing Morto Bay thereby assisting B and C Coys in landing, for as soon as they, the Turks, find that we have reached the top of de Tots Battery they commence to retire, but the leading platoons of B and C Coy are on them with the bayonet before they can leave their trenches killing or wounding most and taking seven prisoners. These platoons then occupy the trenches, covering the landing of the remainder of their Coys. D Coy had very few casualties but we were unfortunate to lose our Coy officer, Major E C Margesson, who hearing the heavy firing going on in the valley below 15 Platoon ran to a breach in the wall to see how B and C Coys were faring and was immediately shot through the chest, dying within an hour. Lt Blake RAMC was unable to do anything for him. He was buried in the evening on the top of the cliff at the entrance to the Dardanelles about three yards from the wall of de Tots Battery.

The assault up the steep cliff had the great virtue of surprise and the wall defences of the battery were quickly taken. Lieutenant Desmond Henry Sykes Somerville led his platoon forward to a position about 50 yards beyond the battery from which he could see B and C Coys assaulting across S Beach. He placed rifle sections and snipers to bring fire down on the enemy who were withdrawing in front of the coys and organised field telephone communications with the beach so as to order up machine guns and additional ammunition. At this stage they were under fire from Turkish positions to the north and from Turkish guns firing from the Asiatic shore. When Major Margesson was killed, Lieutenant Somerville took over command of D Coy.[3]

Major Edward Cunninghame Margesson's untimely death at such an early stage in the campaign was keenly felt. The loss of any soldier, irrespective of his rank, is a tragedy, but here was a senior officer with a wealth of experience who would have contributed much to the battalion's conduct during the coming battles. Born in 1871, he was commissioned into the South Wales Borderers at the age of 20, became the battalion adjutant soon thereafter and saw active service at Tsingtao.

---

2   The tactic of firing across the front of the enemy, rather than head-on, so as to cause maximum casualties.
3   Royal Welsh Museum BRCRM 2004.90, Diary 77. Extract from the Somerville family history.

Image 11. Major Edward Margesson, 2 SWB, killed at S Beach on 25 April 1915 (Major H Margesson).

Image 12. Captain Desmond Somerville 2 SWB, who was awarded the MC for his actions on 25 April 1915 (Sir Nicholas Somerville).

Although he was buried close to where he fell, he has no marked grave and his name is inscribed instead on the Helles Memorial, a very large white plinth erected close to the shore of the peninsula after the war and which dominates the sky line, recording the 21,000 British and Commonwealth soldiers who lost their lives during the campaign, but who have no known graves. Major Margesson's heritage was to live on however as his son John became a lieutenant colonel in the regiment, serving as the regimental secretary on retirement for seven years and was awarded the MBE, while two of his grandsons, Hugh and John were also commissioned into the Royal Regiment of Wales.

Returning to Sergeant Bean's diary:

> By 7.30am we have got a footing on the peninsula, the right of D Coy resting on the straits at the top of the cliff and the left of C Coy on the beach at Morto Bay, and now we have to wait until the troops landing at Cape Helles and Sedd el Bahir have made good. We can hear heavy firing in that direction but can see nothing of what is happening, so we put our position in a state of defence in case of a counter attack. The Turks were evidently not expecting us to land where we did, thinking perhaps that the cliff would prevent us, for although they were well entrenched along the coast of Morto Bay there was no sign of a trench or even a sniper on the cliff a little further up the Straits. B and C Coys who went straight for the Bay suffered very heavily, a great many being killed or wounded in the boats, including Lt Behrens killed and 2Lt W Chamberlain wounded. As soon as the Coys were properly reorganised parties were sent to the beach to get up the reserve ammunition and water, and the seven prisoners who were interrogated by the CO were set to work on this. Several of our boats have gone adrift; the seamen who were supposed to look after them when they were beached, having landed the ammunition and water then joined us in the advance, picking up the first casualty's rifle they could find, leaving the boats to look after themselves.

It is a matter of regret that some historical accounts of the Gallipoli campaign make scant reference of the capture of S Beach, almost as if it was of little consequence in the greater scheme of things. While admittedly on a smaller scale it was in fact one of the few unqualified successes of that first day and the battalion's assault up the cliff to de Tott's Battery was no mean feat. A 200 foot climb, in soaking wet equipment, against an unknown enemy position, requires physical fitness and courage, mental determination and strong leadership and there is no doubt that all these qualities were in evidence on the day. As one observer of this assault reported:

> It was an unforgettable experience to watch this well trained battalion working its way methodically and without confusion to the top of the battery from both sides. A party of Marines had landed almost immediately after D Company and followed them up the cliff watching them literally fly on ahead, line a wall at the top, place machine guns in position, run telephone communications down the hill and station snipers on a line running by a wall at right angles to the position.[4]

Second Lieutenant Hugh Nevile was an officer in B Company, which had been assigned to clearing the enemy trenches on the beach. Aged 35 and formerly a stockbroker from Birmingham, Nevile had applied for a commission in the special reserve of officers on the outbreak of war. Initially assigned to 3 SWB (Special Reserve) which had mobilised at Brecon, he was transferred to 2 SWB

---

4   C T Atkinson, *History of the South Wales Borderers 1914-1918* (London: Medici Society, 1931), p.105.

in early 1915 to supplement the number of officers required when that battalion was earmarked for service in Gallipoli. He was killed at Scimitar Hill later in the campaign, but until then he maintained a diary and his entry for 25 April is of interest:

> Breakfast at 4.0 Landed at 7.0. Opposition luckily fairly slight but losses in landing and there was a good sniper or two who accounted for M, B & C & J (*Major Margesson and Lts Behren, Chamberlain and Johnson*); two good men scrapped unnecessarily at night. Sad. This place could easily have been held with a few men with a m.g. (*machine gun*). Luckily only few men in trench who scooted very soon; apparently had a m.g though did not use it while we were in boats. (Later found m.g. had caused casualties; Lt Chamberlain and others.) We left the Cornwallis at 4.45 or 5am and got into trawlers holding company or so. Steamed slowly to near Sedd el Bahr stopping from time to time. There we saw Wooden Horse (*SS Clyde*) rammed on beach but further off than we had anticipated. She lost from m.g. chiefly men. Then on NE corner of Sedd el Bahr where K (*his brother in law, Captain Robert Cathcart Kemble Lambert DSO RN, attached to the Queen Elizabeth for disembarkation duties*) was to land; boat loads were having a thin time; hope K wasn't there. They got to quay but could not get out of the corner there. When we landed we cleaned up the trench on the beach where we took a few prisoners. D Coy taking small hill right flank without opposition to speak of. Sniper caused some loss, at least one man, being a very good shot.[5]

Ernest Laman's diary also adds to the drama of the moment:

Sunday 25 April 1915

> The Day. Rose at 4am. Had breakfast, meanwhile getting under weigh (sic). The bombardment started at 5am and we were to disembark at 5.30 in order somewhat as follows: 'S' Beach ourselves in four trawlers under the lee of the battleship Cornwallis. D Coy under Major Margesson leading – other Companies following at intervals of 5 minutes. The Cornwallis took us in as close as she could meanwhile the forts at Kum Kale on the Asiatic side bombarded us. Several shells struck very close to the trawlers, which caused some amusement. This however ceased when one struck my trawler in the steam pipe, which nearly caused a panic for a moment as someone called out that the boiler was going to bust. One man's leg was badly shattered. The trawlers took us in to within about 100 yds from shore when we took to the boats and pulled for all we were worth. The Cornwallis meanwhile swept the beach and cliff with shrapnel and thanks to her we escaped being scuppered. My boat grounded some distance from shore and so the men had to drop into the sea waist deep and then haul the boat up. One of B Coy's boats had seven casualties including 2/Lt Chamberlain. Poor Behrens in another boat was killed. Their boats happened to come under fire from the enemy lying in trenches under the lee of the cliff where the ship's guns could not reach them. These trenches were rushed however and seven prisoners taken.
>
>   D Coy meanwhile climbed the cliff on the east side and got into the old ruined fort (De Totts Battery) practically without opposition. One cannot understand why the enemy did not rush us as soon as the shelling ceased. Had they done so we ought all to have been scuppered. B & C Coys collared the Turks trenches on the west side of the Fort. D Coy with one platoon of C Coy held the Fort. We soon had evidence of the sniping qualities of the

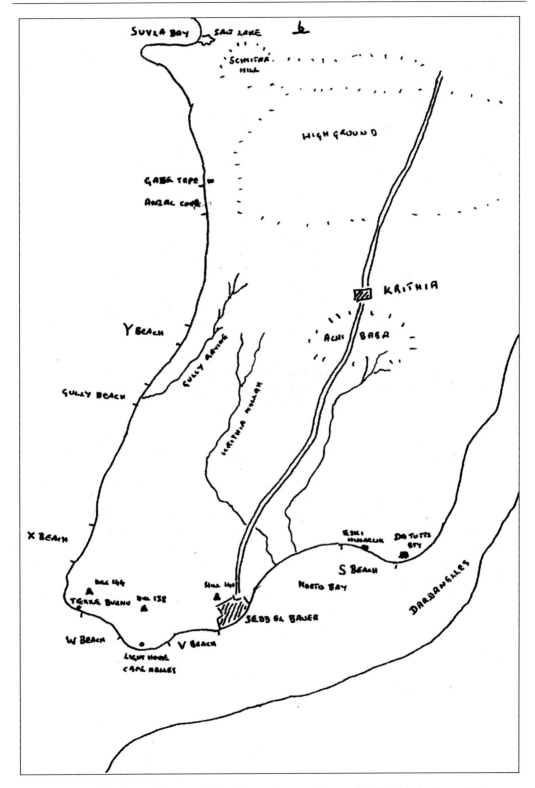

Map 5. A sketch map of Cape Helles by Captain Desmond Somerville (Sir Nicholas Somerville).

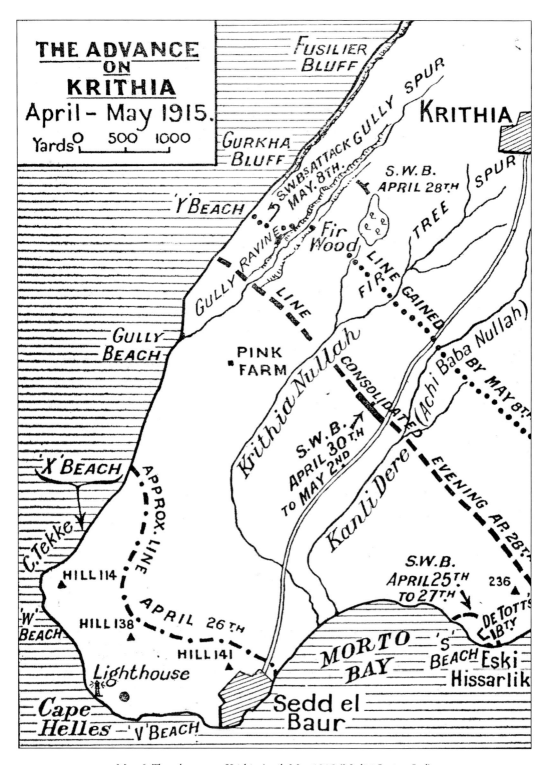

Map 6. The advance on Krithia April–May 1915 (Medici Society Ltd).

Turk, for every head above the parapet became a target. Poor Major Margesson standing in a conspicuous place was hit in the shoulder and unfortunately the bullet glanced and passed through his lungs. He died an hour and a half later. We buried him same evening overlooking the sea along with Pte Goulston who was shot through the head. Capt Birkett has a slight wound in the hand, but was able to carry on till next morning when he was sent off. Captain Johnson[6] was more seriously wounded, but I hear since he is doing well. I had an opportunity of potting Turks myself as the snipers withdrew from the trenches. A most exhilarating feeling one gets as you see a man go down. One sniper however we could not get, nor find out where he was and he caused us a lot of annoyance. A Coy was away with the KOSB at Y Beach and we could learn nothing about them. The view of the Peninsula was good from our position and we could see that things were not going quite so well as was anticipated. We ought to have trekked across to our own Brigade same day, but no order came to move.

Ernest's comment that elsewhere *"things were not going quite so well as was anticipated"* is an understatement if ever there was one and this is a convenient moment to look briefly at the remainder of the initial invasion, starting first of all with General Hamilton's diversionary plans.

* * *

In his own appreciation of the forthcoming battle, General Liman von Sanders had considered Saros Bay at Bulair to the north of the peninsula as a likely landing place by the Allies and had allocated a strong force in reserve for its defence. When the invasion came and the Royal Naval Division was seen steaming into the Bay in the early hours of 25 April, the German general felt that he was right in his assumption and kept his reserve in the north longer than he should have and he spent most of the day in that area in case a major assault developed, despite reports of enemy activity further south. To this extent, Hamilton's deception plan was a success.[7] In similar vein, the French diversionary attack at Kum Kale assisted for some time in holding down Turkish reserves on the Asiatic side of the Dardanelles and while the enemy's artillery was still able to impede allied movement on the other side of the waterway, there is no doubt that this part of General Hamilton's strategy was of benefit to the main body making its way ashore at Cape Helles.

The main battle itself however began with the ANZAC force and their assault of the west coast of the peninsula. Designated to be the spearhead of the invasion, 3rd Australian Brigade under the leadership of Colonel E G Sinclair-MacLaggan (ANZAC brigades were initially commanded by colonels) was to land on Z Beach to the north of Gaba Tepe and the covering force of 1,500 men embarked on the *Queen, Prince of Wales* and *London* at Lemnos during the night and steamed to within five miles of the shore. At this point they would transfer into 12 tows, or rowing boats, attached to steam pinnaces to get within rowing distance of the beach. They were to land at 4:30 a.m. with the second wave of 2,500 men of the brigade following up at first light and their objective was to seize the three main ridges from Gun Ridge in the south to Chunuk Bair in the north. This sounded very straightforward but it did not take account of that well known military adage *" a plan seldom survives contact with the enemy"* as things went wrong from the outset, because instead of coming ashore where it was originally intended, they actually landed about a mile to the north between Hell Spit and Ari Burnu in what was to become known as Anzac Cove. Why did this

6   Later Major General Dudley Johnson VC CB DSO (and Bar) MC who became colonel of the regiment in 1944.
7   Moorehead, *Gallipoli,* p.130.

happen? Some contend that insufficient allowance was made for the current which flowed in a northerly direction, but surely the Royal Navy would have known about this and built this into their calculations. Others suggest that it was due to the inexperience of the young midshipmen piloting the tows who, in the early dawn and the silence, lost their bearings so that the boats bunched and crossed paths, causing confusion and a change of direction; a plausible explanation. It is also maintained, especially in some Australian historical reports, that the final landing place was within operational parameters anyway and as this part of the coast was not so strongly defended by the Turks, it made sense to come ashore there. Wishful justification perhaps, for the size of Anzac Cove is hardly conducive to landing a brigade as the rest of the day was to confirm. As always, the truth, no doubt, lies somewhere in between.[8]

For all that, the Australians stormed ashore with relative ease but the problems began as they started to scale the cliffs. The terrain in this part of the peninsula is particularly hostile, being a series of sharp cliffs and deep gullies filled with coarse, stubby gorse bushes which made movement and visibility, as well as command and control, very difficult indeed. As a result of the confused landing, units were not in their correct formations and were becoming entangled with each other and commanders were separated from their men. The bravery and courage of the individual ANZAC soldier, most of whom were facing battle for the very first time, was not in doubt at all and they stormed the cliffs and gullies with incredible determination. However, as the day wore on, confusion gathered, lines of communication were over-reached and casualties mounted. Once the Turks had overcome the shock of the invasion they began to launch counter-attacks and the Anzac casualties mounted. The dying and wounded being returned to Anzac Cove only added to the confusion as more men and stores were being landed at the same time. Throughout the day, fortune changed hands repeatedly as attack was met with counter-attack on both sides and while the Turks could not force their assailants back into the sea, the ANZACs could not make headway inland for more than about a mile.

There were mixed fortunes as well farther south as the remainder of the assault developed. The first scene of action was at Y Beach where, as the left flank of the main assault, the intention was to draw the enemy away from the principal beaches of Cape Helles and to link up with the battalion landing to their south. The troops involved, 1 KOSB under the command of Lieutenant Colonel Coe, the Plymouth Battalion of the RMLI with Lieutenant Colonel Matthews leading and augmented by A Company 2 SWB led by Captain R G Palmer were brought ashore by the cruisers *Amethyst* and *Sapphire* with *Dublin* and *Goliath* providing close gun support. This was a small, inconspicuous beach with a steep cliff leading to the top and one which the Turks did not consider a likely landing place, and by first light the allied force reached the top unopposed. Patrols were sent out and no contact with the enemy was made, but unfortunately Lieutenant Colonel Matthews did not build upon the success of the situation by preparing a strong defensive position or by calling for reinforcements to capitalise upon their initial superiority. To his credit, General Hamilton, who was cruising the shoreline on board HMS *Queen Elizabeth* and who could see what had happened, *offered* (but notably did not *direct*) GOC 29 Division reinforcements to take advantage of this bonus (*"Would you like to get some more men ashore at Y Beach? If so, trawlers are available"*) but his offer was ignored; considered by some to be a major strategic blunder which could have materially affected the outcome of the war from the outset, although this is countered by the view that this is a *"mixture of fantasy and hindsight"*[9] The Turks however soon realised the significance of the situation and by the evening had started to put in a number of counter attacks

8   Robin Prior, *Gallipoli – The End of the Myth* (London: Yale University Press, 2009) Chapter 8.
9   Prior, *Gallipoli – The End of the Myth*, p.98.

against the allies. The inadequate defences were no protection against enemy machine gun fire and casualties began to mount. The steady trickle of wounded back to the beach and removal by ship somehow gave the impression that an evacuation had been ordered and Lieutenant Colonel Matthews seemed incapable of reversing this and although the Turks took heavy casualties as well, by the following morning Y Beach was empty again. With no tactical gain at all, this fiasco saw the loss of some 700 troops along with the death of Lieutenant Colonel Coe KOSB. As far as A Company 2 SWB was concerned, Captain R G Palmer the company commander was killed, Captain C M Tippets was wounded and 17 soldiers were also killed, 42 wounded and nine recorded as missing.

The next assault position was X Beach, where the 2nd Battalion the Royal Fusiliers, commanded by Lieutenant Colonel Henry Newenham, was to come ashore supported by the 12 inch gun fire power of HMS *Implacable,* whose name became immortalised in the sobriquet attached to this action "*Implacable Landing.*" This was a spirited assault, and once again the Turkish defences were weak, so by 8:00 a.m. the battalion had reached the top of the cliff and were on the way to Hill 114 which was their objective. Seizure of this feature would mean that the entire Turkish position at Cape Helles would be outflanked so heavy opposition was soon encountered, despite the support of the Border Regiment and the Royal Inniskilling Fusiliers as divisional reserves. Headquarters 87 Brigade was to come ashore here later and in quintessentially British style, Colonel Lucas (then brigade major) recalls:

> The landing of the 87th Brigade Headquarters differs from some others. I recollect a bright sunny morning, dead calm sea, not a shot fired. I had a bag in one hand, a coat over my arm, and was assisted down a plank from the boat by an obliging sailor, so that I should not wet my boots. The only thing missing was the hotel.[10]

The harsh reality is the fact that a significant opportunity to outflank the Turks was lost (although there were no specific orders to achieve this) and no contact was made with the force at Y Beach on their left flank which may have had a bearing on the exploitation of that landing.

On their right flank and further round the peninsula was W Beach, where the 1st Battalion the Lancashire Fusiliers were to experience a far more deadly and vicious baptism of fire. The beach itself was about 400 yards long and only some 50 yards in depth, leading up to some steep ridges where the Turks, correctly anticipating this as a likely landing place, had positioned a company of infantry from 3/26 Regiment with machine guns placed to inflict as many casualties as possible. Embarked on HMS *Euryalus*, which was also GOC 29 Division's flagship, the battalion downloaded into cutters at dawn to be towed towards the shore by steam pinnaces, and then eventually cast off to be rowed ashore by naval sailors. Unbeknown to the battalion, the beach was laced with mines, while barbed wire entanglements had been constructed underwater at tide level. HMS *Swiftsure* was designated to give covering fire but with little effect, for as the boats approached the shore the Turks opened fire and the carnage began. Sailors were shot dead at their oars, soldiers who jumped into the water were dragged down by the weight of their equipment and drowned and more perished as they became entangled on the wire at the water's edge and were shot dead where they lay. The battalion took over 500 casualties – almost half their strength – that morning but with incredible courage and valour they had taken the beach by 10:00 a.m. and by 12:30 p.m. they had linked up with X Beach. Assisted by one platoon of the Anson Battalion (RND) and the 1st Battalion the Essex Regiment they had secured Hill 138, their initial objective,

10   Capt Stair Gillon, *The Story of the 29th Division* (London: Thomas Nelson and Sons Ltd, 1925), p.21.

by 4:00 p.m. Their heroic actions this day were to culminate in the award of six Victoria Crosses (giving rise to the well known saying "Six VCs before Breakfast") and their beach was to be renamed the "Lancashire Landing."

Image 13. V Beach from the Helles Memorial. The SS *River Clyde* was beached close to the small headland in the middle distance (Author).

As if all this was not enough, the worst was yet to come at V Beach, which was in effect the principal landing place for the whole assault. The size of the area was similar to that at W Beach and was overlooked on the left by steep cliffs and on the right by the old ruined fort of Sedd-el-Bahr. There were two aspects to this assault. First of all, the 1st Battalion the Royal Dublin Fusiliers were to come ashore in tows, as on most of the other beaches. Then, to overcome the shortage of ships, and no doubt influenced by the classical exploits surrounding the ancient city of Troy nearby on the Asiatic coast, it was decided to recreate a naval version of the Trojan horse. The SS *River Clyde*, a former collier ship with Lieutenant Commander Unwin as its captain, was cleared out and filled with some 2,000 troops of the 1st Battalion the Royal Munster Fusiliers, the 2nd Battalion the Royal Hampshire Regiment, the balance of the Dublin Fusiliers who could not come ashore by tows, and the divisional signallers and engineers. Large ports were cut into each side of the ship with narrow gangplanks leading down to the front, the idea being that the ship would be run aground close to the shore and the soldiers would stream out of the ports, run across lighters which would have been dragged into place to cover the gap between the gang planks and the shoreline and storm onto the beach in force. What folly this turned out to be. First of all, the *Clyde* did not beach itself far enough forward, there was considerable difficulty in getting the lighters into place and once the Turks realised what was happening they trained their machine guns onto the ports of the ship and the soldiers were slaughtered as they attempted to run down the gangplanks. Very few of them made it to the shore-line and their saving grace was a low bank on the beach behind which they could shelter, along with those who also got ashore via the tows, from the withering fire of the Turkish defenders. The despatch of troops from the *Clyde* was soon stopped and those inside the hold had to sit there until the end of the day when they could be brought ashore under the cover of darkness. Those on the beach likewise had to take whatever shelter they could find, with no opportunity of evacuating the wounded and dying until night came.

Image 14. V Beach close to the location where the troops came ashore from the SS *River Clyde* (Author).

By any definition, V Beach was a disaster and by putting all their eggs into one basket as it were, there was no scope to redeploy those soldiers stuck in the bowels of the *Clyde*. Also GOC 29 Division, Major General Hunter-Weston, must be criticised for a distinct lack of flexibility and his inability (or refusal) to exploit windows of opportunity elsewhere. In hindsight, had he reinforced the initial success of Y Beach at an earlier stage, it is possible that this could have altered the whole outcome of the battle. On the other hand, there was a lack of intelligence about enemy dispositions before the assault and the limited means of communication between units on the ground and the staff officers in divisional headquarters was not conducive to keeping pace with the ebb and flow of the battle. However, by the sheer bravery, as ever, of the soldiers on the ground, Sir Ian Hamilton had achieved his objective of securing a landing on the peninsula so his first phase could be called a success – but at a price; almost 4,000 officers and men, some 20 percent of the division's strength, became casualties that day and this was only the beginning. This, then, was what Ernest Laman meant when he wrote in his diary that day:

the view of the peninsula was good from our position and we could see that things were not going quite so well as was anticipated.

* * *

Back at S Beach, the battalion's war diary takes us through the main activities of the day as the beach landing was being secured:

25 April 1915

4.30am. Stood by ready to get into the Trawlers. Cornwallis signalled to trawlers to come alongside about 5 am. Men rapidly changed into trawlers & Cornwallis steamed slowly in towards Morto Bay – two trawlers on her port side & two starboard side.

7 am. Cornwallis made signal for men to enter small boats.

7.30 am. Landing effected as follows. Trawlers in succession steamed in towards shore, on getting in as close as possible a stern anchor was thrown out and small boats cast away. These boats rowed for the shore as quickly as possible. D Coy first to land and made for De Totts Battery at once. C & B Companies on landing made for trench in front of beach at a range of about 100 yds. Manoeuvre completely successful. D Coy cleared De Totts & B & C Companies took trench with the bayonet capturing about 15 Turks.

8.30am. Our position secured. D coy on De Totts Battery & B & C Companies on a ridge about 400 yards to the north west. Some Marines of Cornwallis land with us to assist with the boats, these men did excellent work. Our casualties were not heavy considering the position we attacked. Had it been held by resolute men we should never have been able to capture it without severe loss.

Casualties. Officers
Major E.C. Margesson & Lieut R.P. Behrens killed. Captains D.G. Johnson & G.H. Birkett & Lieut W.J. Chamberlain wounded.
Other Ranks: killed 12. Wounded 40 missing 6.

9am. Watched for landing at Sedd El Bahr, this however did not appear to be a success, we could see troops trying to work up through the ruined village but without success.

10am. Troops observed moving from X beach moving East – this attack however appeared to be diverted towards Sedd El Bahr. From this fact we gathered that the landing at Sedd El Bahr had failed & we were quite isolated. Steps at once taken to consolidate our position, especially as prisoners informed us that 2000 Turks were in our vicinity. Position taken up as follows. D Coy & ½ platoon "C" Coy in De Totts Battery – 3 platoons B Coy ½ platoon C coy on small ridge N.E landing place with 3 platoons "C" Company & 1 Platoon B Coy & R E Detachment in support. Field Hospital detachment with Naval Detachment remained in trees just beneath De Totts where there was an excellent supply of water. Guns from Kum Khale continually shelled our position but without doing much damage. Snipers from Hill

236 very busy indeed. Our orders were to push on towards N.N.W. & join up with our Brigades, but in view of state of affairs the C.O. decided to remain where he was.

12 noon. General situation appeared very involved. Troops appeared to be moving towards Hills 138 & 114 and Turks retiring from 114 were heavily shelled by "Queen Elizabeth" & "Cornwallis".

2 pm. Message received – "On W & Y beach landing is progressing favourably but on V Beach attack is held up by wire – Australians doing well.[11]

These diary entries warrant some comment, as Lieutenant Colonel Casson receives criticism in some quarters for an apparent lack of pro-active determination in capitalising on his initial success. Given the relatively short distances involved, the CO could see across much of the southern face of the peninsula and he was aware of what was happening on some of the beaches and, more importantly, the disaster building up on his left flank at V Beach. His initial orders had been to move on northwards to join up with the other brigades in the division but it was quite clear to him that to do so without support on his left flank would leave him isolated and in danger of being cut off. There was also sniper activity to his front from Hill 236 and his Turkish prisoners led him to believe that there was an enemy force of some 2,000 in the vicinity. The reality was of course nowhere near this figure, but Lieutenant Colonel Casson had no way of verifying this. He had one company detached to Y Beach and he had already sustained 14 dead, 43 wounded and six missing so in the circumstances he quite rightly decided that the wisest thing to do was to consolidate his present position until the outcome across the peninsula clarified itself. Additionally, GOC 29 Division made no attempt to build on the success of 2 SWB at S Beach and it would have been foolhardy for three companies to advance into unknown territory with no definite objective or instructions. The situation which had arisen across the beaches does not seem to have been anticipated and therefore no provision had been made for it.

Next there is the message received in the afternoon regarding the state of the battle on some of the other beaches. Y Beach had gone well at this stage, but only because their landing had been unopposed and it was only later in the day and during the night that their success was to turn to ashes. The Lancashire landing on W Beach had been hard won but as V Beach was a disaster, the proposed link-up of all four beaches across the southern edge of the peninsula did not occur until the following day and then not on the scale that had been originally intended. With regard to V Beach *"being held up by the wire"* the reality was quite different. It was not the wire so much as the inability of the troops on the SS *River Clyde* to come ashore due to the murderous fire of the Turkish machine guns. Those who did make it to the beach had to shelter under a small sand bank until the hours of darkness when the main body could at last consolidate itself in readiness to break out the next day.

And then to the *"Australians doing well."* If by this is meant the fact that the Anzac force had come ashore and was fighting with incredible courage, tenacity and determination then of that there is no doubt. But if this message was to imply that they were on their way to success in taking their objective then that is another matter. As the day progressed, the Turkish counter attacks gathered momentum and the Australians were hard pressed to gain any further ground. As fate would have it, one of the Turkish commanders in this sector was Lieutenant Colonel Mustafa Kemal (later to become Ataturk, President of the Turkish Republic) who urged his troops into

---

11   R Welsh Museum, 2nd Bn South Wales Borderers War Diary 1915 (BRCM: d.1949.8).

battle with that famous exhortation *"I don't order you to attack, I order you to die. In the time that passes until we die, other troops and commanders can take our places"*.[12]

As the day drew to a close the Anzac force was almost spent. Casualties were high and medical facilities were inadequate, command and control was difficult due to the dispersed nature of the troops on the ground, and ammunition, water and food were running short. The two divisional commanders on the ground, General Bridges and General Godley, were coming to the view that their troops might not be able to withstand a concerted counter attack or further heavy bombardment by the Turks and that an evacuation of the Anzac force was the only option. At first, General Birdwood, the Anzac commander, refused to accept their view but as the evening wore on he reluctantly became persuaded and sent the following message to General Hamilton:

> Both my divisional generals and brigadiers have represented to me that they fear their men are thoroughly disorganised by shrapnel fire to which they have been subjected all day after exhaustion and gallant work in the morning. Numbers have dribbled back from the firing line and cannot be collected in this difficult country. Even the New Zealand Brigade, which has only recently been engaged, lost heavily and is, to some extent, demoralised. If troops are subjected to shell fire again tomorrow morning there is likely to be a fiasco, as I have no fresh troops with which to replace those in the firing line. I know my representation is most serious, but if we are to re-embark it must be at once.[13]

The commander in chief was asleep on board the *Queen Elizabeth* when the message arrived, but he was quickly aroused by his very anxious chief of staff and the ball was now in his court. The final sentence of this message laid any suggestion of evacuation clearly at the general's door, but it was one he could not countenance, strategically or logistically. Any plan to evacuate the whole of the Anzac force, even if it was possible at such short notice, would take some time to put into effect and it would be well into the next day, in full view of the Turkish army, before it could be carried out. Casualties would be high and the impact on the remainder of 29 Division elsewhere on the peninsula would be disastrous; indeed it would probably signal the complete failure of the campaign itself. In what was to be one of the most momentous decisions he made during the whole campaign, the general's reply was:

> Your news is indeed serious. But there is nothing else for it but to dig yourselves right in and to stick it out...Hunter-Weston despite his heavy losses will be advancing tomorrow which should divert pressure from you. Make a personal appeal to your men and Godley's to make a supreme effort to hold their ground...you have got through the difficult business, you have only to dig, dig, dig, until you are safe.[14]

This was quickly conveyed to General Birdwood, who accepted the directive he was given and who in turn briefed his two commanders on the ground. From this point onward there was no turning back; the Anzacs were never dislodged from their small stronghold for the remainder of the campaign and from this message grew that famous Australian nickname – Digger. After the war, the Turkish general staff noted in its history of the campaign:

---

12   Moorehead, *Gallipoli*, p.140.
13   Moorehead, *Gallipoli*, pp.153–154.
14   Moorehead, *Gallipoli*, p.155.

Had the British been able to throw stronger forces ashore at Gaba Tepe (the Anzac sector) either by reinforcing more rapidly those first disembarked, or by landing on a broader front, the initial successful advance of 2,500 yards in depth might have been extended so as to include the ridges overlooking the Straits and a serious, perhaps fatal, blow struck at the heart of the Turkish defences.

During the first night ashore on S Beach, there were several heavy bursts of fire from the Turkish positions to the front, which, as 2 SWB had confirmed, ran along a ridge some 800 yards away, but battalion patrols held their fire and the Turks were kept at bay by a few rounds from the ships. One patrol from B Coy became engaged in a fire fight with one enemy patrol and brought in two prisoners, and the only other event of the night was the arrival of a ship's pinnace, loaded with rations and extra ammunition.

* * *

And so, as night fell across the Gallipoli peninsula, it was clear that the allied forces had paid a heavy price for their endeavours, a consequence of the lack of time and resources to plan effectively for this campaign. Insufficiently detailed intelligence about enemy dispositions from the start led to confusion and missed opportunities, while lack of artillery support hindered the attacking forces in their attempts to establish secure bridgeheads on each of their beaches. Casualties had been high and the medical services, with a lack of basic facilities, had struggled to cope with the weight of numbers. But of the sheer bravery and determination of the allied soldiers, under the most arduous and terrifying conditions, there was absolutely no doubt. Despite the numerous setbacks that the day threw at them, they were at least ashore and the enemy had been unable to repel them. General Hamilton saw this day as but the first step on the way to achieving his strategic aim and as he wrote in his diary that night:

> - so now we stand on Turkish terra firma. The price has been paid for the first step and that is the step that counts. Blood, sweat, fire; with these we have forged our master key and forced it into the lock of the Hellespont, rusty and dusty with centuries of disuse. Grant us, O Lord, tenacity to turn it; determination to turn it, till through that open door Queen Elizabeth of England (sic) sails East for the Golden Horn!

Dramatic script indeed and very much in keeping with General Hamilton's somewhat rose tinted spectacles, but to his credit he was confident that his mission could be achieved. Sadly however his optimism was not matched by the reality of inadequate planning and provision by the home team, nor the unexpected ferocity of opposition from an enemy fanatically determined to protect their very homeland. In the days and months which followed, his dreams were to fade inexorably under the weight of unrealistic expectation.

5

Krithia

No sound in all the stagnant trench
where forty standing men
endure the sweat and grit and stench
like cattle in a pen

Robert Nichols
War poet
1893–1944

General Hamilton may have been relieved that his army had a toe-hold on the peninsula at last, but this was only the beginning. He had suffered heavy casualties in the initial invasion and he knew that it would take some time before reinforcements could be sent out by sea from England. On the other hand, General Liman von Sanders could reinforce much more quickly from the Turkish mainland and a further six divisions were already on their way to the peninsula. It was now a race against time and if the Allies were to avoid being driven back into the sea – a very real prospect – General Hamilton had to seize the initiative and strike his way further in-land before the Turks could consolidate their defence. The initial objectives of 25 April had not been taken but if 29 Division could capture the village of Krithia and the Achi Baba hill feature behind it, then they would be in a much stronger position to repel any Turkish counter-attack.

The night of 25 April was far quieter for 2 SWB at S Beach than it was for much of the division and the next morning the battalion heard that the hills near W, V and X beaches had been captured. However, as the ships still continued to shell the Sedd-el-Bahr fortress, this information was clearly not correct and as they could see across Morto Bay to V Beach, the battalion spent much of the morning trying to direct fire from the ships onto the Turkish troops who were beginning to retire from that area. By early afternoon the shelling was starting to take its toll on the Turks and by about 2:30 p.m. Sedd-el-Bahr was eventually rushed by the Dublins, the Royal Hampshire Regiment and the Inniskilling Fusiliers. GOC 29 Division seemed quite content to leave 2 SWB where they were for the time being, sending the message:

Well done SWB. Can you maintain your position for another forty eight hours? I am sending you another 4 days supplies plus the 50 rations lost in the boats to you tonight. Send report of situation twice a day." General Hunter-Weston

As will be seen shortly, this also fitted in with Major General Hunter-Weston's plan for the assault on Krithia, as the general wanted the French Brigade to relieve 2 SWB, once they had extricated themselves from their diversionary assault at Kum Kale. General Hunter-Weston wanted to advance on Achi Baba as soon as possible, but it would take until 28 April until he was in a position to do so, due to limitations of transport to ensure that everyone was in the right place at the right time.

2 SWB spent a further night at S Beach, during which they expected to be assaulted by the Turks at any time, but no such attack materialised. Of course, the commanding officer had a certain freedom of movement within his directive to hold S Beach; he could remain where he was or he could move forward to see what was beyond Hill 236. Not knowing the enemy's dispositions however, he could be cut off and not be able to return to his original position, so the wisest course of action was to remain where he was. At mid-day, orders arrived to say that the battalion was to rejoin 87 Brigade on the west of the peninsula for a new initiative and it would be relieved by a unit of French troops. Their advance party arrived at about 3:00 p.m. to say that the remainder would be there an hour later, but owing to delays in the landing of the French in Morto Bay from Kum Kale, the main body did not arrive until about 7:00 p.m. Then, as Colonel Phillipe, the French commanding officer was very anxious for Lieutenant Colonel Casson to assist his battalion in securing the position, it was well after midnight before 2 SWB could move off towards X Beach. Ernest Laman records the day:

Tuesday 27 April 1915

Witnessed some fine fighting above W beach. The troops drove the Turks out of the fort and they could be seen trying to get across the barbed wire into the communication trenches only to be shot down. They trekked away in hundreds through the woods and the Colonel was able to give valuable information to the battleships who pelted the Turks with shrapnel.[1] The same evening a battalion of French Infantry disembarked and came to relieve us.

A night movement of troops on foot is not the easiest of tasks, even during peacetime. To do so across hostile territory where the route had not been cleared in advance and with battle weary troops who had not slept properly for the best part of 72 hours, was fraught with great difficulty. A small guard of two NCOs and six soldiers was left behind to secure some ammunition and stores at S Beach and the rest of the battalion set off at 1:15 a.m. There was no clearly defined route to follow and the battalion had to move around the coast line of Morto Bay, then behind the lines of allied troops at V and W Beach. They eventually arrived at X Beach at 5:30 a.m. on the morning of 28 April after a four hour march, only to be told that they would be taking part in an assault in less than three hours at 8:00 a.m. with little or no time for any proper preparation. The purpose of this operation, which was to become known as the First Battle of Krithia, was to capture Achi Baba, one of the original objectives of 25 April that had yet to be taken.

Preparation for this battle was scrappy to say the least, but to be fair to the divisional staff, they had little information to give. They did not have accurate positions of their own troops, let alone enemy dispositions, they were unaware of the ground features to their front and they were uncertain whether any opposition would be encountered within the limits of the day's advance.[2] The outline plan was for 87 Brigade to take up the left flank astride Gully Ravine and to advance northwards, with Sari Tepe – Hill 472 – as its objective. The brigade would advance with the Border Regiment on the left, the Inniskilling Fusiliers on the right and with 2 SWB in reserve. The fourth battalion to make up the brigade, 1 KOSB, had yet to return from Y Beach. There was also a contingent of

1   An artillery shell which scatters lead balls like a shotgun on explosion, which is lethal against troops in the open. The 18 pounder shrapnel shell contained 375 half ounce balls.
2   Aspinall-Oglander, *Official History.* Vol 1, p.286.

the Anson Battalion, Royal Naval Division, which was attached to the Border Regiment, while the Drake Battalion, which landed on 26 April, was attached to the brigade for beach duties. Given the attrition rate of senior officers so far, Lieutenant Colonel Casson had taken over command of 87 Brigade and Major Going stood in as 2 SWB commanding officer. 88 Brigade would be on the right with Krithia as its objective and the whole action depended upon a rather complicated right hand pivoting move, hinged upon the French Brigade on the far right astride Kanli Dere (the Achi Baba Nullah).[3] This brigade was made up of three battalions of the 175th Regiment supported by two battalions of the Metropolitan Brigade, under the command of General Vandenberg. Finally, 86 Brigade was the divisional reserve.

There had been no time for any reconnaissance, the strength and location of the Turks was not known and fire support was limited to the very few artillery guns, some sixteen 18 pounders and four 4.5 inch howitzers with scant ammunition, which had so far come ashore. The Royal Navy could of course provide some support but this would be very limited as there were no definite targets for them to engage. At first the advance went well with little hold up, but by about 11:00 a.m. the Border Regiment on the left was the first to meet any serious opposition and B Coy 2 SWB was sent forward as reinforcements. Then, as the right wheel tried to take effect, a space began to develop between the Borders and the Inniskilling Fusiliers, so C Coy under Capt Greenway had to move up to plug the gap. With A Coy still at Y Beach, this left only D Coy as any meaningful reserve and with the brigade under strength after the initial invasion, the whole assault was beginning to waver. The brigade commander now committed D Coy to the centre, thus using up the whole of the brigade reserve and his only option now was to call upon the divisional reserve. The situation was becoming critical as the line on the left advanced and retired depending upon the enemy weight of fire and the crunch came when the line in the centre finally broke. This was caused by the collapse of the French Brigade, which in turn exposed the flank of 88 Brigade, making the whole line untenable. The unrelenting heat, a shortage of water and exhaustion contributed as much to the ineffectiveness of the advance as did the Turkish firepower and by about 5:30 p.m. the allied troops were back at their original positions. Despite the best efforts of the men on the ground, the first battle of Krithia had been a failure with the loss of almost 3,000 British and French soldiers, killed or wounded.

As far as 2 SWB was concerned, half of A Coy, under Lieutenant Silk, rejoined the battalion from Y Beach soon after noon leaving the other half, under Captain Habershorn, still with 1 KOSB. The battalion was largely responsible for keeping the line in place facing the enemy; on the left of Gully Ravine B Coy did very well after the Border Regiment had lost very heavily and in the centre C and D Coys at one time seemed to be the only ones not retiring, these two coys being the last of the Division to pull back. Lieutenant Desmond Somerville[4] and Second Lieutenant Hugh Nevile had been wounded, while 16 soldiers had been killed, 86 wounded and 39 were reported as missing. From Ernest's perspective:

Wednesday 28 April 1915

At about 3am we marched NW to join our Brigade, passing along the firing line of the 86th & 88th Bdes. It was broad daylight when we arrived at our own part of the line and we were ordered to attack at 8 am. Just had time to scramble some tea from the beach for the men before they went. We heard that A Coy had had a rough time with the KOSB landing

3   A water course or ravine, which may vary in size and length, depending upon the local topography.
4   Lt Somerville was badly wounded in the leg and was evacuated to hospital in Malta for two months, returning to 2 SWB on 30 June. He was eventually awarded the MC for his part in the Helles landing.

at Y Beach. Capt Palmer killed, Capt Tippetto severely wounded and 70 casualties in the Company. More than the remainder of the Battalion lost at De Totts Battery (64). A Coy did not join up till a day or so after this. In the attack on the 28th the Battalion did well, although they were so tired – not having had any sleep the previous night and carrying their heavy packs. We lost 140 in casualties – From the beach we had to get up all available ammunition, each man carrying 1000 rounds in bandoliers to the reserve trench. Rations were difficult to get up also, as only half a dozen mules were available for ourselves and the Inniskilling Fusiliers, but we managed to carry a lot, sufficient to keep the men going. Firing continued through the night again.

The next day was relatively quiet, but there was no respite for the battalion. The sub units needed reorganising after the chaos of the day before and then there was the perennial requirement for trench digging – the constant lot of an infantryman in a defensive environment – to make the position secure. A trench would be anything from six to eight feet (about 2.5 metres) deep and about half as wide depending on the time available to prepare it. The spoil would be used to reinforce the parapet and there would be a step to enable soldiers to fire over the top if needs be, but this was a dangerous practice as it exposed a man to Turkish sniper fire. Trenches would be dug in a zigzag fashion rather than a straight line so that the enemy could not fire down the length of it should they penetrate at any point. Recesses were then dug into the wall of the trench facing to the rear – known as dugouts – where a soldier could take shelter during incoming artillery fire or where he could tuck himself away for odd moments of rest.

There were four categories of trenches. First of all, the fire trench. This was the forward line of defence, often very close to the enemy, and from which assaults on the Turks could be launched. Soldiers were continually on the alert and movement and noise were kept to the absolute minimum. Machine guns would be dug in to give oblique, or crossing, fire across the space in front of the position (often known as no-man's land) to have maximum killing effect should the enemy try to charge the trenches. Troops in the fire trenches would be replaced from time to time to relieve the strain and pressure.

Behind the fire trench would be the support trench, the distance between the two being dictated by the contours of the ground and the dispositions of the enemy. As its name implies, the troops in these trenches were there to provide support to those in front in the fire trenches and to launch an immediate counter attack if the enemy had overcome their front line. They too were on a high state of alert and would need to be relieved on a regular basis and would usually move back to the third category, the rest trench. Ideally out of the range of enemy rifle fire, the troops did not need to be on a high state of alert and hopefully could relax somewhat, but more often than not they would be needed for other essential administrative tasks such as the movement of stores and ammunition, so rest was often at a premium.

The three trenches mentioned would normally be parallel to each other and face on to the enemy. To enable the troops to move in relative safety between these layers of trenches there would be one more category, known as the communication trench. Dug at varying angles between the main trenches so as to disrupt enemy fire, their depth and width would be determined by the traffic which used them. This of course was mainly soldiers on foot, but mules and horses were often used to pull carts of supplies from one location to another and there was a constant flow of casualties on stretchers. The communication trenches would also continue beyond the rest trenches back to the beaches where the unit quartermasters had their administrative bases, or to the respective brigade and divisional headquarters and they would also be the route for the field telephone cables between units. For identification purposes, trenches were given numbers – J9 J10, for example – or names – Turkey Trench or the Boomerang – and these were used in operational orders for ease of reference. For all these reasons, communication trenches were vital and much time was spent by already exhausted soldiers, who should have been resting, in keeping them open and repaired after frequent enemy shelling.

To ease the stress and strain of combat, units would be rotated through the three sets of trenches on a regular basis, the amount of time spent in each being dictated by any battles being fought at the time and the availability of troops to replace them. To do this, there was a set procedure, known as relief in the line. First of all, an advance party from the relieving unit, made up of representatives from each of the sub units taking part, would move up the communication trenches to the front line, or support line, to familiarise themselves with the layout of the trenches, if they had not been there before, and to be briefed on enemy dispositions. Then, the sub units would be called forward one at a time, with the advance party acting as guides, and allocated to their relevant trenches. Once they were in position, the outgoing sub unit would then pull out along the communication trenches, they too having sent back an advance party to prepare wherever they were moving to. While this procedure happened on a regular basis, it was always a very vulnerable time for both the incoming and outgoing units and had to be done as quickly and as quietly as possible so as not to alert the enemy, who might be inclined to put in an attack while the units changing over were not fully in control of their defences. Ideally a relief in line would take place under the cover of darkness, but this was not always possible.

Medals and awards are very much part of the military psyche. Prior to the Crimean campaign in the mid 19th century, such awards tended to be the preserve of officers, but with the introduction of the Victoria Cross in 1854, to which any rank of soldier was entitled, medals became more egalitarian. There are, generally speaking, two categories of medals. The first are campaign medals which are struck for a particular battle or war and to which all soldiers who are present in that theatre of operations for a given period of time, are entitled. There were three such medals authorised for the Great War, namely the 1914 15 Star, The British War Medal 1914 1918 and the Allied Victory Medal, affectionately known as Pip, Squeak and Wilfred, after popular cartoon characters of the time. These medals were designed to cover all theatres of war, so there was no specific medal for the Gallipoli campaign, which was a great disappointment to those who had taken part, as if their contribution to the war effort, in completely different circumstances to the Western Front, was of little consequence. On 25 April 1990, the 75th anniversary of the war, the Australian authorities introduced a Gallipoli Star which was presented to their 200 surviving veterans. Interestingly, this medal was originally approved by King George V, but was never issued at the time.[5]

The second category is a bravery award, or decoration, given to an individual officer or soldier for a specific act of courage, above and beyond the call of duty. For such an award, the event itself has to be witnessed first of all, by someone who is then in a position to report the fact. This could be for just one action, or for a series of actions over a period of time. The incident is then reported to a senior officer, normally the commanding officer, who will then write a citation on the incident which is then considered at various stages by a panel of staff officers and at an appropriate time a general officer commanding will make the final decision and probably present the medal as well, often in the theatre of operations. In the case of the Victoria Cross, this is personally endorsed by the Sovereign who will also present it at an appropriate stage. Not every citation is successful and an individual will not be told until the award has been confirmed. As a result of the first battle of Krithia, the

5   *The Medal Yearbook* 2008, p.385.

following names from 2 SWB were put forward for recognition of their gallant conduct: Captain TC Greenway, CSM Smith, Private Millward, Private Spinks, Private Hendy and Private Clent.

Meanwhile, daily routine kept Ernest busy:

Thursday 29 April 1915

Went up early from X Beach with more rations and was surprised to find nothing doing. Everyone was walking about outside the trenches although no armistice had been declared. I found that our line had had to retire a certain distance through the night giving way. Bad luck on our fellows. Went up with Capt Foley Army Service Corps in the afternoon to see the dumping place for supplies for 87th Bde. They could hardly have fixed on a more conspicuous place had they tried. Tiers of white boxes glistening in the sun. They afterwards put Bde HQ in a building close by! A number of our unburied dead lay about.

Evacuation of the wounded is always afforded a high priority in battle, not only for the soldier concerned, but also as a morale booster for his comrades who may well need such help themselves at any time. Today's soldier is treated to a much more sophisticated system, but in 1915 casualty evacuation was quite rudimentary. They would either make their own way back, or be carried by stretcher bearers if unable to walk, to a first aid post, which would be just out of battle range. Here they would be treated and returned to the front, or if more serious, be evacuated further back to a dressing station or field hospital. Space was at a premium on the Gallipoli beaches and medical facilities were inadequate because of poor planning initially, so many a casualty died through lack of attention, or inadequate treatment. There were no antibiotics available, nor were blood transfusions possible, and the excessive heat exacerbated the situation. Even if a soldier made it out to a hospital ship he often fared no better and many soldiers were buried at sea as a consequence.

For those killed on the battlefield, their bodies quite often had to be left where they fell as to attempt their recovery invited the attention of an enemy sniper. In the meantime they would putrefy in the oppressive heat or be blown up by constant artillery shelling, so that bodies of both sides were, quite literally, strewn all over the place. Body parts could be in the trenches, on the parapets or out to the front in no-man's land and the stench of death was everywhere. Occasionally, and as happened just twice at Gallipoli, there might be a short truce just to remove and dispose of bodies and those who could be identified might receive a decent burial at some stage, but many have no known grave – a harsh reality of the price paid by so many soldiers, friend and foe alike.

Having returned from the debacle of Y Beach, 1 KOSB had been moved into the brigade's front line of trenches during the night as the other battalions continued to reorganise, but the next morning they were withdrawn and replaced by most of 2 SWB and a company of the Inniskillings; it was not unusual for battalions to be grouped in this way. A Coy remained behind as the CO's reserve, with battalion headquarters positioned some 400 yards to their rear. That night, at about 9:30 p.m. the Turks opened up on 2 SWB's front line and then began an attack with artillery cover, but the battalion's machine guns forced them back. Meanwhile the Quartermaster continued with his administrative duties:

Friday 30 April 1915

Bde HQ would not allow us to draw our mules at X Beach and find our own way to our Battns. I moved up to Bn HQ near trenches. The ration party brought up the bacon etc in the evening and just missed the shelling, which prevented our going back to Bde HQ for the following day's rations till late. Got back there eventually and found the place congested with men, mules and boxes. What an opportunity for a well directed shell! One or two did come over just afterwards which helped them to make up their minds that something ought to be done, although they wanted to wait for the QMs of the Inniskilling Fusiliers and Border Regt so as to march off together I suppose. Eventually persuaded Bde HQ to let us get on.

The previous night's attack was the prelude to a concerted counter attack which the Turks began against the divisional position on the night of 1 May. General Liman von Sanders was anxious to capitalise upon the failure of the allies to take Krithia and he hoped to be able to drive the invaders off the peninsula. An assault by day would leave the Turks very vulnerable to artillery and naval gun fire as they crossed the open ground and although a night attack can be fraught with all kinds of difficulties, he decided that this was the more prudent option, taking advantage of the cover provided by darkness and the inability of his enemy to see their targets. The attack began at about 10:30 p.m. with a heavy artillery bombardment followed by a headlong rush by some 9,000 Turkish troops. From the battalion's perspective, the attack started against the French on their right followed by an attack on the left against the Inniskillings. These were evidently simply feints as later the whole weight of the attacks was thrown against 86 Brigade on their right. As far as the battalion was concerned there was never any real danger of the Turks being successful. They did not come closer than 100 yards (60 metres) and a brisk fire was maintained by both sides until morning. The right hand machine gun directed its fire right across the front of the Lancashire Fusiliers onto the enemy, with great effect. On the right the Turks made repeated bayonet charges and on one occasion penetrated that battalion's line, but were thrown back by those in the support trenches with heavy loss. Because they knew where the allied trenches had been dug, the enemy's artillery was very effective and the attacks continued all night. Determined not to be left out of things, Ernest wanted to make a contribution to the battle:

Saturday 1 May 1915

Saw the Fusiliers bringing up rations early by hand, cursing their luck. On questioning them I found that the ration dumping place and Bde HQ had been shelled, ration boxes smashed to smithereens and the staff had to shift. Consequently the fatigue party had to go right back to X Beach for more rations, as did the Scottish Borderers. This put an end to the senseless arrangement of dumping stuff in the open and since then we have had no trouble. The Turks made a determined effort to break through the line, so that a constant fusillade was kept up all night. I once more became a combatant and formed all the cooks of ours, KOSB and Inniskillings in the nullah which appeared the most vulnerable spot, with orders to go in with the bayonet should any of the blighters get through. However, the long weary night came to an end at last with the line still intact.

As dawn broke over the peninsula, the Turkish attacks seemed to falter and General Hunter-Weston was keen to take advantage of this by forcing an attack along the line against the retreating enemy. He took no account of the fact that his troops were shattered from their exertions and were low on ammunition, so just before daylight the Border Regiment were sent up to support the Lancashire Fusiliers and they were ordered to make the counter attack assisted by A Coy 2

SWB. The battalion's war diary was not exactly flush with optimism – *the position did not admit of much likelihood of success, but however the effort was made* – and as the Border Regiment rushed out from their trenches they were at once in difficulties and were held up after covering only about 30 yards. They formed to the right to face the enemy on their flank but this exposed their left flank and consequently they suffered very heavily. A Coy were luckier on their ground and found good cover in a small nullah from which they were able to bring fire to bear on some Turks who were inflicting damage on the Border Regiment. Before long, A Coy and the Border Regiment were withdrawn back to their trenches. The whole brigade was then ordered to advance to straighten the line and clear the ground in front and if possible establish a new line. 87 Brigade was held back until 86 Brigade were established to the front. A long wait ensued, but at last troops on the right began to come up into line, whereupon two platoons of C and D Coys 2 SWB were pushed out to form a firing line. However it quickly became apparent that 86 Brigade had not yet moved and that the troops advancing were in fact 88 Brigade supported by the French on their right. By 9:30 a.m. 86 Brigade made it to their start line and the attack started. Hardly had the advance begun when both the French and 88 Brigades met heavy opposition and were forced to pull back. Turkish guns opened up on the retiring troops with great effect which only added to the confusion and at one time it looked as if all troops on the right were going to desert their trenches and retire behind them. However, 86 Brigade saved the situation by extending to their right and filling the gap. To the right of 2 SWB, the Inniskillings had advanced only about 400 yards (250 metres) and when the withdrawal on the right took place, all units had to return and re-occupy the trenches they had left only two hours beforehand. The French suffered badly during this abortive attack, losing some 2,000 men dead or wounded. 29 Division's losses of 700 were light by comparison, while the battalion's casualties over the last two days were remarkably slight, with Lieutenant C R MacGregor and nine soldiers killed and 41 wounded. Attacks on the battalion position again resumed and continued all night with varying degree of intensity but, apart from artillery bombardments, less so than previously.

Ernest was able to witness most of the attack from a vantage point on one of the nullahs:

Sunday 2 May 1915

Went to top of the nullah and saw the Inniskillings forming up for a charge. The Turks chucked in when the boys were 100yds off and they made a bag of 123 including an officer. All the front was strewn with dead and wounded. They were ordered back to the trenches again and the Turks started sniping as usual, and shrapnel prevented men coming back for their breakfasts. They had to attack shortly afterwards without any Artillery support and consequently had to retire again before the enemy's shrapnel to their old position. This took a lot out of the men for nothing and spoiled what would have been a nasty reverse for the enemy. The men eventually got their breakfasts in the afternoon, and an easy night was hoped for. However, we were to be disappointed for we got shelled in the Gulley as badly as the worst night we experienced at Tsingtao. Shrapnel simply swept through the nullah and I was forced to seek a healthier spot twice, but each was as bad as the other, so stuck it the last time and was covered in dust next morning – better than bullets anyhow. Luckily no-one was hit although we had had a few casualties in the afternoon. Several however occurred in the trenches, mostly arm wounds.

On the morning of 3 May, an event took place which, surprisingly, receives minimal coverage by professional historians. According to the battalion war diary, at 10:00 a.m.:

> Turkish burying parties under cover of white flags searched the ground in our immediate front. We accordingly sent out parties also to bury Turkish dead of whom there was great quantity just in front of our right flank. We counted about 150.

Unlike the truce which was to take place in the Anzac sector three weeks later for a similar purpose and which was well documented, this one does not even figure in the official history, yet it is highly unlikely that it would have taken place without official sanction at the highest level. As The Story of the 29th Division recounts – *"the Turkish corpses now accumulated upon our front were removed with permission,"* but with whose permission is not clear; even Ernest makes no reference to this in his diary which is unusual.[6] Military history in general has witnessed any number of truces over the years for various reasons, but they can be fraught with difficulty as it has been known for one side to use this as a ruse to take advantage over their enemy. For this reason they need to be carefully co-ordinated with a given start and end time, the latter being critical for start of hostilities once more. It is known that the Turks took heavy casualties during their counter attacks of the previous few days and the putrefying bodies in the heat of the sun would have only added to the stench and carnage of the battlefield, but apart from the next truce on 24 May, when over 3,000 Turkish bodies were buried in the Anzac sector, no other truce took place during the whole campaign.

By mid afternoon, the battalion was back in its trenches once more and hostilities resumed. At 3:30 p.m. orders were received that the Border Regiment would relieve the battalion after dark. At 8:30 p.m. the Border Regiment came up to relieve them, but unfortunately the Turks began firing once more so it was a long time before the relief could be completed. This was done by 11:30 p.m. and at last the battalion was able to pull back to become the brigade reserve at Gully Beach, this being the first time since the start of hostilities on 25 April that the battalion had been away from the front line. During this move, just one man, Sergeant Fairbrass, was wounded. The activities of enemy snipers, some of whom had been able to infiltrate behind the battalion's lines were a constant threat as Ernest tells us:

Monday 3 May 1915

> Poor McGregor unfortunately was killed by a sniper whilst talking to Morgan. This makes the 10th casualty amongst the officers – four of which have been fatal. Had three Turkish wounded lying near my cookhouse. One was shot through the stomach and shoulder and seemed to be dying. The interpreter said all he asked for was to be put in the sun as he was cold. He lay there all day in the glare of the sun with only a sip of water, which of that even he wanted but little and in the evening got up and walked over to a fire! Wonderfully recuperative powers they have. His was not the only instance either. (It makes one bitter to hear though how they treated our wounded left behind in our retirement. Stories are rife that men known to have been only wounded were afterwards found with their own bayonets stuck into them – others horribly mutilated although this has not since been proved) and none are known to be alive in the hands of the enemy at all. Yet we have their snipers actually behind our own lines in nullahs and scrub who snipe at stretcher bearers and who when taken prisoner are allowed to live! God save me from being captured that's

---

6   Capt S Gillon, *The Story of the 29th Division* (Thomas Nelson, 1925), p.37.

all. Began to look out for a healthier site for one's bivouac in case of heavy shelling when news came through that the Bn had to go into Brigade reserve. Their turn for a rest had come at last and it was much needed. We didn't look much like getting it though for as soon as we reached the mouth of the Gulley, snipers started paying attention to us. There was so much potting going on that it was hard to tell how many snipers there were. Certainly four shots came down in rapid succession like a ragged volley and immediately afterwards it was reported that Sgt Fairbrass was hit in the head. Ellis was in an awful stew about it, so I went for a stretcher, but luckily he was only scalped. Had to send off a couple of sections to stop the blighters. A few shells came down mighty adjacent, but eventually everyone got down to rest.

Early the next morning, A Coy, which had been left behind to support the Border Regiment rejoined the battalion. At last, the soldiers were able to have a complete rest and bathe in the sea, a dangerous occupation at the best of times as enemy shelling continued and spent bullets landing in the water were an occupational hazard, but the risk was well worth it. But it was not peaceful for everyone; at dusk C Coy was sent up the line once again to support the Border Regiment and two platoons of D Coy were despatched to brigade headquarters as ammunition carriers for those units in the front line. It was also an opportunity for the Quartermaster to catch up on his administration:

Tuesday 4 May 1915

Our second day in reserve. It is surprising how soon everyone forgets his troubles and wears a less worried look. I went down to X Beach to see what was being done about our kits in the sunken lighter. This I forgot to mention before. On the morning of the 28th April after I reached Beach X from De Totts Battery I was informed by the Colour Sgt and Sgt Press that, contrary to orders, the Chief and 1st Officers for the 'Alaunia' had put the officers and men's kits and blankets off in lighters to send ashore. The Beach master Major Jones RMLI quite rightly refused to take them ashore and ordered them back aboard again. The lighter containing all the officer's valises and 100lb kits and Bn blankets, besides some men's kits got adrift and struck a reef about 50yds or so from the shore and sank. Most of the kit was salved and some put onto other lighters and sent back to the 'Alaunia' where the process of drying is gradually going on; the weather then prevented further operations for a few days and nothing was done. On my arrival, on hearing the tale, I asked the Beach master to kindly lend me a cutter to go to the lighter which he did and more salving operations were made, several kits and rolls of blankets being got off. Later however the lighters and cutters were required for carrying wounded and the kits had to remain wherever they happened to be and consequently some were eventually dumped at W Beach instead of back on the ship. The damaged lighter meanwhile settled down still more until quite awash and it was considered useless to try for more. However, a lot of blankets have since been got out and a few kits. The former have come in very useful since to cover the wounded at night and much they were needed too, the wind being somewhat keen after hot days. Neville's brother in law, Captain Lambert RN promised to send a diver to try and save the remaining stuff (as Neville's valise is still missing – what luck!) But the diver hasn't turned up yet – too rough I suppose. My valise is still there. Have got the remains of my kit but all spoilt. Good enough to wear on active service though. Have a good excuse to grow a beard as my razors are done for. Am afraid my beard doesn't enhance my appearance, but there are no ladies about. However, I'm digressing …

The apparent lull in battle activity within the division was short lived however, as plans were being drawn up for a second attempt at securing Krithia and the hill feature of Achi Baba. The urgent need for reinforcements was high on the agenda and General Hamilton was given the East Lancashire Brigade which had been part of the Egyptian garrison in Alexandria. This was a territorial force, made up from volunteers who had elected to serve overseas, and what it lacked in training and experience it certainly made up for in enthusiasm and determination. The general also assembled a composite division, made up from 2 Australian Brigade and a New Zealand brigade, shipped round from the Anzac sector, along with a Naval Brigade of the RMLI, Plymouth and Drake Battalions.[7] Within 29 Division, 86 Brigade had taken such a mauling during the early days of the invasion that it was temporarily disbanded and its units dispersed amongst the other brigades. At 10:00 a.m. on 5 May, orders were received for 2 SWB to replace the Inniskillings in the front line and at 2:00 p.m. D Coy proceeded up the nullah and took over on the left flank at 3:00 p.m. Hardly had this happened when orders were received that the move was cancelled and that the whole of 87 Brigade was to be relieved after dusk by the East Lancashire territorial brigade.

Wednesday 5th May 1915

Still in reserve – expect to go up today unless reinforcements come up. All sorts of rumours have come in that large reinforcements are coming – certainly four battalions of Native Infantry are landed – as I saw one of the 14th Sikhs yesterday who said that, besides themselves, the 69th & 89th Punjabs (sic) and a battalion of Ghurkhas (5th I think) had landed two days ago. Right enough our orders to go up to the firing line were cancelled after the Bn had marched off and the Inniskilling Fusrs had started to come down. For some reason the 'Skins' had to remain until relieved by the Lancashire Fusiliers Special Reserve. Bad luck on their Regimental staff for they already had their cooking pots and rations down, and back they had to go again. The KOSB came down afterwards and filed along the beach which is becoming pretty congested. As usual, the German (or Turk) gunners in some mysterious way derived that troops were moving through the nullah for they commenced shelling. One shell in particular came plumb into the centre not far from where we were sitting. Private Claffin, the CO's Orderly was digging a pit for himself, luckily not near his kit, which was blown to atoms. We had to send him foraging for a complete set including rifle and bayonet. A spent bullet passed my head and settled on the Sgt Major of the Border Regt who was lying in his dug-out – catching him in the bum. He yelled out, didn't think he was wounded, thought a cricket ball had struck him. The Turks don't play cricket however.

By 6 May, the allies were ready – if that is the right word – to launch a second attack on Krithia and Achi Baba. While the divisional commander's orders may have been a bit more comprehensive this time, the concept was little changed from the first abortive attempt, so confidence was not high, although there were more artillery pieces available, but not much more ammunition. The attack was to take place in broad daylight with 125 (Territorial Force) Brigade on the left flank, 88 Brigade and the composite brigade in the centre and the French division on the right flank. 87 Brigade was in reserve. The objectives were for 88 Brigade to advance towards Krithia, while the East Lancashire Brigade was to advance and make good a line extending from the sea through Point 472 to the knoll just beyond Krithia. Meanwhile, Ernest was experiencing the battle back-stage as it were:

---

7   Aspinall-Oglander, *The Official History,* Vol 1, Chapter 18.

Thursday 6 May 1915

Woke up awfully cold. Found the nullah full of youngsters of the Lancashire Brigade which had come in during the night. They moved up the nullah shortly afterwards to the attack. One felt sorry to see such a lot of boys going up to tackle a job so difficult, although of course they had nearly, or quite, four times the number of men to do what ours and the KOSB had been holding. An attack developed soon afterwards and the wounded started coming in – luckily most of them are slight. It is surprising how many of the wounded have been hit in the hand, arm and leg. Night came and we heard that although the youngsters had been plucky enough they couldn't get on very far. Firing went on hard during the night. We couldn't get much information. The wind was very cold and the sea too rough to embark wounded from Gulley Beach and so the minor cases had to make the best of their way to X Beach, a pretty trying ordeal for some no doubt. Met one of the officers of the Lancashire Regiment, wounded in the arm. He was very cold as half his jacket had been torn off to get his wound dressed. Lent him my Cording and fleece lining to go to X Beach which he promised to send back. I felt too cold to wait for it and went over afterwards myself and had the greatest difficulty in finding that man; everyone for himself more or less on these cold nights, so I probably shouldn't have seen it again as he gave it to one of his own NCOs to bring back. Not a very pleasant walk back alone with so many snipers about and one has to cough discreetly when nearing troops in order to avoid being potted.

At 10:00 a.m. on 7 May, 2 SWB followed 1 KOSB up the nullah to support the attack with the special task of supporting the East Lancashire territorial brigade and push forward if they failed. If they were successful then these two battalions were to push through 88 Brigade and capture Krithia. They moved very slowly up the nullah but could get no information as to what was going on in front. At 2:00 p.m. the battalion received orders to move up and take over the Inniskillings' trenches. It was very hard to follow what was going on. 88 Brigade, supported by the Essex Regiment advanced a good 400 yards, but then being unable to get on, dug themselves in. The Inniskillings and Border Regiment advanced a similar distance. The East Lancashire Brigade was more or less pinned to their ground by machine gun fire and at 7:00 p.m. the battalion moved across the nullah and took over trenches from the territorials. Not being satisfied with the layout however, it was decided to dig a new line of trenches some 200 yards further in. During the night they advanced to link up with the Inniskillings on the right of the nullah. Digging went on all night and despite their obvious exhaustion, the men worked extremely well and an excellent fire trench was dug right across from the sea to the nullah and a communication trench was constructed linking up the fire trench with the trenches used by the East Lancashire Brigade. Command of the battalion now fell to Captain Greenway as Major J. Going, (who had moved up to command 87 Brigade in lieu of Lieutenant Colonel Casson who was now commanding the composite naval brigade), was himself slightly wounded, along with four other soldiers. On this day, Ernest also became a casualty as his diary entry tells us:

Friday 7 May 1915

Awoke with feet like frogs. Major Going was promoted early as he had to go up and take over a Brigade somewhere, the Adjt said. Greenway left in command. He went off for orders too – and came back with orders to pack up – follow the KOSB as we were to support the

Lancs Brigade if necessary in the attack. My orders were to follow later and bring the cooks to the top of the nullah, probably in our old place. I gave the Bn about a quarter of an hour's start and went ahead of the cooks to find a suitable place. As one proceeded along the nullah the singing of bullets became more audible and several struck very close. Crossing an exposed place I fully expected to be hit but got through alright and had almost reached the tail of the Bn, when getting into the nullah off the bank I thought I was hit by a stone in the right calf. Luckily Blake RAMC was nearby and he fixed me up. Found a bullet had gone in and he thought it was still there. Felt sick for a few moments – damn silly of me I know, but right again afterwards and was able to hobble down alright. But it was most unpleasant getting back through the same danger zone and was jolly glad to see the beach. Had a bit of tiffin[8] at the doctor's place and afterwards made for X Beach as the sea was still too rough for go from Gulley beach. On reaching X Beach found Major Going who had come down with a shrapnel wound in the thumb. We were both sent off with a lot of other wounded to the "Southland" which was full up. They sent us on to find the B6. We eventually fetched up at the B3 my old friend the "Alaunia" – also full up. They said it was the N6 not the B6 we should go to. Pretty rotten piece of bungling on somebody's part to send three boatloads of wounded drawn by a rickety pinnace in a fairly rough sea to find a haven of rest. A lot of the men were sea sick – no welcome addition to a wounded man. Eventually we fetched up at the "Franconia" where another couple of boats had pulled up and at last we got on board. What a relief it must have been to some of these poor fellows. Had a wash and enjoyed my dinner immensely. Found only a few officers aboard.

By now, the battalion was positioned in the main fire trenches between Gully Ravine and the sea, about 500 yards south of Y Beach. At 10:00 a.m. on 8 May a message was received to say that the New Zealand Brigade was about to attack in the direction of Krithia and that the Inniskillings would cover the left flank of this Brigade. 2 SWB and the Inniskillings would also push out scouts and small patrols up the cliff and nullah to dig in as near the enemy as possible and contain the line in front. They were given the task of reporting all hostile movement and to take any opportunity of pushing larger bodies of troops forward. This was contained in the Order received from HQ 87 Brigade at 9:25 a.m. which read as follows, the abbreviation AAA representing a break, or full stop, in the message:

> To SWB. Sender's Number BM2. 8 May 1915. Time 9.25am. Ships will carry out Bombardment from 9.45 till 10 a.m. and again from 10.15 onwards AAA The New Zealand Bde. is advancing to attack Krithia at 10.30 a.m. AAA The R.I.F. will cover the left flank of this Bde. AAA They will not do this by attacking position in front but by pushing out connecting posts which will entrench themselves AAA The SWB and RIF will push scouts and small patrols up the cliff and nullah to dig in as near the enemy as possible and contain him in front AAA They will report all hostile movements and take any opportunity of pushing larger bodies forward AAA The KOSB are in reserve sending one half Battalion. across nullah to occupy R.I.F. reserve trenches AAA The Borders will remain in their present position awaiting further instructions to rejoin 87th Bde. AAA As 88th Bde does not advance R.I.F. may have to push posts forward through their line to connect.

8   An Indian Army expression for a snack or light meal.

At mid-day, the CO spoke to the brigade major on the field telephone, and assured him that he would do his best to push forward, but he impressed upon him that any general forward movement on the left flank was out of the question on account of the enemy's machine guns. At about 3:30 p.m. the brigade major spoke to the adjutant, again by telephone and asked him to report the situation and urged an advance. It was promised that the battalion would do its best to keep up with the advance, although it was pointed out that no advance could take place by day, but that after dark a further line would be dug linking up with the Inniskillings on the right. At about 4:30 p.m. the brigade major again spoke to the adjutant and informed him that he expected to receive orders for an advance but that this would not affect the battalion as the general was satisfied that any further advance by day was impossible on the left flank. Then at 5:25 p.m. the battalion received the following message from brigade HQ:

> To 2 SWB, RIF, KOSB and Borders. Sender's Number BM6, 8 May 1915, time 5.07pm. At 5.30 p.m. 29th Division will advance NE direction AAA General Paris's Division will attack parallel to it on the right AAA 87th Brigade will attack to their front AAA SWB will advance between the nullah and the sea AAA The RIF will advance up the nullah keeping touch with the New Zealand Brigade on their right AAA KOSB will move forward in support both sides of nullah AAA The Borders will move into reserve in old RIF trench just E of nullah AAA The attack will be made by the bayonet.

Consider for a moment the sequence of events. The message was written at 5:07 p.m. which was, no doubt, the time at which it was finalised in brigade HQ. It was then despatched to the four battalions and arrived with 2 SWB some 20 minutes later at 5:25 p.m. with a start time for the attack just five minutes after that at 5:30 p.m. The CO would then need to make his battalion plan and issue orders to the coys, all of which would have to be rushed if the start time was to be met. It is no wonder that confusion and chaos reigned during these attacks and it was the soldiers on the ground in the front line who were to suffer and pay the price too often with their lives. Then consider also the order that *the attack will be made by the bayonet.* In preceding centuries when the infantry would form its legendary square box formation to repel an enemy assault, the bayonet fixed to the end of the rifle was an essential weapon of war. Just as the Zulu armies of King Shaka were experts in the use of the short stabbing spear, the British infantryman was skilled in the use of the bayonet at close quarters with the enemy. There were even occasions when the infantry would advance on the enemy – as in the battle of Chillianwallah against the Sikhs in 1849 – with rifles unloaded and only the bayonet as their means of assault. What was needed at Krithia however, was weight of rifle fire to suppress the Turks and it is inconceivable that it was ever intended that outmoded tactics should be resurrected here. What is more likely is that General Hunter-Weston intended that the assault should be made figuratively *"with bayonet fixed"* – a martial call to arms and an idealistic view that every possible means should be adopted to ensure success.

As always, the battalion worked with a will and orders were issued. C and D Coys were to advance from the trenches in two lines with D Coy on the right. Their objective was to take the Turkish trench in front at a distance of about 1,000 yards. A and B Coys were to be in reserve and to occupy the front trench as soon as C and D Coys had vacated them. At 5:40 p.m. some 10 minutes late, C and D Coys under the command of Captain R K B Walker advanced. Immediately they were hit by a severe cross fire from enemy machine guns, their losses were very heavy and the attack was completely held up. Battalion HQ moved up into the front trench with A Coy, while B Coy remained behind in reserve. The CO decided that it was simply madness to send forward any more troops to support the attack and the only thing to do was to prevent all movement until dusk. At 7:30 p.m. orders were received from brigade HQ for the battalion to be relieved by 1 KOSB and to go back into reserve. This took some time and by 10:00 p.m. the battalion was back in the support trenches next to the 89th Punjabi Regiment of the Indian Brigade. The battalion's casualties, especially in C and D Coys, were very heavy. Second Lieutenant G Bruce and Second Lieutenant W Ross were killed, while Second Lieutenant C H Heal and Second Lieutenant W J Stanborough both died later from their wounds. It was customary at the time, in any written despatch, for officers to be mentioned by name but for soldiers to be listed in number only, so the records of the day state that 14 were killed, 83 were wounded and 34 were missing, presumed dead.

Sergeant Bean recalls the second battle of Krithia with a first-hand account from his diary:

Thursday 6 May 1915

Coy joined Battalion and moved back to reserve on Gully Beach again and had another easy day. During the morning the Lancashire Fusilier Brigade (Territorial Force) moved up the Gully and also one battalion of Ghurkhas. These pushed forward about 1000 yards beyond the line already held by us and entrenched. We are ready to move up at a moment's notice but are not required. We can hear heavy fighting during the evening but get no news as to what is happening.

Friday 7 May 1915

There was almost a continual fire during the night and we had several men wounded by stray bullets. The advance which commenced yesterday is continued this morning and we receive orders to move up the Gully and be ready to push forward through the Lancashire Fusiliers line as soon as they have reached their objectives, but owing to severe opposition they are unable to gain ground; it is not for the want of trying for their wounded are coming back in scores. So instead of advancing through them, we relieve them and they are sent back to the base for reorganisation. They cannot stand the knocking about the same as our troops do. At 9pm we try a little ground snatching as taught us by the Japanese at Tsingtao. Our part of the line – the left resting on the north west shore of the peninsula – being some distance behind that on our immediate right, it is decided that C and D Coys will go forward about 300 yards and entrench under cover of the darkness and a small covering party is sent out to prevent us being rushed. Second Lieutenant Ross goes forward with CSM Millichamp and a few men and mark out the trench. In the meantime Lt Stanborough sends myself with a few men to gather up picks and shovels which have been discarded by the Terriers. We soon have enough to equip the Coy and when we return, everything is ready for the digging to commence, so C and D Coys go forward, leaving A and B Coys to man the trench in rear. The left of C Coy rests on the northwest shore of the peninsula and the right of D Coy on the Gully Ravine. We have just got to the position of the new trench when a shell bursts killing Private Carty and seriously wounding Private Woffenden to whom I was explaining the position of a traverse. The force of the explosion knocked the three of us to the ground, and although I felt bruised all over I did not appear to be hurt except for a small graze on the left thumb. These were the only two casualties all night and only one more shell was sent over.

Saturday 8 May 1915

By daybreak our trench is completed and C and D Coys remain to hold it, with A and B Coys holding the trench in rear and forming our supports. When I look round to see what damage the shell did last night I find I had a very narrow escape. One bullet entered the top of my cap on top and came out at the left hand side. One went through my left breast pocket, through my AB64[9] note book, cardigan and shirt and dropped down inside my trouser leg without even causing a bruise. There are several in my pack, one being embedded in a half bar of lifebuoy soap which was in an aluminium box in the centre of the pack, and in my mess tin, which was also in my pack, are three more. The troops on our right continue to advance during the day but we did not move. At 5.30pm we were ordered to leave the trench and rush the Turkish position in front, about 700 yards away. At about 5.20pm our artillery opened a violent fire on this position and sharp at 5.30pm No's 13 and 14 Platoons of D Coy under Second Lieutenant Ross and two platoons of C Coy under Second Lieutenant Heal jumped the parapet and rushed forward followed closely by the remaining two platoons of D Coy under Second Lieutenant Stanborough and two platoons of C Coy under Capt R K B Walker. A and B Coys took our place in the front trench ready to support us when necessary. We were no sooner out of the trenches when we were met by a perfect hail of shrapnel and machine gun fire which bowled our men over like skittles. When we got to within 100 yards of the Turk's position they commenced to retire but their machine gun fire became more deadly than ever. These machine guns were evidently well concealed in positions probably 550 yards or more in rear of their front line; at any rate our artillery could not locate them. About this time Second Lieutenant Ross was wounded in the head and foot and as there appeared to be no officers left I took charge of the front line which by now was a very scattered one. The shrapnel fire was still as violent as ever but directed on our trench in rear and seeing that it was impossible to advance further until we were reinforced and knowing it was impossible for reinforcements to reach us through such a fire I ordered the line to hold on where they were and scratch up head cover as quickly as possible. LCpl Millward showed conspicuous gallantry running down the line to make sure that C Coy got these instructions. The Turks seemed to concentrate their whole fire upon him as he ran but he got through without a scratch, only to be killed a little later. We hung on in this position until dark and then as no reinforcements arrived I ordered the line to retire. There were only about 40 of us altogether and we reached the trench without a casualty. Here we found a few men who had straggled in before us and were told what had happened. It appears that the first four platoons to advance had got off best, for by our rapid advance we escaped a large amount of the shrapnel. The second line, ie. 15 and 16 Platoons of D Coy and two platoons of C Coy were mown down almost as they left the trench, so accurate was the Turkish fire and on this account A and B Coys were not allowed to leave the trench.

Sergeant Bean had been particularly courageous on the night of 8 May and was put forward for a bravery award with the following citation:

No 8206 Sgt Bean 2 SWB, who on the evening of the 8th May when all the officers in the firing line of C and D Coys had either been killed or wounded, took charge, taking the men he still had under a very heavy machine gun fire and after dusk brought back to safety

9   A soldier's individual Record of Service and Pay Book, which he would normally carry with him at all times.

all that had remained of these two Companies in the firing line. This NCO by his steady example maintained the line in front although it was under an exceptionally heavy fire and undoubtedly saved many lives as any man who moved at all was at once shot down.

The outcome would be announced when GOC 29 Division visited the battalion in the following week.

Once again the assault on Krithia had come to nothing and it beggars belief that GOC 29 Division could continue to expend the lives of his soldiers with impunity in *"one of the most misconceived episodes in a misconceived battle"*[10] where the Australian Brigade lost about 1,000 men and 2 SWB alone took over 100 casualties. Although the fighting had died down for the time being, the battalion could not relax. It was essential that the defensive position was ready to repel any further attacks, so the next day was spent in repairing and cleaning up the trenches. At 5:00 p.m. the battalion was able to return to its rest camp at Gully Beach. For the next four or five days there was little or no enemy activity, but still the battle preparation continued unabated. Much as the battalion needed some much earned rest, a big working party of 300 men was needed daily at W Beach to assist in the movement of stores from the supply ships, while the remainder spent their time improving their spartan living accommodation and tidying up the neighbouring ground which was in a filthy condition, no doubt covered with the detritus of war. On 11 May Lieutenant Colonel Casson resumed command of the battalion and also took over as the Area commandant, an additional responsibility which involved ensuring that all administrative tasks in his sector of the beaches ran smoothly and efficiently.

Meanwhile, Ernest was still away from the heat of the battle as a result of his injury, which fortunately was not that serious. The staff of the hospital ships were under severe pressure trying with inadequate resources to cope with large numbers of casualties, as the next few entries from his diary explain:

Saturday 8 May 1915

Had a very comfortable night. Managed to tub alright and am going to have my wound dressed at 2.30. Not been able to yet, since Blake, our medical officer, did it. The poor doctors are over-worked, however I think I'm alright for it gives me practically no trouble and as I found a second hole in my sock last night I conclude that the bullet went straight through. Can't understand how Blake missed the outlet.

Monday 9 May 1915

A large number of wounded came aboard during the night including a lot of our own. C & D Coys; the latter especially – appear to have borne the brunt of it. Saw several of our men who state that poor Stanborough was killed and they think Heal also. Ross also badly wounded. That leaves no officers in D Coy at all. Major Going tried to get us both transferred to the "Alaunia" as we hear the Franconia is going to Alexandria – the skipper refused to take any more wounded – something over 1500 on board and he had only three doctors till this morning! Two or three Naval doctors came on today to assist. Some of the men had not had their wounds dressed for two to three days – that means since they received first aid. Four buried yesterday evening and four more died during the night. Have just come up from dinner and find we are moving.

---

10   Prior, *Gallipoli*, p.144.

Tuesday 11 May 1915

Arrived Alexandria at noon – just forty hours since – nothing eventful happened. About twelve died from wounds altogether. However as there were only three medical officers assisted by the ships medics – to dress the wounds of 1700 patients, we were very lucky. Two trainloads proceeded to Cairo. I managed to arrange to go back on the same boat, as also did Major Going and Captain Bromley, Lancashire Fusiliers; afterwards awarded the VC.

On 13 May, GOC 29 Division came to visit the battalion at Gully Beach. While in hindsight his tactical handling of the last two assaults on Krithia left much to be desired, he was the senior officer in the division and it was his duty to visit the men under his command whenever he could, to talk to them, and to keep them in the picture about the overall state of the battle. He also needed to assess their morale and to recognise and thank them for their efforts under trying circumstances. On this occasion he addressed all the men who could be collected and he congratulated the CO and all ranks on the splendid manner in which the battalion had upheld its proud traditions in the severe fighting of the last fortnight. He referred especially to the professional manner in which the landing at S Beach on 25 April had been carried out and also to the gallant charge made against the Turkish machine guns in the previous week.

Administrative fatigues continued without letup and at 4:00 a.m. on 16 May, a party of 280 men was sent to W Beach, now known as Lancashire Landing, for work there. During the day a small, but much needed, reinforcement in the shape of Captain H G C Fowler and 46 other ranks joined the battalion from England. There was also some good news in that Sergeant Bean, Private Millward, Private Spinks, Private Hendy and Private Clent had all been awarded the Distinguished Conduct Medal for their conspicuous bravery since the invasion began.

Meanwhile, Ernest was on his way back to the battalion:

Friday 14 May 1915

Left Alexandria again after taking on a small reinforcing draft of various regiments. Fowler came with ours. The Battalion will be glad to see him I am sure. Found to my surprise and pleasure my old batman Joynes also. He was wounded in France while with the 1st Battalion. Glad he is alright again. Had two alarm parades – one can only imagine how helpless we are should we be attacked. Can't think why a gun is not mounted on these troopers [troopships]. We might stand a ghost of a chance, then.

Sunday 16 May 1915

Arrived Cape Helles at about 9.30am. Disembarked in a trawler after lunch. Were sent to V Beach where after waiting for a battalion of New Zealanders to get away who were embarking. We eventually disembarked alongside the old "Iron Horse." (Clyde her correct name) which had taken such a tragic part in the landing. She had the Dublin and Munsters aboard and it was intended to beach her high and dry and for these two Bns to rush out of her. I remember as we went forward to S Beach seeing the old "Iron Horse" trying to get up steam to ten knots to charge the beach. She looked as if she was only making about three or four knots. Anyway she stuck further out than was evidently intended. Holes had been made in her and a gangway built for the men to run off by. From what I was told afterwards, the Turks had the range of these gangways beautifully as soon as the attempted landing took place and the men were knocked down as soon as they appeared. Those that were wounded and could not stand up were drowned by the weight of their packs. How many were killed I don't remember but the two regiments lost so heavily that they have for the present been merged and are now called the "Dubsters." Only one officer and the QM of the Dublins that have not been hit.

The draft under Capt Fowler, Major Going and self rejoined the Bn at Gully Beach. Found on arrival that things are just about the same as when we left. Krithia is still untaken. Williams has kindly had a dug out made for Fowler and me. As expended bullets kept dropping over during the night (a sharp fusillade continued practically all night) it was not very comfortable and so I didn't sleep much. It isn't very pleasant to hear the "phut" of a bullet striking your parapet and if you are sleeping on the off-side it's quite possible to get an unlucky one.

Tuesday 18 May 1915

Orders came to clear everything from X Beach – awful nuisance – we have about 15 cartloads of stores there. Was awaiting instructions near the Colonel's dug out and was watching the puffs of smoke caused by shrapnel fired at one of our aeroplanes, when whoosh! Plug! Three yards off a time fuse struck the ground and went in four inches or so. It would have made pulp of the spot, if it hit one. Luckily the Quarter Master Sergeant who was standing near me was the only other near one to it. Had another experience about 12pm when superintending the removal of baggage from X Beach to Gully Beach. Cpl Jennings was standing near when the usual fusillade started at the trenches. He was unfortunately hit by one of the dropping bullets which passed through his lung from the shoulder. I thought it was not serious.

Wednesday 19 May 1915

Heard, on getting up, that Jennings had just died. Rotten luck after surviving the ordeal D Coy (his Coy) went through the night after I was hit – when C & D Coys had to advance under a murderous fire of four machine guns and shrapnel. The two companies had about 130 casualties. Stanborough shot through the jaw – died on board. Heal died on the way down to the beach. Poor Bunce killed – also Sgt Millichamp. Ross wounded. He had a lucky escape as he was slightly wounded in the head - and places – one in the shoulder also slight – and painfully in the foot. As he himself put it – "They got me with an Upper and Lower Band" – old musketry term.[11] Ross says funny things at times.

Despite the intense heat and the need for rest, most men in the battalion were working almost all day, either tidying up space needed on W Beach which was becoming a central administrative area, or making a roadway up Gully Ravine. All of this was back breaking work which only added to the stress and strain of living under the ever present threat of another Turkish attack at any time. Then, on 22 May, the battalion suddenly received orders that afternoon to move up in support of the Indian Brigade which was being heavily attacked. The battalion was split into two groups; Major Going took A and B Coys to support the Inniskillings near Y Beach, while Battalion HQ with C

---

11   This is a reference to grouping rifle shots above and below the intended target, to increase the likelihood of a successful hit.

and D Coys made their way up the Gully to support the 14th Sikh Regiment. In many ways this was a welcome relief from endless administrative chores and it took the battalion just 20 minutes to get ready to move off at 6:00 p.m. It was planned that the battalion would remain in support, but at 11:25 p.m. they received an urgent call for reinforcements from the CO of the Royal Fusiliers in 88 Brigade. This caused some confusion as the battalion was not a part of this brigade but the CO sent off the coy asked for and reported the matter to General Cox, commanding the Indian Brigade, who confirmed this action.

Ernest's diary continues:

Tuesday 25 May 1915

Nothing of any importance has happened during the last five or six days – except perhaps on the afternoon of the 22nd, when we suddenly saw one of the battleships (Swiftsure I think) open fire seawards and then made off across towards the island about 5 miles away, followed by destroyers at full lick and an aeroplane. We guessed that a 'Squarehead' submarine had been sighted, but we couldn't see the result and shortly afterwards a message came through for the Bn to go up to the trenches in support at once. They were soon off, leaving me the unenviable job of sending up ammunition, tools, rations etc, not easy when you have half Bn in one place and the other half in another. Besides all the spare kit to gather in, washing etc. However, we managed to get everything fixed. Sgt Ellis in charge of the ammunition to Y Beach unfortunately got hit rather badly with shrapnel in about four or five places, but none of them serious I hear. The cause of the trouble appeared afterwards to have been caused by the Inniskillings having their forward trenches rushed. No one appears to have been on the lookout. Their MG section got badly scuppered and altogether they had about 60 casualties. They recovered their lost trenches themselves I heard afterwards. A good many more casualties – native troops – came through during the night, but none of ours. The 7th Fusiliers also had a bad time that night. Next morning I went to 'W' Beach for stores and heard first that one submarine was sunk and one captured. This good news however was soon negatived by Capt Lambert RN who informed me that they hadn't seen one. I heard afterwards the upstanding leg of a dead horse looked like a periscope!

Gully Beach is becoming uncomfortable at times, what with shrapnel by day and falling bullets by night. One can hear the plop plop of the latter into the sea from one's dug out and occasionally one just over the parapet behind strikes very near, but I think my dugout is fairly safe – the head part anyhow. Nowhere is safe for that matter – for two men were struck by shrapnel whilst going along the seashore (below the cliff) from Gully to 'Y' Beach. One of my cooks (Adams) was badly hit in the head with shrapnel – the Doctor is afraid he is a goner. This happened this morning and they are still pelting occasionally. The most disgraceful thing is that we can't reply, because we haven't enough gun ammunition. Heard yesterday that some of the Batteries are tied down to two rounds per gun per day! I certainly heard one of the Battery Commanders say here at 10am the other day that he had his sights laid on to a Turks gun which was plainly visible and was not allowed to fire at it for the same reason. What a lot we have to thank our patriotic labour politicians at home for with their petty squabbles about pay. Could one imagine a thing like that happening in Germany? I'd like to rope the blighters in, give them three months trench warfare and send them back to work.

The next morning the battalion returned to Gully Beach and later that day received a welcome boost of reinforcements. There were 15 officers – Major Jones, Lieutenants K French, R C Inglis, and L J F Bradley, Second Lieutenants B I L Jones, C H Nicholas, S H Berger, S H Geldard, H J Inglis, H L Cass, M Spartali, J C Roberts, P E Burrel, H C Griffith, P H Turner – and 208 other ranks and they spent the night on the beach before being allocated to the various coys. On 27 May a further draft of reinforcements of 1/9 Manchester Regt – a territorial force and part of 20 Brigade – consisting of four officers (Captain G H Okell, Lieutenant J M Wade, Second Lieutenant A E Stringer, Second Lieutenant A W F Connery) and 132 soldiers came through the battalion, but stayed only for two days before moving on to their own units. Finally, a third group of additional troops were attached to the battalion, this time from 5 East Lancashire Regiment, namely Captain A H Roberts, F V Rushton, Second Lieutenants J Baron and G G H Bolton and 120 men.

Administrative chores continued apace with a lot of time being spent around the Gully Beach area making roads which were vital for communication to and from the trench system. Although not in direct contact with the enemy there was still the threat of being hit by stray bullets and over the previous week, two men were killed and 19 wounded in this way and strict orders were given about movement by the fatigue parties. Meanwhile Ernest had the headache of administering this large influx of reinforcements:

Sunday 30 May 1915

Am getting lazy – find I have left my diary for five days again. Little has happened on land since the 25th and we are in the same place – Gully Beach. We had orders to go to 'W' Beach the other day, but as usual orders are countermanded and we remain as before. I nearly forgot to mention that we had a big draft of 222 in on the 27th including Major Jones and 14 subalterns from the 3rd Bn. This brings us up to about 750 and the Mess is at full strength again. On top of this we had 130 men and four officers from the 9th Manchesters attached to us and also 4 officers and 120 of the Lancashire Terriers. They have been splitting up the brigade of Territorials and dividing them between regular battalions. A very good thing for them too, for I hear that most of them haven't cleaned their rifles for a considerable time and they have had no issue of oil or flannelette since they left Egypt! They will soon learn – those that are left with us – the 9th Manchesters were suddenly ordered yesterday to go off somewhere else on the night just as the poor beggars were settling down. They have been badgered about from pillar to post since they landed – one can't help but feel sorry for the young ones – only boys they look and they had a hard time after landing too, going up into the trenches by themselves. Things at sea have been bad – the "Triumph" our old friend at Tsingtao was torpedoed on the 26th at about noon – fortunately nearly all hands were saved. On the 27th the "Majestic" was torpedoed just off 'W' Beach about 400 yards from the shore and her hull upside down is just about ten feet above water at the bow.

On the 28th however we had a set off against this – one of our submarines in the Sea of Marmora captured and sank four Turkish Transports full of guns and ammunition – one at the quay at Rodosta, one at a quay near Constantinople and the other two at sea. I wish we could settle the last of these "Squareheads" submarines though. One hears rumours of one having been captured, but it is not confirmed. Am afraid we are in for some bad weather tonight. We had a bad half an hour a few days ago when a cloud burst somewhere up the Gully and shortly afterwards the tiny rivulet was a foaming torrent about four feet deep which practically washed away the road at the bottom of the nullah. It was the most extraordinary rainfall I've yet seen in so short a time. At 'W' Beach two miles away they got no rain at all. Tonight however portends to be windy and stormy, hope I am wrong however.

From the beginning of the invasion, battleships of the Royal Navy had been anchored close off-shore to give whatever gun support they could to the battles taking place on land. They could be seen quite clearly by the troops on the peninsula and to many soldiers they provided a sense of reassurance, being so far away from home. However, their static presence was not lost on the enemy and it was not long before they became targets to marauding submarines. In the middle of May, the *Goliath, Triumph* and *Majestic* were sunk by torpedoes and it was decided that all battleships should be withdrawn to safer waters. Not only did this reduce the available fire power, but it inevitably had a detrimental impact upon morale. Compton Mackenzie, the well known author who served at Gallipoli made the following comment in his memoirs:

The sense of abandonment was acute. There was a sudden lull in the noise of the beach as if every man had paused to stare at the unfamiliar emptiness of the water and then turned to his neighbour with a question in his eyes about their future here. It is certain that the Royal Navy never executed a more demoralising manoeuvre in the whole of its history.[12]

Meanwhile, Ernest records the death of a friend:

Tuesday 1 June 1915

Went over to 'W' Beach for stores as usual – Lofthouse my old batman and who was Palmer's groom accompanied me to hold the horses. Found a big draft of over 500 Dublins. They say there are thousands at Lemnos waiting to come over. Tonight my batman informed me that poor Lofthouse had shot himself – can't understand it, as he always seemed such a cheery fellow and a rattling good soldier. Heard since that he had been seedy for some days. Touch of the sun I imagine. I shall miss him on my jaunts over to W Beach, he always seemed to like accompanying me. There has been a good deal of firing on this side this afternoon and evening and an Armenian who surrendered says they intend to attack tonight or tomorrow night.

Private Lofthouse's suicide was a sad but somewhat inevitable consequence of the pressure inflicted on some individuals on active service. Today, post traumatic stress disorder (PTSD) is a recognised illness, but in 1915 "shell shock" was the only psychological condition that warranted any consideration. The sordid conditions of trench warfare – the relentless heat, primitive sanitary facilities, unappetising food, sleep deprivation, lack of personal privacy, constant artillery bombardment and the ever present threat of being shot at any moment – were a lethal cocktail which some soldiers could not cope with, so it is not surprising that men like Lofthouse succumbed to the pressure and saw taking their own lives as the only way out.

General Hamilton was fully aware that his last two abortive attempts to capture Krithia and Achi Baba had served only to cause General Liman von Sanders to reinforce his divisions on the peninsula and the threat of an overwhelming assault by the Turks was a real and present danger. The arrival of 42 East Lancashire Division had bolstered his numbers but more reinforcements would

---

12   Compton Mackenzie, *Gallipoli Memories* (London: Cassell and Co Ltd, 1929), p.75.

not arrive for the time being, so another pre-emptive strike was essential if he was to regain the initiative. Thus, the third battle of Krithia was set in motion, to start on 4 June, with a more realistic objective of forcing the Turks back in a northerly direction so that Krithia could be overcome. On the eve of battle, General Hunter-Weston, who had been promoted to command VIII Corps, was replaced by Major General Beauvoir de Lisle, fresh from the Western Front.

By 3 June, Lieutenant Colonel Casson was back commanding 87 Brigade again and the battalion received orders for another attack on the Turkish line the next day. At 11:30 a.m. all COs were called to brigade HQ to go over the plan. At 8:30 a.m. heavy guns were to bombard enemy redoubts, or strong points, and trenches. Between 11:05 a.m. and 11:20 a.m. there would be a preliminary bombardment and final registration of targets and then from 11:20 a.m. to 11:30 a.m. there was to be a feint attack, by the fixing of bayonets and loud noise, with the hope of getting the enemy to expose themselves. This would then be followed immediately by a heavy bombardment for 30 minutes by all guns, howitzers and ships. At 12 noon, with the enemy hopefully disorientated from the intense shelling, the front line was to attack and capture the Turkish first main line of defence, followed by supporting troops advancing through the first line to attack and capture the second main line of Turkish trenches. As soon as these Turkish trenches had been captured, 87 Brigade was to advance through and make good a position ahead of Krithia. The brigade commander informed 2 SWB that no movement was likely for them until 11:30 a.m. the next day. This meant that the remainder of the day could be spent in making preparations and organising working parties, bomb throwers etc.[13]

Thursday 3 June 1915

A good deal of firing took place on night of 1st June. The enemy's fire however soon slackened when the "screw" guns opened (mountain battery). One could hear little authentic news. Our "day" is tomorrow. We move up from here, but no fixed time is given, nor where we go. It's about time we did go however. Tempers seem to be getting rather on edge back in the nullah due to enforced idleness and consequent "livers." The Colonel has taken over the Brigade – cheers.

At 7:30 a.m. on the morning of 4 June, all the battalion's stores were moved further up the Gully to a new administrative position, then at 9:30 a.m. there was a final conference at brigade HQ to co-ordinate last minute arrangements. According to the battalion's war diary:

Judging by the firing, the attacks appeared to work out according to programme arranged. The only information coming back was quite unreliable and was based on what could be got from wounded men. Infantry attack must have begun on time at 12 noon, as a very heavy enemy bombardment and rifle fire soon started up and then, an hour later, about 100 Turkish prisoners were marched down the Gully to 'W' Beach.

Then, as was inevitable, the plan changed and the following order was received from HQ 87 Brigade:

To SWB. Indian Bde held up in front of J10 AAA 88th Bde have occupied H11 and H12 AAA 5th Gurkhas have been placed under Gen Cox's orders AAA S.W.B. will move

---

13   Due to a shortage of issued hand grenades, improvised devices were made by packing explosives into jam tins, with designated soldiers appointed to throw them.

up and occupy trenches just vacated by 5th Gurkhas near Indian Brigade HQ. AAA Dublins will advance up east side of ravine and develop strong attack against east flank of J11 AAA Borders will occupy trenches vacated by Dublins AAA Acknowledge. From 87th Bde. Time 2.35pm.

It is not uncommon for units to be transferred from one brigade to another as reinforcements, or in support of an unexpected development in the battle plan. Early that evening a message came in to the effect that the battalion was now under command GOC Indian brigade:

To CO SWB. The Lt Gen Commanding 29 Division has placed your Battalion under my orders. The left of the 88th Brigade has reached a point near Ravine, either in trench H11 or H12, not quite certain which. In front of Indn. Bde. J10 & J11 have not been captured.

The Dublin Fusiliers have been instructed to join up the advanced portion of the 88th Brigade and dig in at dusk on a line facing, and wherever possible commanding, the Ravine, so as to prevent enemy either turning left of advanced positions of 88th Bde by coming down the ravine, or operating from eastern end of Trench J11. At dusk your battalion is to dig in on a similar line facing Ravine joining on to left of Dublin Fusiliers and prolonging towards our old first line of trenches thus closing the gap. Lieutenant Colonel Palin with about a company of the 14th Sikhs is holding a point in the ravine south east of the eastern end of J10 and you should connect up with & reinforce him there.

Acknowledge & report progress. From Indian Bde. Time 7.15 pm. 4 June 1915

Ernest was now busy providing logistical support:

Friday 4 June 1915

The attack is in full swing. Two battleships (Swiftsure and probably Cornwallis) turned up with a good escort of destroyers to help. Our batteries opened up and then suddenly ceased after ten minutes when the infantry took it up. The bombardment sounded like the Japanese at Tsingtao only on a smaller scale. It was good to hear them however and from reports of the wounded who began to come back we heard the guns were doing fine execution – after an interval of about ten minutes infantry fire – the guns opened with a burst again. Four men were hit at Gully Beach from falling bullets. We managed to get dinners up early and then prepared tea. Unfortunately just as these were being wetted down (sic) the order came to move. Ten minutes more and the men would have had what they like most. Nothing beats a drop of tea. The battalion left at about 2.45 and I followed with two water carts and a few pioneers etc half an hour later.

The Gully was perhaps a little livelier than ever with falling bullets and one could hear them whizzing by, some uncomfortably close. Twice the rear water cart was held up on the way, owing to ambulance wagons which are moving up and down without any regulation of traffic. We all arrived at the place below the White House, my old base in the Gully. One hardly knows it now; so many troops have been through and it looks decidedly worn. It's marvellous how few people are hit with the bullets which go sailing down the nullah. Most of them are going high no doubt but they sound close enough. Where we shall be tomorrow one can't find out. A good many casualties have gone down, mostly Sikhs and Worcesters. One hears that several trenches have been taken and over 100 prisoners have gone back through here. Still, I was hoping that we should have been advancing hard all along the line. Things appear somewhat held up at present – practically no gun fire, only rifle – now 7pm. Must try and answer dear old Puss's letter.[14]

In the early hours of 5 June, an urgent message was received from Lieutenant Colonel Palin for reinforcement. Lieutenant Rawle was sent up at once with one platoon but before he could reach the Sikhs they had retired. Then another message was received for further support. Capt Greenway immediately took up the remaining platoon of C Coy but once again the Sikhs all retired back through the battalion. For the remainder of the day A Coy and half of C Coy were engaged in improving the position covering the nullah.

The Turks continually threw grenades and sniped, but did very little damage. Captain Walker tried to drive a sap[15] through into the trench vacated by the 14th Sikhs and recover a machine gun. At 2.30 pm, orders were received from General Cox to link up the battalion's forward position with the trench occupied by the Lancashire Fusiliers. Major Going and the adjutant went up to arrange details for this sapping with CO Lancashire Fusiliers. During battle, what is known as "the fog of war" – a euphemism for chaos and confusion – is not uncommon. During the space of an afternoon, B Coy and half of D Coy were ordered to relieve A Coy and half of C Coy. Then orders were received for half of the battalion to return to Gully Beach and half to the Indian brigade, with battalion headquarters as reserve. Then at 7:00 p.m. another message was received to say that the battalion was not to return after all, but was to take over Lancashire Fusiliers trenches, under orders to be received from 87 Brigade. Soldiers are a stoic breed who are willing to put up with hardship and privation, but muddle and chaos are not high on their list of tolerances!

Having returned from yet another briefing at brigade HQ, the CO told the battalion that it had been decided to withdraw from the forward post and build a barrier across the inside of the Ravine between the line of trenches to provide protection from enemy fire. B, C and D Coys were on the west of Gully Ravine with D Coy linking up with 5th Gurkhas, while B Coy joined up with the Border Regiment by means of a small detachment on the east side of the Ravine. According to the Bn war diary, General Cox, commanding the Indian brigade, had originally said that *"he did not care whether this forward post was held or not as he attached little importance to it"* – a surprising comment indeed from a senior officer. Casualties were particularly light on this occasion with Lieutenant Rawle and Captain TC Greenway wounded with just three soldiers killed and six wounded.

On the morning of 6 June, information was received that the Turks had driven 1 KOSB out of the most advanced positions and that three coys of Inniskillings had been sent up to support 88 Brigade. Later that day, the battalion received orders to close up to the right and take over from the Border Regiment. By this stage, the battalion was now occupying most of the southern end of the Ravine.

Monday 7 June 1915

Have been too busy since to do much writing. After getting everything fixed up at the last place, got orders about 10 pm on the 4th to move another mile up the Gully nearer the battalion. Eventually found a small place near the KOSBs to settle in about 1 am. As usual the rifle fire was continuous and this part of the Gully has received a good deal of shrapnel

14   This was Ernest's nickname for his wife, Sybil.
15   An engineering term for digging a deep and narrow trench, usually from the cover of an existing fire trench, to approach or undermine an enemy position, without being seen or coming under fire.

the day previous. One was however able to get meals up to the men. Next day (5th) we moved up another 300 yards or so, right under the support trenches. We are now as far as we can get up the nullah. No doubt later on we may be able to proceed still further. Capts Greenway and Rawle both wounded today. Found the sanitation arrangements bad. No Sanitary Officer appears to have been appointed to supervise a system and the Medical Officers all being Territorials wouldn't exercise their authority. The flies around the latrines and dugouts, cookhouses, in fact everywhere are appalling. There is positively no rest by day, for the sun strikes into the dug outs and in conjunction with the dust flying and the flies, keeps one in a fever of irritation. On the 6th we went up into the trenches with Major Going to see if any improvements could be made to sanitary arrangements there. The smell in places was positively awful. Half buried bodies in the parapets in places especially by D Coy were added to the foregoing troubles. This can only be overcome by using plenty of chloride of lime. Had two barrels sent up the same day. Today went over to W Beach for stores – managed to have a dip at Gully Beach on the way back. Over at Ordnance had a chat with a Battery Quarter Master Sergeant of an Artillery Column. Heard from him the comforting intelligence that we have no lyddite (high explosive) for the Guns – only shrapnel. The latter is very good naturally but only against troops in the open. But for turning them out of the trenches we have nothing! It is a deplorable state of affairs. He also told me that a 5 inch enemy shell (shrapnel) caught his horses so well the other day that it killed 20 and wounded 40, besides wounding five men.

By 8 June it was clear that the objectives of the third battle of Krithia were never going to be achieved and all that the allied division had to show for a casualty list of 4,550, not including 2,000 French losses, was an extra 500 yards of the peninsula. Hostilities were to continue of course, and in the case of 2 SWB, the battalion was back on the daily chore of improving trenches. Such was the movement of troops between positions that their fire trench was continually being used by several other regiments as a communication trench. Also the constant hazard of snipers remained a threat but on this occasion the war diary laconically records *"18 snipers shot,"* which was a good haul by anyone's standards and a welcome boost to morale.

As Ernest records, the threat of yet another Turkish attack was ever present:

Tuesday 8 June 1915

Had a sleepless night. An attack was expected owing to the Turks having been observed pulling back their wire entanglements from the front of their trenches. Heavy fire started with darkness. The lights for use with the Verey pistols did not turn up from Brigade HQ until after dark. There are three pistols only in the battalion instead of three times that number and the cartridges are dealt out with a very sparing hand. It's the same with bombs. The R.E. are making them as fast as they can here out of old jam tins and we get up about 25 for the use of the battalion instead of about 250. The Turks have specially manufactured ones apparently in plenty. Took a turn at the telephone for Williams who was looking fagged out and who had to get up every five minutes to get reports from the Trenches. So had my things moved again to be nearer. Lay on the pathway near the operations dugout till dawn and managed to give the CO and Adjt a fair nights rest. Also managed to put in an hour myself after dawn. Have had plenty of opportunity since all day – but the heat and flies, especially the latter (my pet abhorrence) prevents any chance of sleep. With the going down of the sun the "Squareheads" have started shelling our gully again. Some well-timed shrapnel have come over making a pathway of bullets right across the open. Am afraid one or more of the ambulance men have been hit just fifty yards away as a group appeared to be bending over someone in a dugout. Why more have not been hit is a marvel to me. Another one just behind us this time and the bits are falling all around, burst a bit too high up though. Don't mind so long as they don't put them over after darkness sets in. Have just heard that one man was killed by the shrapnel first shot and two wounded by the second.

General Hamilton's strategy was now at a crossroads. At the southern end of the peninsula, 29 Division had not taken any of the initial objectives anticipated on 25 April and its advances inland were minimal, while the Anzac force was still precariously, but doggedly, perched on the slopes of Sari Bair, repelling every Turkish effort to dislodge them. Casualties were high, artillery ammunition in particular was low and it was now for the war cabinet at home, renamed as the Dardanelles Committee, to decide on the next course of action. The whole enterprise could be abandoned and the peninsula evacuated, the allies could push on gradually with minimal reinforcements, or a large injection of fresh troops could be sent out to Gallipoli to force the issue with one new, major, offensive. The last of these options was finally decided upon with three, later increased to five, new divisions (one of which was to include 4 SWB) to be sent out to the aid of the beleaguered Allies in the anticipation that this would ensure the success so desperately needed.

6

Gully Ravine

The most fatal heresy in war
is the heresy that battles can be won
without heavy loss

General Sir Ian Hamilton
Diary Extract
29 April 1915

The third attempt to capture Krithia had ended in failure, but General Hamilton had to keep the momentum of offensive action going if he was to have any chance of seizing the initiative by driving the Turks from their stronghold at the southern end of Cape Helles. At the same time, the Turkish army remained determined to force the Allies off the peninsula altogether and Turkish reinforcements were arriving without hindrance. The Dardanelles Committee had confirmed that help was on its way in the shape of three divisions of Kitchener's new army. These were to be 10, 11 and 13 Divisions respectively, the latter including 4 SWB which was part of 40 Brigade. Such a large force was more than welcome and the general now had to draw up plans to make best use of this valuable addition. The logic of his initial invasion plan still applied, in that a major assault to the north of Bulair, or a landing on the Asiatic shore might not achieve the success he so badly desired. He therefore settled on two options.

The first of these was another frontal attack on Krithia from the southern end of Cape Helles, with the aim of driving the enemy northwards towards the Kilid Bahr plateau. This was, essentially, a repeat of the first invasion and not only had three such attempts failed already, but the Turks were reinforcing their position in and around Krithia and Achi Baba almost on a daily basis. His second option was to use the reinforcements to create a breakout from the Anzac sector to seize the central heights of Chunuk Bair from where he would virtually dominate the whole peninsula. The Turks to the south would be cut off and starved of any reinforcement and the allies would be able to sweep down to capture the Narrows of the Dardanelles, so that the allied fleet could proceed unhindered along the waterway to Constantinople, as originally intended. It was still only early June and given the time it would take for these new divisions to arrive and complete their battle preparation, such an invasion could not be launched until the end of July at the earliest. However, General Hamilton did have 52 (Lowland) Division, commanded by Major General G A Egerton, recently arrived on the peninsula as reinforcement allocated to him earlier, so he was in a position to launch limited offensives against the enemy in the meantime.

A significant feature of the Cape Helles region is a number of ravines, or gullies (known in Turkish as *deres* and also referred to by the British as *nullahs*), of varying size and depth and which run in a north-south direction and which, in 1915, intersected the opposing lines of trenches.

During the winter, these gullies would be flowing streams or rivers, but in the summer they were often barren and dry. By far the largest of these was *Zighin Dere*, known to the allies as Gully Ravine. Almost three miles (5kms) in length, Gully Ravine rises on the southern slope of Hill 472 and then makes its way in a south westerly direction between Krithia and the west coast of the peninsula, letting out into the sea at Gully Beach, situated between X and Y beaches. A formidable natural obstacle, it is some 200 feet (70m) wide in places and up to 100 feet (35m) deep. Its slopes are steep and sandy and it is interspersed with numerous re-entrants – recessions into the banks of the feature – and these re-entrants were the scene of most of the intermittent fighting in the middle weeks of June. During the campaign the gully was like a bustling town, with its terraced dugouts, scattered little cemeteries, open canvas dressing stations, various headquarters and numerous supply dumps. Deep inside the ravine the dry sandy streambed road paved the way for horse drawn ambulances, busy stretcher bearers and marching troops. This road wound its way gently up to a steep zigzagging path that climbed up the cliff face and into the firing lines.[1]

One of the actions in the ravine took place on the night of 10 June, involving 2 SWB and the Border Regiment. At this stage, 2 SWB was dug in on a frontage of about 500 yards to the east of Gully Ravine in an area which became known as the "Boomerang". It was also close to a position referred to as "Turkey Trench" which was being used by enemy snipers and which was to be the centre of attention over the next few weeks. A, B and C Coys were in the front line with D Coy in support. The CO had received his orders from the brigade commander that morning and the

Image 15. Lieutenant Rupert Inglis 2 SWB who died from his wounds on 29 June 1915 (R Welsh Museum).

1   Stephen Chambers, *Gallipoli – Gully Ravine* (Barnsley: Pen and Sword Books Ltd, 2003), p.14.

aim was to dislodge the Turks from a sap opposite the angle of 2 SWB's firing line in conjunction with the Border Regiment who were on their right. As it got dark at about 10pm, Lieutenant Rupert Inglis and a party of 10 men, including some bomb throwers and Royal Engineers, crawled forward across the open ground to the sap which was about 100 yards away. They could have been spotted by the enemy at any stage, which would have meant instant death from heavy rifle fire, but luck was with them and they made it safely to the other side. As soon as they arrived, they leapt into the trench and with guns blazing tried to force their way along its length. Despite their best efforts, enemy bombs and machine gun fire forced them out, with Rupert Inglis being badly wounded in the process. A second attempt was made immediately, this time led by Rupert's brother, Lieutenant Harry Inglis and Second Lieutenant Michael Spartali, but again without success. This abortive operation had achieved nothing, yet Spartali, who had only recently arrived in the battalion, was killed along with six soldiers and Harry Inglis was also injured. Rupert Inglis died of his injuries a few weeks later on 29 June, having been evacuated to a hospital ship, and was buried at sea. (He is commemorated on the Helles memorial.) The next day, Sergeant Rogers led a small party out in an attempt to recover Spartali's body, but he too was killed by enemy fire in the process. Both Inglis brothers were recommended for the MC for their actions, but only Harry Inglis was to receive a decoration.

Ernest makes mention of this episode in his diary:

Thursday 10 June 1915

Birkett and Silk arrived from Alexandria this morning and after lunch went up to join their companies. Poor Silk was killed by a chance bullet about three hours later and buried shortly afterwards. Rotten luck. Another sound fellow gone. Had a night attack by A Coy on the enemy's sap. They got there alright but were bombed out again. Took it again with the same result. Poor Spartali, one of our recently joined was killed – a very able fellow. He was only in the dugout the night before plotting off a sketch of our trenches. The next day an effort was made by Sergeant Rogers and a couple of men to recover Spartali's body with the result that Sergeant Rogers was killed and so two are out now.

In the early hours of 12 June, 2 SWB was relieved by the Dublin Fusiliers for a five day rest period at Gully Beach. While this may have been a break from direct combat with the enemy, it was anything but a rest in the accepted sense of the word. Working parties would be sent out daily to repair trenches in other positions which had suffered from enemy bombardment and to prepare a second line of defence known as the "Eski Line" or "Old Line," this being the line across the peninsula held by the allies on 28 April and now forming a reserve position. Then there was the continual requirement to move supplies, which had been offloaded from transport ships at W Beach and Gully Beach, forward to the various brigade administrative areas. All this had to be done under the ever present threat of sniper fire, stray bullets from the front line which still had the capacity to kill or wound the unsuspecting victim, along with the regular bombardment from "Asiatic Annie," the artillery fire from Kum Kale on the Asiatic shore of the Dardanelles. The weather did not help either. By mid June, the temperature was soaring into the mid 80°F (30c) and the constant wind created persistent dust from sand or dry soil. There was one compensation however – the dust restricted the visibility of Asiatic Annie so that the troops working on the southern beaches were afforded some respite from the shelling. It also gave a welcome opportunity to have a quick swim in the sea off Gully Beach, which was the closest they might come to having a bath.

Consider for a moment, the living conditions endured by soldiers in combat on the peninsula. As well as being frightening, war can be uncomfortable, dirty, chaotic and unhygienic and a soldier spends a lot of his time and energy in just keeping himself alive. This is why both corporate and personal discipline are vital ingredients of life on the battlefield, yet there are some circumstances which are beyond the control of the individual. Today's soldiers have far more resources at their disposal to ameliorate the strain of battle, but in 1915 life was very basic indeed. Apart from rudimentary dugouts in the sides of trenches or gullies, or some sheets of canvas to put over the tops of rest trenches, there was little or no shelter from the blazing sun of the Aegean summer; consequently lethargy, sunburn and heatstroke took its toll. The issued clothing of the time was not designed for the baking hot conditions and the heavy flannel shirts would cause soldiers to sweat profusely, even when resting, which brought on the danger of dehydration and it was not uncommon to go without fresh water for several days at a time. There was certainly no air conditioning, nor was there any ice to keep water and food cool, so drinking water was nearly always brackish and tepid.

Tins of meat would regularly heat up from the sun into a glutinous mess, which, more often than not, was inedible. The battalion quartermaster would do his level best to provide food which was appetising and units which had their food cooked centrally, rather than left to the individual to cope with, fared better. As Sergeant Bean explained in his diary:

We were always well fed after the early days of the campaign. In this respect our battalion was far ahead of any other on the peninsula as we kept up our system of Coy cooks whereas in most other Regts rations were issued to individuals and each man was responsible for his own cooking. Consequently the bacon ration was often wasted and a man very seldom went to the trouble of warming his preserved meat ration even when he had the opportunity which was not often. Of course we never had fresh meat but after about the first month we had a part ration of bread instead of all biscuit. As the preserved meat ration was far in excess of requirements, Col Casson made arrangements whereby the excess was exchanged for condensed milk, rice or dried fruits (raisins, figs etc).

When trench warfare developed the following scale of diet was adhered to as nearly as possible:

Breakfast 7am: - Tea. Bacon (fried or boiled), Biscuits
Mid-day:- Cold preserved meat, boiled rice pudding or stewed fruit
Tea 3.30pm: - Tea. Biscuits and jam
Supper 7pm: - Hot Stew (preserved meat and preserved vegetables)

As the days were extremely hot, cold meat at mid day was much more acceptable than hot meat would have been, the latter being more palatable in the cool of the evening when the flies had ceased to torment.

Although Sergeant Bean gives an outline timetable for feeding, the reality is that meals were not always taken at set times, nor were they served in canteens with tables and chairs. Food was eaten out of small metal containers with a folding handle, known as mess tins. Meals were taken wherever or whenever they could, often at the bottom of a trench, accompanied by hordes of flies. Flies in their millions gestated in the corpses of dead soldiers scattered across the battlefields, lived off the faeces in primitive latrines – often merely holes in the ground, or even just out in the open if a soldier stricken with illness could not get to one in time – and then swarmed all over the food of the soldiers, who could nothing to keep them at bay.

Then there was the smell. The smell of rotting corpses in the sun, the smell of open latrines, the smell of thousands of men, who could not wash on a regular basis, confined together. Worst of all was the spread of sickness, diarrhoea and dysentery from unhygienic living conditions. Dust and dirt got into everything and there were no facilities for washing on a regular basis, apart from the occasional dip in the sea during a rest period. Widespread dysentery was inevitable and at the height of summer there were 5,000 cases a week. With medical facilities stretched to breaking point, it is surprising that the allied army could stand up, literally, but stand up they did and with typical ingenuity, resourcefulness, courage and determination, they managed to retain some degree of normality. The British soldier is blessed with an irrepressible sense of humour which is at its best in times of adversity and so they continued to take everything that the enemy, who was no doubt suffering in equal measure, could throw at them.

Ernest also appreciated the opportunity of some rest:

Saturday 12 to Thursday 17 June 1915

Were relieved shortly after dawn by the Dublins and came back to Gully Beach for a rest. We have been very fortunate I must say in comparison with the Inniskillings who have had a long time up, due to their having been attached to the Indian Brigade and passed back again, in time for another tour. We are to do five days up and five days back I understand in future. Awful dusty weather for days. The wind never seems to go down except for a few hours at night. Remained in the Gully in reserve for the next few days and had a quiet time except for spare falling bullets, especially at night. Had three or four men wounded. The Dublins had a bit of a "dust up" with the Turks judging by the number of wounded who came down on the 16th. We then left our bivouac the next day at 4.15 am and returned to trenches relieving the Dublins. CSM Alabaster got a spare bullet through his arm just before parade. So he is out of mischief for a while again. Everything was pretty quiet that night except for the usual sniping.

At 4:30 a.m. on the morning of 17 June, 2 SWB moved back up to the front line and took over the trenches they had held previously from the Dublin Fusiliers, in the area known as Geoghegan's Bluff. Hardly were they back in position than a particularly aggressive action began to develop. On the evening of 18 June, while General Hamilton was hosting a dinner at his base at Imbros to commemorate the centenary of the Battle of Waterloo, the Turks commenced a very heavy bombardment on the battalion's trenches to the east of Gully Ravine, beginning, according to the war diary, at 6:45 p.m. This lasted for about half an hour and the parapets of both the fire trenches and the support trenches were badly damaged. This seemed to be the prelude to an enemy attack, during which all telephone lines between battalion headquarters and the four companies was destroyed. Linesmen were sent out to repair the cables and it was not long before communications were re-established. This was no easy task however and it required nerves of steel to crawl across open ground, often in sight of the enemy, to find where the cables had been destroyed by artillery fire and then replace them. There are numerous occasions of linesmen and signallers being awarded medals for bravery, often posthumously, for their outstanding courage in attempting to keep vital lines of communication open.

At about 8:30 p.m. the enemy infantry began to attack, but were driven back by heavy fire from the battalion. Half an hour later, the Turks attacked again, this time in greater strength and by 9·15 p.m. they had succeeded in getting in to the northwest end of Turkey Trench. The battalion took casualties and Lieutenant Jordan, who had only arrived on the peninsula 10 days earlier, subsequently died from severe wounds. Bombing by the enemy was very heavy and the allied soldiers holding Turkey Trench were forced back to the main defensive line. As a result, a gap developed between the battalion and Inniskilling Fusiliers on their right, which could have had drastic consequences had the enemy forced their way through. By 9:45 p.m. however, the gap was reported to have been closed and a party of Inniskillings and some of the battalion managed to bomb their way back along Turkey Trench.

This success was short lived and at 10:30 p.m. the Inniskillings reported that they were being driven back and asked 2 SWB for support. The brigade commander stated that they must be supported at all costs and by 11:15 p.m. Captain Walker with a bombing party had advanced about 50 yards up the sap recently dug connecting the main fire trench with head of Turkey Trench, but this was in vain. At 11:30 p.m. Major Going, the battalion 2IC was sent over from the west to the eastern side of the nullah to take charge, as the situation was becoming very confused. Just after midnight, the Inniskillings were again reported to be suffering heavily on the left of their main trench. Preparatory arrangements were made for a charge by one of the SWB coys against the flank of Turkey Trench to relieve pressure on Inniskillings. For the next hour, fighting continued but as the enemy pressure slackened, it was considered better that a counter attack by 2 SWB should wait until 3:00 a.m. except in case of urgency when it would take place at once, so that another gap in the line of defence between the battalions could be made good. This was done by 2:00 a.m. and another 20 yards of Turkey Trench were seized, but yet again the assaulting troops were forced back by Turkish rifle fire. While 20 yards might not sound very much, given the close proximity between allied and Turkish trenches, it was a significant achievement.

At 3:00 a.m. on a prearranged signal the 2 SWB coy charged the flank of Turkey Trench. The moment the assault began, the enemy sent up a rocket flare which illuminated the battlefield and the attack came under heavy rifle fire. The officer leading the attack, Lieutenant Cass, was shot dead and 30 soldiers killed or wounded after charging only a few yards and by 3:25 a.m. the attack had failed. A few men got into the trench although they were killed in the process, but this assault undoubtedly relieved the pressure of the enemy attacks. At this stage, Lieutenant Colonel Casson, the commanding officer moved up into the fire trench to take personal control of the situation and at 4:15 a.m. he asked for artillery support to be directed on the northwest half Turkey Trench. At 4:45 a.m. Captain Fowler, supported by Captain Walker and a small party of men from both 2 SWB and the Inniskillings, advanced down the trench with bombs and bayonets but again were forced back. Although exhausted by a long night of battle, Captain Fowler went out again, this time accompanied by the RSM, WO1 Westlake. The party was headed up by Pte Woods, who cleared the way using his bayonet, while Pte Matthews kept down the enemy's enfilading fire.[2] Over the next hour or so, slow but steady progress was made and by 6:30 a.m. the whole trench was back in the battalion's hands once again. Captain Fowler's bravery during this assault was an inspiration; as his own supply of bombs ran out he would pick up those thrown by the enemy and hurl them back against the Turks with no regard for his own safety. Captain Fowler was later recommended for the VC for his gallantry, but was awarded the DSO instead, while Privates Matthews and Woods were awarded the DCM.[3]

By now, the enemy was in disarray and as they retired across the open ground in daylight, they took heavy casualties from 2 SWB machine gun fire. It was then noticed that the Boomerang was full of enemy and the CO was asked to call for howitzer fire on it. About two hours later reports of

2   A body of troops or a defensive position is "in enfilade" if enemy fire can be directed along its longest flank, thus causing the maximum damage possible.

3   C T Atkinson, *History of the South Wales Borderers*, p.122.

Image 16. Captain Hugh Fowler 2 SWB who was awarded the DSO for his outstanding bravery on the night of 18 June 1915 (Mrs J Copping).

an impending counter attack were received, and a feeble effort was in fact made against the head of Turkey Trench. This was at once repulsed, and the battalion was then in a position to regroup its coys, repair its defences and attend to its casualties. As well as Lieutenant Cass, Lieutenant Lewis Jones was also killed and Lieutenant Jordan died later from his wounds. Major Going and Captain Paterson were wounded, along with 72 soldiers who were either killed or wounded. The enemy lost a similar number in and around Turkey Trench and this figure may have been twice as high if casualties in the vicinity were included.

Ernest witnessed this battle as well:

Friday 18 June 1915

Waterloo Day.[4] Quiet day till evening, then suddenly the Turks opened up with a furious bombardment at our trenches. How many guns they had in all is hard to say, but they ripped out like M.Gs and there were certainly four "Jack Johnsons" with them. These came over with a tremendous clanging burst, all the shrapnel and the high bursting shell of the smaller pieces falling round Bn HQ like rain. As they burst on the trenches the falling pieces just reached our Headquarters, only being about two or three hundred yards behind the trenches. C & D Coys again got the brunt of it. After about an hour's heavy bombardment the Turks attack opened up. It must have been a relief for our poor beggars in the trenches after crouching to avoid or try to avoid being pulverised to get up and hit back. As the Turks

4   The centenary of the Battle of Waterloo – 18 June 1815.

came on at the same old bone of contention (their lost trench) our machine guns caught them beautifully. Morgan (MG officer) asserts that out of 60 which crossed the open he got 50 at point blank range. All night the tornado lasted and the Turks managed to bomb their way into their trench again and captured part of it. We were unable to shift them. Cass was killed and then Lewis Jones. The Inniskillings who were next to us had a go and managed to get on but were forced to retire again.

By "Jack Johnsons" Ernest was referring to the nick-name given to a large artillery shell. The power and large amount of dark smoke given off by the big shell was reminiscent, apparently, of the first black world heavy weight boxing champion, Jack Johnson, in 1906.

The battalion spent the next day repairing the damage caused to their trenches by enemy fire the day before, although they were still under constant fire from the Turkish front line. The next day, with the exception of B Coy who stayed in position on the western side of the ravine, they were relieved by 1 KOSB for a welcome break back in the rest trenches and on Gully Beach. Ernest's diary covers the aftermath of the battle and the rest period:

Saturday 19 June 1915

The Colonel and the Adjt went up and another counter attack was made which was successful. Fowler and the S.M. of the Inniskillings had done some good bomb throwing and when the trench was re-captured it was found to be literally choked with dead Turks. Williams phoned down to me that we had it back again and Gen Marshall our brigadier who was up with me at the time was pleased. After breakfast I had orders from Williams to come up to the trenches as combatant in case of another attack.[5] So hastily getting my actual necessities together went up. Heard that Jordan had been hit by bombs in both legs severely and Captain Patterson and another officer were also wounded, so we were running short of them. The Colonel sent me round to assist in squaring up the trenches, which were sadly knocked about, and C Coy's were a perfect shambles. The men did not get all their breakfasts till about 12 o'clock and the equipment and kit of British and Turk was mixed up. Dead bodies lay about. Two decomposed legs had become unearthed in the centre of the trench floor and the men were just too tired to trouble about these little things and breakfast and rations were issued at about the worst smelling part of the trench (except the Turks trench). We managed to get a working party from the KOSB which I started on parapet repairing and took a portion to make a hole for reception of dead Turks. I shall never forget the sight of that trench. Our bombers had done their work well and the difficulty of burying was enormous.

After swallowing a little lunch, started with another platoon and hoped to get things ship shape. At about 3 pm however the infernal bombardment started again. I was in D Coy's trench at the time and the parapets were simply crushed-in in places. They seemed to come everywhere. Over, behind, in front. One got smothered in dust and the black smoke from the "Jack Johnsons" prevented one from seeing anything for a time. The gorse also got on fire, which made matters worse. One could do nothing while this was going on so made my way back to the CO who was just outside the fire trench. Major Going was standing there talking to him when another "Jack Johnson" came over. He being hard of hearing could not hear its approach I suppose. It burst just over the same Company and next moment the Major was on his knees hit on the side of the head by a fragment. He tried to

5   By combatant, he means that he was to be employed in a fighting, rather than an administrative, role.

make light of it and cursed very solidly while Williams was bandaging him. The wound is not serious fortunately but he is sadly missed at such a time. After the Turks had finished we started once more to clear up, repair breaches etc. They did not come on to attack again – they had had enough. One of the prisoners taken said they were very disappointed, as they had hoped to blow us out of the trenches. They did their best. By passing along the casualties rifles and Turks guns and equipment etc one managed to clear the trenches of a good deal of rubbish and by nightfall things looked fairly ship shape again.

Got the fatigue party to drag some of the dead bodies into an old trench, but there were still about forty more to come out. I expected to stay up for the night but the Colonel told me to come down. It was a treat to get a wash and a clean or fairly clean bit of food away from that trench. My stomach must be getting stronger with approaching age. I'm sure I couldn't have believed I could stick such sights and smells without being ill. The night passed quietly enough and I wasn't called to the phone till about 3am. The CO and Adjt had earned their rest. We had had the agreeable news that we were being relieved on the right of Gully Ravine at 9 am by the KOSB.

Sunday 20 June 1915

Came back in support trenches to the old White House and my dug out is near my old one of nearly two months back. B Coy remain on the left of the nullah and will be relieved by A Coy tomorrow afternoon. Went down with Walker this evening and had the most enjoyable swim I've had here yet. We have lost about 60 casualties in the two days. About twenty were buried by us including two officers, but some are still missing and presumably are lying outside the trenches. Have heard that we have accounted for 200 or 300 Turks besides wounded. Poor Jordan has since died. So our number of officers is being sadly depleted again. Of our original battalion, only Col Casson, Captains Williams and Walker, Lieutenant Morgan and self and Blake the MO still remain. Fowler commanding D Coy came out with a draft recently and has had a pretty rough time lately. Walker has too and has done jolly well through it all.

Monday 21 June 1915

Went down for an early morning swim with Williams, after being up on the trenches watching the French bombardment of enemy trenches. I hope they put the Turks through something like they gave us, but with better results. Feeling a bit slack today and awfully stiff – what from I can't imagine. Had a bullet just by my ear, which buried itself in the ground 10 feet away, and 10 feet below my dug out. It seemed to have come from the direction of the French lines, but it's a Turkish bullet alright. Can't understand what's wrong with the mails. Haven't heard from Puss for ages. Have just been told there's a mail in at W Beach. Let's hope it's true. Must write this evening in any case.

Soldiers are a stoic breed and will take the privations and hardships of active service in their stride. However, if there is one thing that they treasure most of all, it is letters from home. The arrival of a letter, a parcel, or a copy of their local newspaper, no matter how out of date it might be, lifts morale immensely and reminds them that there is a world of normality outside the confines of combat. It also comforts them to know that someone beyond the field of battle is thinking of them. All mail to and from Gallipoli had to travel by sea, so it could take some time to arrive and then be distributed to individuals, but it was always welcome no matter how long it took. Mail sent home had to be censored for reasons of security which added to the delay, but it was appreciated by their families and friends who were always anxious to know if their loved ones were still in one piece.

On 23 June, the battalion was relieved by the Lancashire Fusiliers and moved back into reserve into their old lines near Gully Beach. Being in reserve meant the never-ending round of administrative tasks (known in military parlance as fatigues) such as the movement of supplies and the restoration of trenches, in the area of Gully Beach and X Beach. Ernest makes comment on the lack of laundry facilities compared with those on the Western Front:

Wednesday 23 June 1915

Came back to our old place in reserve in the Gully, starting at 4am. Went to W Beach after breakfast for more stores such as shirts, socks etc. It's a pity we haven't a huge laundry for men to get their clothing boiled after coming down from the trenches. Our comrades in France have a great pull over us in this and many other comforts. We score over weather conditions easily however, so mustn't grumble.

And then news started to come in about a new offensive:

Saturday 26 June 1915

Quiet so far. Enemy sending over "black marias"[6] but am pleased that most have been "duds" so far. We are preparing for a big attack on our left and the 24th are to have the honour I hear. Let us hope we get a good initial performance by the guns and then we shall go through. One hears all sorts of rumours of the Division being sent away for a rest. It would be a welcome change. Certainly the Colonel is in need of one – quite seedy today. Perhaps if all goes well on this next advance and we can consolidate we might get a spell.

While unsuccessful overall, the third battle of Krithia on 4 June had made some progress in the centre of the line at Cape Helles but had failed on the left flank (west) along Gully Spur and Gully Ravine and on the right flank (east), where the French contingent were confronted by a number of strong Turkish redoubts on the feature known as Kereves Spur. Encouraged by the recapture of Turkey Trench on 21 June and the heavy casualties inflicted on the enemy during that action, General Hamilton decided to make another attempt to push forward. The aim was to straighten out the allied front line from Gully Spur on the left flank to Kereves Spur on the right flank. Keen to retain the initiative, the general wanted to launch this new assault as soon as possible, but the governing factor was the time required by the French to organise the fire of their heavy howitzers, which were to assist with the British attack. This would not be done until 27 June, so the attack was fixed for the morning of 28 June.

On the evening of 27 June, orders for the attack were received. 2 SWB was to capture the enemy trenches numbered J9 and J10 on the western side of the ravine. They would be the lead battalion within the brigade, with the Border Regiment across the ravine on their right flank. Then 1 KOSB and the Inniskillings would pass through to take trench J11, followed by 86 Brigade who would move on to the final objective of J12 and J13. To complete the picture, 156 Brigade from

6   A slang expression for a German artillery shell, which gave off black smoke.

52 Division would pass through the Border Regiment on the right to attack trench H12 while 88 Brigade would remain in reserve.

By 6:00 p.m. on 27 June, 2 SWB had taken over the fire trenches from the Lancashire Fusiliers and 5th Gurkha Regiment on the west of Gully Ravine and then started to prepare the trenches for the assault. Trench bridges and ladders were borrowed from the French for this purpose. Ernest fills in some of the details:

Sunday 27 June 1915

The battalion was sent up to take over first line trenches. A Coy relieving R Fusrs, B, C & D Coys relieving 5th Ghurkhas. Had to divide cookhouses – sending A & D to the barrier at top of Gully and B, C & HQ to the head of Y Ravine. Everything for the latter phase had to be transported from the Gully up the mule track by mule or by hand. This made the water question a difficult one, as there is only sufficient water in Y Ravine for the Indian Brigade. All our water had to be carried in camp kettles for nearly a mile and with the extremely hot dry weather, it was a problem on the following day during the attack. However, we did manage to cope with it. The Turks gave us a few shells occasionally just over the parapet, which struck pretty close to HQ bivouacs. These are very primitive affairs, merely being holes in the ground. Had a quiet night.

At 9:00 a.m. on 28 June, the artillery bombardment started. Owing to the short distance between the battalion's line and that of the enemy, 2 SWB were obliged to withdraw their men out of most of the firing line during the bombardment so as not to be shelled by their own side. The bombardment appeared to be an excellent one, quite unlike any other during this campaign, and considered to be a very significant change in artillery tactics. At 10:45 a.m. the Border Regiment attacked the Boomerang trench as arranged. This trench was a very important one to the battalion as it flanked the whole ground between their line and J9 & J10 and any attack without first taking the Boomerang would probably be very costly. Just before 11:00 a.m. most company commanders took their coys back into the fire trench as they considered it better to risk a few of their own shells than to advance out of the support trenches thereby putting another 50 yards of very broken ground between themselves and the enemy's line. At 11:00 a.m. the battalion attack began. Despite the very heavy shrapnel fire the men advanced across the open ground with great determination. They bypassed J9 trench as ordered and took J10. Then at 11:05 a.m. the Inniskillings and KOSB advanced through the battalion and went for J11 trench which they captured without much difficulty. The KOSB suffered heavily however from machine gun fire from H14. At 11:30 a.m. 86 Brigade passed through the lines of 87 Brigade as planned, and advanced with the aid of the Indian brigade who worked along the cliff to take J12 & J13. The rest of the day was spent in consolidating J9 & J10 and in collecting the wounded. 2 SWB losses were heavy. A Coy lost the most due to the fact that the Border Regiment had not quite completed the capture of the Boomerang and its satellites by 11:00 a.m. which made the battalion vulnerable. Lieutenant Joseph Budd was killed, while Lieutenant John Bradley was wounded but died four days later from his injuries. Captain Habershon and Second Lieutenant Nicholas were also seriously wounded, while Captain Williams and Lieutenant Ffrench escaped with only minor injuries. Of the other ranks, 160 were either killed, wounded or missing.

The whole attack, however, achieved its aim and was the most successful battle of the campaign so far. On the left, or west, of Gully Ravine, five significant lines of enemy trenches were taken and in the centre 156 Brigade took H12 trench with the exception of a small section. According to the 2 SWB war diary:

The 29th Division again proved what it could do in spite of its enormous losses.

In his role as Quartermaster, Ernest had a good overview of the battle and his diary entry for the day complements that of the battalion's record:

Monday 28 June 1915

Whether the enemy knew that we had an attack in store for them this time I don't know, but at 9am on the 28th we started a splendid bombardment with high explosive shell against their trenches J9 – J10, followed by 11, 12 & 13 – also on the right of the Gully at H10 – 12. The French had brought around some of their guns to assist. Our 5 and 6 inch howitzers did splendid work. The infantry attack was timed to start at 11 am sharp and so the bombardment of two hours was a really effective help this time. The objective of A, C & D Coys was J9 followed by J10. The 86th Bde to then go through and take J11 & 12 and the Ghurkhas pushing on to get J13 if possible. B Coy was timed to start at 11.10 am in support.

The top of Y Ravine was a tight place to be in – all the ground over 50 yards from the trench was plastered with shrapnel and when B Coy were ordered to fall in they got it as soon as they put their heads out of the dugouts. Two or three were killed and several wounded. Unfortunately two of the casualties or three (not certain which) were Sergeants – a serious loss before going into the attack.

Captain Williams came hobbling back from the fire trench, having got a thump on the knee, luckily only bruised. Our fellows took their trenches alright, and with few casualties on the left, considering the amount of shrapnel the enemy was using. Petre told me on the phone afterwards that we had J9, 10, 11, 12 & 13 or part of the latter. Our job consisted of taking J9 & 10, the KOSB & Inniskillings to go through and take J11 & 12 and the Indian Brigade J13. On our right the Border Regt had the job of settling the "Boomerang" trench and H11 & 12.

Our casualties were Lieutenant Budd killed, Captain Habenshon, 2Lieutenants Bradley, Nicholas and Inglis wounded, the latter very badly in the stomach, a good promising fellow to lose. These were all lost in the charge of the rank and file in the advance and holding of trenches gained on the 28th & 29th. Forty were killed and about 130 wounded. A Coy caught it rather badly as their right was in the nullah, the most difficult place owing to ravines and barbed wire and naturally held in great strength.

The next day, the battalion was ordered to take over trenches occupied by the Borders, Dublins and Lancashire Fusiliers. The trench west of Gully Ravine was very bad indeed and in most places only about six inches deep as a consequence of heavy shelling collapsing the sides and the parapet. The whole place was littered with dead bodies and stench almost unbearable. The men worked day and night and improved the trenches enormously. During the night it appeared as if the Turks were about to make a counter attack but they never came really close to the battalion position, although they did retake a part of J13. Throughout the day, working parties had the grisly task of collecting and burying the dead from both sides and it is recorded that the battalion burnt or buried at least 50 Turkish corpses.

Once again, Ernest was in the thick of it, especially when battalion headquarters returned to the administrative area on the beach at the mouth of Gully Ravine:

Tuesday 29 June 1915

Got orders to move HQ to the Gully. Personally I was glad to say goodbye to Y Ravine, the water difficulty and men's meals apart from the unhealthy shrapnel, which was mighty adjacent, did not leave many happy recollections. Dumped the Battn cooks at the old place at the barrier and walked on up the captured portion of the nullah. Round the big bend about 200 yards up, a sickening sight and stench met me. A strip of stagnant slimy water contained a couple of Sikhs bodies which had been there since the 4th June, whilst another couple, mere skeletons in clothes were hung up in the barbed wire and they could be seen on the bank on the right. Further up behind the bends of the Gully were rough shelters which resembled an Indian bazaar before the Duty Sergt had been round in the morning – pots & pans, great coats, rifles, equipment and dead bodies already putrid. A few poor wounded devils were lying in one of the shelters with a guard over them; they had received first aid but had to wait till later in the day when one was able to get them removed. I wonder if the Turks treat our wounded as well? I hope I never have the bad luck to try it anyhow. Some of our fellows have been getting shocking wounds lately. I saw a bullet yesterday, which had evidently struck base first, for it was mushroomed, and the point undamaged.

The Turks tried a counter attack at night, but were repulsed and were caught trying to get away on the morning of the 30th. Started to clean up the Gully in earnest. By nightfall we had dumped sufficient arms, ammunition and equipment to fit out a battalion and had big fires burning up the rubbish and filth.

On 30 June, time was spent on further improvement of the trenches and cleaning up. Captain Elgee arrived from Egypt and Captain Somerville returned from two months in hospital at Malta, having been wounded at the first battle of Krithia in April. GOC 29 Division, General de Lisle, ordered a defensive barrier to be put further up the gully to impede any surprise attack by the Turks. This was done as soon as it was dark, without any loss of life. The remains of 30 dead Turks were collected and burnt while 10 bodies of the Dublin Fusiliers were found and buried. On the evening of the next day, The Turks put in an unexpected attack against J13 and re-took most of it. They also advanced on J12 and drove the defending Gurkhas out of it, but the Inniskilling Fusiliers were called up in counter attack and recaptured the position.

Ernest adds to the trauma of the day:

Thursday 1 July 1915

Still cleaning up. Found the bodies of Lieutenant Col Jacques and Captain Meade of the 14th Sikhs. The former (both were killed I believe on 4th June) was decomposed beyond recognition except for clothing and a letter found on him, whilst the latter was burnt all except one leg and head, remainder practically a charred skeleton. Wrote to the Adjt of the Sikhs who asked me to bury them. On turning Meade over into a Sikhs blanket I found Meade's gold watch and £3 odd in gold and silver under the body. Strangely though, his watch had only been slightly burnt at the winding stem, which had probably caused the main spring to break, otherwise it was undamaged. There are quite a number of Sikhs lying about near the same place, poor fellows, they made a fine charge I believe but apparently were not reinforced and so suffered severely. Only a remnant of that fine Corps remains.

Then, at 3:30 a.m. on the morning of 2 July, with the battalion occupying a firing line between J11 and J12 (known to them as J11.b) heavy firing broke out which served to portend a general attack by the enemy. When day broke Turks could be seen massing in the Gully at the eastern end of J13. Artillery fire was called for and very heavy shrapnel fire was turned on to them. Machine guns also opened up and it soon became apparent that the Turkish commanders were having considerable difficulty in persuading their men to advance. When they did finally advance against the end of J12, they came under very heavy machine gun fire from the new cross cut trench and were simply mowed down. The Turkish losses were catastrophic, estimated at 4,000 killed and up to 10,000 wounded. In an attempt to seize the initiative, at about 11:30 a.m. and after a bombardment by trench mortar guns, 88 Brigade tried to capture that portion of H12 still occupied by the enemy, but without success.

Ernest fills in some of the detail:

Friday 2 July 1915

More cleaning. Had a pot at a snipers dugout from a loophole in D Coy. I suppose the light must have shone through for a bullet struck the edge of my loophole and the side of my rifle – a pretty near thing. However, a miss is as good as a mile, but these fellows are remarkably keen shots. Had another go from the Machine Gun position and stopped the firing from that quarter. Three new officers joined in the afternoon – Lieutenant Bickley, 2Lieutenants Kerr and Knowles from the 14th Cheshires, with Lieutenant Frodsham having joined the day before. Nearly forgot to mention that on the 30th who should turn up but Captain Elgee, from the Egyptian Army, on a month's leave (jolly sporting of him) and Captain Somerville returned from Malta, his wound being quite alright again. Both were most acceptable. That makes six additional officers in three days. Captain Walker went down to Gully Beach for a rest; the past week or two has been very trying for him and he has not quite survived the strain. He fully deserves his rest and something more too, which I am sure no one will grudge him.

Given the casualties that the Turks had just taken, it is not surprising that they kept a low profile for a day or so, but they could still be seen putting a great deal of work into securing a knoll, subsequently called the Gridiron, not far to the front of trench H12 and which commanded the Ravine. Ernest mentions these efforts in his diary entry for the day:

Saturday 3 July 1915

The night of the 2nd passed quietly except for rain. Thought we were going to have another cloud burst. It started very hard with thunder and lightning, but quickly passed over thank goodness. Day uneventful – a few sniper casualties. Tried a shot at a fellow using a pick 250 yards away – couldn't see his head, but stopped his picking – I hope for good. Individually I think they are wonderful fellows. One chap has been sapping about thirty yards from B Coy and no one can touch him. I imagine a rush by a few men would work wonders and might save a lot of life and annoyance at night.

By the following day, the Turkish saps approached still nearer to the battalion position and continual bombing took place all day, witnessed by Ernest once again:

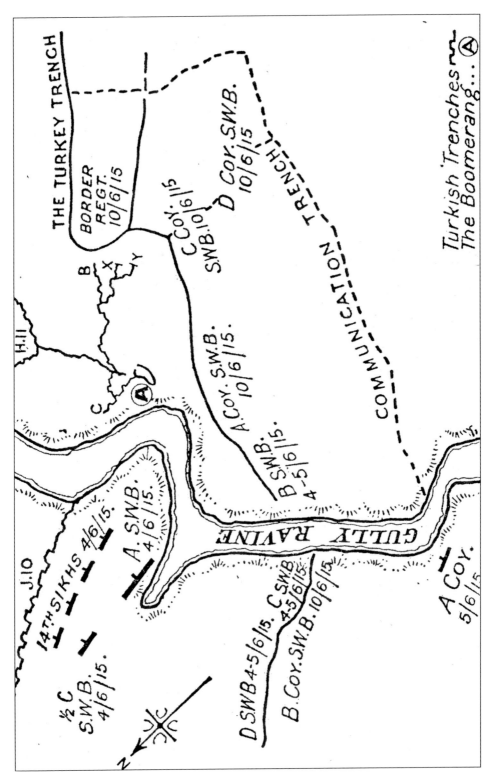

Map 7. Gully Ravine – the Boomerang June 1915 (Medici Society Ltd).

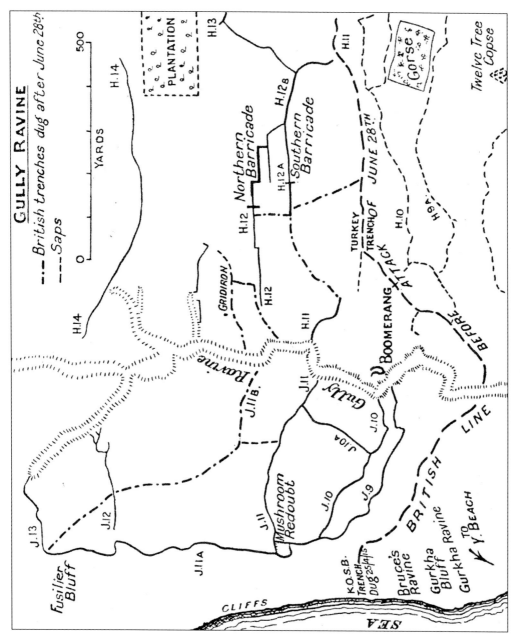

Map 8. Gully Ravine – British trench layout (Medici Society Ltd).

Sunday 4 July 1915

Turks opened the dawn with a terrific bombardment, followed by heavy bursts of machine gun and rifle fire. Went up and had a "look see." Saw one M.G. position and fired about twenty rounds at it, but as it was firing through a loop hole and was heavily sand bagged, could not see results. The range was only 200 yards. We hoped they would attack but they didn't. Later in the afternoon went up and did a bit of sniping from B Coy's trench. Pte Sweet did the spotting for me. Used a Turk's Mauser rifle, which fires with a flatter trajectory than ours. Had some good targets at 800 yds and one good one at 250, when a Turk who was making a sap looked round for a shot. Sweet said I got him alright. After finishing my available ammunition, I turned round to look for more, and poor Sweet at that moment said Oh! and fell across my front, shot through the head. He had been standing too high in the trench and I had told him so once. One couldn't tell from which direction it came. Rotten luck. Fine soldier.

By 5 July, the effects of the Turkish sapping brought them within bombing distance of the battalion forward trenches, so it was decided that Lieutenant Turner should lead a party of 10 picked men to attack the enemy sap head with the aim of forcing them back down their communication trench. This was then to be wired up, while a second party built a sandbagged wall on top of the sap. The attack began in the early hours of 6 July at 2:30 a.m. and was immediately successful, though Lieutenant Turner was shot dead after killing four Turks himself. Sergeant Lucas took over and carried on with the assault, wiring up the communication trench as directed. As soon as this was completed, the second party under Sergeants Bell and Stratford proceeded to make the sandbag wall. The Turks opened up with very heavy fire from three machine guns and the battalion's casualties were considerable. The Turks then counter-attacked and having a superiority in bombs, ultimately forced 2 SWB back. As well as Lieutenants Turner and Kerr, 13 men were killed in this action, with a further 30 being wounded, but the defensive wire and machine gun and rifle fire denied the knoll to the Turks.[7] Once again, Ernest's diary adds detail to this action:

Tuesday 6 July 1915

A small party from A and B Coys under 2Lieutenant Turner went out about 2.30 am. It was disastrous from what one could gather afterwards from Sergeant Lucas who did good work there. It appears that Turner used his revolver on seeing the Turks and was almost immediately shot. Sergeant Lucas got into the sap with a couple of men but a heavy enfilade fire drove the remnants out of it where they held on behind the sandbags they had put up. Another officer was sent out, Kerr – only joined a few days before from the Cheshire Territorials – he was also killed. Our party eventually had to retire to their trench again. Turner's body was carried back early, but Kerr was not recovered, nor the men who were killed behind the sandbags. Later on in the morning there was another misfortune. Captain Elgee standing on the fire trench was hit through the head. His loss was deeply felt. Turner had evidently fired five shots from his revolver before he fell. They were buried side by side near Col Jacques and Captain Meade of the 14th Sikhs. Went up in the afternoon with a Christmas tree arrangement round my helmet on the hill above the Colonel's dugout and reconnoitred for a beastly sniper what had been sniping down the Gully during the day.

7   C T Atkinson, *History of the South Wales Borderers 1914–1918*, p.126.

Found the spot and gave the "Khabar" to our men who kept a very lively eye open for him.[8] He had an iron loophole, which had been well masked. Found a place in an old Turkish trench for a similar arrangement, but heard later the welcome news that we were being relieved next morning and that we were being sent to Lemnos for a complete rest!!

As Ernest mentions, the battalion was at last to be taken out of the line for a complete rest. At 12 noon on 8 July, after 11 days without a break in the trenches, which was perhaps the most tiring time of the whole campaign so far, 2 SWB was relieved by the Hampshire Regiment and pulled back to Gully Beach, before moving off the peninsula entirely to Lemnos. With a frontage of over 600 yards of trenches and only 366 men fit for duty, virtually every soldier had been in the firing line without a break since 29 June. To say that they were tired would be an understatement in the extreme; they were exhausted physically and mentally, unwashed, plagued by flies and dysentery, and resigned to the fact that death, or life changing injury, was a constant reality. Once again, the strength of military discipline held them together as a cohesive, fighting unit and whenever the enemy, equally exhausted, decided to assault their positions, they were ready and willing to give their all.

The battalion withdrew to Gully Beach and established a temporary camp next to 87 Field Ambulance, hoping to get away to Lemnos that same night. The beach was crowded ("*beastly, dusty and crumbly*" as Ernest described it) but for those who had the opportunity for a quick bathe in the sea, it was absolute heaven. However, and as a military person will appreciate only too well, the best laid plans never seem to work when it comes to getting away for some leave, and it was not until the evening of 10 July that the battalion actually found themselves on the move at last. Even then, things did not run smoothly. First of all, the battalion left Gully Beach in two parties, one at 11:00 p.m. and the second at 11:45 p.m. and proceeded to march around the southern tip of the peninsula to V Beach where they were to embark on trawlers for Imbros first of all. Then they had to wait for two hours before they could get on board. Eventually, the first group got away at 2:30 a.m. on 11 July, arriving at Imbros at 7:30 a.m. where they found they were not expected. The second party arrived shortly afterwards and it was not until 4:00 p.m. that they re-embarked on trawlers for Lemnos. Some-one had evidently made a mistake and sent them to the wrong place. Finally at 8:00 p.m. they sailed for Lemnos.

Ernest adds to the frustration of the move:

Saturday 10 July 1915

A hope of moving tonight – windy but not nearly so bad as yesterday. Captain Ellis returned yesterday – his teeth are not much improved. As usual he is overloaded with comforts which he has been distributing with his usual generosity. The wounded coming down to Gully Beach since our arrival have been few, so our successors must be having things pretty quiet at present. The trawler which takes off the wounded was hit the day before yesterday – testifying to good Turkish (German?) gunnery. Three shots fell very close and the fourth hit her in the fo'castle – don't know if there were any casualties. Yesterday while a couple of us were sitting on the pier to get away from the flying dust – a shell came onto the edge of the hill into someone's dug out, without hurting anyone I heard afterwards. One of the pieces passed just over my shoulder into the water close behind us. One hasn't heard a shot from them yet today.

---

8   Khabar is a corruption of a Hindustani word for news, or inside information.

Sunday 11 July 1915

Had orders to move last night at 11 pm, embarking at 12.15 am. However, there was a lot of delay and embarkation was put off a couple of hours. Imbros is only about ten or twelve miles away, but it was long after daylight when we arrived in harbour. The guns were very busy at "ANZAC" when we passed. Arrived in camp about 9 am and proceeded to settle down. Had orders however to embark again at 4 pm in two trawlers for Lemnos. Most disappointing and annoying, for everyone was dog-tired. Embarked at 4 pm and had to wait till 8 before moving – nothing of incident occurred. The small crew kindly offered us tea which was most acceptable. The cook's bread was the best I think I have ever tasted. Makes his own yeast.

In the early hours of 12 July, at about 7:00 a.m. the battalion eventually arrived at Lemnos after a very uncomfortable journey overnight, packed into a trawler like sardines. Their bivouac site was between the fork of two dusty roads and the water supply, much needed as the weather got hotter and hotter, was inadequate. The water cart, needed to move water in bulk, had to be shared with another battalion which was most unsatisfactory and as Ernest said in his diary:

found we had no camp to go to, no arrangements made for water, in fact no arrangements at all for anything were made until we arrived: the usual British way. However, after a very tiring day, managed to get most things.

Indeed, it is surprising that Ernest, as the Quartermaster, had not been sent on ahead of the battalion to ensure that arrangements were in hand for their reception, but such is the 'fog of war' that it was not always possible to follow such routine administrative procedures, particularly as it meant providing additional boats for transportation. Things were so bad that in the end permission was given to move to another camp site, as Ernest explains:

Tuesday 13 July 1915

Saw Godwin-Austin – also Gen Travers and Marr. Also Miss Smith; one of the nursing sisters who came home with us from Hong Kong. Went on board the "Aragon" on my way to the "Minnetonka" the ordnance ship, and had a topping lunch with an iced beer! Could get no stores away from the "Minnetonka" – not a boat to be had anywhere and no stores ashore. In the evening had another visitor, young Ivens – stayed (or billeted rather) with his people at Rugby. Funny that one had only hoped when talking to his mother and sisters that we should meet out here, never dreaming that it would come true though. Hope to goodness he won't get bowled over.

Wednesday 14 July 1915

Moved bivouac nearer to Brigade HQ. Dusty place the old one, so we were not sorry. Hope however that we are not going to be constantly window dressing. Went over to find Ivens after dinner, but was too late – he had already gone. Sorry I missed him.

Thursday 15 to Tuesday 20 July 1915

Quiet time at Lemnos. Found it very hard to get water transport – so one's efforts to complete kit etc of the men coming from hospital etc (some of whom came along just with the clothes they stood in) was rather wasted somewhat. Got a big draft of three officers and 199 men arrived on 16th, Lieutenant Tragett and 2/Lieutenants Mumford and Saul the officers – two other young officers joined on the 14th, 2/Lieutenants Evans and Paterson, from the Ceylon Tea Planters Corps. On the 19th just as I was looking for a boat to take me off to the store ship Minnetonka got a fleeting glance of an old friend I thought was still at Hong Kong – Woods of the Naval Victualling Dept – or some such thing – had no chance to speak as he was just pushing off in a pinnace.

So, after a chaotic move from the peninsula, the battalion was able to switch off for a while. Creature comforts were very limited and it was certainly no holiday camp, but at least they were away from the constant threat of Turkish attacks, shell fire and snipers' bullets. There was the opportunity to sleep without interruption, to wash in hot water and to change out of dirty, sweat caked clothing and everyone took advantage of such simple pleasures, as it would not be long before the battalion had to move back to the reality of war on the peninsula again. There was still time for some amusing diversions however, one of which was a brigade sports competition, where the most popular event was the bomb throwing event!

While 2 SWB was at Lemnos there was a change of commanding officer. On 19 July, Colonel Casson returned to the peninsula to join 52 Division where he had been selected to command 157 Brigade in the rank of brigadier general. Lieutenant Colonel Ward of the Denbigh Yeomanry came in to take over command, as it was not unusual for officers to be transferred between battalions, particularly if there was no-one of the right seniority or experience within the unit to take over. Seniority versus selection had been a serious debate in the army late in the 19th century; it ended in agreement that selection was better.

If the battalion was enjoying the opportunity of a few days inactivity, General Hamilton's staff, also based on Lemnos, certainly were not. General Birdwood's plan for an August offensive, put together in May 1915 and accepted by General Hamilton the following month was largely the brainchild of Colonel Skeen and the general staff of the Anzac headquarters. Following the appalling results of daylight attacks against the Turks at Cape Helles during the previous months, it was accepted that the best hope of success lay in a combination of surprise and darkness. What was now envisaged was a left hook out of the northern flank of the Anzac beach-head with the aim of scaling the heights behind the main Turkish position, thus rendering them untenable. The way would then be clear for a general advance across the peninsula to Maidos and the Narrows.[9] There was a considerable amount of planning and preparation still needed to be done by his staff officers, but General Hamilton now had the extra divisions that he had been promised. Therefore, with good planning, strong leadership, the necessary will and motivation, there was no reason why the forthcoming second invasion should not succeed.

9   Michael Hickey, *Gallipoli*, p.237.

7

The Fourth Battalion

Theirs not to reason why,
Theirs but to do and die

Alfred Tennyson
Poet
1809–1892

It came as no surprise that their sojourn at Lemnos was brought to an abrupt end on 21 July when 2 SWB was ordered back to the Gallipoli peninsula at short notice, apparently in anticipation of another major drive by the Turks, coinciding possibly with the festival of Ramadan, to force the allies off their beachhead. At 9:30 a.m. orders were received for the battalion to be on the Australian Pier at Mudros harbour, ready to embark for Gallipoli by 11:00 a.m. This did not leave much time, but with a bit of pushing and shoving, the first two coys were at the beach, ready to embark, just five minutes late. The battalion and half of 1 KOSB then embarked on Patrol Ship *Rowan*, leaving Mudros harbour at 5:30 p.m. with most of the soldiers wondering why there had been such a rush in the first place. Four hours later, at 9:30 p.m. they were back at W Beach once more and then marched around the coastline to Gully Beach, arriving at about 1:30 a.m. Once again, confusion reigned as their allocated bivouac site was already occupied by 86 Brigade, so a makeshift camp was set up in front of divisional headquarters. Hardly had they got their heads down than it was time to "stand to" at 4:15 a.m.[1]

Ernest endorses the chaos of the day in his diary:

Wednesday 21 July 1915

Rose as usual – nothing seems to disturb the calm scene, except perhaps the high wind which had raged all night – at about 9.30 am or perhaps a little later – Williams told me that orders had come for us to embark immediately for Gallipoli again. The Bde Major (Lucas) told me to be at the pier by 11 am. We managed it or thereabouts after a huge struggle. Got aboard the SS Rowan (a former cross channel packet I believe) with 750 of ours and about 250 KOSBs, not satisfied with packing us or the men rather like sardines. The powers that be have been putting water carts aboard ever since and the kit etc already seems to smother the well deck. Left Lemnos just after 4 pm, zigzagging across at about 16 knots arrived off W Beach about 9.30 pm. We were lucky in transport – found 18 carts for use of two brigades and we wanted the lot. Were sent to Gully beach. Eventually settled down at about 2.30 or 3 am. Stood to arms at 4.15 am.

---

1   First and last light are renowned times for an enemy to attack, so troops in a defensive position will always be up and alert at such hours; known as "stand-to."

The anticipated attack did not seem to materialise after all, at least not in any strength, apart from some enemy shelling and an attack on the left of the battalion's line, so the next two days were spent making new terraces in the sides of Gully Ravine and improving the road structure which was growing around the southern coastline of the peninsula. This was used both for the movement of troops between unit locations and by mules who were used to transport supplies.

As ever, Ernest used these couple of days to catch up on much needed administration:

Friday 23 July 1915

Dustier than ever, not a meal in comfort – everything filthy. Had to go off for ammunition and sandbags last night with 4 carts and 8 mules had to go to "Pink Farm" and bagged 10 cartloads which had not been off-loaded – got back at 12.30 am this morning – lucky I found carts or I'd have still been going now. Turks bombarded and attacked left of our line – J13 I believe – but were driven off. Day ended in dust only as it began.

Saturday 24 July 1915

Thanks to Tragett who volunteered to get the road watered, the day started with less dust, but of course it soon dried and we are as filthy as ever. Got a night's rest last night otherwise it would have been telling on one by now. Have a sore throat as it is, dust the cause I suppose. The Turks have been busy shelling us just after tea and have been making damn good practice unfortunately. Just bursting their shrapnel on the edge of the cliff – stretcher bearers are having a busy time lately – 12 casualties altogether – one killed and 11 wounded – not bad for a "resting" place.

The following day, Second Lieutenant Hugh Nevile, who had been wounded on 28 April, returned to the battalion from Alexandria, while Major Going also returned to take over command of 2 SWB from Lieutenant Colonel Ward, who had been standing in as CO in the previous week. In the meantime, Ernest was as busy as ever collecting stores from W Beach, in amongst enemy shelling of the beach and the coastal road. Here he met up with Lieutenant John Mellsop, Quartermaster of the 4th Battalion the South Wales Borderers, who had only recently arrived on the peninsula and who, as Ernest says in his diary, *was held up by the shell fire close to the scene of the "accident."* The details of the accident will be revealed later, but this is an appropriate time to introduce the 4th Battalion, who were also to play a significant role in the remainder of the campaign.

* * *

After 1918, all regimental war diaries were collated and archived centrally at the War Office so that there would be a lasting record, not only for historical purposes, but in the hope that lessons could be learnt to improve training, or for the development of new strategy and tactics. As well as the official diaries, there were numerous other accounts written, along with letters and individual diaries at regimental level for similar purposes, or perhaps just as a personal reminiscence. 4 SWB kept an official battalion war diary of course, but perhaps of more significance is a separate, comprehensive, document, which gives a most fascinating account of the battalion's activities during the Gallipoli campaign.[2] Whether it was compiled during or after the war is not clear, but

2   War Records of 4 SWB. Narrative account up to end of Gallipoli. R Welsh Museum r1948.16.1/r1948.18.iv.

when it came into the possession of the regimental museum at Brecon, it had no title page, nor was there any indication of who the author might be. For many years it had been assumed that this had been written by Captain C E Kitchin formerly OC C Company 4 SWB. However, a closer examination of the text and the manner in which it is written, suggests that this is unlikely to have been the case, and for similar reasons it is not considered to have been written by Major Beresford, the battalion second in command. By a process of elimination of the other officers who served with the battalion, either because they were killed, did not serve for the whole of the campaign, or because they were too junior to be able to take on the task, it is reasonably assumed that it was compiled by Lieutenant John Mellsop, the battalion Quartermaster, and for convenience hereafter is referred to as the Mellsop paper. In the same way that his counterpart in 2 SWB was able to maintain a diary, Lieutenant Mellsop had a much better overview of his battalion's activities than any other officer who survived the whole war, and the style and content of the paper is that of an officer of his status and position. Just as with Ernest's diary, extracts from the Mellsop paper, hitherto unpublished, are included from now on and where possible they are inserted verbatim, with only the occasional change where the text may need amplification, or to assist the general reader. His account begins with the raising of 4 SWB as part of Lord Kitchener's new army, followed by its deployment to the Gallipoli peninsula:

After Great Britain declared war against Germany on 4th August 1914, Lord Kitchener decided to create new armies quite distinct from those already existing and for this purpose he commenced by appealing to the country for 300,000 men, this force to be formed into three armies each of 100,000 and each army to be divided into six Divisions. These new armies became popularly known as "Kitchener's Armies" and the first 100,000, to which the 4th South Wales Borderers belonged was generally known as "K1". On 21st August the Depot at Brecon became crowded with all sorts and conditions of men who had volunteered and a few days afterwards about 1400 were sent into camp at Parkhouse on Salisbury Plain. These were to form the nucleus of the first two service battalions called respectively the 4th and 5th South Wales Borderers, the former under Major Gillespie, the latter under Colonel Trower.

The men were crowded into the few tents available, they had no uniforms and there were hardly any officers or NCOs. Hundreds more men came pouring in daily, all in plain clothes and by degrees more officers began to arrive – some regulars, some from the Reserve and younger ones from the Universities, Officers Training Corps etc. Uniforms began to appear gradually and after a week or two began to look more ship shape. Eight hours a day on parade soon began to show results, but many of the men were quite unfitted for soldiers and out of the 4th Battalion alone 200 men had to be got rid of for physical defects. Most of the recruits had never had a rifle in their hands before and their ideas of discipline or anything appertaining to the art of soldiering were indeed most weird. All the more credit to them that they improved so rapidly for by the time the 4th Battalion was moved to Draycot Camp near Swindon at the end of September they were quite a promising array who swung along on route marches as if they had been born and bred with rifles and uniforms. By this time the 40th Brigade had been formed comprising the 8th Cheshire Regiment, the 8th Royal Welch Fusiliers, the 4th South Wales Borderers and the 5th Wiltshire Regiment – the whole under Brigadier General J H Travers.

The weather being very wet, Draycot Camp soon degenerated into a quagmire of mud. It went from bad to worse until one night the camp was entirely swamped out. The Battalion was then put into some very hastily constructed huts through which the wind whistled and the constant rain oozed whilst the mud outside became indescribable. From this inhospitable spot the Battalion was moved to Cirencester about the middle of December where the men were put into billets and were very comfortable. From Cirencester they moved to Woking Barracks (the old Workhouse) in February 1915 till the end of June when the home training came to an end, the 40th Brigade forming part of the 13th Division under Major General Shaw. The Brigade had had 10 months of training and it is perfectly extraordinary what fine Battalions had been trained in that time.

On June 29th 1915 the Battalion and the 8th Royal Welch Fusiliers left Avonmouth on the SS *Megantic* for the Dardanelles. The following Officers and Warrant Officers of the Battalion sailed with it:

Lieutenant Colonel F M Gillespie - Commanding
Major M J de la Poer Beresford - Second in Command
Captain H P Yates - Adjutant
Hon Lieutenant J A Mellsop - Quartermaster
Lieutenant W N V Beckford-Smith – Machine Gun Officer
Lieutenant S Hemingway – Transport Officer
WO1 (13852) G Halford - Regimental Sergeant Major
WO2 (14883) J Halford – Regimental Quartermaster Sergeant

A Company

Major Sir William Lennox Napier Bart
Captain A W Hooper
Lieutenant N Y Tassier
Second Lieutenant E P Bury
Second Lieutenant D A Adams-Williams
WO2 C Parish – Company Sergeant Major
WO2 H Wakefield – Company Quartermaster Sergeant

B Company

Major F W Birch
Captain J Fairweather
Second Lieutenant J H Stockwood
Second Lieutenant O S Phillips
Second Lieutenant A Buchanan
Second Lieutenant G M Owen
WO2 J Maher - Company Sergeant Major
WO2 J Callaghan - Company Quartermaster Sergeant

C Company

Captain C E Kitchin
Lieutenant J H Hillman - Miller
Lieutenant T C M Austin
Second Lieutenant L G Cooper
Second Lieutenant E G Staples
Second Lieutenant C M Lucas
WO2 A A Cornish - Company Sergeant Major
WO2 R J Goodchild - Company Quartermaster Sergeant

D Company

Captain P R M Mundy
Captain J B Blaxland
Lieutenant J Farrow
Second Lieutenant A F Bell
Second Lieutenant T M Jenkins
Second Lieutenant J W L Napier
WO2 T Bush - Company Sergeant Major
WO2 D J James - Company Quartermaster Sergeant

They were delayed in starting for a few hours as a large steamer with 1400 mules from the Argentine had been sunk by a hostile submarine that morning off Lundy Island which was on their direct route. Leaving under cover of darkness they were escorted by two torpedo destroyers as far as Ushant, whence they proceeded without any escort during the rest of the voyage. Each of these transports was provided with a gun at the stern for protection against submarines, the gun being manned by an infantry crew, trained "en voyage". Maxim guns were also put in readiness to fire bullets and create a splash in front of any hostile submarine periscope in the hopes of baulking the aim. Happily however neither of these devices was required and the vessel, after touching at Alexandria, entered Mudros Harbour on 14th July."

The commanding officer of this newly raised battalion was Lieutenant Colonel Franklin Macauley Gillespie. He was commissioned into the regiment in 1891 and saw active service as a captain during the Boer War in South Africa. He was promoted to lieutenant colonel in August 1914, just after the outbreak of war, at the age of 43. He kept a personal diary about the battalion's move to Gallipoli and its early days on the peninsula. His reminiscences, abridged for convenience, add to the atmosphere of preparing for war:

On the 28th June, we left Woking in two trains at 9am and 11am arriving at Avonmouth 2pm and 4 pm embarking immediately on the White Star liner Magentic [sic]. She is a fine boat about 15000 tons with roomy cabins and not over crowded. The men are also in cabins and feed in the saloons (2nd and 3rd) in batches. The Sgts feed in the first saloon before us. There are about 1930 troops on board. The Royal Welsh Fusiliers and ourselves. At 9.30 pm we started but shortly afterwards tied up for the night. At 8 am on 29th we returned to our berth alongside the wharf. Remained alongside all day and started again about 8.30 pm, met by two destroyers who escort us. They are about 300 yards on either side of our bow.

Was up at 3 am on the 30th, to see that everyone on the alert, as daylight is the most dangerous time for submarines. The ship has a 4.7 inch machine gun and we have lent them some of our gunners to help work the gun. We have our six Maxims mounted round the ship – belts in and gunners sleeping with the guns. In addition there is a guard of 100 men with ammunition to be ready at any minute to fire on the submarines. We have a post of signallers on boat deck to communicate with the destroyers. Ship seems to be doing about 13 knots against a strongish head wind. The destroyers are having a rotten time going nose under to every wave but we are not moving at all, though some of the men are already sea sick. Our work is physical training 6 - 8 am. Parades and lectures 9.30 – 12 and again from 2 – 4 pm so the men will be kept busy – not much room on deck so the work is done in relays.

In addition we have started a new MG section, the officers are learning the Maxim, map reading and plotting bearings. The Doctor gives lectures on sanitation and first field dressing. We have a boat station parade daily. The signallers are training, the men are taught how to put on respirators and lectures on Turkish army are given. Our escort left us at 1 pm and returned to England. We hear that they picked up the survivors of the Armenia when she was torpedoed off Lundy Island. This was the cause of our delay on 29th apparently. 29 of the crew were killed in the boats by shell fire after leaving the ship.

Went all round the ship with the Purser to show the way. Poor Burt nearly succumbed from the nasty smells we met. Many of the officers and men are now ill although there is practically no motion beyond the quiver of the screw. We are doing about 16 ½ knots now and shall average that in the future. All lights are put out at night or screened from view. The men don't seem to realize the danger and some of the ports are continually being unscreened. The spy trouble seems rampant on all transports. The Captain tells me they have caught a spy on every trip. The last they caught was signalling to someone on or near the Welsh coast. When searched he was found in possession of flash lights, camera and many notebooks stolen from officers. He had a bathing suit on under his clothes ready to jump over board if necessary. I daresay we have some with us on this trip.

The 1st July was a beautiful morning and distinctly warmer. I have a very comfortable suite now. Bed, sitting, and bath room; would probably cost a lot of money in peace time. I allow Burt[3] the use of the bath room as he has the cabin next door. The sea certainly does not suit him – he is never fit. It is doing me good. I slept 6 hours last night for the first time in months. The Captain turned up to breakfast – his first appearance since we started. Had a practice alarm yesterday which went off quietly. Of course Napier[4] got his men all mixed up although they went to the right boats before he interfered. He is very nautical now but was looking a little green I thought yesterday. The next day was much hotter as it is getting tropical. No land sighted since we left England. We are keeping a long way to the west of the Spanish coast. Expect to reach Gibraltar tomorrow morning. They tell me Crippen was brought to England from the USA on this ship.[5]"

The Napier family has had a long and distinguished connection with Wales and its regiments since 1859, when Lieutenant Joseph Napier, was commissioned into the Royal Welsh Fusiliers. On the

---

3   A reference to Major Marcus John Barré de la Poer Beresford, (1868–1944), his second in command.
4   This could be either Major Sir William Lennox Napier, or his son Second Lieutenant Joseph Napier, both of whom were together in the battalion at the time.
5   Dr. Crippen, was an American homoeopath and ear and eye specialist, who was hanged in Pentonville Prison London on 23 November 1910, for the murder of his wife, Cora.

death of his father, Sir Joseph Napier, the Lord Chancellor of Ireland, in 1882, he inherited the family title as second Baronet of Merrion Square Dublin. When he died two years later in 1884 at the age of 43, his eldest son, William Lennox Napier, assumed the third baronetcy. Then only 17, Sir William eventually became a barrister on the Welsh circuit, but he was also a keen volunteer (territorial) soldier and was commissioned into the South Wales Borderers. He rose to the rank of lieutenant colonel and between 1908 and 1912 commanded in turn both 5SWB and 7RWF, which were battalions of the territorial force. Thereafter, Sir William retired from soldiering, but only two years later he was called up once again in 1914, as part of Kitchener's new army. It was not unusual for reservists being recalled to active service to rejoin one rank lower than that in which they had retired, so Sir William, now aged 47, was commissioned into 4 SWB as a Major and he took over command of A Coy. By coincidence, his son Joseph had also been called up into the battalion, where he was a platoon commander in D Coy, in the rank of second lieutenant.

Returning to Lieutenant Colonel Gillespie's diary:

Sighted the Spanish coast early on the morning of 3rd July. We turned round in a circle at Gibraltar waiting for orders but got none so proceed on our way to Malta. During the evening we passed a mine layer towing a monitor, I suppose for the Dardanelles. We have had no news for days. One misses the papers to start with. Could not post a letter at Gibraltar as we did not stop. The next day we put the men into thinner khaki drill uniform as it is getting very hot now. This is about the hottest time of year in these parts and I expect the men will suffer a bit to start with. There is a small breeze now but when that drops we shall feel the heat a lot as this ship is built for cold weather. Arrived Malta about 9 pm on the 5th July, but the port was closed. We cruised round for the night. This does not seem wise with a ship full of troops as one would suppose the enemy submarines would be near our base. During the afternoon our officers pulled RWF officers at tug of war. We lost being 4 or 5 stone lighter.

Entered Malta harbour at 6 am the next morning and tied up in the commercial harbour. No one allowed ashore. We were immediately surrounded by the usual boats selling cigars, fruit etc. The men soon began to exchange their shirts and boots for a cigarette so had the hose turned on the boats to keep them away from the ship. The P&O Media arrived just after us – outward bound. At Malta we heard many rumours but little news. Several naval officers came on board but forgot to bring papers. We were off again at 10.30 am. I don't know why we went in at all as we took nothing except these 5 naval officers on board. In the afternoon we began a boxing tournament for the men and had some quite good bouts and many the reverse of good, but very amusing. About 70 of our men have entered and 17 of RWF. The temperature has been well over 80 F for some days now. It is hot at night in the cabins and one can't sleep on deck as they start scrubbing at 1.30 am.

John Mellsop continues with his account:

The port of Mudros on Lemnos had been selected as the subsidiary base for the Gallipoli expedition. The town itself from which the port is named is a small collection of wretched houses inhabited by Levantines who live by fishery, petty commerce and a few olive gardens and vineyards. It offered nothing but a safe anchorage to the allied fleets. It could not even supply the ships with fresh water, let alone meat, bread and vegetables. Everything necessary for the operations had therefore to be brought by sea and stored at Mudros until wanted. On arrival, the troops on the *Megantic* were ordered to disembark and Col Gillespie and Captain

Yates had gone on shore to look for a camping ground, when about two hours afterwards a fresh order was received on board to proceed at once to the front.

The Battalion left Mudros in two parties, on two small steamers with other troops. The first party under Major Beresford and Captain Yates left at 4.30 pm and arrived off the Dardanelles about 1.30 am the next morning with covered lights. The Turkish fort on the Asiatic shore had however spotted the vessel and the troops thereon received their baptism of shell fire in the shape of shrapnel and high explosive shells, which however did little damage on board. One of these shells hit a magazine on shore which caught fire and the cartridges in it kept exploding for about half an hour.

The troops were landed at V Beach in the Helles sector and after marching to Gully Beach, a distance of about 1½ miles, they were joined by the rest of the Battalion under Col Gillespie at about 6 am. At 8 am, after a sleepless night the whole Battalion started up the big Gully for the front line trenches. The 13th Division had been detailed to relieve the 29th Division in the Helles sector and this movement was now in progress. A short march up the Gully brought the Battalion to the commencement of the communication trenches which had been hastily dug and were then more or less in their pristine condition – in places very shallow, very irregular and affording but indifferent cover from the numerous Turkish snipers who were at that time in pits etc, at many points behind the firing and support trenches. After traversing these trenches for about 2 miles the Battalion arrived at the support trench just behind the firing line where it remained for 24 hours. A grim relic of the 2nd Battalion was found in one of these trenches. One of the men had been buried in the parapet – perhaps through the explosion of a shell – and one of his legs was partially sticking out from it; but it was impossible to take him out from it as that part of the parapet would then have fallen down. The heat in these trenches at this time was very great, the flies were in millions everywhere and the scarcity of water was a very serious matter.

At 4.30 am on 16th July the Battalion relieved the Royal Dublin Fusiliers in the firing line about one mile south of Krithia. The Turkish troops in front were not the worn out troops who had been fighting throughout, but were two fresh Divisions who had come south to Helles to replace those who had been severely depleted. The greatest distance of these trenches from the Turkish lines was about 120 yards and at one place called the "South Barricade" the distance was only 15 yards and the Turks could be heard distinctly talking at this point. They had erected a stout sandbag parapet on their side, as our own men had done on ours, and there were a few yards of unoccupied space in between each. As it was quite easy to throw bombs from one trench into the other, this pastime was much indulged in by both sides and so it was a post of considerable danger and activity. At no place in the line was it possible to look over the parapet except through a periscope and many of these were hit by snipers, in one case the holder being struck in the chest by a glancing piece of bullet, which however did not seriously damage him.

Back to the Commanding Officer's account:

On the 8th July, we arrived at Alexandria in Egypt at 3.30 pm. Were immediately signalled to by another ship. This was the Brigadier who wanted me to come and see him at once. Having borrowed a launch with great difficulty went over. He did not really want anything at all. His ship left at 6 pm. We hand in our surplus kit and leave the Orderly Room Sgt and store man to look after it. Alexandria is a big port, much larger than I expected and is full of shipping. We are now alongside the wharf. We leave most of our wagons behind here as they will not be of any use on Gallipoli. We leave about 50 our horses and mules here too and Hemingway has to remain to look after them.

Having arrived alongside at Alexandria the evening before, we started unloading most of our 1st line transport this morning. This meant unpacking the wagons ashore and taking the contents on board again and took up to 4 pm to complete. We left here 9 limbered wagons and are taking with us 2 water carts, 4 cookers and MG limbers, mess and maltese carts.[6] Some of our horses and mules have been sent on for these wagons. We left 16 more transport men and 4 store men at Alexandria. All the mess kit bags and officers' surplus baggage was landed here. I went ashore to the embarkation office but did not see the town. At 6 pm we pulled out into the harbour and anchored. None of the men got away from the ship. I heard Birkett was in the town wounded but could not see him. He is evidently nearly mended.

We then sailed at about 6 am on the 11th July and arrived in harbour at daybreak on the 12th. Mudros is a fine natural harbour. In afternoon went to report to HQ and then went to see the Brigadier. Found Casson, Somerville and Williams on board, the 2nd Battalion having come over for a rest. Quite hot here, now we are not moving. Two days later and we are still on board. Wanted to teach the men rowing and lowered the boats but the wind was too strong and the boats got adrift and then was some difficulty in getting them back to ship. The Captain was rather angry. Went for a sail in harbour after dinner, with the Chief Officer. Great difficulty in looking after men bathing – they are so thoughtless and swim as far as they can, to find they can't get back to ship. One fool who could not swim jumped in, but at least was wearing his life belt. The temperature was 88 degrees at dinner tonight.

On the 15th July, we left for Peninsula, arriving the next morning going straight into the trenches where we remained until the night of 28th with half a day off to bathe. Left 7.30 pm on the 15th in the destroyer Savage. Arrived 2.30 am. We were shelled on beach. No casualty in ours but some others hit. At 8 am we march from beach to the support trenches. Very hot, Mundy overcome. Snipers all night. One man wounded on beach, which is shelled daily. Took over fire trenches early on 17 July. Smells are bad as dead men lie all around and corpses are buried in many of the trenches . Flies are very bad and it is very hot. The men are enjoying themselves but feel the heat. Jenkins and 6 men wounded, nothing very serious – one Sgt lost two fingers.

Turks had a scare last night on 18 July and heavy firing went on all night. Only one man hit. There are several snipers behind our lines who we are trying to catch. 3 wounded. Relieved in morning of 19 July by Wiltshires. Reached beach 2.30 pm. We all bathed and had a good night in bed. Two shells came over while the men were bathing. No one hurt. Left beach 7 am on the 20th to relieve RWF in support trenches. 2 men wounded. Took over fire trenches by 9 am on the 21st – quickest yet. Dug all day and night, making second line of trenches. 2 men wounded.

Still in fire trenches the next day. 2 killed 3 wounded. Expecting attack as 100,000 Turkish reinforcements have arrived. Were shelled for two hours. Captain Kitchin lost a few men. 23rd July and still in fire trenches. The Turks attacked 39 Bde on our left at 3pm but were driven off with loss. We chipped in on their left which advanced across our front. Mail

6   A limbered wagon is one which has been set up, usually with an additional two-wheel frame, to carry extra heavy loads.

arrived. There was an unfortunate accident on the 24th July. Regt Sgt Major Halford, Sgt Ryan and 3 men severely wounded by a bomb dropped by Ryan. Both RSM and Ryan died from their wounds, which was a great loss.

On Sunday 25th July 1915 and another man killed this morning. Relieved by Wiltshires and move into support trenches. Want rest badly. Have had sand colic for last 2 days and have "plenty trouble for belly". Support trenches the next day. Still got colic and am going both ends! During this time we had three men killed and two officers (Birch and Jenkins) and 25 men wounded.

John Mellsop's paper adds to the detail of the CO's diary:

For some reason or other the Turks kept up a continuously hot rifle fire on these trenches by day and night and it is difficult to understand the object of this vast expenditure of ammunition which chiefly damaged the upper row of the sandbags, made an unholy noise and apparently did little else. Previous to being relieved the Dublin Fusiliers had endeavoured to rush the Barricade, but their attacking party had been killed to a man the moment they left their trenches and dozens of their dead bodies could be seen through the periscopes lying as they fell immediately below the parapet. It is quite impossible to bury them.

The young and inexperienced soldiers of the Battalion soon settled in to their new surroundings and but for the lack of water and cigarettes – their two chief requirements – took their baptism of trench fire coolly and philosophically.

On July 19th the Battalion was relieved by the 5th Wiltshire and marched down the Gully to Gully Beach, a place constantly shelled by the Turks. The bathing here was much enjoyed by the men, who although often shelled whilst in the water soon became accustomed to it, and worried little about it. Two of the Wiltshire who had dug a hole to sleep in whilst they were here had been buried alive through the earth falling in on them so even a night's rest in reserve contained elements of unforeseen danger.

At 6 am on the 21st the Battalion again took over the same line of the firing trenches and later in the day the Turks attacked some trenches on its left. They were simply pulverised by shells and bullets and after about half an hour what was left of them retired back to their trenches. In order to stir up the Turks a bit in the South Barricade, a field battery about 300 yards behind the Battalion – after giving due warning to the troops in front – started firing shrapnel, bursting their shells beautifully over the sandbags and of course just skimming over the Battalion trenches, the garrisons of which had been withdrawn for the time being. Later on in the day, one of our own bombs exploded prematurely injuring the Bombing Sergeant and severely wounding Regimental Sergeant Major Halford, who unfortunately died later on from his injuries.

Here then, is where Ernest met up with John Mellsop and learnt of the death of the RSM of 4 SWB; not only a personal tragedy, but a significant loss to the battalion at such an early stage in its arrival at Gallipoli. On 25 July, 4 SWB was again relieved by 5 Wiltshires and went into Brigade reserve.

As the Mellsop paper continues to recount:

Life in these reserve trenches, except that the men are not kept so much on the alert, has few other attractions, as fatigues are heavy and the shelling and sniping is often worse than when in the firing trenches. There was a beautiful view of Achi-Baba from these trenches and also right back to the end of the Peninsula, the mouth of the Dardanelles, the Plains of Troy and the coast of Asia Minor and except for the firing all seemed peaceful enough. The deep blue of the sky and sea, the sandy soil, the isolated trees and patches of scrub, the Dardanelles like an English river, with a background of high and irregular hills in on the mainland; these, in the evening and early morning – leaving out the clouds from bursting shells – might constitute the setting for a scene of perfect peace. But the dust storms at times were very annoying. The dust would blow around in constant eddies; it fell into food and water and was eaten and drunk (like the flies) at each meal, causing symptoms like those of dysentery. After July, nearly every man in the Gallipoli army suffered from this evil; many died and nearly all were ill and the battalion began to be universally affected by it.

On the 28th July, the battalion was relieved by the Dublin Fusiliers and again marched back to the sandstone cliffs near Gully Beach. On the evening of 30th July it was sent back to Mudros as was the rest of the Division. The experiences gained by the Division while at Helles in looking after themselves, in forgetting the thousand and one details of peace soldiering and in grasping the two or three elementary rules of conduct in war soldiering were, it turned out to be of priceless advantage to the 13th Division throughout the heavy fighting of the following month. During their short stay the battalion lost four men killed and one officer (Major Birch slightly) and 25 men wounded. Mudros was now a scene of great activity. Its harbour was crowded with shipping and the rest camps were overflowing with men – reinforcements for the main part, recently arrived from England – namely three Regular Divisions plus the infantry of two Territorial Divisions; the looked for reinforcements which were to enable a further effort to be made in the great adventure.

Lieutenant Colonel Gillespie completes the picture:

On the 28th July we were relieved and moved to the beach. Men very heavily loaded just now. In addition to ordinary pack and equipment, they carry 220 rounds of ammunition, a blanket, groundsheet, two iron rations, two sandbags and a few other trifles. The men feel the heat a bit and are looking washed out. I hope they will get used to it as Lemnos is worse.

Got orders to move to Lemnos on the evening of the 30th. Started for beach 11 pm. News of victory in Persia received today. All troops fired a feu de joie. Sailed 3 am in the Aboukir, a small liner, to Lemnos. Put on board by trawlers, after long wait. Landed by boats at Mudros and bivouacked about 2 miles inland on bare plain. Had decent breakfast on the boat. Hear 200 Turks surrendered last night, probably because of the feu de joie.

* * *

Returning to 2 SWB, at 5:30 a.m. on 28 July, the battalion moved up to Y Ravine as the reserve to the main firing line, which was taken over from 39 Brigade of 13 Division by 87 Bde. Although it was not as dusty as it was at Gully Beach, the water supply was very scarce as it was not sufficient for all the battalions of the brigade. The battalion was therefore ordered to obtain all its water from Gully Ravine, which was a laborious and back breaking task having to carry cans of water over considerable distances under the relentless baking sun. A Coy was placed in immediate support in trench J.10 which was found to have been practically demolished, with all the sandbags having been removed. Consequently, the trench had to be entirely reconstructed. As if all this was not enough, the battalion was ordered to find working parties to assist the Inniskillings and KOSB, as well as having to improve the mule track to Fusilier Bluff, which required deepening. On 30 July, the battalion took over a portion of firing line held by Border Regiment, which was practically the same line they had held some three weeks earlier, and indication of how little progress had been made in the intervening time.

As Ernest recollects:

Wednesday 28 July 1915

Proceeded to Y Ravine. Same spot we had such a dose of shrapnel on the 28th last month. It certainly hadn't improved in appearance – dug outs just the same, miserable tiny pits. However we settled down – water supply rather precarious.

Thursday 29 July 1915

A quiet day. Had a topping bathe most enjoyable after being seedy for a few days – tummy trouble. Everybody suffering more or less with it, especially the New Army. Got our second dose of inoculation of anti cholera vaccine. Suppose they will give us the anti plague serum next followed by anti tetanus etc. Anyhow it's worth being done.

Friday 30 July 1915

Moved us up to our old place in fire trenches across the Gully. We find that the sniper has made things hum somewhat since we were last here and the Turks trenches are only about 25 yards from ours. Must go and look at my old sniper's post tomorrow and see if one can get a good target. The enemy's artillery has been very lively both on the trenches and our own immediate vicinity, which after all is only about 150 yards in rear. At 5 pm by a prearranged signal the whole line cheered and fired a "feu de joie" to commemorate the victory in Mesopotamia, which has opened the way to Baghdad.[7] The Turks naturally got jumpy and opened fire with machine guns and other guns along the line. The night I hope will close in peace and harmony.

The last day of July saw the battalion hard at work in the burning sun on the perennial task of improving firing platforms and rebuilding parapets. That afternoon, the Royal Engineers, who had been tunnelling under the Turkish defences, exploded three mines beneath a Turkish trench about 30 yards in front of C Coy's firing line. A portion of the Turkish trench was demolished, but in the process Sergeant Stratford and another man were wounded.

One of the drawbacks of Kitchener's new army was their lack of experience in battlecraft as Ernest observes in his diary:

Saturday 31 July 1915

Night passed off quietly. Enemy appears to either have an unlimited supply of gun ammunition or a new stock for we are getting a good deal of shelling. The 13th Division

---

7   This is a reference to the progress of the Indian Army invading Persia up the Tigris River. Amara had been captured on 3 June 1915. The invasion ended in siege and surrender at Kut al Amara.

appear to be a most disappointing lot. The trenches are (or were rather) in a shocking state. One would not have thought Kitchener's Army would have been behind in matters of sanitary importance and apart from this the enemy appear to have had matters much their own way since we went down. While one admits the Turk to be an indefatigable digger one didn't expect to find such a labyrinth of trenches and barbed wire so close to our line. It makes one positively sick to read the tosh in the papers about the Territorials etc being as good as regular troops. One does not expect them to be; and to give them an inflated opinion of themselves does more harm than good.

The concept of General Hamilton's second invasion was a breakout from the Anzac position to seize the heights of Hill 971, Hill Q and Chunuk Bair, while the newly formed IX Corps, under the command of General Stopford, would assault across the flat ground of Suvla Bay to capture the summit of the Anafarta Ridge, thus cutting off any further Turkish reinforcement from the north of the peninsula. As a prelude to these assaults, there were to be diversionary attacks on the right flank of the Anzac stronghold by the Australians and to the south in the Helles sector by 29 Division. It had been General Hamilton's original intention to launch the second invasion as soon as possible after the last of the three new army divisions had reached Mudros, but the choice of the actual date was determined by certain factors. First of all, large numbers of men and equipment had to be brought ashore at Anzac before the operations could begin. To avoid alerting the Turks, this had to be achieved in complete secrecy so could only be done over a succession of moonless nights. Similarly, the Suvla landing would call for a moonless night, or better still, a night when the attacking troops could approach the coast in the dark, but have the advantage of moonlight after getting ashore. With a full moon due on 27 July, such an opportunity would offer itself in the first week of August and would not occur again for another month. Therefore it was decided to land the reinforcements at Anzac on or about 3 August and to begin the main attack on the night of 6/7 August, when the moon would rise about two hours after midnight.[8] Every effort was made to keep the plan as secret as possible, to the extent that senior commanders were not briefed about the breakout until almost the last moment. While this was understandable in principle, it made forward planning very difficult, which, as will be seen, had calamitous consequences later on.

The first week of August was unusually quiet for 2 SWB in their fire trenches. At one stage during the night, the Turks opened up with artillery and rifle fire, but it soon died down and there was little response from the battalion. As usual, a great deal of work was done in improving the trenches which seemed to have deteriorated into a bad state of repair. There was also a welcome reinforcement of four officers – Captains Davies and McShane, Second Lieutenants Gibbs and Creaney – and 100 soldiers. During this period the battalion was ordered to prepare a plan for the attack of the enemy trenches to their immediate front. The objective was to be trenches H13c, H12 w and y and H14. What they did not know at this stage was that this was to be part of the diversionary plan in the Helles sector, but it gradually became apparent that some sort of assault was in the wind. Ernest, a keen rifle shot, also wanted his part of the action, so he started to build a sniper's post of his own just above battalion headquarters. This turned out to be more of a challenge than he anticipated however:

Monday 2 August 1915

Hoped to have finished my sniper's post last night but the trench proved to be a much more formidable affair than I had anticipated. Must try and finish tonight. We have had a lot of shelling today, both sides very active. I managed to stop a shrapnel bullet today, which is jolly painful but luckily didn't cut through my knicks or shirt but did break the vest somehow – caught me on a bony part on the back near the lumber region – made a huge bruise which broke. However it struck ground first so although it made me yell out hasn't done much damage. Got some "black marias" over just afterwards one of which struck down just below near our water cart and another just behind Bn HQ. Most unpleasantly close but no damage done. Tomorrow my bet with Blake (our Doctor) expires. We bet at Lemnos, he for the taking of Achi Baba by 3rd August. I wish he had won.

Tuesday 3 August 1915

My bump has gone down but too painful to lie on. Find it pretty stiff bending. A day or two more however will put it alright again. Nothing unusual – a bit quieter perhaps.

Wednesday 4 August 1915

"A year ago today." One can hardly realise we have been at war for a year. I wonder if we will finish inside another? My sniper's post is still unfinished. Awful ground. Have made the approach to one at the bad corner of the gully safe now, but the field of fire is very close to our own trenches and one has to be very careful, rather a bad place for shrapnel too.

Thursday 5 August 1915

Heavy firing from the direction of "ANZAC" early this morning. There has been an air of mystery about for days, so something's brewing. Had to go over to Bde HQ at 10.30 am where we QMs received instructions what to do in the case of a move. Everything still vague though.

Meanwhile, both 2 SWB and 4 SWB were as ready as they ever would be to carry out their part in the second invasion. 2 SWB would be part of the diversionary attacks in the south of the peninsula to distract the Turks in that region, while 4 SWB were an integral part of the Anzac breakout.

* * *

John Mellsop's paper captures the mood within the 4th Battalion:

As the Army's task was to help the Fleet through the Narrows, it had to operate in the south western portion of the Peninsula. Further progress against Achi-Baba in the Helles sector was hardly possible for the Turks had added too greatly to their trenches there since the attacks of April and May. Operations on the Asian coast were hardly possible without a second Army; operations against Bulair were not likely to help the Fleet. Operations in the Anzac sector offered better chances of success. It was hoped that a thrust south west from Anzac might bring our men across to the Narrows or the top of the ridges which commanded the road to Constantinople. It was reasonable to think that such a thrust, backed up by a new landing in force to the north in Suvla Bay might turn the Turkish right and destroy it. If the men at

Helles attacked to contain the Turks in the south, and the men on the right of Anzac, backed up by a new force marching from Suvla might give a decisive blow. At the same time, Suvla Bay was to be seized and prepared as a harbour at which supplies might be landed, even in the stormy season.

The vital point, where, if all went well, the Turk right was to be bent back and broken, lay to the north of Anzac on the spurs and outlying bastions of Sari Bair. It is not high. Its peaks range from about 250 to 600 feet; its chief peak (Koja Chemen Teppe) is a little more than 900 feet. Nearly all of it is trackless, waterless and confused, densely covered with scrub (sometimes with forest) and littered with rocks. The gullies on its northern side drain towards Suvla Bay and it was in one of these (the Aghyl Dere) where the Battalion had its severest fighting. Dere means watercourse, but they were all quite dry in August.

The 6th August was picked for the first day of the attack from Anzac and the landing at Suvla was to take place during the dark hours of the night of 6th/7th, the moon at that date being favourable. The vital part of the fight was to be fought by troops from Anzac and it is with this sector that the Battalion became associated. The Anzac position was an open book to every Turk aeroplane and every observer on Sari Bair. The reinforcements for this part of the battle had to be landed in the dark some days before and kept hidden during daylight so that the Turks should not see them and suspect what was being planned. Very nearly 30,000 men – one whole Division (the 13th), one Brigade of English soldiers and a Brigade of Gurkhas with their guns and stores – had to be landed unobserved and hidden away. The only place to hide them was underground.

The Battalion was suffering considerably from dysentery, and when at 10.30 am on 3rd August it sailed again for the front, a great many of the men were quite unfitted for an arduous campaign, but every man who could stand up was required and every man who could stand up went. They were crowded on a boat called "The Partridge" – originally plying between Ardrossan and Belfast – together with the North Staffordshire Regiment. The men were warned not to move about much as the vessel might capsize but as they were wedged together like sardines this danger was hardly likely to occur.

Their arrival off Gaba Tepe about 10pm was hailed by the Turks with several shrapnel bombardments and an abundance of sniping, two men being hit by bullets whilst on board. It took three hours to complete the landing and the Battalion was then conducted by an Australian guide up a gully to its bivouac where the men started digging for all they were worth to hide themselves away before dawn.

In the afternoon a party of two or three of the senior officers of the Battalion were taken around some of the Australian trenches. They were splendidly organised, wonderfully clean and afforded magnificent shelter. They were certainly models of their kind and the Australians themselves gave one a most favourable impression of a splendid type of fighting man. Later in the day there was a good deal of Turkish shelling.

On 5th August, officers were sent out to reconnoitre and make maps. Col Gillespie and Captain Yates were taken along the coast in the Torpedo Destroyer "Charmer" to gain as much information as they could for the advance of the battalion the next day. It was impossible to go over the ground as it was occupied by the Turks and this reconnaissance, together with what could be seen through field glasses from the higher ground nearby was all the information possessed by the battalion when it started out on its special mission.

At a little before 4pm on the 6th August 1915 commenced the mighty struggle of the next few days. It started by an assault on the Turk positions below Krithia in the Helles sector and an hour later the Australians at Anzac advanced to attack the Lone Pine, which had been bombarded by the warships for some days. When the sun set upon this fight, many thousands of men fell in for the main battle, every man wearing a white band on his left arm and a white patch at the back of his right shoulder to distinguish from the enemy in the dark. They fell in at the appointed places in four columns, two to guard the flanks, two to attack.

The Right Covering Column under Brig General A H Russell consisted of – The New Zealand Mounted Rifles, the Otago Mounted Rifles Regt, The Maori Contingent and the New Zealand Field Troop.

The Right Assaulting Column under Brig General F E Johnston consisted of – The New Zealand Infantry Brigade, an Indian Mountain Battery (less one Section) and one company of New Zealand Engineers.

The Left Assaulting Column under Brig General H V Cox consisted of – the 29th Infantry Brigade, the 4th Australian Infantry Brigade, an Indian Mountain Battery (less one Section) and one company of New Zealand Engineers.

The Left Covering Column under Brig General J H Travers consisted of – HQ 40th Brigade, half the 72nd Field Company RE, the 4th South Wales Borderers and 5th Wiltshire Regiment.

The Divisional Reserve was made up of – the 6th Bn South Lancashire Regt, the 8th Bn The Welch Regt (Pioneers) at Chailak Dere and the 39th Infantry Brigade and half the 72nd Field Company RE at Aghyl Dere.[9]

It is with the Left Covering Column that we will now proceed. The duties of this column are laid down in Sir Ian Hamilton's despatch as follows "The left covering force was to march northwards along the beach to seize a hill called Damakjelik Bair, some 1400 yards north of Table Top. If successful it would be able to hold out a hand to the 9th Corps as it landed south of Nebrunesi Point, whilst at the same time protecting the left flank of the left assaulting column against enemy troops from the Anafarta Valley during its climb up the Aghyl Dere ravines".

* * *

The scene was now set for what General Hamilton believed would be the decisive battle to determine the outcome of this faltering campaign. There had been a considerable influx of reinforcements and while he may not have had the best choice of senior commanders to take this new force forward, he was convinced that the hour had now come for the allied army to seize the heights of Sari Bair, thus dominating the peninsula and bringing about the defeat of the Turkish army. The offensive at Suvla Bay was about to begin.

---

9   The unusual spelling of both the Welch Regiment's and Royal Welch Fusiliers' titles was adopted by authority of Army Order No 56 of 27 Jan 1920, which indicates that this record of 4 SWB by Lieutenant Mellsop was not written until sometime after the War.

8

Suvla Bay

Once you engage in battle, it is inexcusable
to display any lethargy or hesitation; you must
breakfast on the enemy before he dines on you

Kai Ka'aus ibn Iskander
10th century Prince of Persia
The Qabas Nama 1082

Suvla Bay is about five miles to the north of the Anzac sector on the west coast of the Gallipoli peninsula. It is an attractive, crescent shaped bay, some two miles wide, with two rocky headlands – Suvla Point in the north and Nebrunesi Point in the south – jutting out into the sea. Just behind the sandy beaches is a large salt lake with a small channel letting out into the sea, which, in the summer of 1915, was virtually dry. The land beyond the bay is generally open and flat, interspersed with a number of low hill features, scrub land, gullies and ravines, stretching inland for about four miles. The whole of the bay and the plain behind it is dominated by the ridges of Kiretch Tepe Sirt to the north, Kavak Teppe and Tekke Tepe to the east and then the main Sari Bair feature in the south east. The small hills on the hinterland of Suvla Bay had a variety of names. They were described either by the colour of their features or by their shape – Chocolate Hill, the W Hills or Scimitar Hill for example – or by their position on a map contour line, such as Hill 10, Hill 60 or Hill 70. This could be confusing at times as Scimitar Hill and Hill 70 were in fact one and the same place. Suvla Bay was to become the stage for General Hamilton's August offensive, which he believed would determine the outcome of the war once and for all. How right he was – but not in the manner he expected.

To distract attention away from the imminent landing at Suvla Bay on the night of 6 August, a number of diversionary operations to the south were necessary. There was to be one on the southern, or right, flank of the Anzac sector – immortalised in such actions as Lone Pine and the Nek – while 29 Division was to engage the Turks in the Cape Helles sector. At 2:20 p.m. on 6 August bombardment of the trench complex H12, H12a&b, and H13 began and two hours later, 88 Brigade put in its main attack. It was almost impossible to get any clear view as to what had happened, apart from the fact that the Worcesters and Hampshire Regiments appeared to have taken heavy casualties, but gained most of their objective. During the night, the Turks counter attacked all trenches taken by 88 Brigade the previous afternoon and retook them. The Essex Regiment hung on to H12a, until relieved by the Dublins, but the Turks then counter attacked again taking H12a. They also penetrated the front line of 2 SWB, capturing the Southern Barrier. On the morning of 7 August, at the request of the Dublins, the battalion sent up one machine gun and one rifle platoon to assist them to hold the Northern Barrier and finally the Turks were

Image 17. The view north to Suvla Bay from the heights of Chunuk Bair. Damakjelik Spur is in the lower middle foreground (Author).

driven out of the allied main line with bombs. At 8:30 a.m. on 7 August, the French artillery, in accordance with the general plan, started to bombard the G section of trenches. At 10:30 a.m. the French advanced and took the first line of trenches but were then counter attacked by the Turks and were forced to withdraw to their original line. That morning, news started to filter through that, during the night, three divisions of IX Corps (10, 11 and 13) landed unopposed at Suvla Bay and were pushing rapidly inland. This move was evidently a complete surprise to the Turks.[1] There is no doubt that the divisions had in fact landed, but their rapid deployment inland could not have been further from the truth, as we shall see.

Ernest's diary adds some flesh to the bones of what took place at Cape Helles in the preceding 24 hours:

Saturday 7 August 1915

Firing continued heavy all through the night. Enemy commenced an early bombardment and news began to filter through from the wounded. Some of the Dublins came through our first aid post. They say that the trenches won yesterday have been retaken by the enemy. We evidently haven't got possession of the communicating trenches and consequently the Turks bombed them out. All sorts of rumours regarding the Essex and Hants. The Worcesters were sent up and appear to have been left unsupported. However nothing is known for certain yet. The enemy got possession of our south barricade but were driven out again by the Dubs. We have had practically little or no casualties ourselves yet. A few shrapnel wounds. Two

1   R Welsh Museum, 2 SWB War Diary BRCRM D.1949.8 7 August 1915.

were killed in the Gully yesterday by rifle bullet, whether by sniper again is uncertain but we think so. Our machine guns have been having a busy time today. I hope they have accounted for many heads. Our own HQ has had an uncomfortable time from enemy shellfire, luckily no one hit. Our move down has been cancelled so I suppose we shall probably have to try and do what the others failed to hold. With better luck I hope. However we have heard the good official news that three divisions have landed north of ANZAC and have a good footing and are pushing on. 500 Turks captured and some machine guns. The French are doing a push on the right I hear. Let's hope we cut these blighters off. They are jolly plucky though, one must admit that.

At 3:30 p.m. on 8 August, the battalion was relieved by 1 KOSB and reverted to brigade reserve, where they were to remain for the next two days. The battalion was dispersed with half a coy in Eski Lines, one coy in J10 trench, one coy in Bruce's Ravine and battalion HQ and the remaining one and a half coy in Y Ravine. Most of the time was spent in cleaning up old trenches and at night they had to dig a communication trench back to the Eski Lines. At 3:30 p.m. on 12 August, the battalion went back into the line again and took over the same trenches as before from 1 KOSB. During the night, the Turks were very active and fired continually. A new sap had to be dug to straighten the line east of the ravine started by B Coy. The battalion's line now was now B and D Coys in the firing line, A Coy in immediate support with C Coy in reserve. In the afternoon of 13 August, the battalion trench mortars opened fire on H13c and did considerable damage, so the Turks retaliated by shelling the battalion trenches with small high explosive shells. The battalion then spent the next day and night repairing trenches knocked down by Turkish artillery and in constructing new saps with a view to straightening out the line. They were very lucky during this period and only lost about 10 men killed and wounded. Lieutenant Gibbs was wounded by glass from a periscope. Then on 16 August, orders were received for 2 SWB to move to Gully Beach in readiness for deployment around the coast of the peninsula by ship to Suvla Bay.

Ernest confirms the recent activities of the battalion in his next two diary entries:

Sunday 15 August 1915

It's a week since I looked at my diary. The 88th Brigade lost heavily in their stint on the 6th – 1900 casualties out of 2800. Worcesters alone lost 753 and most of their officers. The Hampshires lost 21 officers killed alone. The Essex also lost heavily. The Royal Scots did not take part. On the 8th we went over to Y Ravine in support, being relieved by KOSBs. We had done nine days this time. Found a new place for the Mess and we enjoyed quite a nice time for the four days there. Practically no shelling took place from that side during our stay. Came away again on the 12th, back to our old firing line in Gully Ravine. I think we ought to call it Borderers Ravine, for with the exception of the Inniskillings, the three Border Regiments have done all the push there. Got a draft of 100 men (and two officers from the 15th Liverpools) on the 10th at Y Ravine and another two officers from the Australians joined same day. We are now well over 800 strong. Hill and Blake are the two from the Kings and Greaney and Gibbs the two Australians. The latter has already gone down with a splinter of glass in his eye from a broken periscope. The Turks must have known we were back, for they gave us a House warming. Stacks of shells came over, bursting all over the place, even into the Mess – the bits I mean. Got a bullet into my dug out the night we came back and another struck ground shortly afterwards. Appear to have come from French side. On the 13th at daybreak we took tea while the Turks advanced, by opening fire with a French mortar throwing a 100 lb bomb. It had come up during the time we were away. The noise was terrific and bits came back into our own trenches. At 11 am we opened up again, so went up to watch it from the left of the Gully fire trench. One would think nothing could live within 30 or 40 yards of the explosion, yet in between the bursts one had an opportunity of sniping at one or two men who crept along the trenches backwards and forwards. Williams spotted for me and assured me I had one fellow plumb. Hope I did. One can't see the result very well oneself.

The French have gone away this morning, taking the mortar elsewhere, as the enemy has this place marked down here. The Turks are hard at it digging again where the parapets were blown in. Had some "Jack Johnsons" over during lunch and luckily they were bursting thirty or forty yards to our left but still any amount of the bits reached the Mess and as I happened afterwards to be down at our transport lines three or four hundred yards down the Gully, had some nasty jagged bits down there too – nearly hit by one piece which would have put an end to the diary had it struck. Walker came back from Alexandria today looking fit again. Hear that Fowler has gone home with his wounds – lucky dog! Wonder if we go back to Y Ravine tomorrow?

Ernest then goes on to talk about arrangements for the move to Suvla Bay as reinforcements to the main effort in that area:

Monday 16 August 1915

On the 16th we suddenly got orders to be relieved by the 88th Brigade – we also received orders to proceed to Gully Beach and hold ourselves in readiness for a move elsewhere within the next twenty four hours. I went down Gully myself and fixed things as comfortably as possible for the battalion, little thinking that we should embark same night. The last of the battalion did not get down till after 5 pm and we had to march at 9 pm for "V" Beach. Kit to be left behind and to come with us had to be sorted and as we had orders to travel as lightly as possible a good deal of necessary stuff was left at the Battalion dump under Allen my storeman. However we did get away alright in two vessels. HQ, B, D and part of C on a paddle steamer and remainder by another boat. Our destination was Suvla Bay where the 10th, 11th and 13th Divisions had landed or thereabouts. We arrived at about daybreak without incident where as normal no one knew exactly where we had to go. Eventually we and the other three Bns of the Brigade were fixed up in a shallow ravine about 300 yds up from the beach.

* * *

While 2 SWB were preparing to move to Suvla Bay, 4 SWB had been fully committed to the breakout from the Anzac sector. Once again, John Mellsop takes up the story, from the night of 6 August:

It has been stated that it was impossible to make a proper reconnaissance of this march and it was more or less a surmise where the Turkish trenches were situated. The ground looks so different in this land of surprises, when viewed from afar, to what it really is, that it was a veritable march into the great unknown in pitchy [sic] darkness.

The column fell in at 8pm amidst the noise of shot and shell at Lone Pine and threaded its way in column of route through the narrow pathways of the rugged hills for the first mile – the Borderers leading; through masses of men resting preparatory to going forward to the attack. Down through a deep gully until at length the sea shore was reached. There was no moon and the darkness had been intense, but here a grand and impressive sight struck all beholders. The search lights from several battle ships were illuminating Russell's Top and the high ground round it, whilst enormous HE shells, one after the other, crashed and pounded all over it, giving the appearance of a volcano in eruption. This scene was soon left behind and darkness once more held sway, except for the rifle flashes on the right which had by now developed into a continuous battle. The left assaulting column had commenced its attack on Bauchop's Hill and elsewhere. Another mile brought the column into the direct hostile fire from this hill, where a terrible fusillade was going on lighted up by star shells and rocket lights. Several of the battalion were hit by Turkish bullets and the whole column had to lie down amongst the prickly scrub along the beach near old No 3 Post. As the fire slackened, it resumed its march, but only for a short way as the firing broke out afresh, compelling it to halt again, still losing men, until at lasts, after about an hour or so, it cleared itself from the zone of fire. The ground now became more open and less densely covered with that annoying species of scrub called a holly oak with which this portion of the peninsula is studded. Attaining a height of about three feet, it is covered with a kind of short holly leaf, very short and prickly and bearing small acorns like an oak tree. It scratches your flesh and tears your clothes.

Image 18. Anzac Cove (Author).

The battalion then formed into lines of companies moving to a flank in fours, at 20 yards interval between platoons and 30 yards distance between successive lines, D Company acting as an advanced guard to deal quickly with any Turkish trench. It was expected that one would be encountered very shortly. The Turks kept up a desultory fire from the low lying hills to the right of the column, but did not seem to be aware of its presence as their firing was in other directions. Its presence had however been detected elsewhere. Suddenly in front from out the darkness flashed rifles from a Turkish trench and several men of the battalion were hit, but D Company under Captain Miller Mundy was well handled by its officers and without firing a shot it rushed the trench with the bayonet, its occupants vanishing like phantoms into the night. This company, which had lost about 50 men in killed and wounded, then continued its advance straight ahead to a position which had been previously indicated to it, whilst the rest of the column bore slightly off to the right, encountering several small parties of the enemy, who, completely surprised, offered little resistance and by 1.30am on the 7th the whole of Damakjelik Bair was occupied.

The operation about the battalion is described in Sir Ian Hamilton's despatch:

The left covering column under Brigadier General J.H. Travers after marching along the beach to No. 3 Outpost resumed its northerly advance as soon as the attack on Bauchop's Hill had developed. Once the Chailak Dere was cleared, the column moved by the mouth of the Aghyl Dere, disregarding the enfilade fire from sections of Bauchop's Hill, still uncaptured. The rapid success of this movement was largely due to Lieutenant Colonel Gillespie, a very fine man who commanded the advanced guard consisting of his own regiment, the 4th South Wales Borderers, a corps worthy of such a leader. Every trench encountered was instantly rushed by the Borderers, until, having marched to the pre-determined spot, the whole column was unhesitatingly launched at Damakjelik Bair. Several Turkish trenches were captured at the bayonet point and by 1.30am the whole hill was occupied, thus safeguarding the left rear of the whole of the Anzac attack. Here was an encouraging sample of what the New Army under good auspices could accomplish. Nothing more trying to inexperienced troops can be imagined than a lone night march exposed to flanking fire, through a strange country, winding up at the end with a bayonet charge against a height, formless and still in the starlight, garrisoned by those species of the imagination, worst enemies of the soldier. The left assaulting column crossed the Chailak Dere at 12.30am and entered the Aghyl Dere at the heels of the left covering column. The surprise on this side was complete. Two Turkish officers were caught in their pyjamas and enemy arms and ammunition were scattered in every direction.

John Mellsop's account continues:

"After capturing the Damakjelik Bair, the column hastened to dig themselves in as soon as possible. The Borderers were lined up on the left, the 5th Wiltshires taking up the line on the right, which they afterwards prolonged to link up with the Australians. Captain Mundy's company had taken up a position about a quarter of a mile to the left of the battalion as a guard to that flank and also for the purpose of occupying a small well close by. The ground varied a good deal, some parts of it being quite easy to dig, whilst other parts were quite rocky and much intersected by small ravines. It was so dark that it was difficult to see whether the new trenches commanded any field of fire or not, but the chief object was to get hidden away before dawn and for this purpose the men worked hard all night.

In order to make the whole position clearer it will be necessary to take a short survey of the battlefield in general. Dimly outlined to the right and the right rear of the Damakjelik Bair lay a huge mass of hill – the hill of Sari Bair – where the main attack was in full swing. The firing was terrific and the hill was lighted up almost from end to end by thousands of rifle flashes and the bursting of enormous naval shells. To the north, the noise of battle could be dimly heard about three miles away; this, though the column did not then know it, was the beginning of the landing of the new Divisions with their 30,000 men at Suvla Bay. By this time the night was over, day was breaking, the Turks were in force and our attacking columns much exhausted; but there was still breath for a final effort.

Looking down from the hillsides, the men could see Suvla Bay full of ships and specks of men on the sand hills. In a flash they realised the truth. A new landing was being made. Taking heart at the sight of help coming from the sea, the Australians and Sikhs, with the last of their strength, went at Koja Chemen Tepe and the New Zealanders on their right rose to the storm of Chunuk. But it was not to be; they could not carry the two summits. They tried a second time to carry Chunuk but the Turks were too strong; but they held on to what they had won. In the evening they hoped that the men from Suvla would join hands and go on to victory with them; they had fought the first stage of the battle, the next stage was to be decisive. But alas, no succour came.

The story of Suvla is not for these pages, sufficient will it be to touch on certain points which were conducive to its failure – a failure which so greatly affected the fortunes of those elsewhere and which was very soon apparent to the anxious watchers at Anzac. On and near the beaches at Suvla there was a congestion of a very hindering kind. With men coming ashore, shells bursting amongst them, mules landing, biting, kicking, shying and stampeding, guns limbered up and trying to get into position, men coming ashore and seeking their battalions in a crowd where all looked alike; shouts, orders and counter-orders, ammunition boxes being passed along, water carts and transports starting for the firing line, wounded coming down, with every now and then a shell from Ismail Oglu Teppe and a blinding August sun. With all of these it was not possible to avoid congestion, an evil which prevented orders being passed quickly, so that the opening assaults were much delayed, whilst the heat and thirst caused much suffering to all.

Chocolate Hill was taken but they were unable to go on against Ismail Oglu Tepe. They were still two miles from the Australians below Koja Chemen Tepe. The Turks soon began to mass their reserves and bar the way. Had time not been lost on the 7th, the task on the 8th would have been to cross the valley at dawn, join the Australians and go on with them up the spurs in a strength which the Turks could not oppose. At dawn on the 8th their path to the valley was still barred by the un-captured fort in Ismail and there could be no crossing until that was taken.

Meanwhile on the 8th the Gloucesters and New Zealanders stormed and took the Chunuk Bair, a hill that rises some 400 feet in as many yards. This, the last step but one to victory, was ours. In the centre an attack on Hill Q was less successful, there the English and Indian regiments assaulting together were held. On the left the Australians tried to storm the Abd-el-Rahman Bair in a pretty desperate assault even for Gallipoli, but were driven back to the Asma Dere from which they had come. By noon, this assault, which would have been decisive had the men from Suvla been engaged with the Australians, was at an end. On the morning of the 9th August Ismail was captured by the troops at Suvla,[2] but they were at once checked and forced back to the Chocolate Hills. The effort had come too late; the Turks were everywhere in force to receive them. The main blow of the battle of Sari Bair was to have no support from Suvla. Nevertheless, the main blow was given by the troops near Chunuk and the following is a brief sketch of what occurred.

At 4.30am on the 9th the naval guns started on the high ground about Chunuk. Men of the Warwickshires and South Lancashires were the first on top of Chunuk, whilst the 6th Gurkhas were the first on the ridge between Chunuk and Hill Q. Our men passed over the crests and drove the Turks down the other side. The third column was coming up the hill below and in a few minutes would have been over the crest, going on to victory with the others. Then came the greatest tragedy of the campaign. Either our men were mistaken for Turks in the early dawn or there was some difference in the officers' watches, causing a few minutes delay in stopping the bombardment; whatever the cause, our own guns fired on the hill top for some minutes too long and decimated the brave handful of our men with a terrible fire. The Turks charged back and beat them off the greater part of the crest. Only a few minutes after this the third column came into action in support: too late. The Turks beat them down to the "Farm." The New Zealanders and some of the 13th Division held the south west half of the top of the Chunuk. After dark on the 9th the 6th Loyal North Lancashires relieved these trenches. At 4am on the morning of the 10th the 5th Wiltshires came to support and there may have been some 5,000 men all told on Chunuk and round the Farm. Before dawn they were attacked by about 15,000 Turks, whose third line overwhelmed our garrisons and destroyed the 5th Wiltshire Regiment almost to a man and fell on our men around the Farm in the most bloody and desperate fight of the campaign. Then followed a long succession of British rallies in the ruined cornfield of the Farm. Our last reserves came up to it and the Turks were beaten back. Their dead lay in thousands all down the slopes of the hill, but the crest of the hill lay in Turk hands, not in ours. Thus ended the battle of the 6th to 10th August.[3]

To return to the left covering column, where the battalion was digging for very life in the early hours of the 7th, there was no cessation of hard work that night and by dawn the men were hidden away in most cases; but here and there the rocky ground had defied the efforts of even the sturdy Welsh miner, whilst the locations of some of the trenches were found to give no field of fire and alterations had to be made.

Koja Chemen Tepe and the long range of the Sari Bair heights loomed ominously on the right flank, everywhere overlooking the under feature of the Damakjelik Bair, with its line of trenches and those still toiling in them. Many stray bullets were flying around, several men being hit, and then as a special mark of recognition the Turkish gunner got to work, whilst his ever ready sniper watched with eagle eye for unwary individuals. It was unsafe to walk about anywhere in the open. Lieutenants Lucas and Buchanan were wounded by shrapnel and Major Kitchin had his equipment ripped but escaped himself. From every direction came the sound of battle and Suvla, just visible to the north, added its quota to the general din. The casualties of the battalion during these last two days amounted to four officers wounded – Lieut W Beckford-Smith and 2nd Lieuts A Buchanan, C M Lucas and T M Jenkins – while 16 other ranks were killed and 74 wounded.

During the evening of the 8th, the 5th Wiltshire Regiment was withdrawn from the

2   In fact, these were troops on the north western slopes of Ismail Oglu Teppe.
3   Most Turkish casualties were the result of Royal Naval gun fire.

Map 9. 4 SWB at Damakjelik Bair – August 1915 (Medici Society Ltd).

Map 10. 4 SWB at Hill 60 on 21–22 August 1915 (Medici Society Ltd).

line and sent back to join the 40th Bde who were toiling on the heights of Chunuk. They had been closely associated with the Borderers since their embodiment and a feeling of comradeship had sprung up between the two battalions. As they left the lines at dusk they received a hearty send off from the Borderers to which they replied with many a friendly jest and hand wave. Alas, in a little more than 24 hours they were practically cut to pieces.

The withdrawal of the 5th Wiltshires necessitated a re-adjustment of the line, as the battalion was now solely in occupation and was too weak to hold it throughout. So in order to join up with Australians on the right, they moved into the Wiltshire trenches, vacating the ridge they had previously occupied, leaving thereon a small observation post. This position was on the extreme left flank of the Anzac line and there was a good one and a half miles between it and the sea unoccupied by any troops, for Captain Mundy's company had been withdrawn on the 8th and placed in rear as a support.

No determined attack in any great numbers was ever attempted by the Turks round this flank, but it was a possibility ever to be considered and one which caused considerable anxiety to the commander of this line during the next few days. Any retrograde movement on the part of the battalion would have placed the Australian left flank in the air. This ridge was afterwards held by more than a brigade, a force which was not considered at all too strong. Apparently the removal of the Wiltshires had been observed, for, at about 4.30 am in the morning of the 9th, the Turks attacked the battalion which had hardly settled into its new trenches, one party getting right up into the position up a gully – afterwards christened South Wales Borderers Gully – lying on the battalion left. These were driven out by a bayonet charge.

And now, on the 9th August, a great tragedy befell the battalion. At the commencement of the firing Colonel Gillespie had hurried over to the right flank of the battalion and proceeded to direct the fire of a machine gun placed there. For this purpose he looked over the top of the parapet and was immediately spotted by a Turkish sniper who was probably anticipating such an occurrence. He fired and Colonel Gillespie, who was shot through the left side of the head, fell dead into the trench.

The writer [Lt Mellsop] had served with Colonel Gillespie for nearly 20 years in the 2nd Battalion. "He was ever a cheery soul and whatever he took up he put his whole heart into. He was ever foremost in any rag or devilment in the battalion – and there was some ragging in those days – a criterion surely of the man with plenty of go in him. He was ever eager for active service, offering his services voluntarily on several occasions. He was also a capital half back at rugby football. He had been with his service battalion from the start, working with unremitting energy, his just treatment of the men and his sterling soldierly qualities having made him deservedly popular with all ranks. He was a loyal friend and a gallant gentleman." The command of the battalion now fell on Major Beresford who had served for 20 years in the 2nd Battalion.

About 7pm, the Turks again made a determined attack the whole brunt of which had to be borne by the battalion, as six companies of Gurkhas which were to have reinforced its left at dusk were prevented from coming. Captain Munday's company was brought up to reinforce the line and on an urgent appeal being sent for reinforcements, 50 New Zealand sappers were sent up about 9pm and two companies of the Kings Own Regiment about 10pm. None of these reinforcements however were brought into action as the battalion after some severe fighting successfully dealt with the opposition. C Company, who were next to the Gully, bore the brunt of the attack. As previously, the Turks rushed up this Gully and

Image 19. Lieutenant Colonel Franklin Gillespie CO 4 SWB who was killed at Damakjelik Spur on 9 August 1915 (R Welsh Museum).

Major Kitchin ordered Lieutenant Farrow to charge through the scrub with his platoon. This he did, driving back some 70 or 80 Turks and inflicting considerable loss on them. After charging about 120 yards, a very heavy fire was opened on this party from the scrub close by. Major Kitchin reinforced Farrow, who just then was wounded in the leg, but continued to lead his men. As the volume of hostile fire increased, two platoons of D Company (at that time the only available reserve) were sent up to reinforce C Company and with this force Major Kitchin was able to hold his own till dark, when he withdrew to a position 50 or 60 yards in rear, taking up there an entrenched position.

For the remainder of the night the line was undisturbed, except for a small attack about 2am which was soon driven back. The reinforcements were sent back just before day break. Besides those already mentioned, the following did especially good work on this engagement: Lieutenant TCM Austin, 2nd Lieutenant AF Bell, CSM W Bush, Sergeant W Myles. Captain Munday had received special mention for his able leading during the night march.

Just previous to this last attack, at about 6pm, the following telephone message was received by the OC Battalion:

'Sir Ian Hamilton sends the following message. Begins. "Well done South Wales Borderers." Ends. General Shaw heartily concurs. The Brigadier congratulates your Battalion on having earned such a message and hopes that it will be made known to all ranks. From 40th Brigade.'

The conduct of the men during these attacks had been most excellent. They fought like veterans and were cool and steady. The battalion suffered very severely, having three officers killed and seven wounded, whilst of other ranks there were 41 killed and 72 wounded. The names of the officers were Lieutenant Colonel Gillespie, Lieutenants Hillman and Miller and Second Lieutenant LG Cooper killed, and Captain Hooper and Lieutenants Fairweather, Austin, Farrow, Jenkins, Staples and Fleming RAMC wounded."

During the campaign there was time to reflect on more light hearted moments, as John Mellsop goes on to explain:

A rather amusing incident occurred about this time. Shortly after the ridge was taken, several Turkish dug-outs were discovered, evidently belonging to officers, who had beaten a hasty retreat and left everything behind. There were waterproof shelters, waterproof sheets and a veritable emporium of articles much needed by the battalion. Major Kitchin had a most excellent servant [Private Fynn who later on was to win the VC] and he took care to see that his master was amply provided with all the pick of the market and had made him very snug and comfortable. On the other hand, I was provided with a hoary old ruffian of 52, who had joined the battalion with a rather unsavoury record from the east end of London. He had grossly neglected to show off the undoubted abilities he possessed for misappropriating other people's property and had entirely omitted to procure me anything. I touched on the matter to him and suggested that a man with his talents might have done better. His professional pride was aroused and he assured me with a rather nasty leer that it would be alright and he therewith left my presence. In a wonderfully short space of time I had everything I could desire, all of the best and cleanest and I smiled contentedly at him. Not long after this, Kitchin in the course of conversation told me that everything that Fynn had procured for him had disappeared, but that he had put his initials on all of them. With a sinking heart I returned and examined all my recently acquired treasures and found them all marked with three letters of the alphabet – CEK – Kitchin's initials. I summoned the aforesaid ruffian of 52 who looked at me with pitying contempt when I ordered him heatedly to take them all back again. 'Sic Transit Gloria Mundi'.[4]

About half a mile in front of the battalion line there was a water well called the Kabak Kuyu which still remained in the hands of the Turks and as the water question was one of great difficulty, it was all important that it should be captured. On the afternoon of the 11th, General Cox, commanding the Indian Brigade, to whom the battalion was now attached, ordered the battalion to swing forward its left flank about 600 yards towards the well, using its right flank as a pivot, the 10th Gurkhas to co-operate on the left. The OC Gurkhas wished this movement to commence about 5pm to enable him to site his new trenches in daylight, but to this OC Borderers objected on the ground that his covering party on moving out would be seen and hotly dealt with by the enemy. As a compromise it was agreed that the operation should commence at 7pm, shortly before dusk, but as it turned out the Gurkhas were nearly decimated and had to retire taking no further part. In the meantime the battalion covering party moved out very quickly at 7pm and took a covering line with practically no casualties at first, but as they advanced too far they were severely dealt with later by snipers and others; Lieutenants Addams-Williams and Bell being killed and Lieutenant Bury wounded. Under cover of this party the line was advanced as ordered and all through the night the new trenches were dug. The Turks attacked the left of the line about 10pm but the attack was repulsed by the battalion.

Next day an attempt was made to rush the well. 250 men of the 9th Worcestershire Regiment were ordered to attack the well on the north, covered by the battalion firing from its trenches, now about 200 yards from the well at one point. At 7.15pm the attack commenced and the Worcesters being driven back they rallied and attacked again at 10pm, but this, like the first attack, was also repulsed and they suffered very severely. Although in

4   Thus passes the glory of the world; or, worldly things are fleeting.

trenches, the battalion had a good many casualties amongst whom was Major Sir Lennox Napier, killed. The total casualties of the battalion during these last three days were – three officers killed and one wounded as already mentioned and of the other ranks 22 killed, 69 wounded and 16 missing.

* * *

Breaking out of the diary for a moment and as previously mentioned, Major Sir William Lennox Napier, 3rd Baronet, had been called out of retirement in 1914 and re-enlisted in 4 SWB, which was one of Lord Kitchener's service battalions. Formerly a lieutenant colonel, he came back in the rank of major and was OC A Company; his son, Second Lieutenant Joseph William Lennox Napier was a subaltern in D Company. On the morning of 13 August 1915 Major Napier was shot dead by a sniper while inspecting his coy trenches and his son was immediately called for. First aid was given, but to no avail and Major Napier was pronounced dead at the scene. His body was removed from the trenches and interred in a makeshift grave near Suvla Bay until more permanent arrangements could be made.[5] His name would then be recorded as killed in action on the daily manpower return and eventually his next of kin, in this case his wife, Lady Mabel, back home in England, would receive formal notification from the war office, all of which could take weeks, if not months, given the number of casualties to be recorded and administered. More often than not however, a friend,

Image 20. Major Sir William Napier 4 SWB who
was killed on 13 August 1915
(Major General LAH Napier).

5   Major Sir William Napier was eventually buried in the 7th Field Ambulance Cemetery at Suvla Bay.

or another officer in the battalion, would write to the family at the earliest opportunity, so that at least they knew what had happened as soon as possible. In this case, Sir William's son Joseph was able to pen a letter to his mother that very day:

Gallipoli Peninsula
Aug 13 1915
Dear Mater,

I daresay by now you will have had the "War Office" telegram about Pater's death; I don't know whether they send them, but I will send one myself at the first opportunity. You see, I am writing the day it occurred and we have no chance of doing so at once. Anyhow, I'll tell you as shortly and as clearly, all I know.

About 6.10am this morning August 13, a Sergeant from 'A' Company came down the trench and told me Pater had been shot in the back. I thought at the time that it was probably an ordinary wound. But on reaching their trenches I climbed out under cover and found Pater's servant Keene and their Company Sergeant Major putting the field dressing round him. His head at the time was covered by his coat which had been put there to get at his body. I still supposed him more or less alright, though there was a lot of blood about, until I happened to pull the coat back from his face, when I saw that he was already dead. He had the ashen colour of death and looked perfectly natural. He didn't live five minutes after being hit and never uttered a word. He was hit somewhere in the back while walking down one of his trenches which at the point were very low (only just dug). A sniper did the work and I shouldn't wonder if he used explosive bullets. Their snipers are rather given to it. I had the consolation of knowing that a Sergeant of 'A' Company later on shot the sniper.

I know it will come an awful blow to you Mater, but you must try to forget it as soon as you can. He died better here than of illness or some other way in England. Quite painless thank God was his death.

Living here as one does in the middle of dead and wounded friends I was not so affected by it as I thought I should be. Nevertheless I feel very much that I have lost something that cannot be replaced. I don't know if I have put things somewhat crudely or severely (I hope not) as I think a frank account of such events is best, though possibly most hurting.

It has made me feel more than ever how much I want to get back to England, as does everyone here. I feel that I don't mind what the cost is (bodily) if only I could get back. The Battalion has had a rough time and very few officers remain. I am the only one in our Company, except Mundy. Jenkins had the back of his right hand blown off. Col Gillespie was the first to die; my servant was shot and died yesterday in a few minutes. In fact, the 13th Division almost ceases to exist.

I took any small valuables that poor Pater actually had on him, such as ring and watch so that nothing will be lost that you may treasure. I will go and see his grave and have some sort of cross put on it if I can. Meanwhile Mater, goodbye and bear the loss as lightly as you can though I know it will be hard. Much love.

Your ever loving son,
Joe [6]

---

6   This letter is included by kind permission of Maj Gen Lennox Napier.

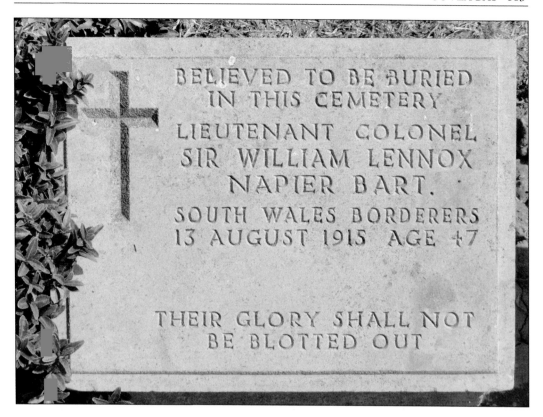

BELIEVED TO BE BURIED
IN THIS CEMETERY
LIEUTENANT COLONEL
SIR WILLIAM LENNOX
NAPIER BART.
SOUTH WALES BORDERERS
13 AUGUST 1915 AGE 47

THEIR GLORY SHALL NOT
BE BLOTTED OUT

Image 21. The grave of Major Sir William Napier at 7 Field Ambulance Cemetery. The stone shows his original rank prior to re-enlistment for the Gallipoli campaign (Major M J Everett).

Although this would have taken the best part of three weeks to arrive, at least Joseph had done all he could to let his mother know the tragic news as soon as possible. This letter does not pull any punches and is somewhat without emotion, but just as any son knows his mother far better than any casual observer, Joseph felt that this was the best way to impart such personal news and we are privileged to share in such a poignant moment. As the oldest son, Joseph now succeeded his father as the 4th Baronet. He continued to serve throughout the Gallipoli campaign and then during the conflict in Mesopotamia, he became a prisoner of war. He left the army in 1920 but rejoined in 1939, finally retiring as a lieutenant colonel, being awarded the OBE in 1944 during the second world war. He later became vice president of the Gallipoli Association, which is still very active in keeping alive the memory of the campaign. He died in 1986 at the age of 91. His younger brother Charles McNaughton Napier also served in the army, as a major in the Royal Artillery and his son, Lennox Alexander Hawkins Napier, born in 1928, was commissioned into the South Wales Borderers, becoming the last commanding officer of 1 SWB prior to its amalgamation with the Welch Regiment in 1969 and retiring as a major general and colonel of the regiment in 1983.

* * *

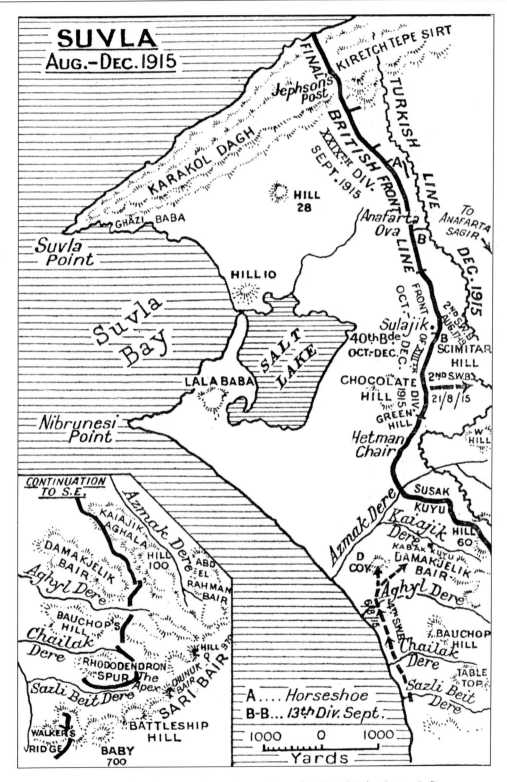

Map 11. The front line at Suvla Bay August–December 1915 (Medici Society Ltd).

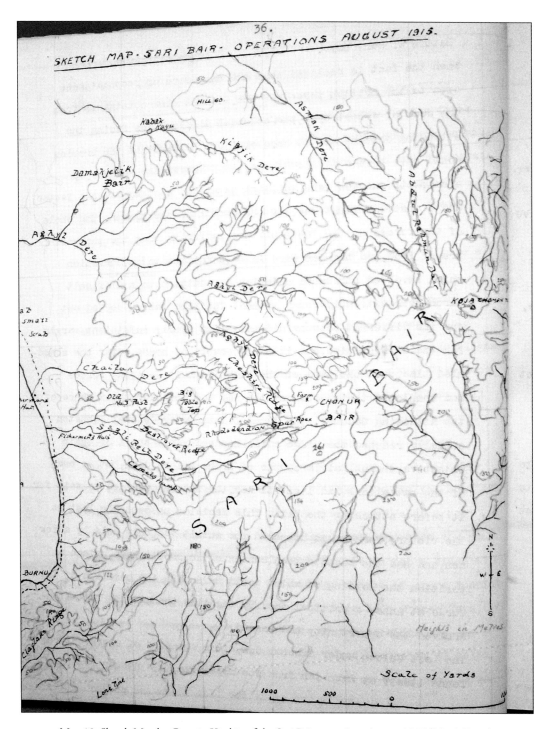

Map 12. Sketch Map by Captain Kitchin of the Sari Bair operations August 1915 (Mrs A Payne).

Back to the 4th Battalion's diary again:

It has been stated that the left flank of the battalion was somewhat in the air, with a considerable distance between it and the sea unprotected and that this was always a source of anxiety at night. Inspecting this flank before dusk on the 13th the OC battalion was much surprised to find the old trenches which the Borderers had originally dug, occupied by about 80 men, who turned out to be part of a territorial battalion who had landed at Suvla. Having lost their bearings they had wandered about until by chance they struck off these trenches and gladly made their home therein. On visiting them next morning not a man of them was to be seen, but the trenches were littered with all kinds of equipment, including rifles, packs, ammunition, shovels, tobacco, razors and goodness knows what else. Apparently, having been hotly shelled at dawn they started off again in their travels unarmed and unequipped.

On the 14th, this left flank was greatly strengthened by some Sikhs and Gurkhas who were brought up to occupy it, General Cox also bringing his headquarters up there. At midnight, 96 New Zealand Mounted Infantry arrived as a support to the battalion and next day they were put into the firing trenches to relieve A Company, which was given a rest for a few days.

The 15th was ushered in by a brisk Turkish shelling on the Suvla Bay landing places, Chocolate Hill, and other selected positions to the north, whilst sniping and occasional shelling were the annoyances dealt out to the battalion. These Turkish snipers were wonderfully persistent and several of them remained hidden behind the firing line after the battalion advanced, causing many casualties before they were eventually seized upon and demolished. A sergeant of the battalion was walking along one day inside the lines, fortunately carrying his rifle, when suddenly he spotted a sniper a few yards in front, lying down and preparing to fire at him. The sergeant, whose bayonet was fixed, rushed at the sniper and bayoneted him before he could fire.

* * *

Returning to the 2nd Battalion, they eventually left V Beach at 1:30 a.m. on the morning of 17 August, distributed on two fleet sweepers after waiting there to embark from about 10:30 p.m. the previous night. It took over 12 hours to make what was a relatively short journey, arriving at Suvla Bay at 4:30 p.m. and then proceeding into rest camp quite near the beach. Major Badcock, of the Army Service Corps and from the divisional supply depot was very good to the battalion and did all he could to help them with transport and so on. At 5:00 p.m. orders were received to the effect that the battalion was to go up into the firing line at 8:00 p.m. and be attached to 53 Division and be split up among the different battalions, to teach them something about trench warfare. At 8:00 p.m. they left the rest camp and proceeded to Hill 10 where they met guides from 53 Division. Bn HQ with A and B Coys were attached to 158 Brigade while C and D Coys went to 160 Brigade. The guides sent to take the coys to their respective battalions took the wrong route on several occasions, so it was very late when they eventually arrived so no work was possible that night, except in improving existing trenches.

Ernest comments on this plan for the battalion in his next diary entry:

Tuesday 17 August 1915

Good landing piers had been erected in Suvla Bay, all in about ten days, with what seemed a good water supply from ships, but everything else was in a chaotic condition. We thought the battalion would have the chance of a rest before going on but for some unaccountable reason, best known to the Staff I suppose, they sent us and the Border Regt up to the trenches again, although we had only just come out in the south, whilst the KOSB had been at rest. Our job apparently was to instruct the "Terriers"[7] how to dig trenches and keep them clean!! The battalion was therefore split up between two brigades and a nice job they had too evidently.

The coys of 2 SWB spent the next day in assisting the territorial battalions to make their trenches safe. Being inexperienced however, they seemed to have very little idea of trench digging and their means of communication was nonexistent, with the result that many men were shot by Turkish snipers who were hidden in the trees. Patrols were sent out to find the best position to dig a trench to link up with 54 Division on the left, as there was a gap in the defensive layout of about 600 yards. To close this gap, 1/6 Royal Welsh Fusiliers (RWF), to which B Coy was attached, had to be withdrawn from the right of the line and the gap caused by their removal filled by 1/5 RWF and 1 Herefords closing inwards. During the night the line was dug without difficulty, with patrols from 1/5 RWF being sent out to cover the front.

Meanwhile Ernest set out from his administrative base to link up with Bn HQ:

Wednesday 18 August 1915

Started out to find Bn HQ but ricked my ankle rather badly just after starting and had to return. The Battalion was to have done only 24 hours up but the plan has changed since and we now have to do another 36 hours. The Turks have the range of the beach and are putting shells into various parts, mostly the Supply Dump. Why they don't wipe the beach out, with all the men mules and stores about, is hard to understand, for they seem to have plenty of ammunition.

The morning of 19 August found the battalion continuing to work on improving trenches. Back breaking work at the best of times, it was now the height of summer and the heat of the day was intolerable. Dysentery was still rife and the water supply was limited to a well to the east of Hill 60, which was being used by everyone, so working conditions were very demanding. Patrols were sent out to the front in an attempt to counteract the enemy's snipers, who appeared rather more active. Eventually, orders were received for the battalion to withdraw at dusk to the brigade rest camp. The plan was to meet guides at Hill 10, but they never turned up so after waiting some time, the battalion moved off towards the beach until they finally reached the place where they were to dig themselves in, with yet more trenches to be prepared. Major Going remained behind to command 158 Brigade.

It is not surprising that that tempers were starting to get frayed as plans seemed to change with frustrating frequency, as Ernest remarks upon:

7   The nickname by which the territorial army was often known.

Thursday 19 August 1915

On the afternoon of the 19th got instructions that the battalion was moving to another place behind Hill 10. I had to move my kit into a brigade dump – awfully fed up, after making everything as comfortable as possible and getting a meal ready for the battalion's return. However orders are countermanded every few hours here. No-one seems to know his own mind for two consecutive minutes. Eventually got things moved and remainder packed on mules and followed the KOSBs to the new bivouac where we found only two Coys had arrived and had scratched up enough earth in the open to give head cover lying down. HQ and the remainder came in shortly afterwards. Everyone seemed to have liver. Not to be wondered at.

General Hamilton's concept to seize the initiative at Suvla Bay, culminating in the capture of the whole of the Sari Bair ridge, never materialised despite the fact that he had a numerical advantage over the Turkish troops in the area at the outset. Lieutenant General Sir Frederick Stopford, a 61 year old staff officer brought out of retirement from his post as Lieutenant of the Tower of London, was, on the face of it, not up to the task of leading such a large force as the British IX Corps on such a critical operation and the plan floundered almost from the outset.[8] Once they were ashore in Suvla Bay, momentum ground to a halt and there was little or no pro-active initiative displayed by Stopford or his divisional generals. Consequently, the opportunity to take the high ground overlooking the Bay was lost, giving the Turks time to rush reinforcements into the area. At the same time, the plan to link up with the Anzac force attempting to capture the heights of Sari Bair failed completely. Just 10 days later, on 15 August, Stopford was dismissed from his command, to be replaced by Major General Henry de Beauvoir de Lisle on a temporary basis, awaiting the arrival of Lieutenant General Sir Julian Byng from the Western Front.

Keen to arrest the inertia that had blighted the landing at Suvla Bay, General de Lisle had ambitious plans to capture the whole of the Tekke Tepe and Kiretch Tepe ridge lines, but General Hamilton directed him to plan a limited advance. 29 Division, which had been redeployed from Cape Helles, was to move forward from the area of Chocolate Hill and on to Scimitar Hill, while 11 Division would take the W Hills. On the right flank and in order to close the gap with the Anzac sector, a composite brigade, under General Herbert Cox, was to capture Hill 60.[9] With 50,000 men at his disposal, this was to be, numerically, one of the largest actions yet fought by General Hamilton since the start of the war on the peninsula. Ever optimistic, he still believed that success was within his grasp.

On the morning of 20 August at 10:00 a.m. a brigade conference of COs was called when probable orders for attack on Scimitar Hill (Hill 70) were explained. 87 Brigade was to proceed first of all to the north of Hill 53 and dig itself in amongst the heather out of sight of the enemy. The brigade moved off at 8:00 p.m. and after many delays, caused by 86 Brigade moving through its position, 2 SWB arrived at its destination near Hill 53 (Chocolate Hill) at about 11:30 p.m. where they proceeded to dig in. The position was a difficult one as just on their right flank was a battery of artillery which was likely to draw enemy fire. C and D Coys were put in a small nullah, with A and B Coys on the slope of Hill 53. Bn HQ was behind the hill. The supply of water continued to be a problem and had to be collected during the hours of darkness as the enemy was reported to be in the habit of shelling the wells.

8   There has been an historical reappraisal of Gen Stopford, especially his reluctance to advance, when his first defined objective was to create a safe base at Suvla, especially with so little artillery support.
9   Michael Hickey, *Gallipoli*, p.308.

As ever, Ernest was in the background sweeping up the administrative arrangements:

Friday 20 August 1915

Got orders in the evening to move to 'Chocolate' Hill and to attack Hill 70 (ie. Scimitar Hill) on the following day, preceded by a bombardment by the ships and gunners. Was not allowed to take on my cooks etc and was ordered to remain with them – had about thirty or more sick men also – mostly dysentery cases. Managed to get rid of a few of the worst cases to hospital, but there's not much room for sick now. Half the battalion is unfit for work really, but most of them stick it uncomplainingly.

At 9:15 a.m. on the morning of 21 August, 87 Brigade's plan for the assault on Scimitar Hill was issued. In outline, the attack was to begin at 3:00 p.m. preceded by a 30 minute artillery bombardment, after which 1 KOSB was to bring down concentrated machine gun fire on the enemy trenches between Scimitar Hill and Hill 112. Thereafter, 1 Royal Inniskilling Fusiliers was to begin the advance, with 1 Border Regiment in support. Once the hill had been taken, 2 SWB were to advance forward as far as possible, linking up with 86 Brigade on its flank. Casualties were to be evacuated from first aid posts to the dressing stations established in rear of Hill 53, while 2 London Field Coy Royal Engineers were to be prepared to go up in the evening to consolidate the position.

This seemed straightforward enough, but as on previous occasions, there were considerable flaws in the planning process. First of all, the orders were not issued early enough.[10] With only six hours before Z hour,[11] there was little time to disseminate the plan down to the soldiers on the ground, so battle preparation was limited. The orders themselves were light on detail, although the soldiers were encouraged to top up their water bottles (as if they needed such telling in the unbearable heat of the day) and the artillery support was very poor. There were around 85 guns available, along with naval support off-shore, but the ammunition allocated was risible. The weather conditions did not help either. In the mid-day heat, a haze blanket rose up from the Suvla plain as the sun disappeared into the cloud. As General Hamilton later wrote in his diary:

I climbed up to the Karakol Dagh, whence I got something like a bird's eye view of the arena which was wrapt from head to foot in a mantle of pearly mist. Assuredly the Ancients would have ascribed this phenomenon to the intervention of an Immortal. Nothing like it had ever been seen by us until that day and the cloud mist call it what you will must have had an unfortunate bearing on the battle. On any other afternoon the enemy's trenches would have been sharply and clearly lit up, whilst the enemy's gunners would have been dazzled by the setting sun. But under this strange shadow the tables were completely turned ; the outline of the Turkish trenches were blurred and indistinct, whereas troops advancing from the Aegean against the Anafartas stood out in relief against a pale, luminous background.[12]

CO 2 SWB and his company commanders did have the opportunity that morning to view some of the ground over which they were to attack and at 2:30 p.m. the artillery bombardment began. Then, according to the battalion's war diary, the main assault began at 3:30 p.m. The Inniskillings'

10   While the 87 Brigade Operation Order was issued at 9:15 a.m. 1 KOSB for example did not receive this until 1:10 p.m. less than two hours before the attack was due to begin.
11   Z (or Zero) hour was the time at which a particular offensive would begin. Currently it is known as H hour.
12   General Sir Ian Hamilton, *Gallipoli Diary* (London: Edward Arnold, 1920) Vol 2: 21 August 1915.

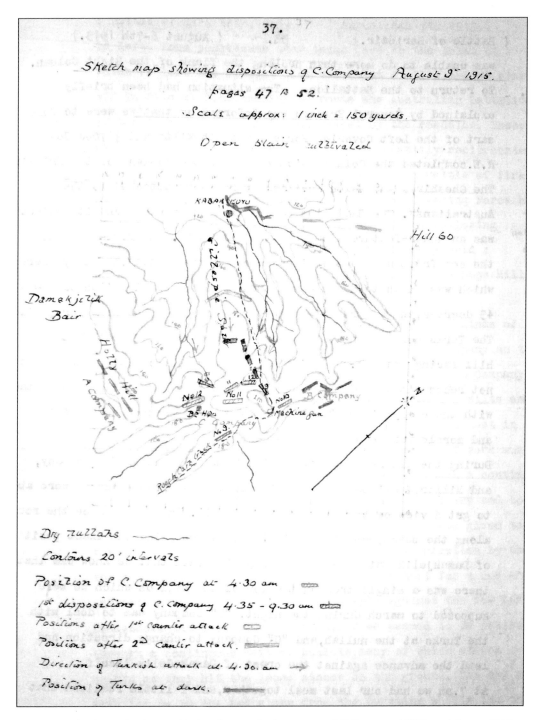

Map 13. Sketch Map by Captain Kitchin showing the dispositions of C Company 4 SWB on 9 August 1915
(Mrs A Payne).

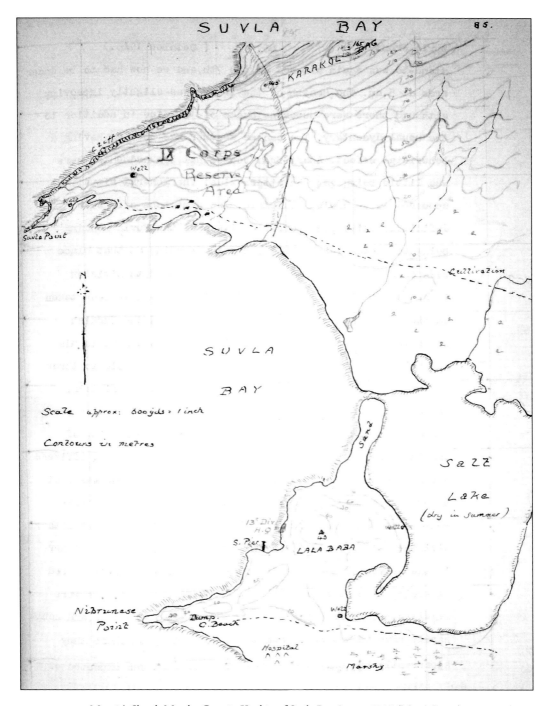

Map 14. Sketch Map by Captain Kitchin of Suvla Bay August 1915 (Mrs A Payne).

attack, which succeeded in gaining a foothold in the Turkish trenches, soon came under withering fire from both flanks and they were driven back from the summit, as was the Border Regiment which was sent forward to reinforce them.

At about 5:30 p.m. the order to advance, which 2 SWB had been expecting since 3:30 p.m. was given. Everyone knew that this was to be the final effort to capture the hill, against which the two leading battalions of 87 Brigade had attacked without success. It was not quite the order they were expecting, as in the original orders they were to attack the southern end of Scimitar Hill and link up with the attacks of 86 and 87 Brigades. They knew that the yeomanry were to operate on their right and left flanks, but very few of the battalion had much idea as to exactly where they were going and what their objectives were. Before long however, some of 2 Yeomanry Brigade, who had veered to their left and also briefly occupied the Turkish trenches on the summit, got intermixed with other units and began coming back, saying that they had been "ordered to retire." There was a thick haze over the whole of Suvla Bay and the Turkish shrapnel was sweeping the space between the front line trench, held by 1 KOSB, and the slopes of Scimitar Hill. The gorse too was burning and an endless stream of wounded Inniskillings and of the Border Regiment testified to the reception awaiting the battalion. They did not appear to have any artillery support and the battalion advanced with C and D Coys leading, while A and B Coys followed in support.

Bn HQ started to advance with the support group, but after a short time the CO decided that it would be better if they remained stationary and tried to keep up communication with field telephone and runner. It was just possible to make out the outline of the hill and the leading coys were given points to advance on. At first, all seemed to be going well and the coys could be seen moving forward through the Turkish shrapnel with surprisingly few casualties. As they reached the foot of the hill, they deployed into line and began the assault. The mist and smoke then obliterated everything and no one could tell what was happening. Not a single message was received at Bn HQ and the only information they could obtain was from wounded soldiers who had only a very vague idea of the situation.

Captain Aubrey Williams, the adjutant, spoke to Captain Walker, who was on his way back having been wounded, and he said that all was going well until the leading line was halfway up the slope, when, according to the battalion war diary *"it was swept from both flanks with enemy MG fire which practically wiped everyone out."* This must have been more or less correct, as every officer in the four coys and the four CSMs were casualties and only about 50 of the men who went over the top, survived. As it was quite impossible to get any information, the adjutant persuaded the CO (Major Going) to let him go up and see what was happening and he started off with his orderly, Private Porter. They passed crowds of wounded and groups of men of different regiments and no-one seemed to have any idea where they were or where the enemy were. Rifle fire and MG fire was coming from both flanks and the men themselves thought they were being fired on from their own lines.[13]

Captain Williams could find no proper firing line so he moved up to the top of the hill to get a better view. He found nothing there but a large number of British and Turkish dead. He and his orderly then crawled over the crest and about 30 yards down the other side he could make out a line of Turks. Many of them were kneeling in the open firing at the top of the hill. Every few minutes bursts of MG fire swept the crest, most of it seemed to come in enfilade from the right. It was obvious that there was no hope of being able to hold the crest, so they crawled back and started to organise a line about 30 yards below the crest.

---

13   From time to time, soldiers are accidentally fired upon by their own side in the heat of battle, known as "blue on blue".

The various units of the brigade had become badly mixed up, so Captain Williams tried to instil some sense of order by positioning 2 SWB on the left flank, the yeomanry in the centre, and the Border Regiment on the right flank. The Inniskillings were told to move back to the bottom of the hill where they were to reorganise. The Turks must have heard them moving as they suddenly advanced to the top of the hill and both lines faced one another, kneeling in the open at about 30 yards apart. The Turks showed up against the sky line whilst the British were in the shadow. The Turks suffered heavily and withdrew, so the adjutant went on with his reorganisation. Moving along the front it was clear that there were no officers or warrant officers in evidence, most of them having become casualties, so he picked out the NCOs and put them in charge of sections of the line. He pointed out the general line to them all, told them to collect ammunition and prepare what cover they could. Everyone seemed perfectly calm and collected and in reasonable safety and the whole centre of the position was defiladed [i.e. covered from enemy view] from right and left by the spurs at the horns of the hill.

As the adjutant received no reply to any of the messages he had sent back to the CO and as the firing line was now stable, he started off back to report in person. On the way he met the RSM, WO1 Westlake and later on a couple of signallers with several drums of wire. They tapped in on a wire which ran past them and found that it was in fact connected to Bn HQ. Having cut onto it, they joined one of the drums to the end and proceeded back up the hill laying out the cable behind them. The adjutant was then able to speak to Major Going who ordered him to return at once. Before doing so, he took RSM Westlake up to the front and pointed out the line to him. He said he would go along and see that everything was all right. It was about 9:00 p.m. when Captain Williams reached Bn HQ and reported to the CO, who then rang up 87 Brigade and spoke to General Lucas. Captain Williams also spoke to General Lucas and told him that it was perfectly useless to try and hold the crest of the hill and that if they were to go down the forward slope they would have to work round the flanks. The brigade commander replied that they were to dig in where they were.

As their main signal station was working well, Major Going decided to move Bn HQ forward. No sooner had they moved than General Lucas ordered the adjutant to go back to Brigade HQ to give a personal report on what was happening on Scimitar Hill. He and his orderly ran back as quickly as they could and on the way stumbled upon the Bn HQ of the Border Regiment. He told their CO what was happening on the hill and that there was not a single officer of his up there. He at once agreed to send someone up to assist Major Going. On arrival at brigade headquarters Captain Williams explained the situation, and was present when General Lucas rang up the divisional commander, General Marshall. From their conversation he gained the impression that the brigade would soon be ordered to withdraw.

Captain Williams then returned to his old Bn HQ position and spoke by phone to Major Going, who told him that a major of the Border Regt had arrived and that they were forming a support line. The adjutant told Major Going that he would gather all available men and start collecting the wounded as soon as possible in case they received orders to withdraw. He assembled about 50 men, including some 20 RAMC stretcher bearers from a bearer post, much to the disgust of a RAMC officer who said [according to Captain Williams] *"it was not the job of the RAMC to work forward of a bearer post."* Anyhow, after a bit of an argument they came with the battalion work party and wonderful work they did too. They started collecting from right to left and working backwards and forwards parallel to the front; in this way they covered the whole area between the front line on Scimitar Hill and their old front line. Sometime during the night, the troops in front withdrew through 2 SWB and as they passed the adjutant made use of some of them to help the wounded back. They remained out collecting the wounded and when they could find no more, started on arms and equipment. They even reeled up a lot of the telephone lines which were lying about in all directions. Dawn was breaking when they finally got back within their own lines.[14]

Being at the hub of the battalion's administrative area to the rear of the battle, Ernest was in a good position to give an overall perspective of the events of that day, including details of the casualties they suffered, as his diary entry explains:

Saturday 21 August 1915

Next day, 21st, the ships and artillery bombarded Hill 70 and from our position one got a good view. Chocolate Hill was plastered by the enemy with shrapnel. The 87th Brigade's attack was originally timed for 4 pm but didn't really commence until about 6 pm. The Inniskillings formed the firing line with the KOSB's, while ours and the Border Regt formed the supports to go through after the Hill was taken and push on as far as possible. As usual the strength of the Turk was underestimated. His troops were supposed to be of poor quality and few. A determined advance was to be made by the 87th Brigade, whatever the Territorial and Kitchener Brigades did. Hill 70 was taken and retaken about four times at least. Twice by our own men. One of the NCOs stated afterwards we could have held on with the assistance of the Yeomanry, only one of their officers yelled 'retire' or 'cease fire' – it is not too sure which. Anyhow, retire they did – damn the word; it ought to be expunged. Got orders from the Adjutant to bring along the rations. Got there with carts and took them as close up to the firing line as possible – it must have been about 11 pm by then. Had to get the rations up into A Coy's support trench and send them out to the firing line as best one could. There was plenty of light – for the gorse and trees had been set on fire in dozens of places by shell fire. The water had to be got up too – luckily we had a new draft of 60 men who had joined that afternoon, otherwise it would have been a sweat! The wounded were coming back as fast as the stretcher bearers could bring them – still, they couldn't cope with the demand so the draft had to help them too.

After getting the rations up we had orders to be relieved by 88th Bde so had to get them all back again and as much of the water as possible. Up to that time we had gained about 500 yds of ground and our men were digging in on the ground gained. The 88th however took over the support trenches and so we learned the next morning that we were back where we started – nothing gained. The battalion lost Lts Burrell and McShane killed – Nevile (?) missing – Captain Walker, Lts Hill, Mumford, Blake, Geaney, Tragett, Evans, Knowles and Philpott wounded – rank and file – 210 killed, wounded and missing. The Inniskillings lost 490 odd and practically all officers and Border Regt nearly as many. The total losses have been given by the Field Ambulance as 7000. Rather think 4000 should be nearer the mark, but don't know how many troops were actually engaged. A former good old 24th officer is among the missing – F W Gray, who left in 1905. Met him quite by accident the morning the Yeomanry Division landed (18th) and took him along to breakfast and a yarn. He joined the Yeomanry owing to being unable to march – through phlebitis and was a full blown 2nd Lieutenant again. Poor fellow, I'm afraid he's a goner. Our first roll call showed a loss of over 300, but next morning a lot came in from trenches of other units who hadn't heard the order of our retirement.

Ernest then went on to follow up some of the casualties sustained the previous day and to explain the rumours heard about further moves:

14   TNA WO/95/4311. Captain (later Lt Col) Aubrey Williams, from a letter written in 1931.

Sunday 22 August 1915

The KOSB only lost about 25 as they were apparently ordered to hold the trenches and not to attack. We were not bombarded with so much shell as one would have expected, but CSM Chaston and CQMS Larley were both badly hit by a shell which practically hit them direct and also smashed every can of water they had for the Company – about 28. Poor Chaston died of his wounds. Our Bde was withdrawn the night after the attack and marched to Point 28. I was left behind to get the cooks and Officers Mess gear along – being promised carts at midnight. I know what these promises are so managed to keep hard on Major O'Hara's tail and eventually got what I wanted. Arrived at our destination about 3 am on the 23rd. Rumours once more of a rest for the Division. One being, that we go to Egypt and do Garrison duty there for the winter and relieve another Australian contingent from there. Another, that we go by Brigades to Imbros for a month – the latter being more nearly correct, except that it boils down to probably eight days – not worth the bother of moving. Why the first proposition doesn't hold water, I can't understand. God knows we want a change. Have to stay on till knocked out I suppose as we are making preparations for a winter campaign.

On 22 August, the battalion was withdrawn into reserve and dug itself in about a quarter of a mile to the west of Hill 28. Two sergeants and about 60 men, who had been listed as missing, eventually made their way back into the battalion's lines, while Lieutenant Byrne joined the battalion with 62 reinforcements. Two days later, Second Lieutenants Hall and Jones joined the battalion with a further draft of 59 soldiers. Still in the height of summer, there was great difficulty in obtaining sufficient water, all of which had to be drawn by hand in bags and cans and carried a distance of about one mile. This had to be done by night, as it was impossible to obtain any by day as the Turkish artillery shelled all the wells. As if this was not enough for soldiers racked with dysentery and a shortage of sleep, every night the battalion had to supply fatigue parties of 300 men for work on new second line of defence across Suvla Bay, marking the extent of IX Corps' limited progress.

On the evening of 27 August, a draft of one sergeant and 10 men arrived, being all that remained of the battalion's reinforcements who survived the sinking of RMT *Royal Edward* when she was torpedoed between Alexandria and Lemnos. Launched in 1907 as the RMS *Cairo*, the *Royal Edward* entered service for the Egyptian Mail Steamship Company and then transferred to the Canadian Northern Steamship Company in 1910. At the outbreak of the Great War in 1914 she was requisitioned for use as a troopship.[15] On 28 July 1915 the ship took on board 1,367 officers and men at Avonmouth. The majority were reinforcements for 29 Division with members of the Royal Army Medical Corps. All were destined for Gallipoli. The ship was reported off the Lizard on the evening of 28 July, and arrived at Alexandria on 10 August, prior to sailing for Lemnos. On the morning of 13 August, she passed the British hospital ship *Soudan*, which was heading in the opposite direction. A German submarine, *UB-14*, was off the island of Kandeloussa and saw both ships. The German Captain allowed the *Soudan* to pass unmolested, and focused his attention on the unescorted *Royal Edward* some six nautical miles away. He launched one of his two torpedoes from a distance of about one mile and hit the vessel in the stern. She sank within six minutes. However, the *Royal Edward* was able to get off an emergency message before losing power, and the *Soudan* returned to the scene as soon as possible and rescued 440 men in six hours. Two French destroyers and some trawlers rescued another 221. The *Royal Edward*'s death toll was 866 and was high because the ship had just completed a boat drill and the majority of the men were below

15   Grammatically, ships of the Royal Navy are almost always referred to in the feminine case.

decks re-stowing their equipment. 56 men destined for 2 SWB died that day and their names are commemorated on the Helles Memorial.[16]

After a brief respite in reserve trenches to the west of Hill 28, 2 SWB moved back into the front line, to relieve the Worcestershire Regiment on the evening of 29 August. With little or no cover, the line was quite impossible to live in, so once again the never ending grind of digging trenches continued into the night, with the aim of preparing a communication trench between Bn HQ and the forward positions. The difficulty of getting water continued to be a problem; the previous evening the Bn was told to get it from Hill 10 and then to try a well at Charak Chasme, but this one was found to be empty. Water could be obtained from the brigade resupply position, but as rations had also to be carried up from the same location, this task took practically a whole company away from work on the firing line. As the communication trench to the front line was not yet ready everything had to be carried up by night. However, the nearest Turkish trench was about 700 yards away, so there was no difficulty in working in the open at night.

Ernest confirms the logistical difficulties in his next diary entry:

Sunday 29 August 1915

On the 29th, we had to go up and take over the fire trenches and supports from Worcesters and Royal Scots, just as we had made some good dug outs. Found the dug outs somewhat primitive again up there – and none at all for the QM as theirs stops on the beach. Their dug outs are nothing but a continuous trench, perfectly safe from fire, but not from water! So we have had some very good ones made higher up on the hill. One each for CO, Adjt, MO and self. The water question at our last place was bad, with the exception of 30 water bags carried on 15 mules which we got after rations came up at night. All the remainder had to be carried by the men in camp kettles etc from Hill 10, the well there giving the best supply. The Division kindly authorised us to use the Charak Chasme well for 29th Div only. They evidently didn't go much into the matter of gauging its supply. It would have taken me 20 hours out of the 24 daily to get my own supply, never mind a Division and we are not allowed to carry by day. Our water parties rarely finished before 3 am. Up here we get it in bulk from the beach carried up in milk cans, kerosene oil tins or camel tanks, whichever they have. This we generally get over by 11 or 12 pm by using a big fatigue party. Then the Companies in the trenches and the outpost and MG Section have to get their gallon a man carried up by night as they are completely cut off by day, there being no communication trench properly dug yet. The only cooking we can do for them is a hot meal at night. They only do 48 hours in, so it is not a great hardship.

Come the end of the month, the only work done during the day was in squaring up the support nullah. Officers reconnoitred the ground with a view to siting a new fire trench to join up with 86 Brigade, as well as a preparing a new communication trench, in which they were assisted by 150 men from the Border Regiment, who were sent up to help later during the evening. There was no let up in the work needed to secure the battalion's defensive position, with B Coy assisting A Coy to carry sandbags and improve the fire trench, while D Coy did all the carrying of water containers and rations. At midnight, C Coy relieved B Coy until 4:00 a.m.

* * *

16 *Journal of the Gallipoli Association* No 136, Winter 2014. The Journal also includes an excellent article about the injustice of the medal entitlement for the victims of this disaster. SWB casualties are listed at the end of this book.

While 2 SWB was caught up in the saga of Scimitar Hill, 4 SWB was still committed to the Anzac sector and was soon to become involved in the equally bloody battle of Hill 60. John Mellsop's account needs little amplification and captures the drama of the event:

The battalion is now the only British regiment in this locality, the remainder of the line being garrisoned by Australians, New Zealanders, Gurkhas and Sikhs. The men by this time had become quite accustomed to their new mode of life and took things wonderfully philosophically. As an instance, several large holes had been dug close together as potential graves for future casualties and two men were observed one day sitting in the bottom of one of these graves playing cards. A short time afterwards a man was buried in the grave next to it.

The field of fire in front of the battalion trenches was by no means good on account of the thick scrub in front of it, so a request was sent to the Gurkhas for the loan of a few Kukris. After dark a party of officers and men from the battalion issued out to cut the brushwood, but being quite unused to these formidable weapons, their efforts were most pathetic and they could make no headway at all. A further appeal was made to the Gurkhas and next evening 100 of them were sent over and working under cover of a party sent out by the battalion, they cleared the way in goodly style and soon got over that difficulty.

On 17th, General Sir Alex Godley, who commanded a long section of this defensive line, inspected the trenches and told the battalion that they had done extremely good work in beating back the Turkish attack on the 9th when unsupported, and that it had greatly assisted the defensive works. Plans for a further advance in this locality had been talked over for several days; the well in front still remained uncaptured and an important under feature of the Sari Bair, called Hill 60, prevented anything like a safe joining up of the forces at Suvla and Anzac. This hill lay about three quarters of a mile to the right front of the battalion.

On 20th, Generals and Commanding Officers held a conference near the battalion lines as the conduct of affairs, which was to be carried out by a considerable force consisting of the Indian Brigade – NZ Mounted Rifles Brigade – 5th Bn Connaught Rangers – 4th South Wales Borderers – 13th and 14th Battalions of the 4th Australian Infantry Brigade – 18th Battalion of the 5th Australian Brigade and 9th & 10th Australian Light Horse Regiments, the whole under Major General C. V. Cox. At 2pm on the 21st, the bombardment was commenced by all sorts of available guns, including some naval ones, and at 3.30pm the Australians and New Zealanders on the right advanced to attack the Turkish left. About 3.40pm, the Connaught Rangers rushed down S Wales Borderers Gully and carried the Kabak Kuyu Well, then wheeling to the right they advanced up some rising ground and gained possession of one of the Turkish trenches. C Company of the Borderers advancing on the right of the Connaught Rangers also rushed and held another trench. As soon as the Well was captured, A Company of the battalion, who had returned to the line, advanced and commenced entrenching around it. It was hotly shelled, losing several men, and Lieut O. S. Phillips was killed by a splinter from a shell. C Company was now really sharing the same trench with the Turks, with a barricade built in between them, and both sides bombed each other unmercifully. Private Beary of the Company, a very fine specimen of a sturdy Irish-Welsh miner, gained great praise for his ceaseless bomb throwing, which caused dreadful havoc amongst the Turks and greatly assisted in retarding their efforts. For this and other good work he afterwards received the DCM. The Company was heavily counter-attacked during the night but held their own, and at dusk the next day they were withdrawn, the trench being taken over by other troops.

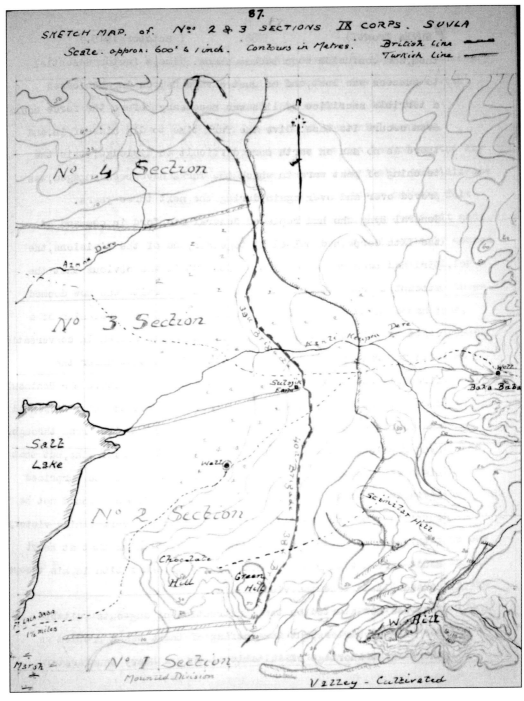

Map 15. Sketch Map by Captain Kitchin of the four sections of IX Corps at Suvla Bay (Mrs A Payne).

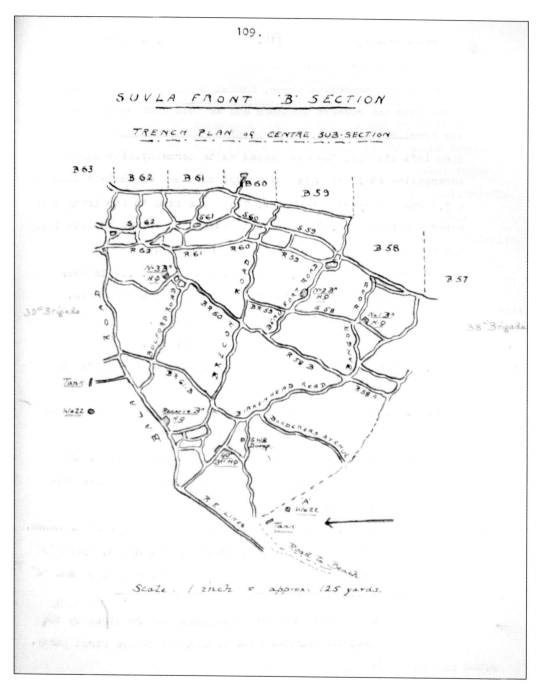

Map 16. Sketch Map by Captain Kitchin of the Suvla front – B section trench plan (Mrs A Payne).

Captain Kitchin, OC C Coy 4 SWB, also kept a diary and his description of the events on Hill 60 adds to the saga being played out that day:

Orders were issued for a forward movement to take place in the afternoon of 21 August. The IX Corps of three Divisions and some dismounted Yeomanry were to attack W Hill, a single ridge running east from Chocolate Hill from the direction of Suvla Bay. General Cox's Brigade, consisting of Australian and New Zealand troops, the Connaught Rangers and 4th S Wales Borderers was to co-operate by seizing the enemy trenches on our front and the hill immediately behind there, known as Hill 60. The Australians were to attack on the right, the New Zealanders continuing to their left whilst the Connaughts were to seize the well on the left front of our trenches and assist the New Zealanders. My Company (C) strength about 60 rifles was to form a reserve to the Connaughts and 'A' Company was to consolidate the ground in front of the well when captured. The remainder of the battalion was to cover the advance with machine gun and rifle fire. On our left a battalion of Gurkhas was to advance up the valley and join hands with the IX Corps. All available guns were to concentrate on W Hill from 2pm to 2.30pm after which they were to switch on to the enemy trenches on our front until Zero Hour at 3pm.

The initial part of the programme was carried out, but the guns continued on their first objective until nearly 3pm and then only a few shots were fired on our front none of which fell near the Turkish trenches. About 3pm we could see the right flank of the IX Corps advancing steadily along the valley under a heavy and accurate shell fire and the Turks retiring in front of them were plainly visible. Meanwhile the Connaughts successfully rushed their objective and captured the well and trenches guarding it; the New Zealanders taking off from my Company trenches made a very gallant advance of some 600 yards in the face of intense rifle and machine gun fire. They lost heavily but established themselves in a section some 300 yards long of a trench about 30 yards below the crest of Hill 60. Unfortunately the Australians were only partially successful and were unable to link up with the New Zealanders from whom they were separated by a broad ravine.

I moved my Company up to join the Connaughts near the well and their CO, receiving news of the position of the New Zealanders with both their flanks in the air gave me orders to reinforce them and detailed one of his platoons to assist me. We were then in a deep narrow lane with high hedges and the only way to get the men into open order was to dribble them into a field and then turn them at right angles to make the advance. This somewhat difficult manoeuvre under fire was carried out quite coolly by the men, ably superintended by the NCOs for I had no officers with me, and we started an advance up the open hill side under a heavy oblique machine gun and rifle fire from the Turks on the right of the New Zealanders. Luckily there were a couple of banks on the way under which we were able to take a breather between the rushes and we reached our objective with a loss of only 10 men. I reported at once to the major in command of the New Zealanders and occupied about 80 yards of trench on his right, our right flank resting on a communication trench which the Turks had barricaded and turned into a bombing post. Unfortunately all my trained bombers were out of action but the New Zealanders kindly provided us with a sackful of 'jam pots' and I had no difficulty in obtaining a couple of volunteers in LCpls Beary and Groucer to handle them. Although never having handled a bomb before they soon got going and judging from the yells of pain and cessation of Turkish bombs undoubtedly made good practice.

Dusk fell rapidly and with it the Turks grew bolder and from their commanding position showered bombs along our trench causing several casualties; we got the upper hand however and things were quiet for a bit. The situation was now somewhat critical as our little force of about 120 rifles all told was isolated in the Turkish main position; we consequently posted every other man on sentry in one hour reliefs.

About 2am on 22 August, word was passed along to cease fire as the New Zealanders thought the Gurkhas had come up on their left and shortly afterwards we saw a considerable number of men on the sky line who rapidly disappeared on being challenged. It transpired that these were Turks who had come up on the left of the New Zealanders and demanded their surrender and the unfortunate mistake as to their identity lost us an excellent chance of wiping them out. About 3.15am an assault on our position was made but our fire was too hot and the attack died away. One enormous Turk remained shouting and waving his arms on the crest line and seemed to bear a charmed life, but at length he fell and we had peace until daylight. It was fortunate for us that the Turks had no other trench above us on the forward slope as they were unable to fire at us by day without exposing themselves.

Having no water we passed a very trying day in the intense heat and also suffered from being heavily shelled out of our trench <u>by our own guns</u> in addition to which a machine gun in rear made unpleasantly good practice on us. The Turks made no further attempt to attack us and at dusk we received orders to withdraw at 8.15pm when the New Zealanders were to be reinforced. The withdrawal was carried out without further loss. Our casualties amounted to 24 killed or wounded – or 40% of our strength.[17]

The 4th Battalion's record by John Mellsop picks up the story:

On the morning of the 22nd a newly arrived battalion of Australians was launched against the Turkish centre, but after capturing a portion of the line they were driven back and coming under heavy machine gun fire they suffered very severely. Although not entirely successful the attack had gained a footing on Hill 60, but the knoll itself had not been captured. The Turks appeared much annoyed at losing the Well and kept up such a hurricane of shot and shell on it that at first no water could be drawn from it in the daytime, but the battalion, aided by New Zealand Sappers soon erected a shell proof shelter around it.

The casualties in the battalion were again considerable. Since the last return mentioned it had lost Major Sir William Lennox Napier and Lieutenant Phillips killed and Lieutenant Bury wounded, whilst among the other ranks there were 12 men killed, 71 men wounded and 4 missing.

As a general re-organisation of this line had now begun, it was expected that the battalion would be shortly withdrawn and sent back to the 40th Brigade and orders to this effect arrived on the 24th. The battalion left the Damakjelik Bair at 7.30pm that evening and after marching about three miles and crossing the Chailak Dere, they arrived in the reserve trenches of the 13th Division, which was holding Rhododendron Spur and the heights around it. This was the highest point on the Sari Bair which we had been able to retain after the big battle and it was about three quarters way up towards Koja Chemen Tepe. The spur was a wilderness of gorse and precipice intersected with deep ravines and gullies, some of them almost un-climbable, rocky in most parts and wild in the extreme, eaten out by the torrential rains, but quite dry at this time. The battalion was met by Brigadier General Travers and spent the night in brigade reserve in one of the steep ravines.

17   R Welsh Museum, Lt Col C E Kitchin's War Diary BRCRM r.1948.16.2.

On the 26th, the battalion was brought up a little closer to the firing line and placed in another stony and comfortless ravine. There was a kind of a Road running up to the advanced trenches. It had at least been beaten down flatter than the rest of the ground by constant use, and it was along this that most of the troops advanced up and down and along which all wheeled traffic proceeded. It formed a long scarp and was just hidden from Turkish view by the formation of the ground. Conceiving the idea that if this scarp could be brought under fire our difficulties would be much increased, the Turk was busily engaged in building a tower of sandbags, which would eventually be high enough to give him all the command he required. This menace was daily increasing, so General Maude – who had lately taken over command of the Division vice General Shaw, invalided – was at first for assaulting the tower, but finally decided that the casualties would be too great. Eventually a mountain gun was placed in one of trenches and very soon it knocked the tower to smithereens.

The battalion was to have taken over a section of the firing trenches on the 27th; the trenches being inspected for that purpose, but before going into them it was ordered elsewhere. From this high ground a battle could be distinctly seen going on around the Damakjelik Bair – the ground the battalion had just left. This was another attack on Hill 60 which was finally taken on the 29th, making the line from Anzac to Suvla impregnable.

On the 28th the battalion took over the trenches on Table Top from the New Zealanders. A truly wonderful piece of ground, it has thus been described – Inland from Old No 3 Post and some 700 yards from it is a crag or precipice which looks like a round table with a top projecting beyond its legs. This crag known to our men as Table Top is a hill which few would climb for pleasure. Nearly all the last 100 feet of the peak is a precipice such as no mountaineer would willingly climb without clear daylight and every precaution. It is a sort of skull of rock fallen down upon its body of rock and the great rocky ribs heave out the gullies between them.

A German Taube aeroplane dropped three large bombs into one of the Table Top gullies on the 29th and several men were wounded by shells and stray bullets from the Turkish lines. It may be said about this time that since no further big attempt could be made by the Allied troops and since no big attempts were subsequently made by the enemy, the fighting had settled down into trench warfare on both sides. There was some shelling every day and night, at times very vigorous, some machine gun and rifle fire, much sniping, great vigilance and occasional bombing and mining. The dysentery which had been present ever since the great heat began increased beyond all measure. Very few men in all that army were not attacked and weakened by it. Many thousands went down with it; Mudros, Alexandria and Malta were filled with cases. Many died.

* * *

If only the principles of war, which should have been well known to any senior commander and his staff officers, had been applied correctly then this operation could well have been the turning point of the whole campaign, rather than yet another failure, particularly given the forces General Hamilton had at his disposal. Objectives were not always fully understood by the divisional commanders; there was insufficient offensive spirit to seize, hold and exploit the initiative; the element of surprise was missing and the enemy was never put on the back foot, especially as the Turkish forces were so thin on the ground at the time of the invasion. Critically, the enemy was given time to build up an unexpected advantage due to the fact that the allied plans were neither clear nor concise;

consequently there was never a thorough appreciation of the overall aim of the offensive. Every operation must be directed towards a clearly defined, decisive and attainable objective, but sadly this was not the case at Suvla Bay.

Failure was not for the want of trying by the South Wales Borderers however, with both battalions being heavily involved throughout the whole of the August offensive. Casualties were appallingly high – 2 SWB lost over 300 at Scimitar Hill, while the 4th Battalion suffered the death of their commanding officer and had in excess of 400 killed, missing or wounded – with little or nothing to show for such a dreadful price.

9

Autumn Stalemate

*From this moment ... the Gallipoli story sinks into
an ugly welter of accusations, personal spite,
dashed hopes and despair*

Robert Rhodes James
Gallipoli (1965)

The August offensive at Suvla Bay and the attempt to seize the heights of Sari Bair had been a disaster. It was clear that General Hamilton had run out of options to alter the course of the war and the dynamics of the whole campaign were about to change. At home in London, Lord Kitchener was under pressure from the French to launch a new offensive on the Western Front, which meant that further reinforcements for General Hamilton were now virtually out of the question, while closer to Gallipoli, Bulgaria, hitherto neutral, had sided with the German axis. This necessitated support to Greece by sending two divisions from Gallipoli to Salonika, denuding General Hamilton's forces even further. Add to this, the uncomplimentary press reports being published at home about the handling of the campaign, the writing was on the wall, both about the general's tenure in command and the very future of the campaign itself.

After their exertions at Scimitar Hill, 2 SWB was withdrawn into reserve and spent the first week of September to the west of Hill 28 on the Suvla Plain. As the British front line had not established itself far enough inland in an easterly direction, the battalion was still subjected to rifle fire from the Turkish position, but more pressing matters at the moment were the provision of water, accommodation and generally making life more endurable. The well at Chanak Chashme was very dry, so water had to be manhandled forward in containers, usually at night, so the opportunity for proper rest was, as always, limited. At 7:45 p.m. on the evening of 1 September, the Turks suddenly opened fire on the left of the KOSB position and on Jephson's Post with trench mortars and field guns for about an hour. The fire on both sides was very heavy, but no signs of an advance by the Turks could be observed. Two hours later, the firing died down and at about 10:00 p.m. the Border Regiment sent up 150 men to assist with the digging of the communication trench, while other work went on as usual. On 2 September, D Coy started to make a new line along the knoll running out towards 86 Brigade and a start was also made on a new communication trench which was likewise to connect up with the brigade. At the same time, a draft of reinforcements from 1/4 Welsh Regiment arrived which, according to the battalion's war diary, brought the battalion's strength up to 19 officers and 1,121 other ranks.[1] These new men were split up amongst the companies and platoons and although work by night continued

---

1   The 4th Bn Welsh Regiment was a local TA unit. See Chapter 12 for further details.

apace, it meant that half companies could at least be sent to the rest camp at the Suvla Bay beach for 24 hours to enable the men to have a bathe and general brush up. Do not be misled by its title however; the beach was still in range of enemy artillery and sniper fire and the soldiers slept in the usual dugouts for safety, with rudimentary shelter from the blistering heat of the day. Food remained as bland and monotonous as ever, accompanied by the incessant plague of flies, but at least it was a break from the pressure of the front line trenches and there was the opportunity to sleep for more than just a few hours at a time.

Ernest picks up the story in his next diary entry. No doubt as a consequence of suffering from the effects of dysentery, he clearly did not seem disposed to having more inexperienced reinforcements thrust upon the battalion, both to administer and to train, despite the fact they are from one of his sister regiments:

Thursday 2 September 1915

Up to yesterday we have had practically no firing our way from the enemy, though if he knows of our position he could give us a very bad time with shrapnel. Yesterday we got a high explosive which we thought was intended for the 86th Brigade but which burst just beyond our cook house. Last night just as we were having dinner two more shells burst almost simultaneously just near the same spot, following by many. The first two however seemed to be a signal for a heavy burst of rifle fire started on our left. In a few minutes the whole line was firing hard although they couldn't see a Turk! The Company Commander asked for reinforcements – just then all our men were away on fatigues and things looked serious. The men of the last drafts made good use of the dug outs for cover! The job was to get them moving. Any amount of shelling took place then by our howitzers assisted by the ships' gun or two and I think they must have been well placed judging by the report. All our water and ration fatigues were at a standstill but luckily everything quietened down by about 11 pm for which one was thankful. Completely off colour for the last three days – can't eat – bile and the usual stomach trouble. Don't feel like moving a yard. Result of last night's rattle – one man wounded and another who had been wounded by one of our own men. Turks loss probably less. There's not much of the old 29th Division spirit left here now. I hear we are to get 250 men and 8 officers of the 4th Welsh foisted on us from tonight to learn soldiering. That will bring us up to over 1,000 which we have never been before. Give me 500 of the old crowd and a few of the officers to lead them. Can't expect to make a silk purse out of a sow's ear.

The next day, Ernest found that he had an embarrassment of riches when more reinforcements than expected turned up:

Friday 3 September 1915

Eight officers and 350 of the 4th Welsh turned up instead of 250. Our numbers are 1150. Serious question of water supply for this lot. Quite a good lot of men though for work. Their chief problem is that NCOs and men come often from the same pits and consequently it is hard for the former to exercise their authority and the officers are pretty young. Still feeling off colour but appetite better – pains in 'little mary' still worry one.

There is no doubt that a full battalion on active service has many advantages. More soldiers means that sentry duties come round less often, giving time for much needed rest; an increase in numbers means administrative duties are shared more equitably, particularly when much of this had to be done under the cover of darkness; but most importantly of all, more soldiers means greater fire power on the front line. On the other hand, the real estate in which to accommodate these extra soldiers had not increased, so the battalion's position became very crowded, which impacted upon space for dugouts, the scarce water supply, the limited latrine facilities and a strain upon the over-stretched medical staff as more men would become susceptible to dysentery and other illnesses in the foul conditions which continued to prevail across the Gallipoli peninsula in the baking hot weather.

Ernest also comments on the matter of command and control. It was not unusual for large numbers of soldiers in Kitchener's new army to be recruited from the same local area and these were often referred to as pal's battalions. The fact that they may have come from having worked together in the same coal mines of South Wales [the pits as he calls them] should not, in principle, cause a major problem; indeed, it could be quite an advantage as the men would not need to waste time getting to know each other as they integrated into their various rifle sections and platoons. What might have been an issue is the fact that their young officers and NCOs were inexperienced as far as command and control – the bedrock of military discipline – was concerned and there may have been instances where they may not have been respected as much as might otherwise be the case where they had been in positions of responsibility for some time already. Respect however has to be earned and the rigours of active service would soon sort this out. War is often said to be "80 percent boredom and 20 percent sheer terror" and no doubt this latter figure would soon distinguish the men from the boys, when it came to command and control under enemy fire. On this occasion, Ernest – himself a very experienced soldier and disciplinarian, having been the RSM not so long ago – was perhaps rather preoccupied by the side effects of dysentery.

Meanwhile, the rifle coys continued to rotate through the firing line. On the evening of 4 September, at about 8:00 p.m. D Coy took over from C Coy while the increased strength of the battalion meant that half of A Coy could go down to the beach rest camp at Suvla Bay. Captain Bayley RE went round the lines and sited a position for a new fire trench to join up the gap between the two brigades. A very good night's work was put in on the new communication trench and on the new fire trench between the two brigades. This continued into the next day when another good night's work was put in on a new fire trench, the trench being marked out and traversed for a distance of about 300 yards. Meanwhile, half of B Coy went to the beach rest camp. On 6 September, some new officers in the shape of Lieutenant B J Davies and Second Lieutenants F Rice, A Ballantine and J E M Cochrane joined the battalion. That evening, A Coy relieved D Coy in the fire trench, while B Coy took over the posts on the knoll running out towards 86 Brigade and left a platoon in support there. The fire trench started on 4 September was continued past the new communication trench and joined up with the left of 86 Brigade, while about 200 yards of the new communication trench were improved. A Coy worked at improving their fire trench, during which they had a man wounded at the listening post by sniper fire. Half of B Coy went to the beach rest camp for a break while the adjutant, Captain Aubrey Williams, left the battalion to join the staff of 29 Division. He was replaced by Captain Desmond Somerville.

As Ernest remarks in his next diary entry, after the dramas of Scimitar Hill, life had become relatively quiet, with more activity happening in the rear echelons than on the front line. It was also his wife Sybil's 28th birthday and like so many other servicemen separated from their loved ones as a result of war, his thoughts were with his family at this time:

Monday 6 September 1915

Times are quite quiet except for the constant sniping. Have had a few casualties only from the trenches. More men are being hit at the Aid post next to my cook House than at the trenches. Have managed to get some medical comforts for the men. The wife's birthday – here's luck old girl!

On 7 September, work continued on improving the overall defensive position and a very good night's work was put in on the same trenches as the previous night. The present fire trench was also improved, during which 1/4 Welsh had one man wounded. Of equal importance, work carried on with a new water well (known as Well 39) near to battalion headquarters, where some blasting had been done the day before. Clearly a vital commodity, the close proximity of a fresh water supply would reduce the need for the tedious and back breaking carriage of water containers at night from other locations. An enemy aeroplane passed overhead during the morning going towards the ANZAC position, but it dropped no bombs. During the afternoon, B Coy worked on the communication trench and that evening C Coy went to the beach rest camp. B Coy then relieved A Coy in the top fire trench, putting one platoon in the bottom fire trench so that it joined up with 86 Brigade. C Coy put a platoon in the posts on the knoll while A and D Coys worked on the communication trench. A hill feature some 200 yards to the left front of the bottom fire trench was reconnoitred with a view to putting a post there as ordered by GOC 29 Division, to provide more cover and advance notice of enemy activity. It was found to be very rocky and digging was almost impossible. During this time, C Coy had one man killed while B and D Coys each had one man wounded.

Two days later, on 9 September, another enemy aeroplane passed over the battalion's position from the direction of Chocolate Hill, no doubt carrying out a reconnaissance of its defences. It was fired at by the battalion's guns and quickly veered off to the north east. There was also a change in commanding officer, with Major Going being appointed as a lieutenant colonel to take over from Brevet Colonel Casson, who was promoted to become the brigade commander. That evening, D Coy moved into the new fire trench on the left of 88 Brigade (who had relieved 86 Brigade) and took over about 250 yards of trenches from the Worcester Regiment. Part of the trenches taken over were in excellent condition. The Border Regiment took over about 75 yards of the top fire trench from B Coy, who kept two platoons in support, one on the knoll, and another in a gully running from the communication trench up towards the top fire trench. At dawn, half of C Coy went to the beach rest camp. Some good work was done by companies in the firing line at improving their trenches. The other half of C Coy worked on the communication trench during the afternoon, while A Coy carried on lower down after dark. Half of B Coy in support worked on the posts on the knoll. That evening, they reported hearing a "brass band" behind the enemy's lines, which apparently had been heard the previous week at about the same time. While unlikely to have been a full band, this could well have been a musical instrument of some kind, marking a Muslim religious festival or perhaps the start of the Islamic new year due the following month. To the Turkish soldier, religion was very much part of his daily life even in combat and there were Imams, or religious leaders, in some of the trenches with the soldiers throughout the campaign to assist with and to promote their faith.

By 10 September, a new well (Well 56) had been dug out by the Royal Engineers. The water had been tested and found to be excellent quality and it was anticipated that it would yield a large supply. At the same time, D Coy in the new fire trench was able to draw water from the Worcesters' well, which saved on the problem of water carriers. That evening, a machine gun opened fire on the battalion's left flank, which was closely followed by the Border Regiment's trenches being shelled by the enemy. This was followed by a burst of rifle and machine gun fire from the direction of 88 Brigade. This only lasted 20 minutes, during which the front companies were not fired at, nor did they return any fire. It was felt that the Turks were doing all the firing, trying to draw fire from the battalion, to test and locate their positions. Resupply was still a problem and it was becoming very difficult to obtain medical comforts and stores. The amalgamated battalions had over 190 men going sick in the morning, and the medical officer reported that he could get nothing to treat them with. A large proportion of the men suffered from diarrhoea and it was impossible to give them anything. Meanwhile, D Coy put in some excellent work on their fire trench, and B Coy carried on with theirs. Half of C Coy started to make communication between the top fire trench and the main communication trench, despite the ground being very hard and rocky. Although the Turks made little effort to interfere with the consolidation of the battalion's position along the eastern edge of the Suvla plain, they were busy putting out new trenches of their own. On 11 September a new enemy trench was spotted on a knoll ahead of their main line and in front of 2 SWB's top fire trench, which meant they could snipe down the gully at a range of 700 yards. The battalion was therefore ordered to draw up a plan to attack the enemy's line.

Come mid September, the weather was starting to turn, with the mornings becoming cold and chilly, plus the occasional heavy shower, which the men started to feel, still being dressed in their summer khaki drill. C Coy relieved their half coy in the top fire trench, while half of D Coy started to connect up Nos. 1 and 2 posts on the knoll. B Coy continued number 3 post on for another 60 yards, giving a second tier of fire. Half of B Coy worked on the coy communication trench, while half of C Coy improved the trench leading to top fire trench. Sandbags were in very short supply, but eventually about 800 new sandbags were delivered from the brigade for use the next day. On 14 September, Captain Brand, the brigade major, came up to the position to site the six listening posts to be put out on the spurs in front of the battalion position. Digging was difficult and the filled sandbags, which were very heavy, had to be carried manually. This made progress very slow, and many of the men were physically too weak to carry the cumbersome sandbags up to the position. Work was stopped about 3:30 p.m. by which time all the posts were well under way and two them were fit for occupation. An NCO and two men of A Coy were put into each of these two, one on each spur, and were left out there for the day and the posts were loopholed for sniping. Although in close proximity to the enemy, the work was not interfered with. One man of C Coy was hit by a stray bullet. Rain started about 3:00 p.m. but not very heavily. A message came up about 1:30 p.m. to the effect that a ship was in with eggs and luxuries for purchase. The battalion sent representatives down, who found only cigarettes, matches and sweets, so nothing was purchased.

On the evening of 15 September, fatigue parties from A and D Coys went down to continue the work begun the night before on the spurs. As the covering parties reached the posts on the first hill, they met a party of Turks just beyond the post, who opened fire on them. After a few minutes the covering parties retired back from the hill. When things quietened down, a patrol went out under Second Lieutenant Ballantine and Sergeant Jackson, who managed to work their way all over the hill and reported it clear. Parties for the posts were got together again and the posts occupied and work continued. Two posts on each hill were made secure and garrisoned by four men in each post. The losses in the covering parties were one killed and one missing, while Sergeant Jackson was subsequently awarded the DCM for his outstanding bravery that night. The next day, C Coy carried sandbags out to what was known as Hill A, and connected up Nos. 1 and 2 posts, turning the top end back to the left. Some wire was put out round the posts and also round Nos. 5 and 6 posts on Hill B. The bodies of the soldier killed the night before and of the missing man were found and brought in. At about 2:30 a.m. after the working party had gone back, a bombing party of the enemy came up from the direction of No. 4 post, which had been demolished the night before, and the party of A Coy in the posts were forced off the hill. Two sections of B Coy were sent out from the fire trench under an officer and they reoccupied the posts, now known as "The Horseshoe," until dawn.

At dusk on 17 September, eight men were sent out to relieve the posts on Hill B and a platoon of B Coy to hold Hill A. As soon as they got on to Hill A, they met the enemy on the far side. Intermittent firing and bombing went on until the moon went down about 11:30 p.m. and continued spasmodically until 1:30 a.m. It was difficult to estimate the enemy's numbers, but it was probably about 50 men. The battalion reinforced the hill with a second platoon of B Coy, making about 60 men in total. Meanwhile C Coy and half of D Coy were filling sandbags and carrying them out to the foot of the hill. With brigade headquarters conscious of the need to reinforce the battalions position, 100 men of the Border Regiment were sent to assist in starting two communication trenches from the bottom fire trench out to Hill A and to a proposed new forward line, while the battalion machine gunners were digging three gun emplacements on the end of the knoll. Likewise, 50 men of the Inniskillings were also employed on the knolls. At 1:30 a.m. work began on the posts and continued until just before dawn. Numbers 1, 2 and 3 posts were joined up and bent back so as to form a partially enclosed defence in the form of a horseshoe, giving rise to its new name. Owing to the activity of the enemy it was not possible to put any wire out. Battalion losses were three men killed and nine wounded, including Second Lieutenant JEK Hall, who died of his wounds five days later.

This fighting had involved a couple of dozen casualties, but sickness constituted the chief drain on the battalion's strength. This was growing serious; the need for rest, the monotony of the rations, the virtual impossibility of getting any luxuries and the natural disappointment at the failure of the Suvla offensive, all contributed to sapping the vitality of the men. Nearly everybody, whether he went sick or not, suffered to some extent from diarrhoea. Medical comforts were scarce, many men were too weak for hard work, especially for carrying fully laden sandbags up to the advanced position, so it was a great relief to learn that they were about to be shipped off to Imbros for a proper rest period.[2] Until then though, there was no respite from working on the defences of the Horseshoe and the enemy continued to put in sporadic attacks, but with little effect. Then, as so often happens in the fog of war, a message was received on the morning of 20 September to say that the move to Imbros was to be delayed by 24 hours. That same morning, another attack came in from the enemy which was quickly beaten off, but five men were injured, including Second Lieutenant Cochrane (who had only joined the battalion earlier that month) whose fingers were blown off on one hand from the premature explosion of the detonator of a mills grenade he was holding. Had the whole grenade exploded, he would have been killed.

In the early hours of 22 September, a party of the enemy came up through the gap in the wire below the Horseshoe with the intention of attacking the post. The corporal in the new post on the Gully saw them, and being afraid to fire for fear of hitting his own men in the Horseshoe he shouted to warn them. The Turks then threw about ten bombs at this post, but they all fell short. Then they retired and he fired at them. At about the same time an enemy's patrol was seen behind the Horseshoe, near the mouth of the Gully, by the officer commanding the bottom trench, who was going out with an orderly to visit his posts. The enemy were about 15 strong and went out over the communication trench back to their own position, without being seen by the post on the right of the Horseshoe.

---

2   C T Atkinson, *The History of the South Wales Borderers 1914–1918*, p.185.

That evening, 2 SWB were eventually relieved by 2 Royal Fusiliers. They marched off by 9:20 p.m. and reached A Beach, one of the former landing sites of Suvla Bay, at about 11:00 p.m. After some delay, they found that embarkation was taking place at West Beach, farther round the bay to the north. However, they moved off and everybody was soon on board SS *Prince Abbas* by 12:45 p.m. which was quick, as the second lighter was not supposed to be embarked until 1:30 a.m. At 6:00 a.m. on 23 September, they arrived at Imbros, but the weather was too rough to land. They had to use up their iron rations until other rations could be got to them in the afternoon. Ernest asked for blankets but none arrived. However, they managed to get the lower holds of the ship open and most of the men were at least put under cover for the night. By 3:15 p.m. the next day, lighters were able to come alongside and the battalion was then disembarked and taken to a brigade camp in a valley about one and a half miles south west of the landing stage at Kephalos. It was a good camping ground with small stream of washing water about 300 yards away. This time, the Quartermaster was able to draw one blanket per man from the ordnance depot. On 26 September, Second Lieutenants Evans and Gibbs rejoined from Mudros, bringing 119 other ranks with them, 85 being a draft from Britain and the remainder being sick and wounded rejoining. That afternoon Lieutenant Colonel Going was sent to hospital with dysentery and Captain Aubrey Williams rejoined from the divisional staff to stand in as commanding officer of the battalion. Although this was meant to be a period of rest, training and administration continued, with the men's clothes being washed in neosole solution for hygiene purposes, while all officers were practiced in marching on a compass bearing by night. Training was delegated to coy level, with drill, weapon training and machine gun classes taking most of the day, with some night work as well. There was also time to get into the sea for a much needed bath.

Ernest's diary has been conspicuous in its absence for the last two weeks as he now explains, as well as filling in the detail of some of the main events, in his own inimitable style:

Tuesday 28 September 1915

Have sadly neglected my diary, principally because one has not been feeling up to the mark and the fly nuisance has been abominable. Can't remember much of any consequence during the remaining days we remained at the trenches. Gen de Lisle came round on several occasions and ordered various improvements and some advanced posts to be made. The latter proved somewhat ticklish. Five new fellows from the 3rd Bn joined. Capt Robertson – 2nd Lieutenants Page, Cochrane, Rice and Ballantyne. The latter went out with a Lance Corporal one night after the working party had been bombed out of the advanced post and found no Turks there. He has been recommended for the Military Cross and the Lance Corporal for the DCM. Pretty quick work for a tyro with less than a week's active service. Awfully jolly fellow and as Scotch as a kilt. Poor Cochrane had a rotten accident while bombing. Kept the bomb too long in his hand and blew all his fingers off. The new bomb – Mills. Had an attack the night before by the Turks on this post which the sight of seems to worry considerably. They hit Hall badly twice – once through the lung – he was doing well, but now I hear he died on the way to Imbros. We lost about a dozen killed up there and about 30 wounded. Several of the latter were hit by the cook House and Aid post. Bullets came from all directions at night except from direct near. Capt Williams (Adjt) was taken from us on 6th September on Div Staff. Capt Ellis to hospital sick the same day and Lt Jones a few days later with dysentery. The men are suffering horribly with the same complaint. Over 200 attending hospital – nearly all with the same trouble.

At last our time came for Brigade rest at Imbros. We left on night of 22nd being relieved by 7th RF and embarked on the 'Prince Abbas.' Arrived at Imbros by daylight or sooner, but found it too rough to land. There we stayed all next day and night. Had a rousing good time in the saloon that night and let off a little steam. Disembarked following evening 24th and marched to camp about 1½ miles from the beach. Got into pyjamas once more! What a treat! On 26th we heard that we were returning on 28th. Spirits down to zero again. Men are still very sick and about fifty have been sent to hospital including the Colonel (Going) and Capt Davies – all same old complaint. Capt Williams returned and took over command. (When Going went sick, Capt Somerville assumed temporary command, having handed over duties as Ack Adjutant to me. The arrival however of Williams the same day cancelled this). Yesterday good news came that we are not going back until Monday 4th Oct. Hooray! Got a good draft of 119 including two ex wounded officers Gibbs and Evans – many of the men are old hands and a lot of them have been in France. Some really good news came in last night from France. The French had broken through the Huns on a front of 50 kilometres. This was confirmed today and a splendid wire from Lord Kitchener about our successes and captures and more to follow. God I hope we keep 'em going now – and they aren't getting it all their own way in Russia either. Greece is mobilising – no doubt because Bulgaria has declared an armed neutrality. Had six hours off today and rode to Panaghir about five miles away. Rotten Road but fine scenery and the wine of the country and omelettes are worth sampling. No improvement in the number of dysentery cases. Handed in 60 odd sets of equipment today of men sent to hospital since we came to Imbros. We seem to have plenty of aeroplanes over here. A school of instruction is in full swing and a miniature Zep makes flights looking for submarines. Have just heard I have another son born on the 11th.

This one short sentence at the end of the diary entry belies the considerable emotion that Ernest would have felt at receiving this wonderful news. His wife Sybil was at home in Brecon where their third son, Eric Graham, was born on 11 September 1915. His elder brothers both joined the services later on, but Eric was the only one to follow his father into the South Wales Borderers, reaching the rank of Major. The "Zep" refers to the German rigid airship, which was being used for reconnaissance purposes.

* * *

Picking up the trail of the 4th Battalion once more, their account tells us that:

On the 2nd September orders for a general move were received. The whole of the 13th Division were to proceed by units to Suvla, their trenches to be handed over to the Australians. Part of the Borderers trenches were taken over this day by the 2nd Battalion Australian Light Horse and the remainder the next day. At 8pm on the 3rd the battalion started for Suvla Bay, a march of about five miles. The night was dark and the going very heavy and sandy, whilst for the first two miles stray bullets whistled and hummed over the men's heads, one man being hit on his canteen. Reaching the sea side of Lala Baba Hill, the men were dumped down to get what rest they could amongst the rocks and quarries along the shore. The roseate hues of early dawn revealed the filth of this horrible spot. It was littered with broken bully beef tins, scraps of meat, old boots, and other discarded rubbish, the dug outs being merely unlighted incinerators filled to the brim with unconsumed fuel.

The late occupants had sorely neglected the regulations, which strongly recommend and indeed forcibly insist that camps and bivouacs shall be vacated in a clean and healthy condition – result, constant fatigue parties to clean up. The Turks delighted in shelling Lala Baba; the landing stages and Divisional Headquarters were close by and as it was always crowded with troops and pack animals they were generally able to bag something or other, aimed they never so badly. On 1st September they killed 100 mules and on the 2nd 26 of the Scottish Horse were knocked out.

At this time the battalion had dwindled down to a mere cadre of its former self. Up to the end of August it had lost seven officers killed and 13 wounded and amongst other ranks 95 killed, 324 wounded and 22 missing. Thus it was reduced in strength on the 4th September to 15 officers and 335 other ranks.

The efforts of the 4th Battalion were much appreciated by their senior officers. When 13 Division left the Anzac force to return to IX Corps, which was still occupying the low ground of Suvla Bay, General Alex Godley wrote to the divisional commander, General Maude and to the commander 40 Brigade, Brigadier General Travers expressing his appreciation:

NZ and Australian Div
1st Sept 1915
To Major General Maude CB CMG DSO

My dear Maude,
I must write a line on the departure of the 13th Div to say how very much I appreciate the honour of having it under my command from 5th to 31st August and to ask you to express to all officers, non commissioned officers and men of all ranks of it, my thanks for all they did during this trying time of particularly arduous fighting. Plunged as they were into the middle of a considerable battle, with no opportunity of becoming acquainted with the country and its difficulties, or of becoming in any way accustomed to their new surroundings and practically no opportunities for any rest or sleep, many of your battalions rendered conspicuous good service, notably in the covering force which occupied Damakjelik Bair (i.e. 4 SWB) and the column which first occupied the advanced trenches on Chunuk Bair. I deplore very much the heavy casualties, which were the inevitable result, but hope that your division will realise how conscious we are of the substantial share which it took in such successes as we achieved during the period that it was here.
Yours very sincerely,
(Sgd) Alex L Godley

And then to the commander of 40 Brigade:

NZ and Australian Div
2nd Sept 1915
From General Godley to Brig General Travers
My dear Travers,
I was very sorry to miss you when you came to say goodbye yesterday, as I wished to thank you very much for all that you and your brigade have done for us during the time you were here. Your occupation of Damakjelik Bair, the work done by the 4th South Wales Borderers

at Kabak Kuyu Well and your subsequent occupation of the "Apex" were of the greatest possible value to the operations and could not have been better done. Will you please let all ranks of your Brigade know how very much we appreciate the work they did here.
Yours very sincerely,
(Sgd) Alex L Godley

4 SWB's report continues:

It must not be supposed that it was a peaceful rest, this stay at Suvla Bay, or that the troops enjoyed a quiet and easy time. On the contrary they had probably more hard work during these three weeks or so than at any other time during the campaign. Trenches had to be dug around Lala Baba and the men had eight hours digging and manning them to do practically every night, whilst the day was taken up in unloading ships, building winter shelters on the cliffs and technical instructions. For some days there were rumours that the battalion would shortly receive a draft to reinforce it and sure enough the draft arrived on the 6th Sept, but it only consisted of one young officer and no men. On the same date the men received their first issue of fresh meat for six weeks, namely about a quarter of a pound per man, but it was so tough that only the most desperate were able to partake of it. On the night of the 12th it rained heavily for the first time and even in this easily drained position it caused much annoyance and discomfort.

On the 18th the Brigadier General, commanding officers and all company commanders of the brigade marched up to the front line trenches – shortly to be taken over – in order to find out all about them. As the ground was very open the party moved up in twos and threes to prevent being shelled. It was a three mile walk to the trenches and the ground passed over was strewn with shrapnel and rifle bullets, relics of the August fighting. The same evening, Gen Maude held a conference at the divisional headquarters at Lala Baba to arrange about taking over these trenches. All the senior officers of the division were present and whilst it was taking place the bullets from Turkish shrapnel struck the roof of the sandbag House they were in, another shell bursting with a loud bang over the House. This apparently inspired a young staff officer with a brilliant idea. He secured an old empty shell case and removing a few sandbags from the roof, he hurled it into a corner of the House. Everyone thought it was a live shell, but no one moved but just gazed at it in dull consternation why it did not explode and get done with it. It was only after quite a considerable time that a daring officer examined it and disclosed the jest. It is not recorded what became of the young officer.

After dark on the 19th, the Division started moving up into the trenches to relieve the 53rd Division and it was whilst the battalion was marching up that CSM W Bush was mortally wounded. Capt Hooper was also hit at one of the halts by a spent bullet. It struck him somewhere in his cap with a particularly loud whack and knocked him over, but a quarter of an hour afterwards, after having his head bandaged, he pluckily returned and led his company into the trenches. He had however to go to the hospital the next day.

In order to supply these trenches with provisions etc. carts were sent up under cover of night from the divisional dump about two miles back with stores which were deposited on an open space of ground in rear of the trenches and transferred thereto after dark. This was a happy hunting ground for the Turkish sniper, who was ever on the alert and who fired at these dumps in the dark, hoping to demolish some man or beast. The trenches were situated due west of Anafarta Sagir, which was about two miles away and although the position was higher than the shore at Suvla Bay, they lay in a hollow as compared with the trenches on either side of them. They were good trenches, nice and clean, and picturesquely situated amidst cornfields and trees. They were full of a kind of long nosed rat, which kept squealing and running about at night, which with an occasional snake, centipede or biting ant, helped curtail the delights of a peaceful night's rest. The men stood to arms every morning at 4.30, receiving then their tot of rum when there was any and after that, those not actually in the firing line were kept busy most of the day with digging and other fatigue work, whilst almost constant shelling and sniping completed the programme. One could not help feelings of despondency and doubt recurring in one's mind from time to time, growing ever stronger as the days passed by and the monotony of trench life with its irksome duties seized and gripped the imagination.

Tied to the positions we had won and unable to advance further – except by spasmodically pushing forward a trench here and there – there came no effort, nor signs of any effort to crush the Turk and push along; the offensive spirit was there, but the force of numbers was wanting. It was indeed difficult to see how an advance could be made anywhere about here without large reinforcements, as the Turkish lines had become most formidable objects; they themselves were in great strength and their artillery was constantly being augmented with small and large calibre guns from Germany or elsewhere. On the other hand our own guns were becoming worn out and inaccurate and the skilful gunners of the earlier days had been largely replaced by men of far less training and experience. As for the infantry there was just about enough to hold the lines and carry on fatigues and those in the front line trenches often had to stay there for weeks and weeks on end without being relieved and there was now so much sickness amongst the troops that their numbers were becoming alarmingly decreased and it was known or surmised that no more help would be sent from home. However there was generally some diversion going on to stifle vain regrets.

At 5am on the 26th, after the Turks had poured a heavy cannonade on this sector, chiefly with French 75s, they rushed forth from their trenches shouting their usual battle cry of Allah! Allah! and looked most formidable and determined as they charged towards the lines. Our gunners got to work on them at once, bursting several shrapnel shells beautifully over them. This, together with the withering fire from the trenches quite deterred all their further efforts and turning tail they simply bolted back to their trenches for all they were worth and the show ended.

The fire from these French 75s is particularly unpleasant as their trajectory is very low and they seem to skim the air just over your head with an extra loud whistle. You cannot hear the shell coming as you can from most other guns and they seemed to be suddenly right on top of you without any premonition. They were affectionately known as "Whiz Bangs." Not content with this defeat, the Turks next night attacked the trenches near Chocolate Hill and for about an hour and a half there was an absolute inferno of rifle firing which however died down at about 8.30, and nothing very much seemed to have happened one way or the other.

On the 29th, preparations were made by the 40th Brigade to push forward some of their trenches, when an order suddenly came for the Division to move elsewhere next day. So on the 30th, the 13th Division once more got on the move for the trenches round and about Chocolate Hill to relieve the 10th Division who were stationed there, while the famous old 29th Division took over the trenches vacated by the 13th Division. In these movements each battalion as a rule marched separately. The Borderers started off at 8pm into the open just behind the trenches and after a march of about two miles in the direction of Anzac over very rough ground they reached their destination , taking over their fire trenches the next day.

The strength of the battalion on the 30th had been reduced to 10 officers and 211 other ranks, but this as in the previous month had not necessarily been caused by casualties in action. Major Kitchin and Capt Hooper had been slightly wounded, CSM Bush, Sergeant Willis and Private Inson had been killed, five men wounded and one missing, whilst some of the men previously missing had returned, but during the month four officers and 132 men had gone to hospital so that the decrease was chiefly owing to sickness and lack of drafts.

The position of the new battalion trenches was immediately under Scimitar Hill and about a quarter of a mile from the Turkish trenches thereon, which overlooked and dominated our own almost everywhere. Scimitar Hill or Hill 70 had been captured by the 29th Division on the 21st August, who however were subsequently forced to retire to the positions now occupied on the outlying under feature of Chocolate Hill, so called from its peculiar brownish colour. The trenches in most cases were badly dug, and in some cases they afforded so little cover as to be positively dangerous, chiefly owing to the stony nature of the ground and here again the troops had to spend much time with pick and shovel. The water question here as elsewhere was a constant source of difficulty as practically all the few wells were overlooked and keenly watched by snipers and four men of the battalion were shot on their second day in this sector whilst drawing water.

The Turks seemed to have been very suspicious of our movements about this time, and evidently anticipated a clash of arms before long. Their constant short bursts of heavy rifle fire, their heavy shelling at times and great vigilance indicated a tension of nerves quite inconsistent with simple trench warfare and a total ignorance of the condition of affairs on our side. Their guns had now become greatly increased and they had planted two horrible fellows somewhere on the heights up north, which were perpetually searching for our batteries on Chocolate Hill, the shells passing over the heads of the battalion en route and very often firing at its trenches also. The shells which were 8 or 9 inch made a most abominable noise and pulverised whatever they hit, and though their effect was fairly local they made sure that the locality was well attended to. Many attempts were made by the Navy to knock out these guns, but never a one succeeded.

* * *

Meanwhile, the 2nd Battalion was coming to the end of its 10 day rest period at Imbros. On 1 October, orders were received to return to the mainland, not to Suvla Bay, but back to Cape Helles once again with the remainder of 87 Brigade. During the morning, the battalion was out practicing with the Mills bomb when two men were badly hurt and five others injured during a training accident. The reason is not clear, but the fact that the battalion was called back to camp suddenly because the commander in chief was about to visit, may have been a contributory factor; unfortunately accidents do occur during training with live ammunition from time to time. By mid-day, the battalion was on parade and General Hamilton walked along the lines and spoke to individual men. He seemed pleased with what he saw and said "If we could only put you into clean clothes and give you two months in England you would face the world. As it is we have to get along as best we can".[3]

No sooner had the general gone than there was the usual unseemly scramble to pack and move to the transport ships. First of all, orders were received for all baggage to be ready for loading by 4:30 p.m. Then at 2:30 p.m. this was countermanded by orders for all baggage to be on the pier

3   R Welsh Museum, 2 SWB War Diary 1 October 1915.

by 3:30 p.m. with 500 men ready by 4:00 p.m. and the remainder by 4:30 p.m. to embark on SS *River Fisher* and SS *Viceroy* respectively. At 5:00 p.m. SS *Viceroy* sailed with Bn HQ and A, B and C Coys, while the balance of 400 sailed in SS *River Fisher*; the baggage came on a separate trawler. SS *Viceroy* arrived at Lancashire Landing (W Beach) at about 6:45 p.m. from where the battalion disembarked and moved into reserve trenches near 52 Division headquarters.

Ernest covers the administrative side of this hurried move in his next diary entry and he was not best pleased with the unnecessary scramble, which seemed to become a prevalent feature of troop movements on the peninsula:

Friday 1 October 1915

Sir Ian Hamilton came and had a look at the troops and a word to say with a few of the men. Orders came about noon to hold ourselves in readiness to proceed to Helles same night. Had to pack in a violent hurry as usual and got baggage to the beach and men as well by 4 pm. Got away in two boats. Our boat with Bn HQ left immediately and was over at W Beach before dark though it took some time to disembark. Got the baggage off the boat by something after 2 am and got to Bn Lines near Pink Farm and unloaded by 4 am, eventually settling down myself half an hour later. We are now on the Plain as Corps reserve – why we were called away from Imbros in such a violent hurry one cannot conjecture. We thought there must certainly be a big "strafe" on. Everything instead is wonderfully quiet. We sent a lot more to hospital before leaving Imbros so our draft was certainly needed and is swallowed up. Ration strength now 570.

By the early hours of 2 October the battalion was in the reserve trenches on the West Krithia Road, to the south west of Pink Farm, where 87 Brigade was part of the corps reserve. The battalion left 47 sick men behind on leaving Imbros, arriving back at Cape Helles with 12 officers, (including the medical officer) and 559 other ranks. The commander 8 Corps, Major General Davies, came to visit the battalion, as did the former CO, Brigadier General Casson, in his capacity as brigade commander. The relentless task of trench digging continued as two groups of one NCO and 24 men were employed for three hours each that evening in digging a new brigade headquarters. Captain E J W Byrne was sent to hospital with dysentery, while the baggage left at Suvla arrived and was brought up to the battalion dump (the administrative holding area) under the control of the quartermaster. On the morning of 3 October, one platoon of A Coy was sent to corps headquarters for reserve duty, to be relieved by 1 KOSB on 11 October. Then there was the new Bde HQ position to be finished, which entailed fatigue parties of one NCO and six men working in two hour shifts throughout the whole of the day. Meanwhile, the proceedings of the board of enquiry into the mills bomb accident on 1 October were forwarded to brigade headquarters for deliberation. Then there was good news in the shape of captured enemy trench maps and Turkish advanced trenches being received.

To familiarise themselves with the remainder of the main defensive position, on 4 October half the officers of the battalion went round the trenches held by the Royal Naval Division in the morning and the other half in the afternoon. This included a portion of the 42 Division's line on the east of Gully Ravine, which the battalion had held, with breaks, from 28 June until leaving for Suvla Bay in mid August. The relentless task of trench preparation continued with reliefs of one NCO and 15 men being employed on digging the new brigade HQ from 9:00 a.m. to 7:00 p.m. while a further two reliefs of 50 men under an officer took over from 7:00 p.m. to 3:00 a.m.

Meanwhile the Quartermaster regained some of his transport in the way of four ammunition carts and some horses by the way of eight pack cobs, and three chargers and there was an opportunity to bathe at X Beach. The next day the trenches of 52 Division were visited, while the preparation of brigade HQ continued unabated, as well as tidying up the beach at Lancashire Landing. Sickness and disease was still a problem with 91 men attending hospital on the morning of 5 October alone, out of 557 – almost 20 percent of the fighting strength. On 6 October, a welcome resupply of clothing and equipment arrived, but, like the curate's egg, it was not all good news. There were 100 service dress (SD) jackets, 300 pairs of socks, 150 SD caps and 100 cap comforters (woollen liners which kept the head warm). However, there were no shirts, trousers nor boots, which were the items most needed. That said, every man was now complete with iron rations, gas helmets, field and iodine dressings, and sandbags of which two were carried tied to the belt for use in case of any attack; presumably to create an instant dugout. Additional officers were drafted into the battalion – Lieutenant OC Bodley from the 9th Battalion and Second Lieutenants DW Mein, RDB Beardshaw, and CF Sutton, all from the 3rd Battalion. As an amusing aside, on 7 October, at about 11:45 a.m. an enemy aircraft appeared to the north east of the battalion's position, which was engaged by a British monoplane and driven off. Bn HQ then received a phone call from bde HQ to say that there was an enemy aircraft to the north east of the battalion's position – news travels fast! Then at 12.30 p.m. another message was received saying that there was an enemy plane moving west from Chocolate Hill, but nothing was seen.

As well as looking after battalion administration, Ernest liked to keep abreast of the bigger picture:

Thursday 7 October 1915

We hear that Bulgaria is in against us and that Greece has backed out just when they are wanted. With a pro-German on the throne, some trouble was expected but I should have thought the voice of the people would be too strong and they are all for war apparently. Had good news yesterday from France, where they have gone through to the last line of German trenches – this evidently means the last line in that particular locality I suppose. A big fight is expected. Another four officers joined today – Second Lieutenants Davies, Edwards, Karran and Mason. This brings us up to 19 now. Over 50 officers have joined since we arrived here in April.

Friday 8 October 1915

With a heavy thunderstorm today, which stopped work on the trenches at about 8.15pm, there are signs of a breakup of the fine weather. Hope it won't come till our new dugouts are ready – when they are, no doubt we will be kicked out and sent to elsewhere as usual – probably back to Suvla. We hear nothing of the rest of the Division coming here, so I suppose we will go back there (i.e. Suvla) in a desperate hurry. Heard yesterday we were getting a draft of 500! This boiled down to 50 today and they are expected tonight.
Saturday 9 October 1915

Draft of one officer (Second Lieutenant Cooke) and 50 men arrived last night from 3rd Bn. The KOSBs got a huge draft of about 500 men which brings them up to 1200. The Inniskillings seem to be out of it and are still only about 250 strong. We are now 625 including 21 officers and another (Briscoe) who joined today making 22. The strongest we have been for some months I think. Briscoe is a survivor of the Royal Edward. Lost everything of course. Tells me he hung on to a piece of wood for four hours. Chilly![4]

All coys put in three hours work during the morning of 10 October on the winter quarters, sandbagging parapets and digging out earth. This continued into the evening with another three hours work put in, as well as on Roads and drains, involving about 320 men. An interesting but sobering manning return was sent to Brigade HQ, showing seven officers (including the medical officer), one warrant officer and 225 other ranks of the battalion still serving on the peninsula, who landed on 25 April. Of these, four officers, one warrant officer and 184 other ranks were still with the battalion itself while the remainder were deployed elsewhere in various locations – all this from an original start state of 27 officers and 1008 other ranks.

The monotonous task of working on the winter quarters continued on 11 October, while the platoon of A Coy detached to corps HQ at the beginning of the month returned to the battalion. A very heavy thunderstorm was about all the afternoon, but only a shower fell on the battalion lines. Work carried on during the evening, with 11 new dugouts started as well as more work on the communication trenches. As ever, the men worked very well, with sickness and diarrhoea much reduced. Since leaving the trenches at Suvla Bay in the heat of summer, the battalion had had a good rest, and was much improved in every way. Two cases of 120 dozen eggs (i.e. a total of 2,880 eggs) were obtained from brigade by the quartermaster and sold to the men at the cost price of one shilling (5p) per dozen, compared with an average price of £1.50p per half dozen today! Not only was this a most welcome supplement to the diet, but it was hoped that it would become a regular supply. Operational training continued, with Second Lieutenant Gibbs and two corporals being sent to the 52 Division bomb school, which was quite close to the battalion lines, for a six day course and then the battalion was warned that it would move into Eski Lines on 14 October; this order was then subsequently delayed by a further 24 hours. The sandbagging of parapets continued apace, with over 9,000 sandbags being used on the winter quarters so far. When laid out flat, a sandbag would measure about two feet long by one foot wide and once full of sand would weigh about 30lbs. Not only were they filled by hand, but they also had to be carried by hand as well, unless a transport cart was available. To assist with this long and demanding task, two coys of 1 KOSB were called on to help, so that the job could be finished before the battalion moved out of the lines.

Ernest had some comments to make on a few administrative issues:

Thursday 14 October 1915

Nothing doing except a few rounds of Arty fire – the French fire about 10 rounds to our one; we take over a part of their line tomorrow. Went round their trenches – very clean, but very narrow. The carrying of rations from Eski line to the firing line (about a mile) is going to be a business as they are too narrow for mule transport. One good thing they have a water supply laid on and pumped from Romanos Well. The supply of clothing and necessaries is quite at a standstill and the men have not had a new shirt or socks for months. Had their shirts and trousers bathed in creosol whilst at Imbros which 'strafed' the close 'friends'.[5] Apparently the breaking of the tic is only temporary however, judging by the number of men one sees hunting through their nether garments. I have been very fortunate and very careful myself,

4   In 1915, an officer had to buy all his own uniforms and equipment, usually from a military tailor.
5   A reference to lice and fleas.

although I could not give a clean bill if asked. One picks one up on the beach occasionally – or did do – have my bath in the bucket now and the frequent use of a little lavender oil has proved of inestimable value. Luxuries what!

At 6:30 a.m. on 15 October, the battalion moved up into the Eski Line as divisional reserve to 52 Division. C Coy moved off first and went into Parsons Road, about 1,500 yards ahead of the Eski Line, close to the headquarters of the Border Regiment who had taken over about 500 yds of the French trenches, and were now on the right of 52 Division. The other coys followed at half hour intervals and took over parts of the Eski Line and trenches round the Brown House from the French. B Coy were in the Eski Line to the west of the Achi Baba Nullah, while A and D Coys were on the east, with Bn HQ at Brown House. Three of the battalion's machine guns were put in the firing line under command of CO the Border Regiment. Most of the baggage had been sent up the previous evening, with the remainder arriving about 6:30 p.m. No sooner had they arrived, than the coys continued to work at improving the existing line and on various other administrative duties; for example, 84 men were employed carrying boxes of ammunition and the ubiquitous sandbags up to the Border Regiment, while water had to be carried forward from the Romanos well, which was about 400 yards to the rear. The water was then chlorinated in the water carts, and water parties were sent down with individual water bottles to top up. Treated water never tastes the same, but it was welcome, whatever the taste or condition. As far as cooking was concerned, the quartermaster provided most of this centrally, but due to their locations, B and C Coys were to cook for themselves. There was little or no enemy activity during this move, apart from one man being wounded by a stray shot. In his usual erudite style, Ernest's diary keeps abreast of international affairs, as well as routine matters. He also adds a poignant note about the late Major Margesson, whom he would have known well:

Friday 15 October 1915

Started the companies off in small batches of six or eight men up to the Eski Lines and took over from the French. This part of the line was originally held by the Royal Naval Division till the 29th Div went to Suvla. This is the first time we have been on the right since we left Tott's Battery on 28th April after the landing. Went over there a few days ago and put new head crosses on the graves of Maj Margesson and the men killed on landing. These were nicely painted with the Regimental Crest by Pioneer Sergeant Kelly. De Tott's Battery is in much the same condition as when we left, but the site of our own trenches outside is all altered now by horse lines and dug outs of the French. We got most of our kit moved up last night. What with trekking down to the beach to see the dentist and twice up to Eski Lines one was quite ready for bed afterwards. News came through that the Austro-German army has invaded Serbia from the north and Bulgaria from the south, so our poor little allies are getting snuff. One hears that we have sent an allied contingent to help them consisting of English, French and Italian troops. M. Venizelos says the Greeks will hold to this bargain to help the Serbs. I wonder if they really will now. We seem to be doing well elsewhere. At present there seems to be no sign this side of any assistance from the Central Powers either in men or munitions. The Turks certainly shell us systematically every day, but not so much as they might do by a long way as if they were well supplied and most of the field gun ammunition is poor stuff – many thanks, too. Unfortunately poor Maj Stoney and another officer of the KOSB were killed this morning by a shell from the Asiatic side into their dug out. Maj Stoney joined some months ago from the Gyppy Army and commanded the battalion till his death. He is a serious loss to the Regiment. The young Adjt now takes command I believe.

The next day work carried on improving trenches, digging a new and secure ration area and a bomb dump. 40 men carried ammunition and sandbags to the Border Regiment in the morning while 100 men took 400 gallons of water up in the afternoon, a back breaking task at the best of times. To give an idea of the length and monotony of battalion administration, two reliefs of 40 men each worked all night from 8:00 p.m. to 4:00 a.m. under the control of the Border Regiment. An enemy aeroplane came over and was fired at by troops in the front line, as they had orders now to open rifle fire on any hostile aircraft within range. Full of enthusiasm after his course of instruction, Second Lieutenant Gibbs held a bombing class for one officer, one NCO and three men of each coy, giving instruction in the making of bombs, as well as forming a bombing section of grenadiers.

Once again, Ernest adds to the round of administrative necessities and has a swipe at the difference in the promotion system between regular officers and those on a late entry commission:

Saturday 16 October 1915

Only one casualty last night. This man was standing near me when we were off loading kits and blankets. I thought the bullet had struck a valise by the sound, until the man fell over. We took him to the dressing station, where Blake the doctor soon fixed him up. He was hit on corner of the chin and the bullet went into the right breast. It was severe but apparently not dangerous. Had a good night's rest in a French dressing station, a well made one with a good roof. They do things rather well and make themselves pretty comfortable. Have just had an enemy plane over, which our men fired at; of course without effect. Our mess is in a rather exposed position and one shell would settle the hash if it came right. An exchange of pleasantries is going on now over our heads. The Turks have got up some better ammunition lately which sings in all sorts of keys on explosion like the wind through the rigging of a vessel during a storm. It sounds better at a distance. Major Lucas who was our Brigade Major before he went to Suvla and then took over the command of the brigade with the temp rank of Lieut Colonel has been appointed temporary Brig General. As this will probably become a permanency, just think of the promotion in one year! He was Capt when the war started. He's a good level headed fellow though and deserves all he gets. I wish they'd think of the poor QMs though who stand still and go on at the same old pace of ten years for a Captaincy and see temporary Second Lieutenants who after commanding a company a month go up to captain.

As the battalion war diary for 18 October records, work continued as ever on the ubiquitous trenches, with a new cookhouse being made at the corner of Central Street and Back House Road to facilitate feeding the battalion when they moved into the firing line next day. This took two reliefs of 20 men three hours each, while working parties carried 200 trench mortars and bombs, along with 120 gallons of water, up to the Border Regiment. In addition, all of the battalion rations had to be manhandled up to the new cookhouse in the evening, while another 80 men started a new brigade headquarters off Leith Walk, working well into the night to achieve this. The next day 9:30 a.m. the battalion moved up into the firing line and relieved the Border Regiment. Their right flank joined the French and their left flank joined 156 Brigade, just below the Eglington Tunnel. They found the trenches very narrow and the parapet too high to fire over; it was also not very bullet proof in places. It would seem that the French did all their observation work through loopholes, rather than periscopes, so the battalion decided to carry on the same way. They also pushed the parapet forward and strengthened it, building a firing step and widened the trench to the rear in a few places. A, B and D Coys were in the firing line; B Coy were next to the French, A Coy was in the centre, with D Coy on the left. C Coy was in support behind the Horseshoe on the eastern side of Achi Baba Nullah. Bn HQ was on Central Street between Parsons Road and Trotman Road. The stretcher bearers and other administrative elements of Bn HQ were also on Trotman Road. To round off the position, a new support trench was dug, which took two reliefs of 200 men from the Border Regiment virtually all night to complete. Ernest confirms the various arrangements, adding a few details of his own:

Tuesday 19 October 1915

Relieved the 1st Border Regiment in the fire trenches while they taking our place in support. We put our ration dump and cook House 400 yds nearer the firing line than they had it. The Turks shelled it with shrapnel this morning – evidently the smoke gave it away. One case came into the trench and a good deal of dust but nothing worse happened. A couple burst while I was there and almost cracked my ear drums. The Greeks appear to be backing out of the show as they don't consider they need hold to their bargain to help Serbia as it is not a Balkan war. I am staying with the Doctor in his aid post up here – a good one built by the French. They seem to get plenty of good material and the CO's place is practically bomb proof. We are told to expect an attack from the enemy in the next few days. The French reported yesterday seeing a battalion massing behind Krithia, but the night passed quietly enough.

It is surprising at this point that Ernest, usually the most perceptive of officers who kept abreast of the bigger picture, makes no mention of the fact that General Hamilton was relieved of his command this week. On 15 October, the General received a personal telegram from Lord Kitchener which read:

the War Council held last night decided that though the Government fully appreciate your work and the gallant manner in which you personally have struggled to make the enterprise a success, in face of the terrible difficulties you have had to contend with, they, all the same, wish to make a change in the command which will give them an opportunity of seeing you.[6]

Wasting no time at all, General Hamilton left Imbros the next day, along with his chief of staff, General Sir Walter Braithwaite and after a farewell dinner on *Triad*, boarded the cruiser *Chatham* on 17 October and sailed away from the peninsula, never to return. Selected to replace him was General Sir Charles Carmichael Monro. Born in 1860, he was commissioned into the 2nd of Foot (The Queen's Royal (West Surrey) Regiment) in 1879 and served in a number of staff positions during the South African War of 1899–1902. Promoted to major general in 1910, he served on the Western Front on the outbreak of war and by July 1915 he was commanding the new British third army in the rank of general. As he could not get out to Gallipoli until the end of the month, General Birdwood was to stand in for him.

6   Alan Moorehead, *Gallipoli*, p.312.

If it seemed that the battle had gone rather quiet for the time being, there was evidence that the enemy were mining under the battalion area, with the aim of creating a large underground explosion, which would cause heavy casualties and a major collapse of the trenches in the firing line. Therefore, on 20 October the 8th Corps mining coy began to drive in a counter mine, in an attempt to beat the enemy at their own game. 2 SWB had four skilled miners working in six hour shifts on the mine by night, with the Border Regiment finding the same by day. The battalion also supplied fatigue parties to remove the earth and had 10 men from C Coy and a bombing party kept ready in a communication trench to rush in and seize the cratered area as soon as the explosion went off. In addition, a new machine gun emplacement was built to sweep the approaches to the area, while a patrol went out to reconnoitre an old trench leading out from the salient; they heard voices about 40 yards out, but no noise of digging. Then on a personal note from Ernest:

Wednesday 20 October 1915

Brother Tom's birthday. Wonder where he is? France somewhere if he has not already been 'strafed.'[7] Went out with the first Canadian Contingent I think. Except for artillery, all quiet this side.

Born on 20 October 1872, Thomas Alexander was three years older than Ernest and this was his 43rd birthday. He joined the Royal Engineers initially, but then emigrated to live in New Brunswick, Canada. He served on the Western Front with the Canadian contingent, but little is known of his life thereafter, apart from the fact that he survived the war and eventually died in Canada.

Enemy aerial activity continued and on the morning of 21 October an Aviatik biplane flew over the battalion position; it was fired at by their firing line, but without success. Then a Taube aircraft was reported coming in from the Anzac area, but did not appear. Later, there were a few shrapnel bursts near the cookhouse, but no damage was caused. The French continued to bombard the enemy trenches to their front with trench mortars, which seemed to have considerable effect. That apart, the day was fairly quiet with little bombing activity by the Turks. By the use of a simple catapult, the battalion could launch grenades into the enemy trenches when the wind was not too strong, but mortars continued to be the most effective. On the firing line, work continued restoring and strengthening the parapet, as well as building the firing step. New machine gun emplacements and sniper's posts were also prepared. The battalion miners continued their work in a race against time, but they heard no sounds of enemy mining. That night, the moon was too strong to do any wiring, but the Turks came out to try on two occasions and were driven in by rifle fire. For his troubles, one eager Turkish soldier was working on his parapet in the early dawn, only to be shot dead. Then, on the morning of 22 October, Major General the Honourable H A Laurence, commanding 52 Division came round the trenches and expressed his great satisfaction and surprise at the work done by the brigade as a whole since its arrival from Imbros.

By 23 October, 2 SWB was holding about 500 yards of the front line at Cape Helles, exclusive of traverses and machine gun positions. The effective strength in firing line however was down to about 320 men; a sobering indication of the effect illness, disease and exhaustion was having on the manning of the battalion. D Coy had one platoon in the Couronne and at night sent one platoon into the Horseshoe. They carried on with the work on the trenches as they had on previous days and as it was very wet that evening with the moon being clouded over, they decided to take the

---

7   A colloquial expression for being shot at, attacked, or even killed.

opportunity to put wire out. Supplies of French wire were used, until the whole front was wired except about 60 yards in front of B Coy. This was because a Royal Engineer sapper was spotted by the Turks and was fired on, thus giving the work away, so that the battalion could not complete the whole length. The Turks took advantage of this activity to work on their own parapet, but as soon as the battalion's own wiring was finished, they opened up on the Turks with a machine gun and stopped them working any more.

The battalion then kept up a good rate of fire, as well as using garland grenades, which were on trial during the campaign. A simple, improvised design, the garland mortar (designed by Herbert Garland) consisted of a smoothbore steel barrel fixed at 45 degrees to a solid wooden base. By means of a powder charge it propelled a variant of the jam tin grenade; so called because when demand for grenades was at its greatest, engineers were encouraged to improvise their own grenades from the tins containing the soldier's ration of jam, hence the name. The grenade was an inner can of explosive with an outer can of metal fragments or ball bearings. The heavier pattern number 9 grenade contained more high explosive and more metal fragments. The fuse was ignited by a friction device or a cigarette. Incidents with the improvised form and the supply of superior grenades led to official withdrawal of the design.

The weather was starting to turn now and the next day was very cold after the night's rain. In preparation for an eight day break, 2 SWB was relieved by a composite battalion of the Inniskilling Fusiliers and KOSB, a reflection yet again of manpower shortages. Relief came up by platoons, starting at 9:30 a.m. and was completed by about 1:30 p.m. The battalion then went back into its new winter quarters on the West Krithia Road, which had been vacated by 1 KOSB. Dugouts had been completed, but no roofs had been put on yet. It was a cold, dull, uncomfortable day and as the soldiers' second blankets and other stores had been left behind at Romanos well in the morning, they did not arrive until that evening.

Ernest adds a comment on the fact that, while this was supposed to be a rest period, administrative work continued as usual:

Saturday 23 October 1915

Came back to rest trenches for eight days so called rest. Still digging daily. However we get our clothes off at night which is a comfort and we are using the old quarters of the 87th Bde staff. Naturally there are some dugouts and they kindly left their tarpaulins. Capt Byrne, Shaw, our new padre and self, stop in a very comfortable one which is quite waterproof.

With the unpleasant weather continuing, one officer and 30 men worked on the new rifle range for 52 Division for most of the morning of 24 October. New clothing was drawn and issued, with shirts, socks, trousers all round and new coats, caps and boots for a good many. Some of the sizes very poor and it wasn't possible to please everyone; to quote the war diary " no use sending 6 ¼ caps when you don't ask for them, as a man who takes 6 ½ or 6 ¾ can't wear them."[8] Meanwhile, a welcome draft of one officer (Second Lieutenant F J L Mayger from the unattached list) and 62 other ranks joined the battalion, most of whom were former soldiers who had been away sick or wounded, along with 12 survivors from the *Royal Edward* disaster back in August.

Still during the so called rest period, on 25 October work commenced on fresh winter quarters about 400 yards south west along the cliff from X Beach. The whole cliff was being terraced starting at the top, which meant moving tons of earth and disposing of it into the sea; all by hand with

8   Cap sizes are given in inches.

shovel and pick. Other fatigues took away a lot of men; for example, six NCOs and men were sent to 52 Divisional bomb school for a six day course, one officer and 50 men worked on rifle range in the morning and a similar relief in the afternoon, 20 men did drainage work for the 52 Division in the morning, and a relief again in the afternoon. The total number of men, on outside fatigues, on a typical day, was two officers and 140 men, who were getting no rest from the rigours of being in the front line. Added to this, A and B Coys started disinfecting their clothing at 2 Lowland Field Ambulance, but it was very slow progress; at only eight men per hour it had to carry on all night. If there is any consolation, it had been a much warmer day, with some bright sun.

As outlined previously, a proportion of an infantry battalion's strength was often siphoned off from the rifle coys for other tasks. In this case it was to establish grenade sections and machine gunners and a grenadier section was to be created in the battalion, in accordance with 52 Division orders. Under the watchful eye of two officers (Second Lieutenants Parry Davies and Gibbs) one sergeant and one corporal, six squads of eight grenadiers each were set up, each squad under a lance corporal or selected grenadier and when – or perhaps if – the battalion was at full strength, there would be eight such squads. Initially, the men remained with their coys and did all the normal duties, except when required for grenadier training. Second Lieutenant Mein was appointed the battalion machine gun officer, with a total of 50 machine gunners to facilitate in the carrying of ammunition as no transport was available for the task. Meanwhile, work continued on 26 October with terracing the cliff, while one officer and 30 men worked for the supply depot at Lancashire Landing for most of the morning. 20 men worked under the commander Royal Engineers of the RND on the pipe line above Lancashire Landing, while 20 men worked on the drainage system at HQ 52 Division all day; a total of one officer and 90 men who, once again, were not resting and would not do so until the end of the month as these fatigues, particularly the terracing of the cliff top, were to continue each day.

Ernest, too, had been feeling less than at his best:

Tuesday 26 October 1915

More signs of bad weather – glorious day yesterday. Have had a touch of Gallipoli fever for the last few days, wet weather and cold the cause no doubt. Feeling better today. Had a few shells uncomfortably close just after lunch and 'Annie from Asia' was busy a little lower down. All sorts of rumours floating of our next move. Anzac-Suvla or Salonika? The betting is on the latter. It will be mighty cold I bet.

As alluded to earlier, Bulgaria, hitherto neutral, had sided with the German axis. This necessitated support to Greece by sending a number of divisions from Gallipoli to Salonika, which had an impact on the force levels of the peninsula. In fact, Ernest was wrong on both counts; 29 Division was to remain at Cape Helles, while a composite Anglo-French force of two divisions was earmarked for Salonika.

On the morning of 31 October, 2 SWB returned to the firing line once again, but hardly refreshed after 10 days of providing a constant round of working parties. With the effective strength of the battalion now 21 Officers and 604 other ranks, they moved up by half companies at half hour intervals, relieving KOSB in the same trenches as last time, with B Coy on the right, C Coy in the centre, D Coy on the left flank and A Coy in support. There was plenty of work to be done improving trenches and making them more secure for winter, and also in case of a big Turkish attack, which was rumoured to be imminent. A good deal of enemy shelling took place during the day, but no damage was done. It was now getting dark by 6:00 p.m. as the nights became longer and longer.

General Monro arrived at Gallipoli on 28 October 1915 and immediately set about the task he had been set by Lord Kitchener, namely to report on the military situation and then to express an opinion whether, on purely military grounds, the peninsula should be evacuated or the offensive battle be continued and, if so, the force level which would be needed to achieve this. What he saw did not fill him with optimism – an army ravaged by illness and disease, worn out by incessant fighting in the most hostile of environments and in a tactical position that "possessed every possible military defect."[9] In the six months since landing at Gallipoli, the allied forces had hardly progressed beyond the fringes of the peninsula and most of their positions, particularly the beaches at Cape Helles, were under constant bombardment from Turkish artillery. Two divisions had recently been diverted to Salonika, while those that remained were, in many cases, augmented by yeomanry and mounted brigade personnel to make up their numbers and they were short of competent officers to command them. Within a very short space of time, General Monro was convinced that there was little to be gained by dragging out the campaign any longer than was absolutely necessary, so, despite some opposition from senior officers on the peninsula, he recommended to Lord Kitchener and the war cabinet back home in London that evacuation was the only sensible option. It was now for the government to make the final decision.

---

9   General Sir Charles Monro, First Despatch (*London Gazette* 10 April 1916). This was not sent until March 1916, two months after the end of the campaign.

10

The Final Decision

You are to report on the best means
of removing the deadlock at Gallipoli and
the means required to carry it out

Lord Kitchener to
Gen Sir Charles Monro
October 1915

After the battle at Hill 60, the 4th Battalion remained at Suvla Bay and, like the 2nd Battalion, who had returned to Cape Helles with 29 Division, their routine became one of consolidation and maintenance, while they waited for more reinforcements. John Mellsop's report picks up again at the beginning of October:

On the 6th October the Naval guns got to work on the Turkish trenches to the north. Huge shells came over one after the other as fast as these warships could let them off and most of them appeared to fall right into or near the trenches from which huge masses of flame, debris and dense columns of smoke soon made the ridge look like an earthquake and volcano combined. The shells kept sweeping the ground from left to right and from front to rear, whilst the land batteries opened with shrapnel, the explosions of which dotted the denser background with small white patches. These bombardments used to last for about an hour and though you would think that the Turkish nation had ceased to exist after one of them, Turkish prisoners told us afterwards that they really did wonderfully little damage. Nine young officers joined the battalion today, making the strength up to 15 officers and 210 other ranks. On the 7th, Pte Druny was very severely wounded by a shell; he just had time to say 'they have got me at last' when he fell back dead.

It is presumed that ordinary trench warfare differed but little in no matter what zone of action the occupants were and it has been so often described that there is but little interest in going over the old ground here, but a walk round the trenches with the Commanding Officer on his early morning inspection may perhaps give one a short glimpse of our splendid "Tommies" during that time. The CO has probably slept all night in his clothes, or in the greater part of them, possibly because he has nothing else to wear or else because he finds it less trouble when he has to turn out; anyway at about 4am his servant wakes him and possibly brings him a cup of cocoa. He turns out, puts on his boots, coat and equipment and staggers out into the pitch darkness where he meets his Adjutant and Sergeant Major and stumbles up the narrow communicating trenches, half drunk with sleep, till he reaches the firing trenches. Here everything is quiet but every man is on the alert, sentries at intervals gazing over the parapet. The mornings are often intensely cold, but the men in these trenches are not allowed any blankets as they might retard their turning out quickly on case of need and so they are mostly huddled up and shivering on the banquette, examining their rifles or otherwise preparing for any emergency at this hour most likely for attack, officers and NCOs seeing that all is well and orderly. The CO passes along keeping a watchful eye on all, stopping occasionally to take a rifle and examine it to see that it is in good working order and that the magazine is charged, or to receive reports of anything of consequence during the night. If there is enough rum every man now receives a small tot, but of course such luxuries as smoking are strictly prohibited at this hour. Then a tour round the support and reserve trenches and so on to the cooking trenches to see that tea is being got ready as soon as possible for the men and that all is clean and in good order. By the time he is finished – perhaps in an hour – daylight will be showing, but still for another hour will the men be kept vigilantly watching, after which, if nothing untoward has happened, the normal day begins. This inspection again takes place at dusk.

On the 13th, by a lucky shot, the Turks disabled one of our aeroplanes, which, descending very slowly, landed inside our lines on the bed of the dry salt lake, about the most conspicuous place it could have chosen. Anticipating further hostile demonstrations, the aviators quickly scrambled out and ran with much speed for cover, only just escaping the furious bombardment which was immediately poured upon it. It seemed to bear a charmed life as shell after shell failed to further damage it until the 65th (the writer counted them) landed under one of the wings and blew it off. The remains of the plane were towed in at dusk and it was flying again in a few days.

It was rumoured that certain German and Turkish spies were in the habit of moving about our trenches dressed as British officers and orders were issued that any officer in the trenches unknown to the men was to be stopped and questioned, but they had become so accustomed to seeing strange officers walking up and down the trenches in the course of their many duties that it was difficult at times to have this important precaution satisfactorily carried out. There was a decided inclination amongst many of the Turks at this time to come in and surrender and naturally this chastened spirit was highly approved of and encouraged. Every night letters in almost affectionate terms were stuck on their wire entanglements offering them the best of treatment should they decide to accept our hospitality. Many did.

On 17th October, Brig Gen J H Travers was invalided with dysentery and the command of 40th Brigade was given to Lieutenant Colonel A C Lewis. On the 18th the Mounted Division on the right of the 13th Division captured a Turkish trench during the night, suffering eight casualties (two killed) whilst the Turks lost 14 killed and three prisoners, the number of their wounded being unknown. On the 19th, Sir Ian Hamilton sent out a farewell message to the troops previous to his leaving for home, being relieved as Commander in Chief by General Sir Charles Monro. By the 24th the strength of the battalion had been reduced to 19 officers and 178 other ranks, the lowest number of men it had yet attained, but a draft arriving of two officers and 68 men – all of whom had been previously wounded or sick – its strength became 21 officers and 246 other ranks, several young officers having arrived during the month. Amongst these young officers was Lieut Caldwell who was a very fine rifle shot and was put in charge of the battalion snipers who had now become quite a formidable force of picked marksmen, who hid in hollow trees and other places of concealment and had already put unholy fear into the Turkish sniper, who was a much more harmless individual than previously. One day, Caldwell was trying to pick off a Turkish sniper and was firing from the parapet, and a man with field glasses was spotting for him about a yard away. Suddenly this man threw up his arms and shouted 'I am not hit' and fell stone dead into the trench. He had been hit through the heart by a Turkish bullet.

On the 31st another draft arrived of two officers and 146 men bringing the battalion strength up to 22 officers and 378 other ranks. During the month of October two men of the battalion had been killed and five wounded and the sick list included five officers and 58 men. During the last 10 days heavy rain had fallen at intervals and the horrid mess it had made of everything gave ominous warning of what to expect later on, when the annual torrential winter rain pours down in all its fury. The men had practically no shelters of any kind in the trenches as the wood and corrugated iron necessary for their construction was almost impossible to obtain and any shelters which the officers had were of the frailest and most primitive kind; in most cases just a covering from the sun and quite unworthy of being called rainproof.

* * *

Back at the Helles sector, the beginning of November saw 2 SWB continuing the never ending work on their trenches. They were digging out machine gun positions under the front line parapet which would be flush with the ground and manned at night while the communication trenches were straightened for about 30 yards just in front of the new support trench, with a T shape dug in at the near end of the straight part. There were filled sandbags ready for barricading the trench, and two bomb throwers in each side of the T, so that if the front line was taken by the enemy, they could at least stop the Turks from moving down the communication trenches. They also worked at driving in posts for wire in front of a new support trench, assisted by two reliefs of 80 men each from the Border Regiment working during the night on continuation of the new support trench between General Street and Oxford Street. The battalion also dug T shapes back from the fire trenches, each able to hold four men, into which they could go during a heavy bombardment. Also by this time, the battalion was issued with a 3.7 inch trench howitzer, which was a very useful addition to their defensive armoury. Meanwhile, four Turks were shot by a battalion sniper using a telescopic sight. There were two casualties, one of whom died of his wounds, while six officers from 157 and 155 Brigades arrived to supplement the battalion strength while in the firing line.

Over the next two days, defensive work continued, especially on creating the T shape trenches and the Border Regiment supplied working parties at night to assist, as well as strengthening the barbed wire defences which were linked up to that of the French. This work was not without its casualties however, with one man being killed and two wounded, mainly when sapping back on the shelter trenches, being enfiladed by the enemy from the left flank. On the morning of 2 November, the brigade commander came round the lines and expressed himself very pleased with the work the battalion had done, especially with the cleanliness and discipline in the trenches – two most essential aspects of maintaining morale in a defensive position. A hostile aeroplane came over the battalion position on the morning of 3 November which was driven off by shrapnel and rifle fire. Clearly on reconnaissance, the plane returned again only to be driven off once more.

On 4 November, 2 SWB was relieved by the Border Regiment and moved down to Brown House and Eski Line. B Coy was in the support trenches to the west of White House, C Coy in Eski Line to the west of the Nullah, while D Coy was in Eski Line to the east of the Nullah. A Coy was in Parsons Road. Four machine guns were left in the firing line, and two squads of grenadiers were attached to A Coy, to work on the bombing stations in Central Street and Oxford Street. Ammunition was needed on the front line, carried up there by a working party of 82 men who then continued to work on trench defences until late that evening. Rain fell in the afternoon but did not affect the trenches.

Ernest had a few laconic comments to make on the situation:

Thursday 4 November 1915

Relieved by Border Regt. Took their place in support trenches. Have lost eight men by sniping in the past four days. One killed, one died of wounds, remainder wounded, nearly all badly as the range is so close. Had nice weather this time up but windy today and some rain – result trenches greasy and slippery. Hope my trench boots come out before the real bad weather sets in. The flies are like the poor – always with us – and the Gallipoli fly refuses to die unless you strafe him.

With no major reinforcements in the pipeline, offensive action across the whole of the peninsula had fallen into a state of limbo, so life at Cape Helles was reduced to a defence mentality. Considerable effort was put into the maintenance of battalion positions, especially as the weather was beginning to change and the prospect of a winter in the trenches was a real one. Over the next week, the battalion assisted the Border Regiment in strengthening the support trench parapets so that they would not collapse in the wet weather. On the firing line, two of the underground machine gun emplacements were finished and a gun was mounted into one of them. At the same time, 16 grenadiers with A Coy worked on bombing stations in Oxford and Central Streets. The six officers who had been attached since 1 November went back to their battalions, their places being taken by seven others from 156 and 157 Brigades to keep the battalion up to a reasonable strength. Carrying parties were also needed to take water and rations up to 1 KOSB. At about 4:00 a.m. on 8 November, very heavy rifle and machine gun fire, accompanied by bombs and trench howitzers, came from the direction of the French on the battalion's right flank. This lasted about 15 minutes, but there was no artillery fire, so it was assumed to be an isolated incident, rather than the prelude to an enemy assault. Later that morning, two officers and 128 NCOs and men left for the beach to take over duties of guard company at Lancashire Landing, while six men joined the 52 Division bomb school for a six day course; all essential duties of course, but a drain on battalion manpower which only exacerbated the pressure on those left behind; for example, 80 men were still required to work on the terracing of the cliffs above X Beach.

On 9 November, the battalion was relieved at Brown House by the Inniskilling Fusiliers and moved back to their winter quarters in the reserve trenches. During the afternoon, the guard company on the beach was relieved by a garrison battalion and also rejoined the battalion. Other commitments continued apace; Second Lieutenants R D Beardshaw and F J L Mayger were sent on a two day course with 52 Division bomb school, while Sergeant Auger and Private Kent, who had done a trench mortar course in the previous month, were sent to join 52 Division mortar battery. Work continued on the cliffs with, as the Bn war diary states, *"all available men, about 80"* – a reflection on the shortage of manpower in the battalion at the time. Then, as if they didn't have enough to do already, the officers had to endure a lecture on courts martial disciplinary procedures by Captain J C Brand, who was the brigade major; all part of military training and education, even though they were on active service. More appropriate perhaps was a lecture given by Lieutenant Colonel Kelly 1 KOSB on bombs, catapults and trench mortars and one from Lieutenant Colonel Pearce, Inniskilling Fusiliers, on musketry and fire control. A sobering reminder of the fact that they were still in a hostile environment was that, during the last nine days that they had spent in

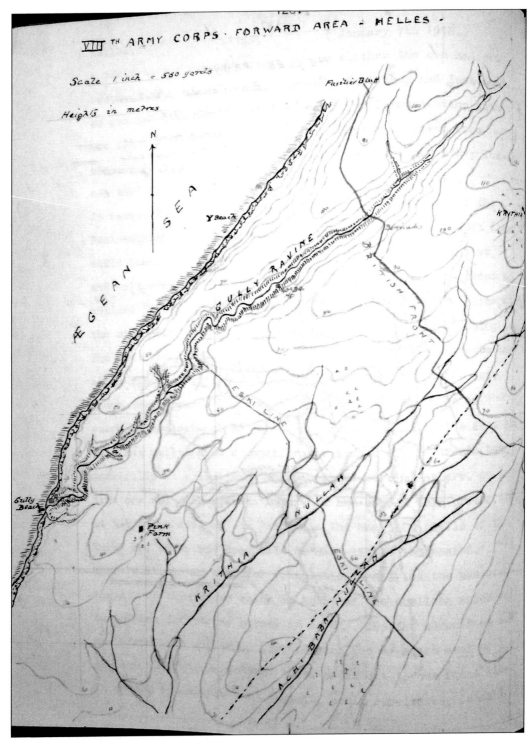

Map 17. Sketch Map by Captain Kitchin of VIII Army Corps forward area at Cape Helles (Mrs A Payne).

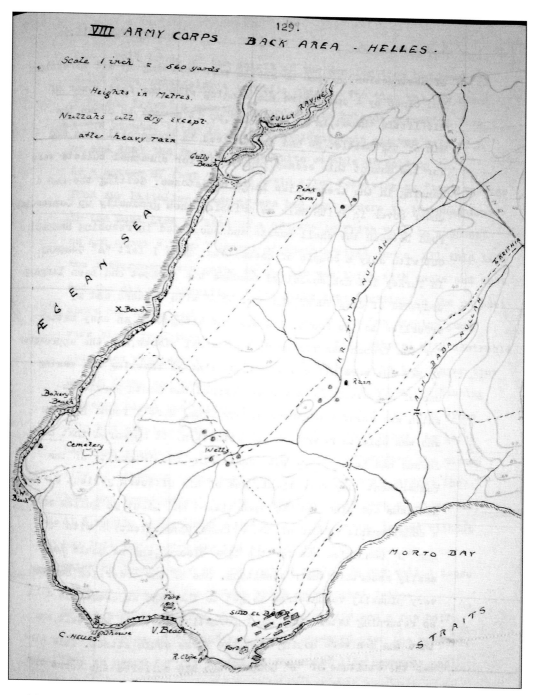

Map 18. Sketch Map by Captain Kitchin of the VIII Army Corps rear area at Cape Helles (Mrs A Payne).

the trenches and in reserve, the battalion had one soldier killed and eight wounded, one of whom died later of his wounds.

The final decision was not without its difficulties and General Monro's recommendation to evacuate the peninsula had a very mixed reception, both at home and at Gallipoli itself. There were political implications to consider and while these are outside the scope of this book, the universal humiliation of what would be considered as a defeat weighed heavily upon both the war committee (formerly the Dardanelles Committee) and the cabinet. Nevertheless, General Monro continued to recommend immediate evacuation as the only option, adding that he felt that there could be casualties of up to 40 percent (some 40,000 men) in the process. Once again, the vacillation seen at the beginning of the campaign set in, with Lord Kitchener stating on the one hand that he was against evacuation, yet on the other, directing General Birdwood to work out, in the greatest secrecy, plans for a potential evacuation.

Such was the level of indecision, that the cabinet sent Lord Kitchener out to Gallipoli to assess the situation himself. He arrived on 9 November and stayed for a week, during which time it became apparent to him that evacuation was almost inevitable, but he was still reluctant to accept this and looked for every opportunity to continue the offensive, aided and abetted it has to be said, by the Royal Navy in particular, who were keen to resurrect the aborted sea-borne invasion of the Narrows earlier in March. Burying his head in the sand, Lord Kitchener tried to sideline General Monro by transferring him to command the Salonika campaign, but this did not transpire, although the general was appointed commander in chief, Mediterranean expedition, with General Birdwood – who was in favour of continuing the campaign - taking over command of the Dardanelles army, as it was now called; perhaps in the forlorn hope that the impetus for evacuation might recede. Indeed, Lord Kitchener tried to alter the balance of persuasion by suggesting a reinforcement of up to four divisions at Gallipoli, but General Monro robustly pointed out that, given the congestion that this would cause on the ground, the winter weather conditions and the time required to turn this concept into reality, such a plan would not work.[1]

All of this planning was supposed to take place in the greatest secrecy, but as ever, rumours started to circulate that something unusual was in the air, as Ernest noted in his diary:

Friday 12 November 1915

Heard that Kitchener had landed on the Peninsula and left the same afternoon. He sent a congratulatory message to the troops. I wonder what is really in the wind this time?

Saturday 13 November

Lord Kitchener reported to be at Imbros.

Sunday 14 November

There's plenty in the wind today, if it's only dust. That means the mails are all at sea and likely to remain there. Great rumours rife about our move to Salonika and two other Divisions from France. Personally I don't think we will go from here. If we do and have to march any distance on landing it will be a sorry looking Division at the end of the day. Went over and had a look around Sedd-il-Bahr yesterday, the French landing place and GHQ. They do

1   C F Aspinall-Oglander, *Gallipoli*, Chapter 30.

things in the building line on a much greater scale than we. Where we use sand bags they use stone and cement. Thousands of tons of building material are stacked neatly on the beach. The best of this is in their large quarter circle sheets of boiler iron – two of these joined together make splendid dug outs and will bear almost any weight on top. Their ingenuity is splendid. One hut had a window made with white wine bottles with their necks cut off; a row at the bottom and another row inserted at the top, the interstices being filled in with cement. The same hut had a tiny lawn in front with old Turkish stone cannon balls at each corner and a stone flower vase in the middle. One could almost imagine oneself off the peninsula but for the 'Annie from Asia' which was then screaming over. The village is in ruins but a lot of the old towers etc have been partially repaired by the French and used for stores. They certainly have the advantage over us for material as there is not a stone or building of any sort on our side.

The smashed guns of the Turks still lie where they originally fell and in addition to the shell there are great numbers of stone balls about 18 to 24 inches in diameter which were used in the old days to roll down the cliff side I understand. Some of these are of alabaster and neatly cut. Nearly all their gravestones are of alabaster – one is pleased to see them wired in to prevent men walking over them. The French cemetery too is well laid out and the graves are well cared for. Some of the headstones and iron railings are splendidly done.

By 15 November the weather really was beginning to change and there had been heavy rain during the previous night and early morning, which turned the top dressing of the parapets into a sea of mud, but at least it remained hard underneath. The men were issued with winter vests and drawers, as well as with ammonia ampoules in case of gas poisoning, as there was the threat that the Turks might resort to its use. That afternoon there was heavy shelling by allied artillery, accompanied by rifle fire, on the Krithia Nullah, which turned out to be a successful attack by 156 Brigade to straighten out part of their firing line.

In his next diary entry, Ernest commented on the damage done to the piers on W Beach by the previous night's storm:

Monday 15 November 1915

Yesterday's damage at W Beach is only a foretaste of what is to come. I hear that one of the three steamers (which were sunk end to end to form a breakwater and which also formed part of the pier) has broken its back and parts from the stone portion of the pier. The mails could not be landed and several bags were lost. One hears that several boats have gone down.

An entry in the battalion war diary for 16 November records "sent off cheque for £37.5.6 to Lord Robert's Memorial Fund, being one day's pay of all ranks." In 1908, Lord Roberts VC, who had served with distinction during the Boer War, launched an appeal to help service veterans who had fallen on hard times and within 12 months £38,000 had been donated, equivalent to £1,500,000 today. The fund was looked after by the Soldiers and Sailors Help Society and at the time assisted over 800 ex-soldiers, many of whom were "taken from the workhouse and enabled to end their lives in dignity and modest comfort."[2] Lord Roberts died in 1914, but the Lord Roberts Memorial Fund was launched in his name and soon £500,000 was raised, mainly from contributions from units, as in the case of 2 SWB described here. This large sum enabled the first workshop for disabled

2   The Soldiers and Sailors Help Society Report 1909. TNA BT 58/1616.

soldiers to be opened in Fulham in 1915. It is fitting that such charitable organisations as the Army Benevolent Fund, SSAFA Forces Help, The Royal British Legion and Help for Heroes continue to carry the flag today, as the need for this support is, sadly, as important now as it was in 1915.

The bad weather continued into 17 November when 2 SWB moved up into brigade reserve at Brown House, where they relieved 1 KOSB. While doing so they carried about 170 loads of ammunition, sandbags, water and rations up to the Border Regiment in the firing line. Then they began work on communication trenches leading into the new Eski Line, which was about 3 feet deep all along, but work had to be stopped after an hour due to a very heavy rain storm which flooded everyone out during the evening. Ernest adds to the drama:

Wednesday 17 November 1915

Back to support trenches. Yesterday fine, but today the windiest day we have had. Rain came on with darkness, at first in spasms but by the time the rations arrived it was driving hard. It wound up at 8 pm with a deluge which nearly filled the trenches. Valise[3] had a quart or two in, which did not add to the comfort. Goodness knows what would have happened had it rained all through the night. The regimental dump with all our spare kit, officers mess stores, signalling gear etc (which were in a large dug out over three feet deep) was full to the top and over. The store man (Allan) managed to save most of the officers' kits but a lot of other stuff is ruined.

The weather was becoming the main topic of conversation on the peninsula, as the battalion awoke on 18 November to find their trenches in Oxford Street and Central Street badly flooded, with many up to a foot deep in places. The wind went into the north after the rain the previous night and the temperature dropped considerably, but the day turned out to be bright, warm and sunny, with no wind. Working parties were set up to drain the trenches as much as they could, while others carried 125 loads of water and rations up to the Border Regiment. This was no easy task in the very muddy conditions and each water party took about three hours to get to the firing line and back. Two more officers in the shape of Second Lieutenant J S Ashford from the Dorset Yeomanry and Second Lieutenant H K Wadams from the Worcester Yeomanry were posted to the battalion and were attached to D and B Coys respectively. As a reminder that there was still a war in progress, sounds of gun fire and bombing came from the left flank but this did not affect the battalion. Ernest could at least see the funny side of things:

Thursday 18 November 1915

Beautiful day – cold but cloudless. What a state the trenches are in! However, we must be thankful that we can dry our blankets. Most of the men sat up all night and sang – God bless 'em. Tommy is a curious creature. Hear that the Bulgarian artillery has arrived at Constantinople. If it's true we shall soon be in for an unpleasant time I suppose. Don't know however how they can afford to dispense with their artillery on their own front just now.

The weather remained fine and warm by day and as the battalion was still in reserve, they continued to bail out the worst of the trenches and take supplies up to the front line. On the evening of 19 November, Second Lieutenant T D Burt 14/Royal Scots arrived with a welcome draft of 110

---

3   A small overnight travelling case.

NCOs and men from the 3rd Battalion. These were battle casualty replacements from 3SWB, some of whom had been on the Western Front; a few were still wounded so they were sent back. The battalion's own casualties were light at the moment, with just two men injured by shrapnel, but they were able to remain at duty. Like everyone else, Ernest was hoping for good weather:

Friday 19 November 1915

Another fine day but cold. The Turks have replied with some vigour to our artillery. Wish I had my trench boots. We go up tomorrow and Oxford St and Central St are nearly knee deep in water and mud in places. Hope to goodness we get no more rain for a while.

On 20 November, the battalion came out of reserve and returned to the firing line to relieve the Border Regiment. Everything was very quiet and had been so ever since they came back from their rest period on Imbros at the end of September; as the war diary comments "no fighting but a lot of heavy work!" A Coy were on the right flank next to the French, C Coy were in the centre, and D Coy took up the left flank, with B Coy in the new E11 trench. Three machine guns were positioned in the Horseshoe and one in the Couronne. B Coy sent 10 men to Horseshoe at night and they also manned four bombing stations in the communication trenches in front of E11. B Coy spent some time pushing back 40 yards of the parapet in E11, as the sandbags had been laid too close to the edge. They also continued a new cut in Oxford Street while C Coy did some work converting Boundary Road into a fire trench. C Coy also started roofing in some of the shelter Ts in the firing line. While battle casualties remained light, two men were wounded when a bomb from their own catapult hit the parapet and bounced back into the trench.

Ernest was also getting his share of the consequences of the bad weather:

Saturday 20 November 1915

Up again to fire trenches in relief of Border Regt. Central Street was not so bad, thanks to the bailing that was done yesterday in certain parts of it. This time I have a dug out of my own which is far better than sleeping in the aid post. One sees enough sick and wounded without sleeping in it. However, even that – with a roof on it. They actually talk of giving a bit of roof for the cooks to put their rations in at night and a place in which they can cut up the fresh meat. The promises we get! This time I have actually been asked to make a suitable plan and we have really started on the digging but no roofing material has come yet I observe. The weather is bitter cold.

The weather was getting colder by the day and on 21 November work continued on the new Oxford Street and a new location was selected for the battalion field cookhouse in Trotman Road. That evening at about 4:15 p.m. the Turkish guns started firing rapidly on the Krithia Nullah and the communication trenches, which was followed closely by retaliatory fire from the battalion's guns and the French trench howitzers. The Turkish fire was converging from different parts of the line, along with rapid machine gun fire apparently from both sides. This appeared to be on the western side of the Krithia Nullah and went on, together with the guns and occasional rifle fire for the next hour, when the shell fire began to slacken. Rifle fire continued with machine guns till about 6:00 p.m. when it became intermittent, but no news about the situation was forthcoming from brigade HQ; indeed the French had to come over to the battalion to find out what was happening. Just before 8:00 p.m. a message was received from 1 KOSB on the battalion's left flank that the Turks

Image 22. The Helles Memorial which commemorates the 19,000 British servicemen who have no known grave at Gallipoli, 423 of whom are South Wales Borderers (Author).

Image 23. The memorial to Colonel Mustafa Kemal at Chunuk Bair in honour of the Turkish war dead (Author).

had attacked in force, but had been repulsed. This was backed up by a French artillery observation officer who came to Bn HQ to say that it was a counter attack on the part of the Turks to force the battalion out of H11 (a) which had been captured recently. Ever conscious of the chemical threat, the brigadier arrived later that evening, and ordered a practice gas attack, which the battalion, according to the quartermaster, responded to with less than their customary vim and vigour. Under the cover of darkness, the enemy attempted to repair their parapet in E13 b but was driven off by 2 SWB's rifle fire and two rounds from the 3.7 inch trench howitzer. During the ensuing melee, Private Llewellyn Jenkins of A Coy was killed. Aged 25 and from Pontnewynydd in South Wales, he is buried in the Skew Bridge Cemetery. The epitaph on his gravestone, which is featured on the rear cover of this book, encapsulates the spirit of endeavour demonstrated by every soldier of the regiment at Gallipoli – Duty Nobly Done.

Ernest's diary for the day adds colour to the battalion's activities and updates some of the ongoing administrative arrangements:

Sunday 21 November 1915

About 3 pm a heavy bombardment on our left started which by 4 pm had increased to a perfect tornado of shells. Couldn't tell from here which side started and everyone seemed to be asking their neighbours what it was all about. It kept up until after dark when the Turks guns shut up as they practically always do at night. Don't like to give their gun positions away. Machine guns rattled away – one specially had a beautiful rhythm – well up to 600 rounds a minute. Had a look over the parapet by Bn HQ and the sight just before dark was magnificent. The French commander even did not know what it was and was rather anxious. We got it later from the next Division that the Turks had attacked in force and were immediately repulsed with severe loss. Probably they tried to recover their two lost trenches which the 157th Bde won whilst we were in rest quarters. I forgot to mention this I see. They were collared quite early one afternoon – first a bit where we are trying to straighten the line. Brigadier Gen Casson is commanding that brigade so he is mightily pleased I dare say.

Forgot also to mention that a draft of 1 officer (Second Lieutenant Burt) and 110 other ranks arrived on 19th at V (French) Beach. I had to go down to meet them in case the powers that rule such things at Lemnos had taken their blankets from them before embarkation – they did this with the preceding draft. This time however they came with one blanket and a water proof sheet and a bag of extra kit! We've never seen ours since we left the 'Alaunia' in April. Due to arrive at 9 pm the draft fetched up at the landing pier at 10.40 pm so we didn't get up to the support trenches till midnight. Several old faces. Sgts Russell (acting CSgt) Irons (acting CQMS) Lamont and Ruffle. Not at all a bad looking lot of men. Burt, the young sub comes from the 13th R Scots. Why don't they send out some of our own 3rd Bn youngsters? A mail was also landed at the French beach – the one we have been waiting for and which was nearly lost at W Beach. The latter looks a shambles after the storm of the 17th. One of the boats forming the pier and breakwater has disappeared; the one with the broken back being the nearest has sagged under water at either end which closes the entrance way cut in the starboard bow and the remainder of the pier is practically washed away – as also are the two smaller piers. How badly we do run our own shows! With all the time we have been here either the R.E. (or a contractor even) could have built a pukka[4] pier – labour is cheap enough goodness knows.

4   Old Indian Army slang for something which is well made, or in good order.

By the next day, good progress had been made on the parapet and shelter Ts, with one being fully roofed over which made an excellent shelter. A sentry post was also completely covered, while the machine gunners had prepared some anti-aircraft emplacements. A new cut for a bomb station had been made from which the grenadiers fired about 150 bombs out of the catapults, knocking down about 10 yards of enemy parapet. Bombs were also thrown by hand from the listening post in front of P7, which drew heavy fire on the post from the enemy, but when even more bombs were thrown, the enemy's fire ceased. The battalion fired about 100 bombs and 15 rifle grenades during the previous night and the day before, with good effect; the Turks seemed to have identified their right catapult, upon which they fired heavily, but the 3.7 inch howitzer put one shell into the enemy's trench and two more onto their parapet and the firing soon ceased.

As Ernest recounts, the practice gas attack a few days earlier did not go as smoothly as it should have done:

Monday 22 November 1915

Heard this morning that the MO and I were the only two absent last night when the gas test alarm was on. The General (Lucas) it seems came up and woke the CO (Williams) and ordered an alarm. Then he went round the fire trenches and today he sent in some caustic remarks about waking men up. Too much courtesy is shown! So next time the butt end of the rifle will be the rib tickler I expect. It is surprising how some of these fellows sleep through – like waking the dead. Only just heard we have a telescopic sighted rifle in use in the trenches. Went up this morning and found it in the forward post. Had to creep in under the fire parapet outside where it is all nicely sandbagged, but found the beastly thing was out of order, and in any case not a Turk would kindly show his head. Had a good spot round with the telescope – surprising how far our position of the line is in front of the bit on our left which still requires straightening. Crawled out still further to our listening post which is into our barbed wire and within hand bombing distance of the Turks trenches by a good thrower. One gets a good view of our own trenches from there.

At 7:00 p.m. on 23 November heavy rifle firing was heard in the Krithia Nullah and a large number of flares were put up, which seemed to indicate that the Turks were making another attack, but there was no artillery fire, and little from their machine guns and some 15 minutes later the fire died away. On the morning of 24 November, the battalion was relieved by the Inniskilling Fusiliers, and moved back to the rest camp. However, with 1 KOSB already in the battalion's lines, they had to go into the Inniskilling dugouts. Casualties to date came to one man killed, two wounded and two slightly wounded, who were able to remain at duty.

Ernest had caustic comments to make about the disorderly method in which units took over each other's trenches on relief:

Wednesday 24 November 1915

Down once more in reserve for our eight days rest, which consists mainly in finding big fatigue parties for the beach or making dugouts for anyone but ourselves. Had to take over spare trenches and those of Inniskillings for the first night, as the KOSBs were occupying ours – a rotten arrangement. One battalion could easily relieve the fire trenches in the morning and the other battalion relieve the supports in the afternoon, thus allowing both

Image 24. Casualty evacuation through a communications trench on the peninsula (IWM Q 3225).

battalions to come down straight into their own rest lines on same day. We have all been up three times to both places and could walk in with our eyes shut – as it is now, only one battalion relieves in one day. Even if they had a cycle order by which we relieved the KOSB, the Border Regt relieving Inniskillings and vice versa it would be alright. However, it is the usual British way of muddling.

On 25 November, 1 KOSB relieved the Border Regiment at Brown House in the morning, so 2 SWB went back into their old lines. They had a very cold four days in the front trenches, but the men were very fit and in good heart. B Coy was sent to live on the cliff to the south west of X Beach, to erect the winter dugouts there and to put on the roofs. An officer and 35 men from C Coy were sent to corps HQ for duty with the cyclist coy as orderlies while two squads of grenadiers under an officer were sent to 157 Brigade to help them in holding their bombing locations. While this was going on, the officers in the rest camp had a lecture on "trenches, their design and construction" given by Brigadier General Lucas, commanding 87 Brigade. The wind rose in the evening and brought rain from the south; more bad weather was expected.

The following day one officer and 50 men, which included as many miners and quarry men as possible, went to the RND RE detachment at Lancashire Landing. Their task was to work in a quarry getting stones for a new pier, the old one having been washed away by storms. At the same time, 80 men worked under the Royal Engineers draining the rest camp, and 50 more on a similar task during the afternoon with CRE 52 Division. They still found time during the day, however, for about 450 men to be sent to wash in hot water baths with disinfectant near 29 Division HQ. That evening there was very heavy rain and a thunderstorm across the peninsula, which lasted about two hours; the prelude of what was about to come.

On 26 November 1915, a raging storm, the intensity of which had not been experienced in the previous 40 years, hit the Gallipoli peninsula. A fierce south westerly gale which started that evening, veered the next day to the north and continued with exceptional violence for the following three days, during which time it was impossible for any boat to approach or leave the Gallipoli beaches. The first thunderstorm was followed by a torrential downpour which lasted for 24 hours, soaking everyone to the skin. An icy hurricane then began to blow from the north, the rain turning first to a blinding blizzard and then to heavy snow; the snow was then followed by two nights of exceptionally bitter frost.[5]

The impact of the storm varied across the peninsula. At the Anzac sector, a large number of the men were able to shelter in the caves and underground defences built to hold the additional division for the summer offensive, so the number of deaths from exposure was comparatively small. Likewise at Helles, where 2 SWB was located, the trenches were mostly on sloping ground, so they too suffered little from the flooding. It was Suvla Bay however which bore the brunt of the storm. The dry water courses on the plain became rushing torrents and on the southern flank a wall of mud and water several feet high came rushing down the nullah, bringing with it drowned bodies of Turkish soldiers and pack ponies. Throughout the Suvla plain, where 4 SWB were still in their defensive position, many sections of the trenches were completely uninhabitable, but if it was any compensation, the Turks were suffering in equal measure with personal survival, rather than warfare, the prime consideration on both sides. The nights of 27 and 28 November saw hundreds of men dying from exposure as well as many being drowned in their trenches, while the hospitals struggled to cope and ordnance tents, supply depots and every place where cover was available, were packed to overflowing. By the time the storm abated on 30 November, there had been more than 5,000 cases of frostbite and over 200 men had been drowned or frozen to death.

This variation in conditions is reflected in the two battalions' war diaries. At Cape Helles, 2 SWB got off fairly lightly and although the conditions were freezing, it did not seem to have a major impact upon the daily routine, with working parties still being sent out to secure defences and to keep drainage ditches open; indeed, there was even time for a football match. At Suvla Bay however, 4 SWB saw things quite differently as seen in their report which follows shortly.

After a particularly bad night, with the wind blowing in all directions and the cookhouse an absolute quagmire, the morning of 26 November could only be described in 2 SWB's diary as "miserable." For all that however and with typical British fortitude, a football match of sorts took place that day between the officers and the sergeants of the battalion. As the adjutant gleefully described in the war diary "the officers' side consisted of babes and ancients, ranging from 20 to 40 years, yet we wiped the Sergeants up by seven goals to one!" It was back to work as normal the next day and luckily the camp was not very wet after the previous night's rain, as the drainage work had held out well. Despite the weather, with more heavy rain in the afternoon, there was an exchange of fire, bombs and machine guns from both sides but there were no casualties. Once again there was another lecture for the officers, this time on the subject of discipline, given by Lieutenant Colonel Pollard, the CO of the Border Regiment. Ernest had taken part in the football match and was feeling the effects by the sound of things:

---

5   C F Aspinall-Oglander, *Gallipoli*, pp.432–434.

Saturday 27 November 1915

Awfully stiff yesterday and today after the footer. The wind has gone round to the north and is beastly cold. Snow fell in the night, mostly sleet.

Come 28 November, the snow at Cape Helles was falling in the morning and lying on the ground. It cleared away later but came down again by about 4:00 p.m. This did not stop the fatigue parties going out in the morning, especially those carrying out drainage work but most came back in again in the afternoon as the snow continued to fall. There was an issue of seven oil stoves which was hardly enough to go round, otherwise there were no winter stores, nor clothing, except jerseys and underclothes available; a sad indictment of logistic foresight and planning. In anticipation of an evacuation, orders had been issued for all surplus stores to be sent back to Mudros and through an unfortunate miscalculation, the first articles to be sent back from Suvla were the latest consignments, which happened to be winter clothing.[6]

How different life was for officers in 1915, where class distinction was still prevalent in most battalions. While the soldiers huddled together in the cold at the bottom of their trenches or in their dugouts, it was not uncommon for the officers of the battalion to enjoy a relatively more comfortable existence, as Ernest's next diary entry confirms:

Sunday 28 November 1915

Still snowing or sleeting as one got up. Went over to the cliff to see B Coy who are in the dugouts with roofs! Had an invitation to tea, cards and dinner with Byrne and Ballantyne. Went over at 4 pm and was nearly blown over the cliff. Had a new loaf with Irish butter for tea. What luxuries! Played bridge until dinner and Byrne made some delicious sauce with French wine, cream (tinned of course) and goodness knows what else, which we had with hot tinned lobster. When I left to come home to bed – ye Gods what a night! Nearly black as pitch except for the snow drifts. However, one was careful to watch land marks on the way over first otherwise I should probably have fetched up somewhere in the same place as Blake did the night before, near Pink Farm about ¾ mile to our left front. He knew he was too far forward when a bullet went singing past him. We are out of bullet range here. Ricked my ankle again coming down the communication trench just within 200 yards of my dug out. That makes the third time for my left ankle since last August. It froze hard during the night and in the morning I found my canvas bucket solid with ice which Barnes had to break up and substitute warm water. Washing is not a pleasant experience just now and I believe the great unwashed are in the majority even in the Mess, certainly at breakfast time anyway. The wind is still blowing hard from the north and one's fingers and toes are stiff with cold. My boots, which normally I wear with two pairs of socks, are now tight with one pair.

The very hard frost continued into the night, with 29 November turning out to be cold but dry with a strong northerly wind as the worst of the storm seemed to abate and life returned to a degree of normality. 130 men carried on with outside fatigues during the day, with 60 men being sent over to the cliff for two hours work in the afternoon. That evening there was a lecture in the evening on trench discipline, given by Major Aubrey Williams, the former adjutant, who was now on the brigade staff. The sharp frost extended into the night, but the morning of 30 November was a brighter and warmer day at last. Training in the use of mortars and grenades was considered to be a vital part of the defensive battle, with two officers being sent on a two-day grenade course, two men sent to 52 Division trench mortar battery for a 10 day course on the 3.7 inch howitzer, and six men sent on a six-day course about grenades.

Ernest then summed up the sad and sorry state of logistic supplies after the storm, with strong words to say regarding the political messages being bandied about in the House of Commons back home in England:

Tuesday 30 November 1915

The wind although still in the north went down last night and today broke with a blue sky once more, but still freezing. Had a bath in the open – ugh! And felt myself a martyr to cleanliness. Could hardly put my boots on – toe joints swelling. Blake, our medico says it is probably arthritis – lively outlook for winter. Robertson went sick yesterday with what he thinks is gastric ulcer. Has been looking ill for some time. Have had a few cases of frostbite already. Also heard last night that the Turks gassed one of our mine galleries over at Fusilier Bluff on the left flank. That is the first time the Turk has used it and now I suppose it won't be the last. We have about 100 gas helmets with the talc broken and can't get new ones because there are none. We are in a pitiable state really after a few days' storm – I hear there's not a bale of hay left. The French have stocks sufficient to last six months and timber and iron in abundance. Our latest report is that 19000 sheets of corrugated iron for us have gone down. How the French must laugh at us! No piers of our own left (have to use theirs). Only last night 1000 mail bags came over from Mudros and had to go back because they couldn't land them. Yet Tennant (I believe it was) stands up in the 'House' and blandly informs his hearers that the British soldier is comfortably Housed for the winter in Gallipoli!! Should like to put him in one of them for a month – not in Corps HQ though. One doesn't blame HQ for making themselves comfortable – and they should be looked after – but their dug outs should not be photographed and the public gulled into the belief that they are typical dug outs.

* * *

The 4th Battalion was still committed to the Suvla Bay area, as their account of the campaign continues to explain:

Every night, officers' patrols searched the ground towards the Turkish lines, encountering in many cases parties of the enemy similarly engaged and almost invariably driving them back with a casualty or two. On the night of 9th November, Capt Farrow went out at 11pm with six men and two bombers on a patrol of this kind. After going a short distance he left the other men behind and creeping up by himself actually got behind two Turkish sentries. Here he waited and presently six other Turks joined the sentries and Farrow who had taken a bomb with him threw it into the middle of them, quickly making his way back to the trenches which he reached about 3am, having obtained some useful information as well as scaring the lives out of eight Turks if indeed he had not wiped their lives entirely out. This promising young officer afterwards obtained the MC for general good work, but was unfortunately killed later on in Mesopotamia. On 10th November the battalion lost their

Adjutant, Capt Hubert Yates, who was promoted to command a unit in 38 Bde – the 6th Battalion the Kings Own Royal Regiment of Lancaster. Major Kitchin took over as the Adjutant.

Hubert Peel Yates was born in 1874 and after a period of service with the 4th Volunteer Battalion the Wiltshire Regiment, was commissioned into the South Wales Borderers in 1896. Promoted to captain in 1907 he was adjutant to a battalion of Indian railway volunteers and then returned to the regimental depot in Brecon in 1912. It was from here, in 1914 that he joined the newly raised 4th service battalion, becoming the adjutant. He was the father of Lieutenant General Sir David Peel Yates, who commanded 1 SWB from 1953 to 1955 and who became colonel of the regiment, first of all of the South Wales Borderers from 1962 and then on amalgamation with the Welch Regiment in 1969, he continued as colonel of the Royal Regiment of Wales until 1977.

Returning to the 4th Battalion's report:

A scheme had been devised for pushing forward some of the trenches closer up to the Turks, so every night marking and digging parties went "over the top" and got to work with tape and shovel. The method adopted for constructing these trenches was to dig several communicating trenches out to the front and when they were sufficiently advanced to dig short fire trenches on either side of them, these being afterwards extended until they finally merged into one long firing trench. In this way a new trench was dug from 40 to 150 yards nearer to the enemy and about 500 yards long, but the last 150 yards were never completed owing to the terrific storm towards the end of the month. On the 11th, the battalion lost two men killed and five wounded whilst digging these trenches.

It must not be supposed that the Turks were idle during all this time. Our lines were subjected to an artillery bombardment every day and though generally it was an intermittent sort of affair, as comprising the whole line, special objects of hatred were daily selected and the battalion lines which were now in a conspicuous position came in for their full share of attention at times, and owing to the peculiar twisted line of the firing trenches, some of the Turkish batteries to the north were actually in the rear of our firing trenches, consequently shells were often taking them in reverse. Towards the end of October the writer was talking to Capt Fairweather in the firing trench when a shell burst into a tree about 30 yards away. We then walked into a communicating trench close by when we fortunately heard the whizz of another shell approaching. I called sharply to Fairweather to crouch and we both huddled into the trench only just in time; a shrapnel shell burst beautifully just over us and the bullets came down in a regular shower all about us with a tremendous bang and swish, the trench just saving us by a few inches. A little further away another shell burst and nearly hit the Brigadier – his Brigade Major – Yates and Kitchen, who were caught unawares and a boy of 17 called Willis, who was an orderly to the commanding officer, was hit in the back a few minutes afterwards. These of course were only a few of the dozens of shells fired that day and this sort of thing was more or less a daily occurrence. Our naval guns however aided by the land batteries used to give the Turkish lines a proper doing at times. And so the scene went on and so the players acted, but the scenery was about to be shifted and the drama transferred elsewhere.

The failure of the combined attack in August, from which much had been hoped and for which large reinforcements had been despatched from England, was a severe disappointment to the Government and to the Country. Doubts arose as to the ultimate

Image 25. Taking a break – life in the trenches (V Godrich).

success of the expedition and alternative courses of action came under consideration. It was open to the Government if the necessary reserves in the way of men, guns and munitions were forthcoming promptly to strengthen the expeditionary force to such an extent as would enable it to drive the Turks out of the peninsula or at least attempt to do so, or our garrisons on the shore of the peninsula might be maintained in the positions they were then occupying until the spring of 1916 provided that the Turks did not bring heavy guns into play and render these positions untenable, or steps might be taken for the evacuation of the peninsula before winter set in. There was much divergence of opinion in regard to these different courses, the General Staff at the War Office being strongly in favour of evacuation. To Sir Ian Hamilton such a step as evacuation was unthinkable and he informed Lord Kitchener accordingly. On 11th November Lord Kitchener also told the Dardanelles Committee that in his opinion the abandonment of the Gallipoli Peninsula would be disastrous. On the other hand Sir Charles Monro strongly urged its expediency and this view, although at first distasteful to Lord Kitchener, was afterwards accepted by him. Late in November something happened, which had perhaps some influence in hurrying on the date of the evacuation. It was the blizzard of the 26th to 28th, described thus by an able writer:

'The 26th began as a cold dour Gallipoli day with a bitter north easterly wind which increased in the afternoon to a fresh gale with sleet. Later it increased still more and blew hard with thunder and with the thunder came a rain more violent than perhaps any man of the Army had ever seen. Water pours off very quickly from that land of abrupt slopes. In a few minutes every gully was a raging torrent and every trench a river. Our trenches were in nearly every case below those of the Turks who therefore suffered from the water far less than our own men did. The Turks saw our men leaping from their trenches and, either guessing the reason or fearing an attack, opened a very heavy rifle and shrapnel fire upon them. Our

Image 26. Captain Charles Kitchin 4 SWB, who was awarded the DSO for exemplary service throughout the Gallipoli campaign (Mrs A Payne).

men had to shelter behind the parados of their trenches where they scraped themselves shallow pans in the mud under a heavy fire. At dark the sleet increased, the mud froze and there our own men lay, most of them without their overcoats and many of them without food. In one trench when the flood rose, a pony, a mule, and pig and two dead Turks were washed over the barricade together.

Before the night fell many of our men were frostbitten, limping to the ambulances under continual shrapnel fire and in blinding sleet. A good many fell down by the way and were frozen to death. The gale increased slowly all through the night, blowing hard and steady from the north, making a great sea upon the coast and driving the spray far inland. At dawn it grew colder and the sleet hardened into snow with an ever increasing wind, which struck through our men to the marrow. The water from the flood had fallen in the night, but it was still four feet deep in many of the trenches and our men passed the morning under fire, fishing for food and rifles in their drowned lines. All through the day the wind gathered till it was blowing a full gale, vicious and bitter cold and on the 28th it reached its worst. The 28th was spoken of afterwards as "Frozen Foot Day." It was a day more terrible than any battle, but now it was taking its toll of the Turks and the fire slackened.'

Probably either side could have had the other's position for the taking on the 28th had there been enough unfrosted feet to advance. It was a day so blind with snow and driving storm that neither side could see to fire and this brought the advantage that our men, hopping to the ambulances two miles or more away, had not to go through a pelt of shrapnel bullets. On the 29th the limits of human strength were reached. Some of those frozen three days before were able to return to duty, but a great number of officers and men who had done their best to stick it out were forced to go to hospital. The water fell during the day but it left on average two and a half feet of thick slushy mud, into which many trenches collapsed. It was at Suvla where the effects of this storm were most severely felt. In the three sectors over 200 men were dead, over 10,000 were unfit for further service, whilst not less than 30,000 others were sickened or made old by it.

On the 30th the battalion was put into the reserve trenches having been in the firing trenches for 47 consecutive days, but really the change made little difference – less sentry work and less responsibility certainly, but the fatigues were much increased and the shelling but little diminished. One good result from the gale was that it destroyed or removed the dysentery which had taken nearly a thousand victims a day for some months. No more fresh cases were reported.[7]

The 4th Battalion's war diary has some horrifying statistics on manpower over the months of October and November which make clear the terrible toll on the battalion during this period. The fighting strength of the battalion on 1 October 1915 was seven officers and 211 other ranks. While several batches of young officers arrived during this period which accounts for the increase in the officer figure, owing to sickness and the lack of drafts, the overall strength of the battalion dropped to as low as 19 officers and 178 other ranks by 23 October. Two drafts of two officers and 68 men arrived on 24 October and two officers and 146 other ranks joined on 31 October, giving an overall strength of 21 officers and 378 other ranks at the end of the month. On 30 November, when the battalion was relieved by 8 RWF and went into reserve, the battalion was down to 15 officers and 236 other ranks, the difference of six officers and 142 men accounted for by six officers and 140 men being in hospital, most of whom were casualties of the great storm.

* * *

The debate between the war committee and the cabinet continued for the remainder of November, with senior members such as Lord Curzon, Lord Privy Seal in Prime Minister Asquith's coalition Government, arguing most vehemently against evacuation. Despite such eloquent appeals and Lord Kitchener's indecision, the final decision in favour of evacuation was eventually made and this was announced by the cabinet on 8 December. There was a compromise however, with the evacuation being limited to the Anzac sector and Suvla Bay, while Cape Helles was to remain in allied hands, for the time being at least, ostensibly to prevent this being used as a naval base for Turkish and German ships, but in reality to ameliorate the opprobrium of a complete withdrawal from the peninsula.

---

7   Whatever the cause of the dysentery, it is unlikely to have been the flooding itself, but rather the de-fouling effect of the flooding and the many days of frost that limited the disease.

11

Evacuation

*After the bungled conduct of the campaign,
the evacuation itself was a flawless example
of a textbook operation that took the Turks
completely by surprise*

C F Aspinall-Oglander
Gallipoli Vol 2

As the effects of the storm subsided on 1 December, the weather at Cape Helles became much warmer again with bright sunshine. 160 men of 2 SWB were employed on outside fatigues tidying up the damage, while the Turks began hostile activity once more, with a plane coming over from the south at mid-day, dropping two bombs, one of which fell 25 yards in front of the battalion's forward line of dugouts but did not explode, and the other burst further forward, to the west of the Pink Farm road. That afternoon, the two squads of grenadiers attached to 157 Brigade returned. The next day, the battalion moved back up to the firing line, to relieve 1 KOSB. A Coy took up the right flank, B Coy were in the centre, while C Coy were on the left flank with D Coy in E11. Brigade standing orders had reduced the manpower levels for sentries, so the battalion were now working only one man in four as sentry at night, with double sentries on machine guns. C Coy had one man killed by sniper fire and the battalion's strength was down to 20 officers and 550 other ranks. Meanwhile, Ernest lamented the aftermath of the storm and the pressure put on the soldiers by relentless fatigues:

Thursday 2 December 1915

Back to fire trenches again in relief of KOSB. Yesterday and today we enjoyed beautiful weather and much warmer. Feet too much swollen to get boots on yesterday morning and had to go to breakfast in slippers. Today one had to wear trench boots (a pair bought by Robertson when he went sick). Luckily they are size 8 – two sizes larger than I normally take. The trenches are in muck. We always have to clean up after other people and it is a most annoying game when you do all you can to leave your own lines above suspicion.

Friday 3 December 1915

Thought it would rain last night it was too cloudy and warm. Today is what the Irishman terms "a soft day your Honour" – a drizzle which makes walking in the sticky clayey mud difficult. Water question is going to be difficult. The pipe from Romanos Well to Tank

Road which is about half a mile back had frozen and no water has been obtainable except that brought up by the Battalion in support, in petrol tins. These are excellent things if the men wouldn't lose the screw stoppers. As a man can carry only two tins and about 270 tins are required for the day that means a big slice out of the available men for fatigues by the support battalion. Not to mention the rations, wood, ammunition grenades, sandbags etc to be carried up. The wonder is how men are found to dig and repair trenches.

Misty rain fell during the night of 3 December and continued throughout the day, which made the communication trenches very muddy and greasy. Work continued on the shelter Ts and a new cookhouse, while C Coy exacted revenge by shooting the enemy sniper who they believed killed their man the previous day. The battalion then carried out a heavy bombardment on the enemy trenches during the afternoon, during which one man in B Coy was killed and Second Lieutenant A Ballantine was wounded and sent to the field hospital. During the night, bombing activity between the two sides became quite heated, with the Turks throwing some bombs at the listening post at P9 which had been pushed forward the night before about three yards down the trench connecting the battalion with the Turks; an indication of how close the opposing firing lines were to each other. About four bombs were thrown, of which one burst and all fell short. A party of grenadiers under an officer went out about 8:45 p.m. and again at 4:15 a.m. and threw about 16 bombs, of which eight went into the enemy's trench. The battalion continued to work on three defensive shafts, but could not hear any noise of enemy mining. On the afternoon of 4 December, there was a heavy bombardment of the enemy in the J trenches lasting about half an hour, to which the Turks replied, putting shrapnel all along the front line and down into the gullies; some 10 of them burst all round battalion HQ but did no damage. At the same time, the French 'crapouillots' burst a number of heavy bombs onto the Turks at the junction of E13e and Achi Baba Nullah.[1] During the evening about 60 yards of fresh wire was put out in front of existing French wire, using small trestles which one man could carry, to link up with the barbed wire. Two men from B Coy were wounded while putting out the wire._

Another milestone in Ernest's life, his 40th birthday, was not spent in the manner he would have liked and with no birthday cards arriving, morale was not high:

Saturday 4 December 1915

Woke today and found I was 40. A mail came in last night which I helped to sort but was disappointed. The last mail we got was landed on the 19th of last month – I suppose this was only half a mail. All I got for my birthday present today was a bombardment from the Turks to show us probably that their supply of ammunition was coming through. They certainly gave us an unpleasant half hour or so at Headquarters. Salvoes of shrapnel came over – about eight striking smack into our parapet but no personal damage was done. There was a heavier bombardment on the left going on from both sides. Tonight the Turks are sending an occasional shell over – rather unusual for them. They have wounded two men out wiring by sniping. Killed one man last night and one the night before. Bad luck to be hit by a stray bullet. However laying out barbed wire in front God I should like to be on the (…) tonight – have been in the blues all day. Of your trenches which are only about 100 yards from the enemy's is bound to bring casualties.

---

1   An affectionate term for *"le petit crapaud"*, the little toad, which was used by French soldiers to designate a small trench mortar.

On 5 December, 2 SWB discovered that the Turks appeared to have built up a heavily timbered grenade head in their front line, opposite to the battalion's listening post at P9. They managed to knock a good number of the sandbags from it with grenades from a catapult, exposing the timber underneath. They then set out to demolish it with a battery of Japanese mortars which they recently had acquired. The following day they moved back into brigade reserve again, at Brown House, being relieved by the Border Regiment. While there were no friendly troops to the west of Achi Baba Nullah, A Coy was in front of battalion HQ and to the east of Regent Street; B Coy were in the Eski Line next to the French; C Coy were near the White House, while D Coy and the spare machine gunners were in Parsons Road. The grenadiers were in front of B Coy, with one squad holding positions on Oxford and Central streets in front of D Coy. There were machine guns in the Horseshoe and 50 men were working with the RE on drainage and mending the pipe line to Tank Road. D Coy spent some time clearing up the mess of empty tins left by previous units around Parsons road and then there was the task of carrying yet another 150 loads of water and rations up to the front line. That night, the enemy maintained a fairly heavy rifle fire for a few hours, and then started again at stand-to the next morning. There was also some shell fire, but none landed on the battalion position.

The tedious and arduous task of trench reinforcement continued on 7 December, with 50 men all day under the Royal Engineers, and a further 60 men in the morning and 40 in the afternoon on the new Eski Line. There was also a further 150 loads of water and rations to be manhandled up to the front line. Enemy rifle fire appeared to have become more intense, with more shells being fired during the day around Parsons Road and about 200 yds in front of Brown House. On 8 December, warning was received from brigade HQ that the battalion was to change positions with the Royal Naval Division; at the same time, guides were to be sent to V Beach to receive an incoming draft of reinforcements. Ernest was not too happy about the somewhat illogical change of location:

Wednesday 8 December 2015

Rotten news – hear we are to relieve the RND over in the left centre on the 10th. They are taking over our line – can't think what the game is unless the RND are so fed up with their part of the line. One hears that it is pretty filthy and the firing line none too healthy both as regards sanitary arrangements and open proximity to the enemy. Several parts can be enfiladed and certainly they get more than their fair share of the shelling. The latter is becoming more general daily.

The disembarkation of the new draft did not go smoothly and it was not until 6:30 a.m. on 9 December that they were all ashore. There were two officers and 90 other ranks, most of whom were from the battalion originally, with Lieutenant F S Blake of the 15th King's Regiment, who had been wounded at Chocolate Hill and Lieutenant T C T Llewellyn, originally from 3SWB. The following day, the battalion moved out of Brown House and returned to the rest camp. Interestingly, the war diary records that no relief arrived to replace them as the brigade reserve, which implies that there was a shortage of manpower and that the brigade staff were taking a calculated risk, based on the assumption that 2 SWB could always be called forward quickly should the need arise. No sooner had they arrived than A Coy, with a platoon of B Coy, were sent straight to W Beach for work under the Royal Engineers; on arrival they were told they were not wanted and returned to the battalion in the afternoon. While at the beach, the enemy shelled the position, which caused some damage and wounded four soldiers, as Ernest explains:

Saturday 11 December 2015

Came down to Rest lines yesterday. What a treat to get out of one's clothes and into pyjamas again at night and have a bath with warm water in the morning, even if only in one's canvas bucket. However there are no ladies about. The Turks have been very busy today with their heavy high explosive shell. They started strafing the lines on the opposite side of Krithia Road – everyone a burster. Went for a walk towards W Beach and had a look at some of the graves just at the top but the shelling got a bit too close. Some men of the 'dug outs' employed at the beach bolted everywhere for cover. Can't blame them either for the day before one shell demolished the Ordnance office another the YMCA tent – casualties were slight I hear. We had four men of a working party hit, one seriously. Omitted to mention that we got another draft of two officers and 90 Rank & File on morning of 9th up at Brown House (support trenches). Lieutenant Blake was one – wounded at Chocolate Hill – the other Llewellyn who came in June or July last from 3rd Battalion and was sent to Essex Regiment I think and went sick just afterwards. He has been doing duty at Mudros for a long time.

An essential part of the logistic network at Cape Helles was a makeshift road, known as the mule track, which ran along almost the entire coast line from Gully Beach around to V Beach and which was used constantly by mule carts, to move stores from one beach to another, depending upon where they had been off-loaded from the supply ships. From here, supplies were then broken down into brigade consignments, from which Quartermasters would collect their unit allocation. As this part of the Cape was under observation from the Turks on the Asiatic coastline at Kum Kale, movement of supplies and any necessary repair work had to be done at night under the cover of darkness. Consequently there were 100 men from the battalion on divisional fatigues and 60 deepening the eastern mule track near brigade HQ during the night of 12 December, with a further 100 men working on the cliff top. During the afternoon, there had been heavy rifle fire from the direction of the French lines, followed by shelling of Turkish trenches from Achi Baba Nullah to the east. Ernest picked this up in his diary as well:

Sunday 12 December 1915

A lot more heavy shelling from the Turks today – these 'black marias' are most unpleasant brutes. Saw the hole on the beach made by the one which damaged four of our men. They were on the cliff side – apparently there are some marvellous seascapes.

Monday 13 December 1915

Heavier shelling near our lines. One has just burst about 300 yards in rear and a piece came singing back over us, at least 400 yards from where it burst.

Must bid farewell to this part of my diary. Hope to read it again many years hence – au revoir old pal.

Compulsive diarists, such as Ernest, can become closely attached to their notebooks, as they are an outlet for personal feelings, which are often quite emotive. They are also an indication of a logical and tidy mind and the commitment to make an entry almost every day can become an obsession. They are not necessarily written for wider publication and one wonders what Ernest might have thought had he realised that, one day, his diary entries would be the subject of a book for all to see. On this occasion, his diary was kept in a military issue notebook and he had simply run out of pages, so it was time to start the next volume. It clearly meant a lot to him and it was something that he intended to put away and read at his leisure in "many years hence" when he felt the need to look back on a dramatic chapter in his life, rather than submit it to regimental archives as an official war diary. How many other people might have read his entries over the intervening years is not known.

Back on the ground, fatigue parties continued at their relentless pace, with 150 men on divisional fatigues and 80 men on the cliff. Turkish shelling had become much more frequent with a larger proportion of shells bursting; fortunately none fell in the battalion camp area, but several among the units to the west of them. Winter clothing had started to arrive, with 650 waterproof capes and 650 pairs of fingerless leather gloves being issued. They also received a certain number of leather jerkins and about 80 pairs of long gum boots. The next day, the Turks put a lot of high explosive over the battalion in the morning; an 18 pounder shell fell among a party of another unit going up on relief, quite close to battalion HQ and hit two of them. Almost half the battalion was on divisional fatigues during the day, draining out the rest camp and then on the beach at night unloading a supply ship. This was to be a similar pattern for the next three days until 18 December, when the battalion moved back into the front line once again, to relieve 1 KOSB. As usual, three Coys were in the front line; A Coy on the right, B Coy in the centre and D Coy on the left flank. C Coy, less one platoon, was in support in Fusilier Street; this platoon being in support of D Coy on the Essex Knoll. The Border Regiment were on the left of the battalion, with a battalion of the Highland Light Infantry from 157 Brigade (52 (Lowland) Division) on their right. There was still work to be done sapping a completely new fire trench 60 yards in advance of the present line, but six saps had been run out and in some cases the saps were nearly joined up.

Drinking water was now more easily obtainable from tanks at the east end of Fusilier Street, with cooking water held in a tank near the brigade administrative area. This at least took the strain off the need to manhandle water supplies, but there was still a large amount of work to be done, particularly on trench defences, which put pressure on battalion manpower. On 18 December, the total strength was 644 all ranks, but of these, about 70 were nearly always away on other duties, all of which took its toll. At this time, the moon was too bright all night to dig in the open which limited the amount of time available to work in. Thankfully, enemy activity was very quiet and while the Turks threw some bombs at the Worcester barricade, it soon stopped when the battalion retaliated; they wanted to keep enemy activity to the minimum until the new trench had been dug. During this time four men were wounded.

By now, Ernest had acquired another military notebook (well, he was the Quartermaster after all) and the next volume began as normal:

Friday 10 to Saturday 18 December 1915

Think I left off my old diary when we came down from the trenches east of Achi Baba nullah for the last time unfortunately. Am writing this in my dug out in the RND trenches which we took over from the KOSBs yesterday (18th) after eight day's rest. Nothing eventful happened down below. The usual 'black marias' came over from Achi Baba and an increased number from the Asiatic side, nearly all of which went to W Beach (Lancashire Landing). Huge bursters of better quality than they have been. On Wednesday 15th went up to look over the new line – new? – Not a stroke of work appears to have been put into those trenches since they were first dug, except what the KOSB have done in the last few days.

What the RND have been doing all the time they held the line except making bomb saps is hard to conjecture. As is usual with these people, cleanliness of trenches is practically unknown. The Turks airmen can have no difficulty in picking out our lines of trenches by the number of tins of all descriptions lying on both sides of the trenches. On the 16th went over to Ordnance at W Beach and was just coming away when "Asiatic Annie" started on the stores and beach. Several horses were killed and it is surprising what few other casualties. Of course, after the first couple came over everyone is away for cover, but still as they are all high explosive shells one would expect more damage. The sound of them coming is worse I think than the explosion. When you hear the latter you are generally safe. 18th December. Relieved the KOSBs had got in without any casualties. They have had about 70 hit during the last eight days, mostly men working on the new trenches in front. A good few have been hit by shrapnel outside Bn HQ too.

By 19 December very good progress had been made with the saps. Each end advanced about eight to ten yards daily, at a depth of about 10 feet, with four rows of sandbags and was deepened and widened by parties working to the rear. The previous evening, the enemy had been spotted working on their parapet in the moonlight and were driven back by rifle fire. The battalion was then warned that at 2:15 p.m. an attack was to be made in the direction of the vineyard and trench G11a. This was preceded by a naval bombardment from a monitor ship, followed by a heavy burst of rifle and machine gun fire away to the left, after which there were two mine explosions and a heavy bombardment by both sides. Almost simultaneously, firing broke out from the direction of the Krithia Nullah, which continued till about 4:00 p.m. when things became quieter and by 5:00 p.m. there was practically no firing. At 9:30 p.m. there was a sudden burst of rifle firing and grenades away to the left, thought to be in the J trenches, with a little artillery fire. This continued till 10:30 p.m. when, for some unknown reason, Turkish cheering was heard from the same direction followed by comparative quiet. By 11:00 p.m. everything had gone quiet, but at midnight, heavy rifle and machine gun fire with grenades broke out in the Krithia Nullah, which continued intermittently all night until about 7:00 a.m. when it ceased. The allied bombardment appeared very effective, and was distributed evenly all along the line, while the Turkish reply was comparatively feeble and concentrated on a few locations. Ernest comments on the effects of the outbreak of enemy activity on his logistic workload:

Sunday 19 December 1915

Awful long job cleaning the blankets rations etc last night at the ration dump. A dozen carts of ours, some of the Border Regt, also Bde carts and some of 52nd Div; they all arrived at about the same time. A few stray bullets fizzed around but no-one hit. This morning it took about three hours to issue rations and stores purchased from Divisional Canteen. Don't know how we should have gone on for room if one hadn't managed to get a few stretcher bearers to dig out a place in the trench. Every available man digging somewhere. We have to hold the same amount of line too as the KOSBs who were 300 stronger up here. We have only half Coy of 'C' in reserve and it would take over an hour to get up reinforcements from our bivouac in the case of anything serious happening. However we have done it before and they always think we can do it again. At 2 pm a heavy bombardment was opened on the Turkish trenches opposite the 157th Bde in order to straighten that portion of the line across the Krithia Nullah. I started to count the shells but soon they were pelting over from both sides almost like bullets. It is now 5.30 pm and it is still unfinished, but much abated. At one time the ground fairly heaved and it seemed as if an earthquake had stepped in to stop the rot, but it was only a mine – what they must have felt in the near vicinity! Our monitors' guns have been hard at it and one pities the Turk having to endure such a crash. We shall want all the pity ourselves shortly if the rumour is true that the 'Square heads' are bringing their heavy artillery down here. 16 inch howitzers will soon level everything. We are withdrawing our troops from Suvla and the 86th Bde are already here, also some guns, so it seems that we have to hang on to this end at all costs. I wonder why? We have evidently failed to save Serbia and incidentally failed to stop the Germans' advance.

* * *

With the decision finally made to begin the evacuation at Gallipoli, life for the 4th Battalion, who were still at Suvla Bay, took on a new dimension, as it did in the Anzac sector as well. It is ironic that the majority of the offensive actions during the campaign were unsuccessful, yet the evacuation, a humiliating defeat no matter what gloss history may place upon it, was a masterstroke of staff planning and an outstanding success. So as not to alert the enemy by any sudden or unusual activity, the evacuation took place gradually from the time that the decision was made, to the moment that the last allied soldier left the shores of Anzac and Suvla Bay in the early hours of Sunday 20 December. The key elements were balance, timing and secrecy. Balance, in that it was essential that sufficient troops remained in the front line, to convince the enemy that nothing untoward was taking place, while there was a steady withdrawal of manpower and equipment at night; timing, in that it was crucial that those being withdrawn did so in accordance with a meticulous programme, so that there were sufficient ships available to take the men off-shore in the right place and at the right time; and secrecy, so that the Turks should have no idea at all that an evacuation was about to happen. The element of secrecy also applied to the allied troops; details were kept under wraps until the latest possible moment so that there was minimal chance of the plan being inadvertently leaked, while at Cape Helles none of the units had any idea that such an event was even taking place. All sorts of ruses, booby traps and subterfuge were put in place to hamper the enemy once he got wind of what was happening under his nose and in contradiction of all the most pessimistic predictions of huge casualty figures, not one soldier lost his life in this phase of the operation.[2]

The 4th Battalion account takes up the story:

The evacuation of Suvla and Anzac commenced on the 8th and on the 10th the Brigadier and commanding officers of the Brigade marched down to Lala Baba where they were allotted trenches in case they were required during the retirement. It would almost seem that the Turks had an inkling of our intentions as their shell fire had greatly increased, and they appeared to be registering on all likely places for embarkation – huge HE shells were constantly coming from the direction of the narrows right across the peninsula and landing with tremendous explosions along the seaward side of Lala Baba. But they had no inkling, and possibly rejoicing in the augmentation of their heavy pieces of artillery, wished to impress us with their ever increasing might.

By the 13th everything which could be best spared from the trenches, such as supplies, carts, valises, cooking pots etc had been sent away and the men had little else than what they

2   Alan Moorehead, *Gallipoli,* pp.340–348.

were actually wearing. On the 14th the battalion was informed that it had been selected as the last to leave the trenches of the 40th Brigade and that it would have to hold these lines alone after the other battalions had been withdrawn. Brigadier General Lewin spoke to all the officers saying that the battalion had a splendid record on the peninsula and that its two line battalions were amongst the best in the British Army and he asked for the battalion's best efforts in the onerous duty which had been assigned to it and it is needless to state the reply.

The Borderers relieved the 5th Wiltshires in the firing trenches on the 15th December and on the 18th the Royal Welch Fusiliers and Wiltshires were withdrawn from the lines, leaving the battalion and the Cheshires without any supports. It would be a false deduction to suppose that no anxiety existed amongst the officers, or, at all events, the more senior officers, during these latter hours of the evacuation. Who – standing in those support and reserve trenches on the morning of the 19th, empty of all save the few men who were sent to patrol up and down them, and the fires that were kept lighted in their usual places – could be free from the doubts and fears which disturbed the even tenor of their thoughts. It seemed altogether absurd to suppose that the enemy were entirely ignorant of our movements, but rather that he was waiting for the psychological moment when he might pounce down on our sufficiently weakened lines to crush us in his strength. The weather was another factor; a breeze of any strength suddenly arising – as it often did – might make it quite impossible to get the troops embarked. All had gone smoothly and well so far, but there were so many possibilities of the unforeseen happening that to those with responsibility the slowly moving hours seemed long and tedious, with an abnormal tension worked up by the imagination. Everything possible was done to deceive the Turk and blind his eyes. The vigilance of our aeroplanes made it impossible for any hostile machine to fly over our lines and for the past 10 days or so our sniping had purposely become less and less, so as to accustom the enemy to the short periods when it ceased altogether.

There was much work to be done; the mines in front of the trenches had been made operative by the Royal Engineers the night before and others were being laid in all sorts of places where the Turk was likely to poke about after our departure. Numerous telephone messages had to be answered and final preparations of all sorts and kinds had to be thought out or attended to. It was known that the Turks were in need of sandbags so for the last day or two our men had been at work slitting our sand bags with their knives and leaving them just sufficiently serviceable to last out our needs; this work was still proceeding in the front trenches.

At 10am on the 19th the enemy started a bombardment from the Chanak fortress on the Dardanelles. Nine-inch shells came whistling over, one after the other, all directed at the landing stages at Lala Baba. 40 of these shells were fired; one of them going right through and demolishing a pier which had been temporarily constructed to facilitate the embarkation, but with the exception of this there was no firing of any consequence. In the light of subsequent events it remains clear that the Turks were quite deceived as to what was going on. The increased shipping in the harbours had led them to believe that we were actually landing more troops and that an attack on their own lines was imminent. Those in our front trenches had noticed an unusual activity in the Turkish working parties; additional wire entanglements were being rapidly constructed in front of their lines, trenches were being strengthened and they appeared to have a general feeling of unrest. They were digging new lines, bringing up new guns and making ready for us in every way. The idea that the

Turks knew all about it, but had been bribed to "wink the other eye" was as foolish as it was unfair to the splendid staff work which enabled the evacuation to be one of the most wonderful of its kind.

At 5.45pm on the 19th the Cheshires were withdrawn from the lines, taking up a covering position about two miles back and leaving the SWB alone in the front trenches of the Brigade, whilst at 7pm the remaining seven maxim guns were sent away. The first party of the battalion, about 250 strong under Lieutenant Col Beresford, silently and with unfixed bayonets glided out of the trenches at 8pm and a second party under Major Kitchen stole away at 11pm, leaving Captain Cahusac and six other officers with 100 men to patrol up and down the otherwise empty trenches until 1.30am when they were to retire and leave the trenches empty.

How curious are the sentiments of the human mind, for when the last moments arrived there came a feeling of positive regret at leaving those filthy old comfortless places which we had loathed when compelled to stay in them. Perhaps the feeling that the task was not completed and that all the previous sacrifices had been in vain, perhaps these, added to the fact that our own very departure was an acknowledgement of failure, had a saddening influence on all that army who had wished 'to see it through.'

The march was slow as the men were heavily laden but the way was comparatively good and the moon, though hazy, was at the full. It was weird and impressive, that march of silent men, for whatever their feelings they kept them to themselves, wondering no doubt in a kind of awe, whether the Turks would discover them and attack, but no shells came, only the usual sniping here and there and the whistling of an occasional overshot bullet. Even when all had departed, our mechanically arranged rifles gave fitful answer to the Turkish sniper. The outer lines of the last defences were passed and several others until at last, after a three mile march, the parties arrived at Lala Baba where they were crowded onto a lighter, the first two parties being embarked on the "Osmanish" and the last party being put aboard another vessel. These parties left Suvla at about 3am on the 20th for the island of Imbros. All the embarkations from other points were successful and so the evacuation of the northern part of Gallipoli was thus accomplished, practically without a casualty and without a hitch.

The two parties of the battalion landed at Imbros about 8am along with many other troops. Everything here was in great confusion as battalions were naturally very mixed up so the men just marched individually or in small parties of their own making to a camping ground about two miles away where they were sorted out and given a meal. They were weary, filthy and footsore from the unaccustomed marching, but soon they were on the move back to the landing stages from which they had come. Here the battalion was put on board the ex North German Lloyd ship "Derflinger" now called the "Huntsgreen" together with the 5th Cheshires, Loyal North Lancashires and South Lancashires, in all about 1,500 and 2,000 men. The orders were to sail for Mudros at midnight, but unfortunately at about 4pm a German aeroplane came hovering right over the ship and dropped several bombs into the water around it. As there were known to be several submarines outside the harbour and as of course the aeroplane would give due notice to them, the captain of the ship was ordered to delay his departure till the next morning. At 7.30am on the 21st the Huntsgreen started, with the Osmanish following, together with the battleships Lord Nelson and another, the whole escorted by three destroyers. A bad storm soon started with a blizzard of rain and wind and as the sea was washing right over the destroyers they signalled that we were going back, whereupon the battleships steamed ahead, the Osmanish disappeared somewhere and the

Huntsgreen remained alone. It was a very unpleasant voyage and the threat of being torpedoed was not the least unpleasant part of it, but all went well and at 1pm the Huntsgreen entered Mudros harbour in fine weather. Next day the troops started disembarking in lighters and after a hot march of three miles the battalion and the Cheshires reached a stony hill called Porteanos where they found the rest of the 40th Brigade and which they were informed was their camping ground. Lieutenant Col Beresford was invalided from this camp, Major Kitchin taking over command of the battalion.

* * *

While the 4th Battalion withdrew to Lemnos, the 2nd Battalion were still under pressure at Cape Helles, as trench work continued at a relentless pace. B and D Coys were getting only six hours rest a day, while C Coy was working up to 12 hours a day. The new trench had to be completed as quickly as possible for various reasons, not least of which was the fear of a concerted attack by the Turks. The secrecy covering the evacuation planning at Suvla and Anzac had clearly been successful, as it was not until 20 December that the battalion knew what had happened. There had been a fair amount of shelling by both sides during the day, none of which affected the battalion; there were reports of heavy howitzers, some of the largest seen on the peninsula so far, firing at trenches on their left flank, in the areas of the Border barricade. That evening, there was a considerable amount of activity, including mortar and artillery fire and it was thought that the Turks were massing in their trenches behind H13c in the Krithia Nullah, possibly preparing for a general attack, thinking that the allies were evacuating the whole peninsula. In the event, however, no attack took place. The battalion suffered five casualties, one of whom died later of his wounds.

Ernest's diary then picks up various bits of news relating to the effects of the storm at Suvla and about the evacuation:

Monday 20 December 1915

Not much rest last night. Turks counter-attacked on the left of our line about 9 pm and soon there was a din of rifles, machine guns and big guns. We have not heard the result. The CO remarked this morning that there was a lot of cheering which he thinks was the Turks shouting 'Allah.' The last time we heard that was in night attack they made on 2nd May. About 2 am had to take my boots off, feet having painfully swollen. Find too that Carding's boots are no good to wear except in water for the rubber and lining get so wet inside when the boots are worn for some hours that they never seem to dry. The Turks are strafing us with HE somewhere on our left, the pieces flying over here. Saw 'Baby' Shaw today – came up to see us and had lunch. He was at Alexandria and went to Suvla about two months ago. He evacuated with the other troops from that part a few days ago. We got a message through today saying that Suvla and Anzac had completely evacuated last night without a casualty. A very gratifying piece of intelligence. The bulk of the troops have gone to Mudros I expect. A few guns which the wire says could not be extricated were abandoned at ANZAC. They were destroyed.

The 86th Bde had an awful time over at Suvla during the blizzard and rain. Apparently the thing was so sudden that the water rushed into dug outs and swept equipment, men, horses and everything in its path. The Turks got it as bad as we did. Over one parapet two mules, two horses a donkey and two dead Turks were swept from the enemy's side. The

86th Bde had 2600 casualties during that rotten time for the blizzard followed the rain and they got frost bite badly. Both British and Turk I'm told got up out of their water logged trenches and stood or huddled on the parados without attempting to fire on one another – I expect they had nothing to fire with. Poor beggars. To make matters worse they had only just sent off their heavy kit pending the evacuation and so had practically only just what they could carry with them. The 88th Bde were better off up in the hillside, having only 800 casualties but even that is a lot. Now that Anzac and Suvla is abandoned we may expect all the big guns over here. However it hits both ways, we ought to have plenty too. Hear that the stunt over at 157th Bde was not quite altogether successful. The HLI took all the trench except one bit on the left which has a brickwork redoubt. They lost all the officers they had in the show. Total casualties about 60 or 70. Don't know what the Turks lost. Have heard nothing about the stunt on our left. I hear that the HLI still hold their trench; perhaps they will be able to blow up the redoubt. The Dublin Fusiliers came up and took over part of the 52nd Div line next to us on our right. Suppose the 86th Bde will take over all the 52nd Div area.

The next day, during the afternoon and into the evening, the Turks kept up salvoes of artillery fire over battalion HQ and the communication trenches, using what appeared to be a new shell with an aluminium fuse; an indication of new stocks of ammunition they were receiving from Germany. Another two men were killed and Captain W Pace was wounded. It was also a wet day, as Ernest records:

Tuesday 21 December 1915

Very little peace last night. We had the report passed along that the Turks were massing opposite Northern Barricade and also opposite 52nd in Krithia Nullah. Heavy firing from both sides nearly all night. Today it is no better. Rather the opposite. Bn HQ is in a most uncomfortable spot. Shrapnel came over four at a time just missing the top but why I don't know. About 2 pm it started to rain, driving hard from the south. Managed to keep my dugout fairly dry but small waterproof sheets are not much use especially when old and perforated. The trenches were soon churned up to a liquid mud and thanks to the rotten way that the RND looked after them they wouldn't drain. Had to go through pools of it nearly up to one's knees in places. The enemy bombarded heavily in the afternoon and our HQ got straffed again – from a Whiz bang! (A small gun which fires at close quarters). There is a battery of them evidently not far away as we got them in fours again. One of these burst its case and a piece went through one of the mess boxes at such an angle that it seemed impossible to do so without cutting through the sand bags at the corner of the dugout. The shrapnel fuse of these guns is of aluminium, probably German. Must try and find one. Went down to meet rations in the evening and a heavy scrap started, first with rifle and MG fire followed by all sorts of artillery. I wonder if the Turk thinks we are going to try and get away from here too by night as they did from Suvla and Anzac? Some very heavy bursters came over and fell short of the ration dump. Was very much relieved to see QMS Hulbert and his pioneers turn up without any casualties. On my way back to HQ found my way barred by the explosion of one of the howitzer bursters which had literally filled the trench in, having pitched into the parapet. Lucky that no-one was passing at the time or there would have been two burials.

While the rain had hindered work on the trenches the previous day, come the morning of 22 December, the new trench, with some 50 wire trestles, was almost complete. The enemy turned a machine gun on the wiring parties, but caused no casualties, while the Dublin Fusiliers took over trenches on the battalion's right flank and Ernest's next diary entry picks up the engagement they had with the Turks on their arrival. He also has some caustic comments to make about General de Lisle coming back to the Cape – renowned for his propensity for trench digging:

Wednesday 22 December 1915

Very little rest again last night. Enemy strafed us once for a long time – about an hour I should say – without any reply from us. In order to make them attack, but except for gun fire there was little doing. We fired a few rounds from the ship only. From information given by a Turkish prisoner it seems rather unlikely that he will try and assault our positions with the bayonet. He says "it is hard enough to get the men into the firing line and to hold it without getting him to attack." They call this place 'The Slaughter House.' He also said that the intention is to bombard us for seven days as soon as they get the Germans' heavy guns up, then to attack. I should think that not at all unlikely. A most extra-ordinary thing happened this morning at about 6.30 just after Stand-to. About 60 Turks attacked the Dublins' fire trench. Can't understand how they crossed over unobserved. They first threw bombs in and then went for the Dubs with the bayonet. The parapet gave way as it was so sodden. Six of the Dubs were killed, don't know how many wounded. They turned the Turks out in three minutes, killing 20. I suppose some of the remainder who got away were wounded. They say a German officer led them and he is lying outside the parapet now. The Dublins are being relieved tomorrow by the KOSB so the latter have had only five days in bivouac. I thought there would be changes as soon as de Lisle came over from Suvla and took command again. We came under his command again today at 12 noon. I wonder if that knocks our rest on the head? We should go down on the 26th but I shall be surprised if we do – how cheerful! Managed to get rid of a lot of the water and mud from the trenches today.

By the morning of 23 December, the remaining portion of the trench between Sap Q and Sap R was cut through, with nine loop holes put in between Worcester Barricade and Sap 30; there was also a good drainage system between battalion HQ and the brigade dump. The enemy had become very active and the rate of his rifle fire had increased; also his bomb throwing was more accurate than before. For example, near Sap 30 they put five bombs out of 15 into the battalion's trench, but luckily without damage. The Turks were seen working on their parapet too and appeared to be roofing in their trench, as well as baling out water. Also during the morning, 1 KOSB took over the trenches held by the Dublin Fusiliers, as well as some of the battalion's trenches. This enabled them to close in to their left and to shorten the line held by the coys. While this was going on, GOC 29 Division came round the trenches on a routine visit.

Once the British public had come to realise that this war was not going to be over by Christmas, as had originally been anticipated in August 1914, a number of voluntary welfare organisations were set up, with the aim of sending gift parcels to the soldiers serving on the Western Front and at Gallipoli, to make their lives a little more comfortable. There was no shortage of interest and enthusiasm, but the reality of fundraising to support the concept was easier said than done. With such a large number of men away from home, money was in short supply in many families and it tended to be those organisations with Royal patronage which had the most success. On this occasion it was Queen Alexandra's Field Force Fund and Lady Hamilton's Dardanelles Fund which were in a position to send some welcome sustenance to those troops who had yet to be evacuated from the peninsula, as Ernest recalls:

Thursday 23 December 1915

Had quite a quiet night, most surprising after the last few nights. Trenches are drying again, but have been constructed so badly that half an hour's rain will make them as bad as ever. I hear we are going to get ½ lb plum pudding per man for Xmas. This is through the generosity of the Q.A.F.F.F. and Lady Hamilton's Dardanelles Fund. I hope they are already cooked otherwise it will be a bit difficult up here. The wind is from the north today but it is not too cold. We have just had three shrapnel shells on top of Bn HQ. The first of course was the worst for several of us were outside and it went all around without hitting anyone. The men don't care much – they are outside again and serving out dinners.

The logistics of steaming the many hundreds of Christmas puddings needed for the necessary hours would indeed be "a bit difficult." It is little details like this that bring home the immense task that Ernest was accomplishing, and the stoic endurance he showed. The ongoing effort to co-ordinate cooking as well as providing for all the other needs of 1,000 men doing hard labour through all weathers for months while under fire is almost impossible to imagine.

By Christmas Eve, the new fire step was complete all along new firing line, with machine guns mounted at regular intervals. Two enemy snipers and a bomber were shot, while four enemy aeroplanes came over very low early in the afternoon; no doubt to check that the allies at the Cape were still in place. They were heavily fired at from the front trenches, but got away unscathed and came back again at about 9:00 p.m. Five men were wounded that day and the battalion was told that they would have another six days to do in the front line.

Christmas Day saw no let up in trench digging or enemy activity. During the morning, the usual improvements to the new trench continued, while the enemy's new work in the Worcester Barricade was severely damaged by grenades from the battalion. In the afternoon, the enemy shelled the Krithia Nullah heavily with both HE and shrapnel for about 15 minutes. They also shelled the battalion's front line and communication trench with shrapnel and a "whizz-bang" gun which had been causing trouble for some time. For all that, the allied artillery batteries made little reply, mainly because they were low on ammunition. Orders then came in from HQ 29 Division that no firing was to take place from 5:00 p.m. until after the moon was well up, at about 9:30 p.m. with orders "to take advantage of any attack by the enemy and to kill or capture as many as possible." The irony of this order was the fact that the Turks took advantage of this to do a lot of work on their own defences, but in any event their fire did not differ much from previous nights. They sent out a strong patrol to the gap between 2 SWB and the Border Regiment on their left flank, but this was fired on and driven back. Likewise, two other Turks came out from the Worcester Barricade to throw bombs and they were also driven back. At about 11:15 p.m. heavy bombing and firing was heard from the J trenches and a number of flares went up from the battalion; this was closely followed by firing from the Krithia Nullah and a quantity of shrapnel bursting over the battalion HQ. The "whizz-bang" started up again, resulting in two casualties, while the enemy to the front opened a brisk rifle fire. They also threw some bombs over their parapet, but this was a very half hearted affair as they were a long way off and caused no damage at all. Christmas Day saw Corporal John Mandall, age 27, die from his wounds in an exchange of rifle fire and a further five were wounded. Ernest recorded the day as follows:

Saturday 25 December 1915

Xmas Day! Who would have thought when we landed eight months ago today that we should be here at Christmas and not more than a mile beyond our line of the 28th April? Yesterday was remarkably quiet really except for a strafe down the Krithia Nullah from about 2 to 3 pm. Two or three enemy airplanes came and circled round very low and must have taken back some useful information. Not an airplane of ours to be seen worse luck but a lot of rifle fire and shrapnel was directed at them from our lines without any appreciable result. Today they have shelled us a good deal at various times – any amount of the Whizz bang variety around our HQ. Someone will get badly knocked out unless we go on being lucky. Was off up this afternoon to try the new telescopic sighted rifle when about eight or ten Whizz bangs came hailing down in rapid succession. They sent their 'Black Marias' along the nullah; I hope without result. Got some news yesterday which if it proves true is really good. We are to move into the old support trench (Fusilier Street).

The "whizz bang" was originally attributed to the noise made by shells from German 77mm field guns, and the name was derived from the fact that shells fired from light or field artillery travelled faster than the speed of sound. Thus, soldiers heard the typical "whizz" noise of a travelling shell before the "bang" issued by the gun itself. Whizz bangs were consequently much feared, since the net result was that defending infantrymen were given virtually no warning of incoming high-velocity artillery fire as they were from enemy howitzers.[3]

On Boxing Day, conscious of the effects of the enemy's increased fire power, work continued on the deep underground bombardment dugouts in the support line, while orders were received to move Bn HQ immediately, as it was becoming vulnerable to enemy shrapnel fire. The new position was not quite ready, so it relocated to Fusilier Street for the time being. Although any political decision to evacuate the Cape had not yet been made public, the battalion was given a long list of work to be done in anticipation of any further move and they were also led to believe that they too might be taken off the peninsula for a time. During the evening, 35 wire gates (gaps in the defensive wire) were put out, as well as an amount of loose wire. Two enemy snipers were shot, while the battalion had one man killed and two wounded. During the night, the rain fell heavily, making all the trenches very wet, so the next morning everyone worked on drainage and also on deepening the fire trench to three feet below the fire step. By 9:00 a.m. the rain cleared and the rest of the day was bright and sunny. That afternoon, the enemy shelled the Krithia Nullah heavily and fired some shrapnel and "whizz-bangs" over the battalion position, to which they replied with heavy gun fire; indeed, the day was characterised by a good deal more rifle fire than usual from both sides. More wire was put out around the head of the Worcester Barricade and along the rest of the line. The Turks appeared to have withdrawn their bomb head from that position and built a new one, as far forward as their fire trench, which the battalion fired on with numerous bombs. They then took over a number of saps from the Inniskilling Fusiliers and 1 KOSB, while 29 Division cyclists attached to C Coy arrived during the day to help with this work.[4]

Ernest commented on the difficulties created by the additional wire defences and the effects of the wet weather; he was also aware of the threat caused by the bigger calibre guns being used by the Turks:

3   Michael Duffy, Firstworldwar.com.
4   The Cyclists were originally Divisional messenger units on the Western Front but were re-roled as infantry at Gallipoli. They were disbanded in 1916.

Monday 27 December 1915

Hardly room to move around the traverses. However, we managed to cover the fire step sufficiently to keep our valises dry. Luckily we did for it commenced raining about 4 this morning and the trenches are full of slush and mud again. One gets smothered from head to foot through brushing and slipping up against the sides. It is now noon and seems to be clearing a bit. One thing this ought to hamper 'Fritz's' big guns again. Whether the enemy can see our covering or not can't say but he has been shrapnelling us. The Border Regt has been relieved by the Inniskilling Fusiliers today. We hope to go down after tomorrow.

While the weather was fine and warm, the battalion was able to push on with deepening the water drains and trenches, assisted by100 men of the Border Regiment. During the afternoon allied guns shelled the enemy in the H trenches to their front, with the exception of the front trenches, and as a precaution, the battalion withdrew most of their men in case any of the artillery shells fell short – an occupational hazard of war! Once again, the Turkish "whizz-bangs" were in evidence and while the battalion's firing line was not affected, the support line took several hits, with three men being wounded. That night, work continued on anew communication trench alongside Central Avenue.

Ernest had a few things to say about a number of rumours circulating:

Tuesday 28 December 1915

No sign of going down tomorrow. The latest rumour from one of the Company Captains, who was speaking to the General today, is that we stay up another three or perhaps six weeks! Must have been pulling his leg. The men couldn't stand it. This morning we got 'Khabar'[5] that we were going to bombard the enemy's trenches in front of ours starting at 1 o'clock. It is now 2.15 pm and there's quite as much stuff coming from the Turk in reply. Some of their HE came too close to our HQ for liking and one of them nearly deafened me. Shrapnel is going hard now fore and aft. Don't mind that so much as long as one is not in the open but their howitzer bursters are most unpleasant.

On 29 December, at 1:00 p.m. 2 SWB put in an attack on the Krithia Nullah. This lasted for about an hour and then at 5:00 p.m. the enemy bombarded the trench, during which time two men were wounded. The battalion then carried on the usual work of strengthening their line of wire.

Ernest was a very keen shot and in peacetime had been a member of the battalion's rifle team, where he took part in a number of inter-unit shooting competitions. He had acquired a sniper rifle with telescopic sights and was keen to try it out on live targets; "good sport" as he called it, but the rigours of war could create a different perspective on life and death, particularly when he had seen any number of his friends and colleagues killed by enemy fire:

Wednesday 29 December 1915

I took the telescopic rifle up to 'Munster Terrace' but found no heads except behind loopholes. Had some good sport at these though at 400 yards range and closed them all up.

5   An Indian Army colloquial expression for news or rumours.

My spotter said I got two hits through the loop holes. One can tell the Turks' loop holes by the light behind as they rarely close them. Then by spotting with the large telescope they can be seen passing and re-passing. As soon as my spotter told me there was a head at the loop hole I fired. Two of these he said were hits – pure conjecture of course – for the fellow pulls his head away naturally if one strikes the sandbags inside the loophole. However it's good sport. When I came down I found I was urgently wanted about stores required to complete. Had to go down to 29th Div HQ and see DADOS who was purported to be leaving Helles. There was nothing worth recording in this except that one wondered why one couldn't go direct to ADOS at W Beach. I found out next night.[6]

By 30 December, news was out that the Cape was to be evacuated shortly and the logistic planning to achieve this was set in motion, along the same lines as it had been organised at Suvla Bay. The battalion was ordered to send in to the divisional ordnance dump everything that could not be carried, along with all officers' personal possessions, for it was the officers, by the very nature of their rank and class distinction, who had more personal items of clothing and equipment with them in the field than did the soldiers. There was no let up on trench defences however and work continued during the day on rebuilding Fusilier Street to the west of Left Avenue. There was a heavy bombardment by both sides, with one soldier being wounded.

Having been safely evacuated from Suvla Bay to Lemnos in the previous week, 13 Division then redeployed two brigades to the Cape to assist in the second phase of the evacuation. As part of 40 Brigade, 4 SWB found itself alongside 2 SWB, an unusual occurrence to have two battalions from the same regiment alongside each other, and the battalion had sent an advance party to liaise with Ernest, to reconnoitre its new defensive position:

Thursday 30 December 1915

On the 30th I had a visitor – Capt Marr. He had come on in advance of 40th Bde to see the firing line and where his machine gun emplacements were to be. He said the 4th Bn were landing same night and were taking over part of our line, so there seemed some hope of our going early after all. After lunch went down to draw up all stores I could from Ordnance at W Beach. I had hardly started getting my stores into the carts when we were bombarded from Achi and from Asia. That meant a general clear out of tents into dug outs and under the cliff. Really one could walk into the tents and take anything during a strafe of the beach. The shelling was a little more erratic than usual; quite a number going into the sea. Two however landed on Corps HQ I heard afterwards. I stayed to tea with Charlton of the Ordnance – an old pal of Ted Bachelors at Kirkee. A German Taube came over to look see and dropped a bomb or two. He was afterwards chased by one of our planes. I proposed to the Ordnance Officer Lancashire Landing that I should draw up my other stores after the gunning had finished but he refused me. Said they were packing up and nothing more would be issued. Said I could draw from the 9th Corps later on. This seemed absurd to me and set me thinking. However when I got back to Bn HQ pretty tired I found I was urgently wanted at Brigade HQ. Back I had to go about a mile again and then my eyes were opened. Had orders to get all officers' kits and regimental stores to the beach same night and any balance on 31st. We are to evacuate the peninsula shortly. Got back to Bn HQ again and after a hasty dinner, during which time Barnes packed my kit, went off down to our

6   See Glossary for details of abbreviations. DADOS was at Divisional level; ADOS at Corps level.

regimental dump. All the officers' kits followed in the ration carts. Twisted my ankle again in the mule trench and had two miles to go. That is the fourth time for the same ankle since August. Hobbled into the dump about an hour and a half later and got the four carts loaded and sent off to the beach.

During New Year's Eve, rifle fire and artillery bombardment continued on both sides, during which time one soldier was killed and three wounded, as 4 SWB moved into position on the left flank of the 2nd Battalion. The supporting platoon of C Coy was regrouped to Fusilier Street and more wire was put out on the eastern flank of the Worcester barricade, should the enemy attempt any major offensive at this vulnerable time. To confuse the Turks and to give the impression that it was still business as usual, orders were received to keep a steady fire going till midnight, and then let it gradually die out until 1:00 a.m. There was then to be no firing until 6:30 a.m. This appeared to achieve its object, as the Turks did not seem to understand it all, and their reaction was to keep up a volley of rifle fire, to no avail, during the night. In the meantime, Ernest was heavily involved with the logistics of planning for the evacuation, but had time to catch up with an old friend of his:

Friday 31 December 1915

At about 1am, 11 more carts turned up with eight men to load. Got those off and at about 3am got another four carts. Then had to send six carts loads of under clothing to the Bn for distribution and got them there by 6am, just time enough for them to get away before dawn. A fair night's work. Sometime in the night two officers of the 46th Bde were heard outside enquiring their way to Gully Ravine. I called them in and one was Casuhac! Adjutant of the 4th Bn looking very fit and cheery. Told me he had been with the 1st Bn for four months in France then got invalided with fever and came out a month ago to join the 4th Bn. He was the last officer left in the trenches to hold the line at Suvla – of his own Bn. To resume: got back to Bn HQ at 6.30 am just as dawn was breaking. Got in a couple of hours sleep but the shelling prevented any more. Major Kitchin, who now commands the 4th Bn turned up for lunch. He looks remarkably fit and young. Told us that H P Yates commands a Bn (I forget which) in 39th Bde. Morgan-Owen Bde Major 40th Bde expects to go to Div Staff as GSO 2. Godwin Austin goes to be DAQMG 13th Div.[7] Our fellows are doing well in staff appointments. Gen Travers has gone home invalided. After dinner, Cahusac turned up and stayed for an hour which he kept merry.

On New Year's Day, firing began again at 6:30 a.m. Hardly had a flare been put up, than the enemy returned rapid rifle fire, no doubt expecting a major attack. 2 SWB wired some more of the right flank of Worcester Barricade and pushed on with work on the new and old Fusilier Street, so as to get two tiers of fire. There was very little artillery fire from either side, nor were any patrols seen. Officers' equipment continued to be moved back to W Beach and the regimental dump was cleared under the arrangements of the quartermaster. 63 men who were deemed to be too sick and weakly and who might be a hindrance in the last stages of the evacuation were likewise moved back to the rest camp. Ernest greeted the new year in his diary:

---

7   Captain Alfred Reade Godwin-Austen went on to become the colonel of the regiment in 1950 in the rank of lieutenant general. For more detail see the list of officers at the rear of the book.

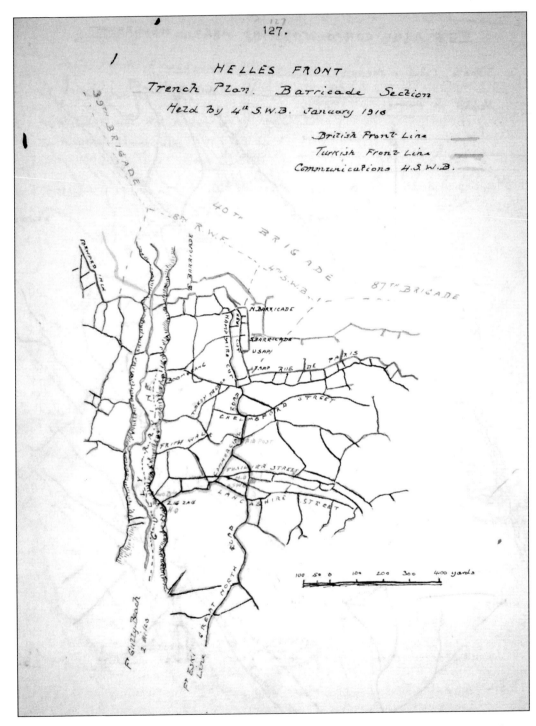

Map 19. Sketch Map by Captain Kitchin of the Helles front trench plan – January 1916 (Mrs A Payne).

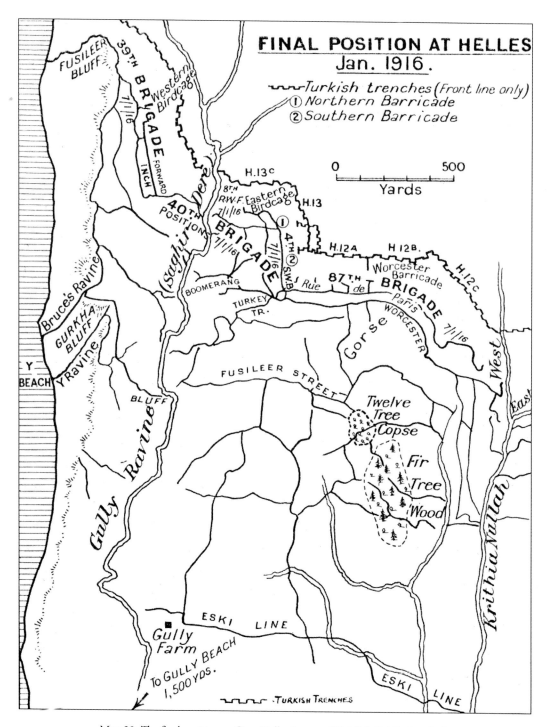

Map 20. The final position at Cape Helles January 1916 (Medici Society Ltd).

Saturday 1 January 1916

A Happy New Year! A fine crisp wind from the north but not too cold yet and the shelling is fairly warm. Have been too busy the last few days to write up my diary till now. Tomorrow we go down to Eski Lines and are being relieved by KOSB. I wonder if we shall come up again and if so what part of the line. The men are guessing hard as to what we are going to do. The Turks have been wonderfully quiet today. Hardly any shelling at all – wonder what their game is.

On 2 January, 2 SWB was relieved by 1 KOSB and moved to the Eski Line, where it cut the eastern mule track. The battalion then set to, clearing the drains in mule track so as to ensure a clean trench if evacuation was to take place on a wet night. As at Suvla Bay, the details of the evacuation were kept very secret, but the commanding officer was briefed on discipline during the withdrawal, and arrangements for forming-up places, which would be revealed to the troops nearer the time. So that they had the minimum to carry at the end, some of the soldiers' personal clothing in the way of gum boots, mackintosh capes, packs and excess tools, were withdrawn to the beach and a further 27 sick men were sent to the rest camp for evacuation. To assist with the withdrawal, a fatigue party cut another communication trench from the brigade dump to Left Avenue. An enemy aeroplane came over and flew very low right down the firing line, no doubt looking to see if any evacuation was in progress. The plane was heavily fired at, but got away.

Still anxious to learn of the allied intentions, another two enemy aeroplanes came over the next day and flew down towards the beach. Parties were hastily clearing out drains in the communication trenches and blocking off side entrances to ensure that there would be no confusion and that everyone would take the correct route on "Z night," as the night of the evacuation was being referred to. In the event of a fighting withdrawal, each soldier was issued with 220 rounds of rifle ammunition while 100 boxes of small arms ammunition, along with a large supply of grenades, were brought down and buried at the beach as an immediate reserve. Two platoons were sent to Fusilier Street as support to the Inniskilling Fusiliers and in Bn HQ, one of the clerks was tasked with collecting up all valuable documents and taking them off the peninsula in advance. Not knowing what the enemy's reaction might be if they discovered that another evacuation was about to happen, every available man worked on the Eski Line after dark, improving communication and support trenches. In the event of having to hold the line in a rearguard action, seven days' reserve of rations were built up into a parados on the fire step. This was a nerve-wracking time for Ernest, as the battalion's logistic plan for the evacuation rested very much upon his shoulders. His diary entries for the next few days capture the mood and tension of the coming withdrawal and need no further amplification:

Monday 3 January 1916

Came down yesterday morning and managed to fix up rations for the men eventually – the first day in a new place is generally a little confusing. We got a lot of shelling yesterday including our own lines, which the KOSB said were generally left alone. In the afternoon came the intelligence that we go up on the night of the 3rd to take over from a portion of 88th Bde. It had been pre-arranged that we should not go up again, but lend men and officers as required to show others the way down when we finally scuttle. This is now all changed and they are putting us up in the worst bit of line of all viz Krithia Nullah which gets all the HEs.

It is an honour for the 24th to be singled out for it though as it is the 'Skins' turn up and they are relieving the Border Regt instead. So the latter will not be in the last stint I imagine unless we get a bad time and are held up. Had to get all the men's packs, water proof capes, gum boots and jerkins taken to Ordnance last night which took 13 carts. Sgt Irons who was in charge of the party informed me this morning that none of our Mess stores or kits, valises (17 cart loads) have gone yet and it is believed they are going to be burned. The Mess stores alone are valued at about £60.[8] We shall have nothing but what we stand up in – cheers!

Got not a wink of sleep last night – went to bed with a head ache and whether it was the plum pudding we had for dinner or the cold or what but had a rotten night. The Turks shelled all night the beaches and several HEs very close to us. They are hard at it now. Don't know what time we go up to take over G11 A (the recently captured trench) and the other bit of the line. C Coy goes down to Rest Camp this afternoon to light fires I suppose to deceive the enemy – they come up to Eski Line by Krithia Nullah tomorrow. Half D Coy go up to be attached to the Skins today – we shan't see them again here. Shall at Mudros I hope. Have sent about 80 unfits away – remainder go up and see the last of it. A Turk aeroplane came so low yesterday that he must have seen everything. Anyhow I hope he saw lots of troops. Three more came over this morning. They were fired at but not hit apparently. It is nippy today but the rain, although threatening is still holding off luckily.

Tuesday 4 January 1916

Had a better night's rest last night but have a touch of rheumatism in my hips or something. Can't sleep on either side for more than half an hour at a stretch. Went to W Beach in the afternoon to see how much stores had gone. Found them still there and Sgt Ellis's party. Carts came up whilst I was there and started taking officers' valises, so we hope to see them again someday. Never have I seen such a conglomeration of stores thrown about. No order – no method – no one seemed to be running the show. Gum boots lying about the road, kits had been opened up and one could take anything away if he could carry it. Saw the Armourer Sgt there who told me the arrangements for destroying the stores, ammunition etc were admirable. Can't say I could agree with him by the look of the muddle. He told me however that everything for the final night was settled. Got back to rest camp and had a cup of tea with Sergeant Press the Mess Sergeant.[9] He and his staff were sent off two or three days ago when we thought we were going up to the trenches on the 3rd. They got the order to proceed to V Beach while I was there. We have six other men staying in Rest Camp whose job it is to go round unoccupied bivouacs and keep fires and incinerators burning so as to deceive the enemy. The French side looks like the "deserted village" – not a fire burning anywhere. Have given our men orders to restart their (French) fires too. Several huge bursters were searching for our Field Guns close to the communication trench on my way back. Some of the pieces take as long as 10 seconds to come down and they can be heard all the time. Various traps have been arranged for Brother Turk to facilitate our getting away. Barbed wire fixed up, rifles fixed up to go off after we have left and some mines also. The communication trenches leading to the beaches have been marked out and side places barred so that the men shan't lose their way in the dark. I wonder if the Turks know when we are going? He is shelling our beaches more now, yet not so much as one would expect, especially at night.

8   At 2015 values, this would be about £6,000. A private soldier was paid one shilling a day in 1915; in 2015 worth in the region of £5.
9   It is customary for an officers' Mess to have a Sergeant as its administrator.

Wednesday 5 January 1916

Another disappointment. Bad weather set in last night, rain and wind. It's blowing a gale now so there won't be much doing at the beach. To cap it all we hear that the evacuation is postponed, why no one knows. It is thought that the Navy aren't ready. The co-operation between the two Services on this campaign has been extremely rotten. I only remember the Navy being up to time once and that was when we left Suvla for Imbros. Went to the beach and found Sgt Ellis, Pte Allan and the baggage guard had gone; our valises and boxes had evidently gone too. Hope Allan got my suitcase away. Must (cost?) my old four year old SD jacket as soon as we get somewhere or it will cost me. The Mess stores do not appear to have gone. There were about a dozen boxes there out of about 24 sent down. The others have been given away I suppose. Got three boxes containing the Christmas dinner sent up on our water carts and the remainder up on ration carts. Had to draw rations from the beach again last night instead of using up our reserve supply here so it looks as if the business is postponed for a week at least. Business at the beach seemed to be at a standstill owing to bad weather but dozens of men were going through kits with no officer about to give them something better to do. Not a staff officer about. If they did a little less writing and a little more work in the open things might go a little smoother and they could see the flaws in their own orders. They want a few more men about like de Lisle our Div Cmdr and Lucas our Brigadier. They get more work done than the whole of Corps HQ together and see it done too. The enemy was expending some of his old gun ammunition along the road as I went back – it does no damage unless it is a direct hit, still it wasn't very pleasant till one had got inside its range.

Thursday 6 January 1916

Had a good night's sleep last night. Managed to find a couple of clean blankets left in a Sgts Mess dug out by the old "White House" which made my bed softer and warmer. The wind went down yesterday evening and with it the sea in a surprising fashion so they ought to have got a lot of stores away in the night. Had no alarming bursts of fire either like we had the night before when it sounded at one time as if the enemy would attack. We are about as weak now as we were on the 28th April, all the 42nd, 52nd Divisions and the French having left and our own Division much depleted in numbers. We have part however of the 13th Div here though, including our 4th Battalion and the RND on the right holding the French line. If our numbers are small we have good trenches and providing the enemy doesn't bombard us too heavily we are alright and should all get away. It is to be hoped it will not be left too long for the bad weather will set in with a vengeance shortly (blizzards are expected about 14th) and our plight will then be a sorry one. We are getting a lot of 'Black Marias' over our way this morning, searching for a battery. I was surprised yesterday at the number of guns we still had left. There was quite a heavy bombardment in the afternoon. The weather today is perfect. Hope it will continue so now for the remainder of our time here.

Ernest's plea for good weather went unheeded as the wet weather seemed to come and go. There had been some rain during the previous night, but not enough to make the trenches bad. Despite the fact that there was only a few days remaining, work continued improving defences, with more wire being put out, in case the enemy launched a last minute attack. As part of the battle procedure for a withdrawal, the coy officers were sent back to reconnoitre the route from G11a via B Avenue,

Leith Walk and the mule track to the divisional RV and the final forming up place (FUP). On 7 January, known as X day, the brigade operational orders for the evacuation were issued, including maps showing communications, time-tables of troop movements, and special instructions for the battalion. They were also notified that they would not be going back to the Firing Line as previously arranged. That afternoon there was a very violent enemy bombardment of the allied trenches near the northern and southern barricades and also on the west side of the Gully Ravine. This was followed by heavy rifle fire, but no shells landed on 2 SWB's position. At 5:30 p.m. three parties of 100 all ranks in each with two machine guns were sent back to the regimental camp under Captain McLaren, leaving the battalion thinly manned on the ground at a very crucial stage in the operation. The administrative arrangements were key to a successful withdrawal, so Ernest picks up some of the detail for which he was responsible:

Friday 7 January 1916

The weather last night changed again and rain started to fall, but although it looked threatening it cleared towards morning. Went down with Gibbs and Maygor to the beach to see what was doing. Found the Mess boxes of provisions still there. Had the others brought back to HQ as there seemed no possibility of getting our Mess stores away. The quantity of army stores did not seem to have diminished to any appreciable extent. French soldiers were allowed to take what they liked so they took motor bicycles, gum boots, mackintosh capes etc. On our way back we called in at the 17th General Field Hospital and had a pleasant hour with our medicos who had a new gramophone and some decent records. Their dug out was made of full lime boxes which had been condemned, including glass windows and blinds made out of a lady's petticoat – or something else – anyhow it gave quite a feminine touch to the place. Arrived at Bn HQ in time for lunch and I got orders to proceed with 300 of the Bn to rest bivouacs near 29th Div HQ and remain there until further orders. The Turks bombarded the 13th Div over by Gully Ravine very heavily during the afternoon. It looked like the preparation for attack. At about 4 pm heavy rifle fire opened up so our move was held up as we had to stand by in case of accidents. However it all fizzled out. We heard afterwards they went for a new trench we had dug by P Sap and had levelled it out and afterwards they tried an attack – about 50 coming over the parapet, thinking no doubt that our line was weakly held but they got too warm a reception. I think it was a most fortunate thing for us that they did die out that day, for things were wonderfully quiet afterwards up at the firing line.

In the evening we got orders to get our packs and the men's kit bags down from the dump at Ordnance where I had previously sent them to the beach between No 2 and 3 piers which had been repaired after the storm. I had to go down to show the Officer I/C fatigue party (Second Lieutenant Mason) where to get them. Of course everything seemed chaos. Horses were being embarked at No 3 pier. I tried to find Mason and his party, as they had preceded me on another fatigue. 'Asiatic Annie' was busy again so after having tried unsuccessfully at the piers to find Mason I made for the 29th Div Train. One of the RE officers took me up a safer and shorter cut to the top of the cliff. On the way up he showed me the quarries which 50 of our miners under Second Lieutenant Beardshaw had been working for a couple of months. They had done excellent work. Huge caves had been dug out of the rock sufficient to put nearly all GHQ in I should think – perhaps that was what it was intended for should the shelling from Fritz's 16½ inchers have become too accurate later on. The rock taken out was used for the piers and for building Corps HQ. As I could find nothing from 29th Div Train I went down onto the beach again to cross over to Ordnance. On my way, two shells came over suddenly and burst right on the beach close by – just had time to fling myself flat and escaped the flying bits. Saw the flash in the sky of another which took 24 seconds then the report and immediately afterwards the distant purr increasing to the sound of something between an express and a ships siren. Only having myself to look after, I got behind an old lighter which was high and dry. No one was hit and as I came out one of the heavy bits came down on the lighter with a whish and a crash – must have gone straight up on the burst. Some of the bits in Krithia Nullah used to go quite 500 yards. Eventually found the party up at Ordnance and they finished their job about 2 am.

The evacuation of Cape Helles began in earnest on 8 January. This was originally to be known as Y day, with Z day being 9 January, but the two somehow merged into one, with the main part of the evacuation taking part overnight. 2 SWB was divided into five groups of 100 all ranks and a further group to which was added men of HQ 87 Brigade. Each officer commanding a group was given seven slips of paper, onto which were written the names of the officers and the total number in that group. These slips were for movement through the control stations, RVs, FUP and at the departure pier. Those men working on Lancashire Landing and other detached parties were evacuated under corps arrangements. At mid-day, the beach party loaded up all packs on to lighters, with every man to leave the peninsula with two blankets and a waterproof sheet. At 5:00 p.m. 2 SWB moved off from Eski Line, after destroying what rations and stores that were left behind and reached the brigade RV at 6:00 p.m. where they joined up with Captain McLaren's party, which had moved back the previous day. They moved on at 6:15 p.m. and reached the FUP half an hour later, where there was an inevitable delay for another hour, until they eventually marched down to the piers on W Beach in single file. A number of shells came over from Kum Kale, landing very near the column, but there were no casualties. The battalion then embarked onto a number of motor lighters, about 200 men on each. The battalion war diary makes an interesting comment in that "after enquiring at every ship in the harbour, eventually got on board the Prince Abbas" as if there was no set plan for which ship was to take the battalion. Ernest explains what actually happened in his next diary entry about his final moments on the peninsula:

Saturday 8 January 1916

Beautiful morning and one could hardly believe that there was such a thing as a war. Later in the day we got orders to proceed to the rendezvous at 6.15 pm. I thought somehow Y and Z days would become one as so many rumours were afloat that Sunday the 9th was the day and W Beach is a likely place for spies, even though all the Greeks had been sent away a couple of weeks ago. The afternoon passed quietly up at the fire trenches, just the ordinary number of shells passing to and fro. We destroyed things we didn't want any more before parading, but the number of fires burning brightly in the various bivouacs after dark ought to have raised the enemy's suspicions. On reaching the rendezvous we started to file past along the railway line along to the top of the hill above W Beach or Lancashire Landing where the forming up place had been made. The progress was very slow and it took us three quarters of an hour to march about 1000 yards. We formed up on top and lay down till such time as the lighters were ready for each party. These were specially built for this place or for the landing at Suvla Bay rather, each one carrying 400 at a pinch and having its own motor. They had to be brought from Imbros after dusk so that probably accounts for their being somewhat late as we were nearly an hour on top and 'Asiatic Annie' had been quiet. Just however as a move was made in front she started. There was the ominous flash followed by another and 24 seconds later the distant boom! Then the sound two seconds later of an express train a big flash and a crash right on the side of the beach where the troops were filing down. Luckily however the bursting quality of these shells was not nearly as good as they had been.

As we passed the last line of trenches right on top we could see the Border Regt in them. They had been in reserve for the last few days so were sent to hold the beach defences. We were rather disappointed – some of the fire eaters exceedingly so – that we had none of the fire trenches to hold till the last as we had done so much work on them. We were to have had the post of honour in Krithia Nullah but it was altered at the last moment. It certainly was a ticklish place, especially as we had not been in that particular portion of the line, but the way back was so well marked that unless it rained very badly and it was very dark we should have found our way alright. One thing to my mind ought to have been done and that was to have a sandbag wall built all the way from the top of W Beach to the bottom. Had the Turks shelled the beach as they ought to have done, we ought to have had a lot of casualties there. When I got to the bottom I found a big gap in the line which ought not to be there and as I brought up the rear of the Bn and the last of ours to embark I had to see that none were left behind. One was not sorry to have to double round to the pier though and get out of the most dangerous zone. I got to the lighter in time to find 12 men and myself cut off as the lighter was full so had to board another and go below where we filled up like sardines and the air was thick.

We pushed off at 8.15 pm to look for HMS 'Mars' an old battleship. After cruising round for nearly three hours in a rapidly rising sea and visiting each ship without any luck we eventually heard the 'Mars' had not arrived so back we had to go to the pier again for orders and were sent to the 'Prince Abbas.' This was the same old tub we had gone to Suvla on from Imbros in Sept. last. We found her full up and the Skipper would not take us at first but eventually we all squeezed on somewhere but the men had no room to lie down and after we started they got wet through with the seas breaking over her. It was 11.45 pm when I eventually struggled through the crowd to the Saloon where I found to my delight the remainder of the officers so we were all together again. How I enjoyed my whisky and soda! In addition to ours I found we had about 300 Essex, about 200 Worcesters, 100 odd Hants about same KOSBs, besides Div HQ, 87th HQ and London RE. Altogether with our 500 a total of about 1300 souls on a small packet like the Channel steamers. Our thoughts were with the troops in the fire trenches as they were due to leave at 11.45 pm from the trenches. They had prepared rifles and bombs to go off after they left and Thorne, our RE officer, had worked hard at prepared mines for ammunition dumps etc. The men wrapped pieces of blankets around their boots so as to deaden the sound, especially wanted too as the wind was blowing strong from the south. I wonder if the Turks heard our guns being removed? About eight passed us at the top of W Beach but unfortunately we never got any of them away owing to the rough sea. We were afraid the last party wouldn't get away for the same reason.

With defences repaired from the earlier bombardments and the communication trenches cleared, giving the impression to the enemy that it was still business as usual, the battalion began to withdraw from the front line in accordance with the divisional plan. The Quartermaster and an advance party of 20 men moved back from the battalion's position first of all, to prepare for the reception of the main body. This was followed by the adjutant, who took 175 men back to W Beach and then by Bn HQ and 77 men from the intermediate line. This left just 80 men, with 8RWF on their left flank, to hold the main defensive position while the remainder of the battalion withdrew to Gully Beach and then along the coastal path to W Beach. Here they embarked onto motor lighters which took them out to the battleship HMS *Mars* for their return to Lemnos. Meanwhile, the small rear-guard withdrew at 11:45 p.m. and made their way silently down the Gully Ravine for the very last time, hoping to embark from Gully Beach. However, the wind had picked up and the sea was too rough for any ship movement from the beach, so they made a nerve wracking march around the coast to W Beach, arriving at about 4:00 a.m. on the morning of 9 January. Here, along with the pioneer party detailed to set fire to the massive dumps of stores and ammunition, they eventually sailed away from the peninsula and it was not until the flames and explosions from the munitions were seen and heard blazing away on the shore line did the Turks realise that, once again, the allies had escaped from under their very noses. The fact that so many allied troops could be evacuated from within such close proximity of the Turkish front line, on two separate occasions, almost defies belief, but the fact is that, as the official history records, after the bungled conduct of the campaign, the evacuation itself was a flawless example of a textbook operation that took the Turks completely by surprise.[10]

After nine months continuous active service, 2 SWB had left the shores of Gallipoli forever and arrived at Mudros harbour at midday on 9 January, with a complement of 19 officers (including the MO) and 585 other ranks; a shadow of the battalion which landed on 25 April the previous year. Ernest picks up the final moments:

Sunday 9 January 1916

Arrived off Imbros early and got into harbour about 9 o'clock. Heard rumours that the last party hadn't got away but after we had been transhipped to the 'Scotian' and Gen de Lisle had come aboard we heard that the evacuation had been carried out most successfully. Brand, our Brigade Major, told us that the only casualties were a few at the beach from falling debris when the magazine was blown up. The last lighter wouldn't go after the fuse had been laid! One man's arm was smashed and several cut heads and the steering gear knocked sideways so the lighter drifted out to sea and next morning was making for Anzac! Rather awkward but for the assistance of a destroyer which got them off. They rendered the guns useless and had to leave them. Have been told there are about 40 guns abandoned altogether – a rather serious number – won't the Turk make some copy out of all this? He will say of course that we were driven into the sea by the unparalleled valour of the Turkish troops etc. However I won't deny that he is a fine fighter and he has fought us in a gentlemanly way too – much more than we could expect from his master. We found that our boat load on the 'Prince Abbas' filled the 'Scotian' and a few over. The 'Scotian' is a liner of about 1200 tons so one can imagine what the packing on the other little tubs was like. We hear our destination is Alexandria. What a treat to get a warm bath and into a suit of pyjamas again. (Managed to get a suit from the MO I/C 17th General Field Hosp just the day before we left Helles). This was the first time we had been out of our clothes since 17th December.

On 10 January, Captain G T Raikes, formerly 1 SWB and who had been serving with the Egyptian army, came on board at Mudros and took over command of 2 SWB from Major Aubrey Williams, who left the ship to take up the appointment of brigade major to Brigadier Casson who was now commanding 157 Brigade. The next day, the battalion sailed away for the last time, but as they were still at war and there was a threat of enemy submarines, they posted four machine guns and 30 riflemen on the forward deck, with two machine guns and another 30 riflemen and a 12 pounder on the rear deck as a precaution. Two days later, in the early hours of 13 January, after a quiet passage, they arrived at Alexandria but it was not until later that night that they eventually disembarked and moved by train to Suez. Ernest's next diary entry gives a poignant summary of the battalion's casualty figures during the campaign:

Thursday 13 January 1916

Saw our ORQMS (Woods) who came aboard and told me who were here convalescent – Ballantine, Evans, Paterson and Davies. He also gave me the total number of casualties since we landed. The numbers are taken up to the 18th December. There have been a few since. His numbers are as follows:

Killed – 187
Died of wounds – 95
Died of disease – 12
Drowned in 'Royal Edward' – 56
Died in Manitou – 1 = 351

Wounded – 946
Wounded 2nd or 3rd time – 36 = 982

Missing – 72 = 72

The missing can all I think be counted as dead, for we have not had any names sent in by the enemy as captured. Still I think we have been pretty fortunate compared with other battalions. The total number of officers who have been with the battalion since the landing including our original 26 is 94. As we have 19 left now, 75 have become casualties. The total number of other ranks is 2410. Total numbers who have proceeded home sick or wounded is 897.

To summarise Ernest's figures, between April 1915 and January 1916, a total of 1054 officers and men of 2 SWB were killed or listed as missing. 982 soldiers were wounded and of the 94 officers, 75 became casualties at some stage. This of course comes to more than the original 1,000 that the battalion started out with, but during the campaign the battalion received reinforcements along the way to make up for their losses, giving a total throughput of 2,410, which means that over half the battalion was either killed or wounded and this does not take into account those who were taken ill through dysentery which was rife throughout the summer of 1915.

It was a long and arduous railway journey to Suez, with the officers and men squeezed into cramped train compartments. There were numerous stops and hold-ups, and after a 39 hour journey they arrived at their new transit camp at about 11:00 a.m. on 15 January. It had not been possible to send an advance party on ahead to set up the camp, so they were greeted with only partial camp accommodation both in tents and sanitary arrangements. However, after the quartermaster had sorted out some breakfast, they managed to get things into reasonable shape. Here they found the sick and injured men in camp who had been sent away from the peninsula prior to evacuation.

Once Ernest had the battalion's administrative arrangements under control, the next day he decided to set out for a change of scenery:

Sunday 16 January

Went in to Suez and on to Port Tewfik in the afternoon. The latter has a nice drive along the canal but there appears to be nothing else. Called in at the French Club and had tea – met the Paymaster of the 'Implacable' (Smith by name) and was invited aboard. Went all round most places on deck and below. He seemed to think we are in for a big scrap here about end of January. 30 years ago today my father died.

Clearly a family man by nature, Ernest still had time to think about his father at such a busy time. By the next day it was time to start getting the battalion back into its normal routine once again, with drill being high on the agenda. They also had to get ready for a parade that afternoon, when General Sir Charles Monro, commander in chief, mediterranean force, came to inspect the division. What he said is not recorded, but it could only have been praise of the highest order for the manner in which the officers and men of the division – and thus the battalions of the South Wales Borderers – endured the most trying of conditions in such a courageous manner, throughout a frustrating campaign which ended in evacuation.

Monday 17 January 1916

Our return requirements called for today. DADOS is in a hurry for it. Believe we get khaki drill so we are not to go to France that's evident. Wish one could get settled in about somewhere. One's things are constantly lying in dust. A huge mail arrived for the division. We got about 90 bags and the KOSB over 200! My trench boots and a parcel containing "medical comforts" arrived from home. What is one to do with two pairs of trench boots now? Our tents are littered with parcels. Forgot to mention that our new CO arrived on the 10th the day before we sailed from Mudros – Capt Raikes my old 1st Bn Adjutant. He has just come down from Khartoum having worked an exchange with Capt Walker to the Gyppy Army. Looks awfully fit as usual and am sure he will make an admirable CO. He gets the temporary rank of major vice Williams who left the same afternoon to take up his duties as Bde Major to Brig Gen Casson 157th Bde. We lose Capt Byrne to hospital at Cairo this evening – got some sort of skin trouble – the result of 'highs' living in the trenches I suppose. Ballantine ought to be back in a few days. He will keep us amused till Byrne returns. Hear we are to get a week's leave, 25% at a time. Wish one could get a month and go home. Had a letter written two days after Xmas from Puss – poor girl! It was a miserable Christmas for her. I wonder where we will be next Christmas and if this damned war will be over?

He was understandably concerned about his wife Sybil, who was on her own with their children at home in Brecon, South Wales and although the battalion was to get some local leave, he only wished there was sufficient time for some home leave, but this was not to be, at the moment anyway.

While the epilogue chapter will draw the story of Gallipoli to its close, for Ernest this was just another day on active service, so his final diary entry is not an emotive summary of all that had happened in the last 259 days. The trauma of Gallipoli was now, thankfully, behind the 2nd Battalion, which had served with distinction throughout the whole of the campaign but there was still much work to be done. Contrary to his prediction about not going to France, the battalion did indeed move to the Western Front a short time later, which is where he was to find himself for the next Christmas, while the 4th Battalion, which had been involved in all the major battles since arriving in July 1915, particularly at Suvla Bay, moved on to the campaign in Mesopotamia. Ernest continued to keep a comprehensive diary about his battalion's activities until the end of the war in 1918 but that, as they say, is another story.

12

Regimental Comrades

these magnificent soldiers of Wales
who, in peace or war, in life or death,
have set us so great an example

Lieutenant General Sir Francis Lloyd
Colonel the Royal Welch Fusiliers
15 November 1924

While this account of the Gallipoli campaign has concentrated primarily upon the South Wales Borderers, for that was its purpose, two other distinguished Welsh regiments also took part, namely the Royal Welch Fusiliers and the Welch Regiment. Since the formation of the Royal Welsh, the present regiment, in 2006, all three of these regiments, through a number of amalgamations, which included The Royal Regiment of Wales from 1969, have become linked as antecedent regiments. It is therefore appropriate and indeed fitting, that their commitment to the Gallipoli campaign should also be respectfully commemorated. The unique spelling of the word Welch in their titles did not become official until 1920, and as this chapter covers their activities at Gallipoli, which was prior to that date, the original nomenclature of Welsh is used throughout.

Taken in order of seniority, the Royal Welsh Fusiliers was raised, in similar fashion to the South Wales Borderers, by Lord Henry Herbert at Ludlow, Shropshire, in March 1689 and was known originally as Herbert's Regiment of Foot. Its inception was part of an expansion of English regiments designed to oppose King James II when he landed in Ireland with a French army, supported by King Louis XIV, in an attempt to reclaim his lost throne. The regiment was soon in action at the Battle of the Boyne, defeating James II's forces. While most infantry regiments of this era adopted the name of their regimental colonel as their title, it was not long before this regiment had a title which, with some minor adjustment, was to endure from an early age. In 1702 the Regiment was armed with the 'Fusil' musket, the most modern weapon of the day, instead of matchlock muskets and so, uniquely, became the Welsh Regiment of Fuzileers. After the War of the Spanish Succession from 1701 to 1714, the Regiment was granted the title of Royal in recognition of its gallant actions during that campaign and became styled as The Prince of Wales's Own Royal Regiment of Welsh Fusiliers. This title remained in place until 1751 when all infantry regiments were directed to dispense with the custom of naming regiments after successive colonels and to adopt a numerical title in accordance with the order in which they were raised. At this point the regiment became the 23rd Regiment of Foot or Royal Welsh Fusiliers. The regiment then went on to see service during the American War of Independence, and the Napoleonic Wars, being the last British regiment to leave Corunna in the retreat of 1809. The regiment also fought at Waterloo in 1815.

The Regiment also distinguished itself during the Crimean War (1854–1856) when Sergeant

Luke O'Connor became the first soldier ever to be awarded the Victoria Cross, Great Britain's highest possible accolade for valour in the face of the enemy. Born in County Roscommon, Ireland in 1831 he enlisted into the Regiment in 1849. He was awarded the VC at the Battle of the Alma on 20 September 1854, for saving and carrying the Colours – sacrosanct symbols of great regimental importance – while wounded. Also he was recognised for his great gallantry during the second assault on the Redan (a Russian fortification) during the siege of Sebastopol on 8 September 1855. His VC embraces two actions which were a year apart, but the former date is the first for an army VC to be awarded. His medal was presented by Her Majesty Queen Victoria at the first public investiture of the medal in Hyde Park, London, on 26 June 1857, when a total of 62 VCs were awarded that day. While an officer usually had to purchase his commission in the mid 19th century, due to his outstanding bravery and example Sgt O'Connor was commissioned without purchase in October 1854 and he rose to the rank of major general. He was knighted, became the colonel of the regiment and died in London in 1915 at the age of 84.

Another act of bravery during the Crimean War was the sad case of Major Charles Lumley. Born in Kent in 1824, he was initially commissioned into the 97th Regiment of Foot, the Earl of Ulster's Regiment and his VC was awarded on 8 September 1855 during the assault on the Redan. He single-handedly attacked three Russian gunners loading a cannon, which was about to be used against the regiment and although knocked to the ground, he recovered and drew his sword to rally the troops. He was then shot in the mouth and had to retire wounded. His medal was gazetted on 24 February 1857 and presented by Queen Victoria at that initial ceremony on 26 June 1857. The following year he transferred to the Royal Welsh Fusiliers and was posted to Brecon in July 1858 to command the detachment there. Three months later in October he put a gun to his head and shot himself. Whether this was a case of post traumatic stress disorder (PTSD) is not known, but the coroner's verdict was "suicide while of unsound mind." He was buried at Brecon Cathedral, (then a priory church), first of all outside the perimeter, as was the case with suicides at that time, but then by public request, in recognition of his outstanding bravery, his body was moved inside the wall, where his grave now is.

In 1881, as part of the Cardwell reforms of the British army, infantry regiments were given geographical titles, linked primarily to their main recruiting areas, which in this case was North Wales. At this point, the Regiment became known as The Royal Welsh Fusiliers, a title it retained (apart from the adoption of Welch in 1920), until 2006, the first time it had ever been amalgamated in its entire history. There were two particular items of dress which distinguished the Royal Welsh Fusiliers from other infantry regiments, both of which are still worn today. The first of these was the "flash", which consisted of five overlapping black silk ribbons (seven inches long for soldiers and nine inches long for officers) on the back of the uniform jacket at neck level. It originates from the time when it was normal for soldiers to wear pigtails and the material on the back of the jacket prevented stains from the grease. In 1808, this practice was discontinued but when the order was issued the Royal Welsh Fusiliers were serving overseas in the West Indies and did not receive the instruction. There then followed some 20 years of wrangling to keep the flash, until 1834, when the officers of the 23rd Foot were finally granted permission by King William IV to wear this non-regulation item, as a distinction, on their full dress uniform. This privilege was extended to all ranks in 1900. When khaki service dress replaced the scarlet tunic as the main uniform, there was an attempt to remove this privilege from the regiment, but without success and the custom has continued to this day. The second item was the hackle, which, to denote a fusilier regiment, was a plume of white feathers mounted behind the cap badge. The full dress of the Royal Welsh Fusiliers, as worn by the entire regiment until 1914, included a racoon-skin hat, with a bearskin for officers and a white hackle and a scarlet tunic, with the dark blue facings of a Royal regiment. Thereafter, the custom was restricted to the regimental corps of drums and the regimental pioneers. The Royal Welsh Fusiliers traditionally had a goat, but it was never called a mascot; the goat was always named 'Billy' and this custom dated back to at least 1775.

The regiment saw service in the Boer War (1899–1902) and was then plunged into the maelstrom of the First World War, when a total of 42 battalions were raised for active service. Four of these battalions were involved in the Gallipoli campaign, three of which were territorial force battalions. The first of these was the 1/5 (Flintshire) Battalion, which was raised in August 1914, as part of the North Wales Brigade. On mobilisation it was located initially at Conway and then spent much of the next 12 months training in various locations throughout England until 13 May 1915, when it became part of 158 Brigade, 53 (Welsh) Division. In similar fashion, 1/6 (Caernarfon and Anglesey) Battalion and 1/7 (Merioneth and Montgomery) Battalion were raised, both of whom were also to join 158 Brigade. Then there was the 8th Battalion, (8 RWF), which was a service battalion, raised as part of Kitchener's new army. This battalion formed up at Wrexham in August 1914 and was assigned to 40 Brigade, 13 (Western) Division, along with 4 SWB.

While the regiment was not involved in the amphibious landing on the beaches of Gallipoli on 25 April 1915, the next day saw an outstanding act of valour by one of its officers. Lieutenant Colonel Charles Doughty-Wylie was a staff officer in the headquarters of General Sir Ian Hamilton and he was sent ashore at V Beach, the scene of particularly bitter fighting the previous day, to assess the combat effectiveness of the troops who had taken part. What he found was that most of the senior officers had been killed or wounded, while those soldiers who had survived the landing had yet to move off the beach and morale was low. Seeing the need for pro-active initiative, he gathered up most of the men on the beach and began to clear the old fort of Sedd el Bahr of enemy snipers. Once this was secure, he then advanced towards Hill 141, which had been one of the initial objectives, launching a number of successful attacks along the way. Lieutenant Colonel Doughty-Wylie was armed only with a wooden cane; having served in Turkey before the war as a military attaché he looked upon the Turks as his friends, so he refused to carry a weapon as he had no intention of shooting any of them. Ironically, as they approached the summit of Hill 141 he was shot and killed by Turkish fire, but his outstanding courage and leadership carried the day, for which he was awarded the VC posthumously. He was buried where he fell and after the war, the Turks left his grave where it was, as a mark of respect; the only British soldier on the peninsula to be buried outside a centralised war cemetery.[1]

8 RWF was the first battalion of the regiment to see action at Gallipoli. Sailing from Avonmouth in SS *Megantic* on 28 June 1915, with Lieutenant Colonel A R Hay as the CO and Capt M D Gambier-Parry as adjutant, the battalion arrived at Alexandria on 8 July and four days later was at Lemnos. On 13 July, 13 Division sailed for Cape Helles to relieve 29 Division and by16 July 8 RWF was in the Gully Ravine, ready to take over from the South Lancashire Regiment in the front line. The battalion remained there until 30 July when it was relieved by 1 Royal Scots (29 Division having returned to the peninsula after a short break) and withdrew to Lemnos again, to prepare for the Suvla Bay offensive. As part of 40 Brigade and in conjunction with 4 SWB, the battalion was in the left covering force for the Anzac breakout, the overall intention being to capture the heights of Sari Bair.

On 4 August, the brigade set out for the Anzac sector and was concealed in great secrecy in specially prepared dugouts, awaiting the launch of the offensive during the night of 6 August. Along with 8 Cheshire, 8 RWF had been assigned to support 3 Australian Light Horse Brigade in what was to become the infamous diversionary attack on the Nek and at 3:30 a.m. on 7 August the

---

1   Battlefield tour guides consider this to be the smallest war cemetery of the First World War.

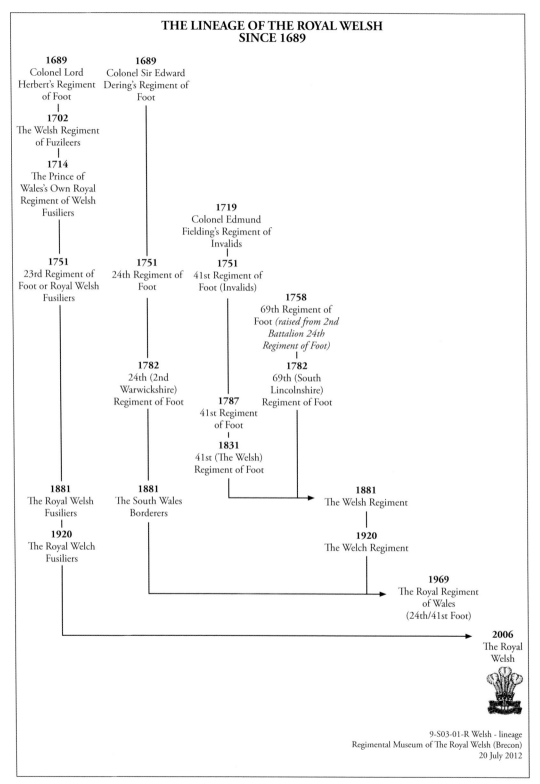

Image 27. The lineage of the Royal Welsh since 1689 (R Welsh Museum).

battalion moved from Russells Top to its allocated location in Monash Valley, on the right flank of the Nek. Immortalised in the Australian film, "Gallipoli", the Nek was a natural killing ground waiting to happen and its futility was ameliorated only by the outstanding bravery of the Australian soldiers who took part. In the space of an hour, in an area not much larger than a football field, 8 Light Horse had 234 of its 300 soldiers killed and 10 Light Horse lost well over 100 of its men. While 8 RWF escaped the slaughter at the Nek, they took heavy casualties in attempting to scale the steep slopes of Monash Valley. Those that managed to get to the top were severely mauled by Turkish machine guns, losing four officers and 61 men in the process. No further advance was made by the battalion and they withdrew to Russell's Top where they remained until 9 August, after which they became part of the corps reserve. The battalion spent some time on Cheshire Ridge until 4 September when it then moved to Lala Baba.

The battalion spent its autumn at Suvla Bay along with 4 SWB, the detail of which has been covered already and also endured the ravages of the winter storm at the end of November. Captain Powell, one of the company commanders, kept a diary and recounts the day of 30 November:

"The men are in a very bad state and I have had to send any amount down with bad feet and rheumatism. One's clothes, already soaking, freeze on one, and the only thing to do is to keep on the move the whole time. We got a certain amount of braziers going in the trenches, but it is very hard getting the men any tea or hot food, indeed, almost impossible. The nights cannot be described. To add to my troubles I have got bad diarrhoea. I hear the Turks are in an awful bad condition and we can see them running about in the open trying to keep warm. However, we try to shoot as many of them as possible, but some of the rifles are in such a condition they won't go off. My feet are agony to walk on."[2]

The battalion was evacuated from Suvla Bay with the remainder of 40 Brigade on the night of 19 December, via Imbros, arriving at Lemnos on 23 December. Christmas day was luxury in comparison with the last few months and the soldiers had the delight of some fresh fruit and a pint of beer per man. The break was short lived however, as 40 Brigade soon returned to Cape Helles to support the evacuation of the remainder of the allied army still there. As previously recounted, the Turks attempted a major attack on the British lines on 6 January but 8 RWF escaped with minimal casualties. The evacuation here went as planned and by 10 January the battalion was back at Lemnos. On 26 January 1916, 8 RWF sailed in SS *Grampian* and landed at Port Said on 30 January in preparation for its next stage in the war, which was to be in Mesopotamia.

* * *

Returning to the other RWF battalions, on 3 July 1915, 53 (Welsh) Division was warned to move and two weeks later, 158 Brigade, consisting of 5 RWF (CO – Lieutenant Colonel B E Philips), 6 RWF (CO – Lieutenant Colonel T W Jones) and 7 RWF (CO – Lieutenant Colonel J Reveley) embarked at Devonport, arriving at Gallipoli on 8 August. Without any period of acclimatisation or adjustment, they were immediately launched into battle, landing at C Beach on 9 August. By this stage, the Suvla Bay offensive was three days old and was already bogged down with inertia, confusion and poor leadership, so it is hardly surprising that 158 Brigade got off to an inauspicious start. Their objective was the Tekke Tepe Ridge, overlooking Suvla Bay from the east *"without*

2   Dudley Ward, *Records of the Royal Welch Fusiliers* (RHQ RWF, 1995) Vol 4, p.54.

the possession of which, Suvla Bay is not safe"[3] but the orders they received were not clear, nor were their lines of advance. Consequently, brigade and battalion boundaries were crossed which meant that units often became mixed up with each other. As an example, in advancing towards Scimitar Hill, 5 RWF had to move through the positions of 4 Cheshire and 5 Welsh (both 159 Brigade) and while waiting for support to assault the hill, their CO, Lieutenant Colonel Basil Philips was killed, along with a number of his officers. In the confusion that followed, the battalion fell back in disorder, which has led to some of the quite erroneous reports about Welsh soldiers pulling out of the battle. 6 RWF did in fact provide support, but it was too little too late and they too had to withdraw. 10 August was a day of disaster at Suvla and it has been alleged that General Sir Frederick Stopford, who himself was sacked for incompetence the following week, sought to blame everyone and everything but his own lack of resolve. His basic premise was that the troops he had been given to carry out the plan were not good enough and had been ill suited for the task in hand. He is quoted as saying:

> I am sure they [the territorial divisions] would not secure the hills with any amount of guns, water and ammunition assuming ordinary opposition, as the attacking spirit was absent; owing to the want of leadership by the officers.[4]

To which Major General J E Lindley, GOC 53 (Welsh) Division, retorted in his diary entry:

> The Cheshires and the North Wales Brigades are in an awful muddle, owing to so many officers having been killed or wounded and the men are lost without them. The NCOs seem powerless and carry no authority – the officers have done wonderfully well, freely exposing themselves to get their men on, hence the heavy casualties.[5]

The fog of war and the heat of battle have to be experienced to be understood. There is no doubt that the failure of this operation was a consequence of the ineptitude of the high command and its senior officers who were clearly out of their depth, not the quality of the soldiers under their command. It also has to be remembered that, as territorial soldiers, these men had little or no actual combat experience and were not practised in responding to events as a team. The high command should have known this was likely to be the case and so it was reckless and irresponsible of them to plan the action using underprepared troops.

By the evening of 10 August, it was clear that any further assault on the Turkish positions would achieve very little, so General Hamilton ordered the corps to halt its advance and to entrench on the positions it held at the time. Once again, the inertia of static warfare set in and no further forward movement was to be made. As the regimental history then records:

> We then had a terrible week, occupying a shallow Turkish trench, very little water, few rations, cold at night and a blazing sun during the day. The smell was indescribable, dead and wounded everywhere and no means of burying the dead. After sweating in the sun all day, the dust caked on everyone's face and for want of water, everyone's lips were black with caked blood; the blood cracked if one opened one's mouth and it streamed down one's chin.[6]

3   General Sir Ian Hamilton, *Gallipoli Diary* (London, 1920) August 1915.
4   Nigel Steel and Peter Hart. *Defeat at Gallipoli* (London: Macmillan, 1994), p.277.
5   Stephen Chambers. *Suvla – August Offensive* (Barnsley: Pen and Sword, 2011), p.110–111.
6   Dudley Ward, *Records of the Royal Welch Fusiliers*, p.40.

Image 28. 5th Battalion Welsh Regiment at Suvla Bay in August 1915 (R Welsh Museum).

On 14 August, 7 RWF was withdrawn to Lemnos where it was involved in administrative duties, returning to Suvla Bay on 14 October. At about this time, the 5th and 6th battalions, their numbers being so low, were amalgamated into one battalion under the command of Lieutenant Colonel C S Rome. The battalions then sat out the autumn of 1915 on the plains of Suvla Bay, while the politicians anguished over their future. Once the decision to evacuate the peninsula had been made, the gradual process to pull back from Suvla Bay and the Anzac sector first of all, began. It was thought that 53rd Division might be one of the last to go, but the troops were so weak that it was decided to send them first. The whole division, 215 officers and 4,522 other ranks, embarked on the night of 11 December and sailed for Alexandria. While their active service at Gallipoli may have drawn to a close, the Regiment's war against Turkey was to continue with the campaign in Mesopotamia.

* * *

And now to the Welsh Regiment. In 1719, it was decided that additional units were needed for garrison duties at home, in order to release active regular battalions for service overseas in the wars against the French. A source of such manpower was identified amongst the more active out-pensioners of the Royal Hospital at Chelsea, in London, who were fit for light duties at home, and so on 11 March that year 10 companies were enrolled and formed into what was to be called Colonel Edmund Fielding's Regiment of Invalids. The term "invalid" did not necessarily imply infirmity, rather that they were pensioners, whether disabled or not, living at the Royal Hospital. While they were probably not fit for active service due to their age, they were all former soldiers anyway, so their induction back into uniform was an easy one and they were soon on garrison duties at Portsmouth. The regiment then followed the practice and precedent all others at the time, changing names, uniforms and Colours with each successive colonel, until 1751 when it was directed to adopt the title of the 41st Regiment of Foot (Invalids). The practice of recruiting soldiers from the Royal Hospital at Chelsea continued until the end of 1787, when all such members of the regiment were finally pensioned off and the 41st Regiment of Foot took its place in the order of line, equal in every respect to all other infantry battalions. In January 1788, the Honourable Arthur Wellesley, later to become the Duke of Wellington, was commissioned into the 41st of Foot and while he did not stay long, the regiment can lay claim to being his first military home.

During this period other events of regimental significance were taking place. With the Seven Years' War with France looming, the government ordered the raising of a further 15 battalions in 1756, one of which was the 2nd Battalion the 24th Regiment of Foot, later the South Wales Borderers. Recruited mainly from the Midlands, this battalion assumed its own identity in 1758 when it took the title of the 69th Regiment of Foot. Later on, in 1881 as part of the Cardwell reforms, it changed hands yet again to become the 2nd Battalion of the Welsh Regiment, so its history is an integral part of the family regiment as a whole. In 1761, the 69th of Foot first distinguished itself at the capture of Belle Île, off the coast of Brittany. Belleisle is the regiment's oldest battle honour although for some reason it was not actually awarded until 1951. During the Napoleonic Wars in the latter part of the 18th and early part of the 19th centuries, infantry regiments sometimes served on board ships of the Royal Navy and performed many of the duties carried out by the Royal Marines. In 1782, the 69th of Foot took part in the Battle of the Saintes in the West Indies, on board HMS *Britannia* and HMS *Captain,* under Lord Nelson. For their part in this victory, the regiment was included in a vote of thanks passed by both houses of parliament, and was awarded a Naval Crown, superscribed '12 April 1782' to be carried on the regimental Colour. This battle honour is unique throughout the British army. Then in 1796, the 69th of Foot moved out to the West Indies again as marines and were present at the Battle of Cape Saint Vincent in 1797, which was also to become a battle honour. The regiment is most proud of its second unique naval award and in 1951 was given permission to associate it with the battle honour of the naval crown.

The Welsh Regiment has been synonymous with the custom of having a goat mascot since about 1842 at the time of the first Afghan war, when it is alleged that the battalion adopted a local tribesman's goat as a pet. This could be hearsay, but there is firm evidence that a goat was part of practice and precedence by the time of the Crimean campaign and remained so up until the regiment's amalgamation in 1969, when the tradition was carried forward into the Royal Regiment of Wales and continues to this day. Originally presented by Queen Victoria from the Royal herd at Windsor, the mascot was first known as Billy, but this changed to Taffy for the regular battalions of the Welsh Regiment and to Dewi and Sospan for the territorial battalions. Likewise, there are conflicting stories about the origin of the leek as a Welsh emblem. Shakespeare's Henry V is a good source of information on the subject and the Royal Welsh Fusiliers claim to have been eating the leek on ceremonial occasions for over 300 years. The Welsh Regiment seems to have adopted this custom after the First World War and this too has been carried forward and continues today in the Royal Welsh.

The regiment took part in the Crimean War of 1854 and had the distinction of having the first Welshman, born and bred, to be awarded the Victoria Cross. This was Captain Hugh Rowlands, who came from Llanrug in North Wales. He was awarded the Victoria Cross at the Battle of Inkerman on the 5th November 1854 when he rescued a wounded officer, Colonel Haly of the 47th of Foot (the Lancashire Regiment) in the face of the enemy. Captain Rowlands was also put forward for a second Victoria Cross, for bravery during an attack on the Redan on 18 June 1855 but this was not awarded. His VC was presented, not by the Queen, but by a major general in Barbados on 5 August 1857, some three years after the event. Such delays were not unusual as the medal had to be ratified and gazetted, i.e. published in the *London Gazette*, before it could be awarded. Captain Rowlands took part in the Zulu war campaign in 1879, alongside the 24th Regiment of Foot and eventually rose to the rank of major general. He died at his home in Llanrug in 1909 at the age of 81. It was during this time, in 1894, that the Welsh Regiment returned home, from two years in Malta, to Pembroke Dock in West Wales. Here, on Saint David's Day 1895, the Officers' Mess was totally destroyed by a fire, losing all its silver artefacts. From the molten silver which was recovered, a new centre piece was created.

After meritorious service in the Boer war, during which it was awarded the Battle Honours of Relief of Kimberley, Paardeburg as well as the theatre honour South Africa 1899–1902, the Welsh Regiment laid claim to the first Welshman to be awarded the Victoria Cross during the First World War. This went to Lance Corporal William Fuller, who came from Laugharne, Carmarthenshire, for attempting to save the life of Captain Mark Haggard, nephew of the author Rider Haggard, on 14 September 1914 during the battle of the Aisne. Though mortally wounded, Captain Haggard urged his men on, shouting "Stick it the Welch!" words which are immortalised below the clock on the main barrack block in Maindy Barracks, Cardiff.[7]

Of the 53 battalions raised by the Welsh Regiment during the First World War, three were to see active service at Gallipoli. The 8th Battalion formed up in Cardiff in August 1914 and was assigned to 40 Brigade in 13 (Western) Division. It spent most of its training period on Salisbury Plain and then re-roled as a pioneer battalion, moving to Aldershot in February 1915. The battalion then embarked with the remainder of 40 Brigade at Avonmouth for Gallipoli on 15 June 1915. 4 Welsh was raised in August 1914 in Carmarthen and then trained as far apart as Tunbridge Wells in England and the Forth and Tay in Scotland until it was posted to 159 Brigade in 53 (Welsh) Division in April 1915. 5 Welsh was raised in similar fashion, but from Pontypridd in the Rhondda valley, and then followed the same training pattern as 4 Welsh, joining 159 Brigade in April 1915 in preparation for their deployment to Gallipoli in July 1915.

The 8th Battalion was the first to arrive at Gallipoli, as part of 40 Brigade and they disembarked at Mudros Bay on 2 July. No sooner were they ashore than they were employed in their role as pioneers, road making, well sinking and creating a causeway to and around Turks Island. Their work was delayed through the difficulty of getting explosives and wheelbarrows from the ordnance supply ship, a situation made worse by the unrelenting heat and a strong north easterly wind. By the end of the month, they received orders to move to the peninsula for the Anzac offensive and on 4 August at 2:00 a.m. 26 officers and 749 other ranks went ashore at Shrapnel Gully, leaving three officers and 150 men behind at Lemnos as reinforcements. Then on the night of 6 August they moved to Chailak Dere to support the attack on Chunuk Bair.

On 7 August the assault began, with the battalion under command of the New Zealand infantry brigade. The first casualty was the commanding officer, Lieutenant Colonel John Arthur Bald, who was severely wounded while out on a reconnaissance, so Major Robert Peel Yates (brother of Hubert Peel Yates of 4 SWB, whose son David eventually became colonel of the regiment) took over. The battalion then went into bivouac on Rhododendron Ridge as the advance which had been ordered for 6:00 p.m. had been put off until the following morning. At 4:15 a.m. on 8 August, preceded by the Gloucesters and the Wellington Battalion, 8 Welsh moved out in support of the attack on Chunuk Bair. It was still dark at first, but by the time the Cheshire Ridge was crossed the light level was fairly good. A and B Coys were in the first line of the attack and soon came under fire the moment they passed the ridge and attempted to deploy. C and D Coys were in the second line and

7   J M Brereton, *History of the Royal Regiment of Wales 1689–1989* (Cardiff: RHQ RRW, 1989), p.475–480.

they too were gradually shot down by machine gun fire and shrapnel fire. Those who remained took cover in the bush of the gullies on the right and left.

Image 29. Presentation of medals at the Barracks Brecon in July 1919. Note the contingent of Womens Army Auxiliary Corps (WAAC) also on parade (Mrs J Copping).

Major Yates continued to advance with a small party and reached a forward position on the slopes of Chunuk Bair and was to the right of the Wellington Battalion which was now in trenches below the crest. With Major Stevens gathering a few more men to fill the gap left by Major Yates, a firing line was formed, but by 8:00 a.m. the detachment under Major Yates had been shot down and dispersed. Reinforcements were assembled with the Gloucesters, but the battalion was suffering badly from enemy snipers who had worked their way around to the rear of the battalion. During this time, Major Yates was wounded and had to be evacuated, with Major Herbert Lyn Stevens taking over. Throughout the day and into the night, the enemy made repeated attacks trying to turn the battalion's flanks and these were successfully resisted at first, but they were unable to hold out indefinitely and by 9:00 p.m. they were eventually relieved by the Otago battalion and pulled back into the Gully. Of the 26 officers and 749 soldiers who started out less than a week before, the battalion mustered just seven officers and 274 men on 9 August.[8] The battalion had taken part in one of the most bloody attacks of the Suvla Bay offensive and having reached the heights of Sari Bair, albeit briefly, can lay claim to being involved in what might have been a turning point in the campaign. This was not to be however, and by 10 August, the Turks had secured the feature which they would dominate for the remainder of the war.

In the meantime, the 4 and 5 Welsh had arrived at Alexandria and by 7 August they were at Lemnos, getting ready to take part in the offensive at Suvla Bay. That said, there was little time for any meaningful preparation, for within 24 hours 159 Brigade had been launched onto C Beach and

8   Royal Welsh Museum, War Diary of 8 Welsh (CARWR 1349-10)

Image 30. Battalion soldiers and ex servicemen falling in for the Brecon peace festivities in July 1919
(Mrs J Copping).

immediately advanced to attack the Turkish positions on Anafarta Ova. They were soon swept up in the similar chaos and confusion which affected the RWF battalions in 158 Brigade, and by nightfall on 10 August, for example, 5 Welsh endured a total of nine officers and 124 soldiers killed, wounded or missing. Such was the stress experienced by the troops on the ground that the next day, the commanding officer, Lieutenant Colonel M Morgan had to be withdrawn, suffering from physical exhaustion and shock.[9] By 13 August, the battalions were digging themselves into a line of firing and support trenches across Suvla Bay and then were held in reserve while the battle for Scimitar Hill began on 21 August. Some reinforcements began to arrive to make up for battle casualties and by 28 August, 5 Welsh were relieved by the Herefordshire Regiment and pulled back to A Beach. While the battalions were starting to get their first decent night's sleep in almost a month, enemy shelling was still a threat and the everlasting chore of trench digging continued unabated.

Such was the drain on manpower through battle casualties, sickness and a shortage of reinforcements that it was decided to link 4 and 5 Welsh into one battalion on 11 October, under the title of 4/5 Welsh composite battalion. This was to be a temporary measure only, until such times as both battalions could be brought back up to their established strength.[10] There were two coys from each battalion and Bn HQ was based on 4 Welsh, with Major H H W Southey as the commanding officer; he was promoted to temporary lieutenant colonel the following month. It is interesting to note however that while this was now essentially one battalion for operational purposes, the element of the 5th Battalion continued to maintain its own war diary, one amusing entry for 13 October being:

In the afternoon, a British airplane was seen to descend into the middle of Salt Lake. The two passengers got out and walked away. It was then wrecked by heavy enemy shell fire.

9   Royal Welsh Museum, 1/5th Battalion Welsh Regiment War Diary (CARWR 1394-1) entry dated 11 August 1915.
10   The battalions were unlinked on 20 February 1916 and reverted to their original titles.

This is corroborated by Major John Gillam, supply officer of 86 Brigade, who also saw the plane make a forced landing. As he says in his diary:

a short pause, during which we notice the pilot and observer climb out, when suddenly shrapnel bursts over the machine. It is quickly followed by another and another, and later high explosive shells when the pilot and the observer scurry away quite quickly. They are wise, for the Turkish artillery are now well on to the machine which is rapidly becoming a helpless wreck. I should think they put a hundred shells on that machine before they stopped.[11]

Clearly the Turks were not short of artillery ammunition! And then on 10 December:

A Turkish prisoner surrendered to us on the left centre of our line, running across the space between the opposing trenches. He was fired upon by his own side, but although he had difficulty in getting through our wire, he was not hit.

Image 31. 4 SWB on parade in Woking prior to embarking for Gallipoli in 1915 (R Welsh Museum).

The autumn of 1915 went the same way for all of the battalions at Suvla Bay. While there was the constant round of sniping and shelling, more by the Turks than the allies as they had better artillery resources, there were no more major battles. Time was spent in digging new trench systems and repairing the old ones and although there was some relief from the plague of flies, now that the

---

11   Major J Gillam, *Gallipoli Diary* (London: George Allen and Unwin Ltd, 1918), p.246.

weather was cooler, there was still a regular admittance to the field hospitals of sick soldiers. After enduring the terrible storm at the end of November, preparations began for the evacuation. On 9 December, 4/5 Welsh were relieved by 2 Scottish Horse and withdrew to Lala Baba where they remained for three days. During the night of 12 December they were evacuated from C Beach, arriving at Mudros harbour at 6:20 p.m. the next day. They were immediately transferred to the

Image 32. 4 SWB parade through Brecon in 1919 prior to disbandment after Gallipoli (R Welsh Museum).

Ascania and set off for Alexandria, arriving there on 18 December.

Meanwhile, after being relieved from its involvement at Sari Bair, 8 Welsh reverted to the pioneer role. After some reinforcements in early September, the battalion's strength was seven officers and 358 other ranks, who were then committed to repairing the piers on the beaches of Suvla Bay. Like all other battalions, hospital admittance was a daily occurrence, with sickness outstripping battle casualties; in the month of September just six soldiers were wounded, while 54 were sent to hospital. Even the commanding officer was not immune; on 11 September, Major Stevens succumbed to dysentery and was replaced by Captain Gordon Williams. He was replaced by Captain W E G Solomon on 1 October, until Lieutenant Colonel Robert Johnson joined the battalion from 8 RWF to formally take over the appointment a week later. Over the next two months, the battalion was committed to numerous pioneer tasks, most of which were in and around the beaches of Suvla Bay, developing piers for the unloading of supply ships at what was now a large logistic base for the administration of all of the divisions entrenched in that sector. After the November storms, 8 Welsh took part in restoring the flooded trenches, for although evacuation was imminent, there could be no let up in defending the area against a Turkish attack. During the night of 16 December, the battalion left Suvla Bay via the south pier aboard SS *Abassia*, arriving at Lemnos the next morning. By 20 December, all battalions of the Royal Welsh Fusiliers and the Welsh Regiment had left the peninsula and, with the exception of 8 RWF, were never to return. Preparation then began for their involvement in the Mesopotamian campaign, in the knowledge that their commitment to Gallipoli had been significant and courageous, yet costly in the numbers killed, wounded or missing.

* * *

On 15 November 1924, the Royal Welch Fusiliers unveiled a regimental memorial in Wrexham. At the service, Lieutenant General Sir Francis Lloyd, colonel of the regiment, said "these magnificent soldiers of Wales who, in peace or war, in life or death, have set us so great an example." In so doing, he enshrined a fitting epitaph to all of our regimental comrades who fought side by side so courageously in a conflict that was beset by so many difficulties and setbacks. Gallipoli was not the finest hour in British military history, but emblazoned on the battle honours proudly displayed on the regimental Colours for generations to come, it was duty nobly done.

Epilogue

The drama of the Dardanelles campaign, by reason of the beauty of its setting,
the grandeur of its theme and the unhappiness of its ending,
will always rank amongst the world's classic tragedies

Brigadier C F Aspinall-Oglander
Official History of Gallipoli

The Great War was to continue until November 1918, but at Gallipoli the guns had fallen silent at last and the senseless killing had ceased. For those who survived however, this was not the end of the matter as most of the allied forces who were evacuated from the peninsula, particularly both battalions of the South Wales Borderers, went on to other theatres of war, such as the Western Front, Salonika, or Mesopotamia.

The Government was quick to initiate an investigation into the disastrous outcome of the campaign and the Dardanelles Commission was set up under the Special Commissions (Dardanelles and Mesopotamia) Act 1916. Those involved in the key positions of expedition were interviewed, and the final report of the commission was issued in 1919. It concluded that the expedition had been poorly planned and executed and that the difficulties likely to be encountered had been underestimated; difficulties which were exacerbated by supply shortages as well as by personality clashes and procrastination at high levels of the campaign. However, these findings did not have any measurable impact on the careers of those investigated. That said, the senior players at Gallipoli experienced mixed fortunes. Before he could give any evidence to the Commission, Field Marshal Lord Kitchener perished at sea on 5 June 1916 during a journey to Russia, when his ship, HMS *Hampshire*, struck a mine and sank off the Orkney Islands. Lord Kitchener, Secretary of State for War, was portrayed as a national hero following his drowning; consequently it would have been unacceptable, at least for those senior officers involved in the war, to besmirch his reputation. Consequently, this restricted the information both Winston Churchill and Sir Ian Hamilton felt that they could give to the tribunal. General Sir Ian Hamilton never served in the field again. He became the Lieutenant of the Tower of London in 1924 and the Rector of Edinburgh University in 1932. He continued to write on the development of warfare and died on 12 October 1947 at the age of 94. General Sir Frederick Stopford, branded as the scapegoat for the failure of the action at Suvla Bay, retired from the army in 1920 and died in 1929 at the age of 75.

The disastrous Gallipoli campaign saw Winston Churchill's departure from the government and he then briefly resumed active service on the Western Front as commanding officer of the 6th Battalion the Royal Scots Fusiliers. He eventually returned to politics as Minister of Munitions, Secretary of State for War, and Secretary of State for Air. In 1921–1922 he served as Secretary of State for the Colonies, then Chancellor of the Exchequer in Baldwin's Conservative government of

1924–1929. Out of office and politically in the wilderness during the 1930s, Churchill took the lead in warning about Nazi Germany and in campaigning for rearmament. At the outbreak of the second world war, he was again appointed First Lord of the Admiralty and following the resignation of Neville Chamberlain on 10 May 1940, he became prime minister and architect of the eventual defeat of Germany and Adolf Hitler in 1945. He died on 24 January 1965.

* * *

4 SWB was redeployed from Egypt to Mesopotamia in February 1916 and was soon involved in the battles fought by the Mesopotamian Expeditionary Force, in the vain efforts to relieve General Townshend who was besieged at Kut al Amara. On 4 April 1916 the battalion attacked the Hanna position and despite severe losses reached a line about 800 yards from the Turkish trenches. During the advance, an officer fell and one of his men going to his help was also hit. Captain Ian Buchanan dashed out from behind cover and not only carried the officer in despite heavy fire, but, going out again, brought in the private soldier as well, for which gallantry he was awarded the Victoria Cross.[1] A few days later on 8 April, during the assault on the Turkish position at Sannaiyat, the battalion gained another Victoria Cross. After a night attack, Private James Henry Fynn, the CO's orderly, was one of a small party which was entrenched in front of the battalion's advanced line and about 300 yards from the enemy's trenches. Seeing several wounded men lying out in front, he went out and bandaged them, while under heavy fire, making several journeys to do so. He then went back to the advanced trench for a stretcher and, being unable to get one, he carried on his back a badly wounded man to safety. He then returned and, aided by another man who was wounded during the act, carried in another badly wounded man. After the failure to relieve Kut, when the British commander surrendered his garrison of approximately 10,000 men to the besieging Turk force, operations ceased until December 1916. Once 13 Division had reorganised, the 4 SWB took a leading part in the second battle for the recapture of Kut and in the advance to Baghdad, became the first British troops to enter the main city on 11 April 1917. They ultimately finished the campaign at Kirkuk, 200 miles beyond Baghdad and over 500 miles from their original base at the head of the Persian Gulf.

No sooner was the war over, than the battalion began its demobilisation process. By the end of January 1919, 4 SWB was reduced to 14 officers and just over 200 men and began its journey home. However, on reaching Karachi, the battalion was despatched up country to Rawalpindi owing to troubles on the frontier and it was not until 26 July that they could move on again. It was then affected by an outbreak of influenza during the sea voyage, so were put into quarantine and it was on 19 August 1919 that the battalion eventually arrived in Brecon for its final disbandment as a service battalion, after a distinguished war record.[2]

Of its commanding officers at Gallipoli, the first was Lieutenant Colonel Franklin Gillespie, who having been killed by a sniper on 8 August 1915, was thought to have been buried in a temporary cemetery and was then commemorated on the Helles memorial. He is also commemorated on the Newtown war memorial in mid Wales and he has a memorial plaque in the regimental chapel in Brecon Cathedral. Major Marcus John Barré de la Poer Beresford immediately took over command and was briefly the CO until being invalided back to England in December 1915 with acute bronchitis. He was admitted to a nursing home and then sent on four months sick leave. He was awarded the DSO for services rendered during Gallipoli and retired as a lieutenant colonel in April

1   Capt Buchanan had also been awarded the MC previously and had been Mentioned in Despatches four times.
2   In 1918, there was a worldwide outbreak of Spanish Flu, which killed up to 50 million people.

1919. He was killed in a German air raid on 26 July 1944 during the second world war at the age of 76. Lieutenant Colonel Charles Kitchin took over command in December 1915 and continued as CO for most of the remainder of the war. He too was awarded the DSO for his services at Gallipoli and he transferred to the reserve of officers in November 1919. He died at Tonbridge in Kent on 25 January 1948 at the age of 71.

* * *

Meanwhile, 2 SWB was preparing to move to the Western Front and in March 1916 arrived in France. Its first experience of the horrors of Flanders Fields was the opening day of the first battle of the Somme on 1 July 1916, when, in the attack on Beaumont Hamel, it lost 15 officers and 384 soldiers killed, wounded or missing, out of a total of 21 officers and 578 men, within an hour. The battalion was eventually reformed and after periods in various parts of the front line fought at Monchy Le Preux in April and May 1917, where Sergeant George White was awarded the Victoria Cross posthumously. During an attack, the leading coy was held up by enemy machine guns and both coy officers were hit. Seeing that all depended upon these guns being put out of action, Sergeant White made for the nearest one, shooting three of the enemy and bayoneting a fourth one. He was within a few yards of another gun when he was caught in its murderous fire, but his self sacrifice diverted the fire of the guns from the remainder of the battalion.

During the summer and autumn of 1917, the battalion took part in the third battle of Ypres and in November and December earned what was perhaps its greatest battle honour, at Cambrai. Starting on 20 November, and preceded by 400 tanks and a massive artillery bombardment, 29 Division broke through the Hindenburg Line to secure the crossings of the Scheldt canal between Masnières and Marcoing, to get a footing on the Beaurevoir canal. The fighting was vicious and relentless, with attack and counter attack taking a heavy toll on the battalion's manpower. Cambrai was not a success for the British, but it was a learning curve for the victories which were to come in the following year and one in which 2 SWB fought with great distinction. The battalion served the rest of the war in France and it helped to stem the German offensive on the Lys in April 1918. It then joined in the final advance to victory, taking part in the re-capture of Gheluvelt, scene of 1 SWB's historic stand in 1914. On crossing the Rhine, the battalion formed part of the army of occupation in Cologne and carried its Colours, which had been brought out from the depot in Brecon, into Germany. Demobilisation began soon after the armistice and on 5 April 1919 the final cadre of the battalion arrived in Brecon, having served in three theatres of war – China, Gallipoli and the Western Front – and had taken more casualties than any other battalion in the Regiment.[3]

2 SWB had three commanding officers during the Gallipoli campaign. The first was Lieutenant Colonel Hugh Gilbert Casson, who had been the CO since 1911. He landed with the battalion at S Beach and was in command until July 1915 when he was promoted to brevet colonel to command 157 Infantry Brigade as part of 52 (Lowland) Division. A much respected and popular officer in the Regiment, he had already been appointed as a Companion of the Order of St Michael and St George (CMG) and in 1918 he became a Companion of the Most Honourable Order of the Bath (CB) for his distinguished service throughout the war. He retired as a brigadier in 1919 and died in 1951 at the age of 85. When he was promoted to command 157 Brigade, he was replaced by Major John Going, who was CO for three months between July and September 1915. He then succumbed to dysentery and had to be replaced, but he recovered and was promoted to lieutenant colonel in November 1915. He continued to serve throughout the remainder of the war, commanding the

3   C T Atkinson, *The South Wales Borderers in the Great War*, p.50.

battalion again for a brief period in 1916. He retired in 1920 and died in 1949, aged 83. The third commanding officer was Captain Aubrey Ellis Williams, who, as a captain, took over from Major Going in September 1915 and commanded until the battalion had been evacuated from the peninsula in January 1916. Captain Williams then went to be brigade major in 157 Brigade. He commanded 1 SWB from 1934 to 1937 where the battalion saw active service in Waziristan.[4] He continued to be promoted and eventually became commander 160 Infantry Brigade in 1939 at the outbreak of the second world war as a brigadier. His final appointment was GOC 38 Infantry Division in the rank of major general in 1940. He retired on 1 April 1941 and died on 25 March 1977, at the age of 89, on the Isle of Wight, where his ashes are interred.

Another officer of note was Captain Dudley Johnson. Although badly wounded at the beginning of the campaign on 25 April 1915, he recovered well and ended the war as one of the most highly decorated regimental officers, having been awarded the VC while commanding 2 Royal Sussex and then the CB, DSO (twice) and the MC. He also commanded 2 North Staffordshire Regiment in 1928. At the outbreak of the second world war he was GOC 4 Division and was evacuated from Dunkirk. He was both the colonel of the Monmouthshire Regiment (TA) in 1941 and the colonel of the South Wales Borderers in 1944. He retired as a major general in 1944. He died in 1975 at the age of 91.

* * *

Ernest Kirkland Laman, one of the central characters of this book, continued as quartermaster of 2 SWB for the remainder of the Great War, being present at all the main encounters in which the battalion was involved on the Western Front. In 1918, he was awarded the MBE for services rendered over the whole period, as well as the MC for his outstanding contribution in the field. Promoted to captain in 1917, he accompanied the battalion to India for part of the posting there after the war and by 1928 was back in Brecon where he was the quartermaster of the training depot in the barracks. He then became the regional recruiting officer in Pontypridd, having been promoted to major in 1929 and he retired on 4 October 1930 after 39 years service with the regiment.

On retirement, he and his wife Sybil (known to their family as Gumpy and Morganny respectively) moved to Dinas Powis, near Cardiff, where they both continued to take an active interest in regimental affairs. He was a fine craftsman in wood, and besides making various small tables, stools and shelves, he made a dolls house for his first grandchild Joanna. His granddaughter Frances recalls being told that Ernest, a man fond of smoking, said that tobacco was so hard to come by during the war that he had tried smoking cabbage but that "it was filthy". He was a keen golfer and made frequent use of the local golf course.

Ernest was fairly deaf in his old age but he remained very smart and upright, as would be the case with any former RSM and Quartermaster. Frances remembers him at the wedding of his god-daughter, where she and her sister Sarah were bridesmaids. Someone was making an overlong speech and Ernest, tired of standing and playing upon his deafness, asked loudly "Is he still speaking?" and then, after the speech had continued for some time, he declared "Is the silly old bugger still talking? I can't stand here much longer." This seemed to work as the speech did end fairly swiftly, to everyone's relief! He became very frail in the last few years of his life and died at the Royal Hamadryad Hospital in Cardiff on 30 April 1961 at the age of 85. This was a double tragedy for the family, as his grandson Nicholas was killed in a mountaineering accident in Scotland on the

---

4   During this time, Capt Frederick Ernest Kirkland Laman, 5th Bn, 1st Punjab Regiment, the eldest son of Ernest Laman, was awarded MC while serving with the Tochi Scouts.

Image 33. Ernest with his wife Sybil and their two
sons Freddie and Bertie (Mrs F Voelcker).

Image 34. Ernest as a member of the Army Revolver XXX at Bisley in 1913 – 5th from left, centre row
(Mrs F Voelcker).

same day. So passed away one of the regiment's most distinguished, respected and popular officers, who had made a significant contribution, both professionally and socially, to the fabric of the South Wales Borderers, a regiment in which he was so proud to have served.

Sergeant S D Bean DCM continued to serve with 2 SWB for the remainder of the war. He was the RSM of the battalion between 1921 and 1928, when he was commissioned as a Lieutenant Quartermaster into 10/17 Dogra Regiment, an infantry regiment of the British Indian army. Having joined the regiment in 1903, he retired in October 1945, in the rank of major, after 42 years unbroken service. An extremely smart, able and much respected officer, he died at Bath on 29 April 1961.

* * *

Being a regular unit, 2 SWB was brought back up to strength after the war and by November 1919 was ready to be posted to India again, where it remained until 1927. This was followed by a short tour in Aden (where 1 SWB was to see active service in 1967) after which it returned to England, being stationed first of all in Portsmouth and then at Catterick until 1935. There were short tours to Malta and Palestine, with three years in Londonderry, Northern Ireland, until the outbreak of war again in 1939. 2 SWB took part in the ill-fated expedition to Norway in 1940 and was the only Welsh battalion to land on the beaches of Normandy on D Day, 6 June 1944, just as it was on S Beach at Gallipoli on 25 April 1915. By coincidence, the only two battalions of the British army to be involved in both the landings at Gallipoli in 1915 and at Normandy in 1944, were 2 SWB and 1 KOSB. In a similar coincidence, Lieutenant Desmond Somerville landed at Gallipoli during the first assault, where he was awarded the MC, while his son Captain Nicholas Somerville (later Brigadier Sir Nicholas) landed with 2 SWB on D Day. Desmond went on to command 2 SWB from 1937 to 1939 and retired as a brigadier in 1945, having been elevated to CBE. He died in 1976 at the age of 77.

The battalion spent the remainder of the war in North West Europe, ending up at Hamburg where it became part of the army of occupation. The battalion returned home to Woodfarm Camp, Malvern, Worcestershire (now the site of the Three Counties Show) on 30 November 1946 where it was to end its days, as a consequence of the reduction in size of the British army after the war. Lieutenant Colonel A J Stocker DSO was the commanding officer from 15 August 1946 until 16 January 1947, when he handed over to Lieutenant Colonel D L Rhys MC, who was to see out the last three months of the battalion's service. The final ceremonial parade was, appropriately, on 22 January 1947, being the 68th anniversary of the Immortal Defence of Rorke's Drift, after which its manpower was dispersed, either to other battalions, or through demobilisation and its administration closed down, until it lapsed into suspended animation on 16 April 1947. The Battalion was officially disbanded on 31 May 1948. The Colours, having been carried by the battalion since 6 August 1880, were laid up in the regimental chapel at Brecon cathedral 10 years later, on 14 September 1958, where they now rest in perpetuity.

* * *

After the Anzac force was evacuated from Suvla Bay, it was regrouped under the title of 1 Anzac Corps in Egypt in February 1916, as part of the reorganisation and expansion of the Australian imperial force and the New Zealand expeditionary force (NZEF). Along with 2 Anzac Corps, it replaced the original Anzac force, which had battled with such tenacity throughout the Gallipoli

Image 35. Captain Ernest Laman at the Depot in Brecon in 1928 – 3rd from the right, front row
(R Welsh Museum).

Image 36. Ernest admiring the garden at home in Dinas Powis South Wales (Mrs F Voelcker).

campaign. The corps initially participated in the defence of the Suez Canal before being transferred to the Western Front in France and Belgium in late March 1916. Here, almost 300,000 men of the corps fought with great distinction, taking heavy casualties along the way. Battles such as Pozieres on the Somme, Bullecourt, Ypres, Fromelles and Paschendale, are but a few which honour their courage and bravery and there are many memorials in France and Belgium, such as that at Mont St Quentin, scene of one of their greatest victories, which stand as sentinels to their outstanding commitment and self sacrifice. In November 1917, 1 Anzac Corps ceased to exist when the Australian infantry divisions in France were grouped together as the Australian corps, while the New Zealand division, then part of 2 Anzac Corps, was allocated to a British corps. Since 1918, Australia and New Zealand have been at the forefront of commemorating the Gallipoli campaign each year, with 25 April known throughout their countries as Anzac Day. While in reality that day belongs to all those nations who took part and should more appropriately be called Gallipoli Day, the significant contribution made by the Anzac Force is respected and it is understandable that each nation calls to mind its particular sacrifice in its own way.

* * *

It would be discourteous if no mention was made of the Turkish army which fought with such fanatical courage to defend their homeland during the Gallipoli campaign and who suffered

Image 37. Ernest with family and friends at Dinas Powis (Mrs F Voelcker).

Image 38. Ernest in pensive mood, recalling duty nobly done (Mrs F Voelcker).

much the same hardships and privations as their allied counterparts. Their casualties were between 300,000 and 400,000 with up to 87,000 of these being killed. The details of their involvement are outside the scope of this book, but their achievements speak for themselves. The allied forces did not capture any of their major objectives, due not only to the inadequacies of their own high command, but also to the tenacity and determination of the Turkish forces opposing them. Much of the credit for this must go to Colonel Mustapha Kemal, one of the senior Turkish regimental commanders. His tactical awareness, vision and sheer stubbornness ensured that the allied forces were thwarted at almost every turn and he was instrumental in ensuring that the assault on Sari Bair in August 1915 did not succeed. This was the pivotal point of the campaign, after which evacuation by the allies was almost inevitable. He went on to become the first president of the newly created Turkish republic in 1923 and in 1934 he made the following speech by way of reconciliation, now inscribed in stone above Anzac Cove at Gallipoli. It is also commemorated on the Kemal Ataturk memorial at Anzac Parade, Canberra, Australia:

Those heroes that shed their blood and lost their lives…You are now lying in the soil of a friendly country. Therefore rest in peace. There is no difference between the Johnnies and the Mehmets to us where they lie side by side here in this country of ours…You, the mothers, who sent their sons from faraway countries, wipe away your tears; your sons are now lying in our bosom and are in peace, after having lost their lives on this land they have become our sons as well.

Honoured by the people of Turkey with the title of Ataturk, which means the "father of the Turks," he remained as president until he died in 1938, aged 57.

* * *

To mark the centenary of the Gallipoli campaign, an act of remembrance took place in the regimental chapel, Brecon Cathedral, on Saturday 25 April 2015 which was well attended by the regimental association and members of the public. While there were a number of events taking place at the same time, both in Turkey and in London, it was felt that it was appropriate for the regiment to commemorate locally the distinguished service of the South Wales Borderers, as well as the Royal Welch Fusiliers and the Welch Regiment, who also served at Gallipoli and who are now all linked together as the antecedent regiments of the Royal Welsh. Major General Lennox Napier, the last commanding officer of the South Wales Borderers and a former colonel of the regiment, laid a wreath in honoured memory of all three regiments and there were readings by Lieutenant Colonel Michael Lewis, High Sheriff of Powys, representing the Royal Welch Fusiliers and Lieutenant Colonel Peter Davies, who represented the Welch Regiment. Major Alan Harrhy gave the exhortation on behalf of the regimental association, after which a bugler sounded last post, followed by a period of silence and then reveille. This author gave the following regimental tribute:

> Of the many battle honours emblazoned on the Colours of the Royal Welsh, a number have particular resonance today and I name but three – Gallipoli 1915–1916, Landing at Helles and Suvla. Etched in the regimental psyche as icons of courage of the highest order, they encapsulate the purpose of meeting here this morning. Gallipoli Day is being commemorated nationally, and it is appropriate that we should gather locally to pay tribute to all ranks of our antecedent regiments, the Royal Welch Fusiliers, the South Wales Borderers and the Welch Regiment, who gave their lives in that heroic but tragic campaign.
>
> By December 1914, the war on the Western Front of France and Belgium had ground to a halt in a stalemate of trench warfare. Anxious to find a way out of this impasse, Winston Churchill, then First Lord of the Admiralty, proposed an alternative campaign to take Turkey out of the war, which would force Germany to fight on two fronts and would free up the Dardanelles waterway for use by beleaguered Russian forces. While the concept was sound, its execution was not, as it was hastily planned, and poorly resourced. The campaign also took part amidst the most appalling conditions, such as the unrelenting heat of a Mediterranean summer, a lack of water, poor food, inadequate equipment and without proper sanitation. Sickness and disease was rife and at the height of the war, there were up to 5,000 cases of dysentery a week. Over half a million allied personnel took part, of whom 420,000 were British and Empire troops, 80,000 French, 50,000 Australians and 9,000 New Zealanders. The cost in human terms was terrible. The Allies had 250,000 casualties, of whom some 58,000 were killed with only 11,000 having known graves, while the Turkish forces suffered similar losses.

There were many acts of heroism and endurance by all those officers and soldiers of our regiments who took part. The 2nd Battalion the South Wales Borderers landed at Gallipoli 100 years ago today, on 25 April 1915, during the initial invasion at Cape Helles and was present throughout the whole campaign. The following day, Lieutenant Colonel Charles Doughty-Wylie of the Royal Welch Fusiliers was awarded the Victoria Cross posthumously for his outstanding bravery in leading an attack onto a nearby hill held by the enemy, armed just with a swagger stick, only to be killed in his moment of triumph. A few months later, a number of other Welsh battalions arrived on the peninsula to take part in the second invasion, this time at Suvla Bay. There were four more battalions of the Royal Welch Fusiliers, one of whom, the 8th Battalion, was in support of the Australian Light Horse during their infamous attack at the Nek, immortalised in the film *Gallipoli*. Three battalions of the Welch Regiment were also present, with 8 Welch, initially a pioneer battalion, taking part in the ANZAC assault on the main hill feature above Suvla Bay which very nearly succeeded and which could have turned the whole course of the war. The 4th Battalion the South Wales Borderers was also part of this action and suffered the loss of their commanding officer, Lieutenant Colonel Franklin Gillespie who was killed by a sniper on 9 August 1915. Also, Major Sir William Lennox Napier, grandfather of Major General Lennox Napier who is with us today, was killed a few days later on 13 August. There are also a number of other local connections. Captain Hugh Fowler, grandfather of Mrs Jo Copping, distinguished himself on the night of 18 June 1915 in a particularly vicious battle when he led an advance into an enemy trench. Capt Fowler's bravery during this assault was an inspiration; as his own supply of bombs ran out he would pick up those thrown by the enemy and hurl them back against the Turks with no regard for his own safety. Awarded the Distinguished Service Order, Capt Fowler's citation actually recommended him for the VC for his gallantry. Mrs Anne Payne's grandfather was Capt Charles Kitchin of the 4th Bn South Wales Borderers, a company commander at the start of the campaign, who became its commanding officer at the end. General Sir William Birdwood was the general officer commanding the ANZAC force and his great nephew, Major Andrew Keelan is also here to commemorate his great uncle's significant involvement.

By the autumn of 1915, it was clear that no amount of reinforcement would change the tide of the battle, and with allied troops required elsewhere, the British government decided that evacuation was the only option. Suvla Bay was evacuated in December 1915 with Cape Helles following a month later. By 9 January 1916 there were no allied troops left on the peninsula and after the failure of the offensive campaign, the evacuation itself was a flawless example of a textbook operation that took the Turkish army completely by surprise. After nine months continuous active service, virtually all of our battalions had been reduced to almost 50 percent of their original strength, many of whom have no known grave. Their names are inscribed on the Helles memorial, sentinel over the beaches and battlefields where they gave their lives in selfless sacrifice. The Great War was eventually won on the Western Front, while Gallipoli was often referred to as the forgotten war. Gallipoli Day ensures that this is no longer the case and those of us who have served, or continue to serve, in our successor regiments have a duty to ensure that those magnificent soldiers of Wales, who, in peace or war in life or death have set us so great an example, will always be remembered."

Today, the Royal Welsh stands on the threshold of another chapter in its illustrious regimental history. Those who serve in its ranks are, quite rightly, focussed on the challenges and responsibilities of the future, while its former members who now support from the sideline are confident that the new regiment will take with it the golden thread of all that has been achieved along the way at such conflicts as Gallipoli. This golden thread, which embodies duty nobly done, will shine like a beacon of light upon the forthcoming journey, just as it illuminated the road which was forged by those who served yesterday, thus ensuring that their noble deeds and all that they stood for will not be forgotten but will remain bright and clear for all to uphold, cherish and respect together.

Appendix I

Officers of the 2nd Bn South Wales Borderers
who served at Gallipoli
25 April 1915–8 January 1916

Name	Service Details	Additional Detail
ASHFORD, James Samuel	Born 1.1890, From Tpr Dorset (Queen's Own) Yeomanry #618, 2Lt Gen List 10.10.1915, To South Wales Borderers 10.10.1915, T/Lt 1.7.1917, To Warwickshire Yeomanry as Lt 28.5.1917, To Remount Service 15.6.1918, Capt 1.9.1921	Son of Edward James Ashford & Anne Challis (née Hilder) Ashford of Zouch Farm, North Tidworth, Wiltshire; Married Keturah Muriel Bown at Sherborne 6.1922; Served Egypt 22.4.1915; Gallipoli 2nd Bn SWB 29.10.1915-5.1.1916; Egypt 6.2.1916 (Sick); Resided: Wylye, Wiltshire; Died Wylye 11.5.1925; Buried All Saints Churchyard Langford Steeple; WO339/48500
BALLANTINE, Aitken	Born Greenock 1876, 2Lt (SR) SWB 13.4.1915, Lt 28.12.1915, RC 27.3.1919	Son of the late John H Ballantine, Sugar Refiner, Glasgow; MID LG 28.1.1916 (1200); Served Gallipoli 2nd Bn SWB 30.8.1915-8.12.1915 (Sick); France 9.2.1916-6.4.1916 (Medically unfit) awarded Silver War Badge; Member Greenock Cricket Club; Resided 99a Eldon Street, Greenock; Died 1937
BARON, James	5th E Lancs, T/Lt 18.6.1916 (or 14.11.1915), To MGC 29.7.1916, A/Capt 17.4.1917, A/Maj 28.3.1918, To 5th Bn E Lancs 13.4.1920, RC as Maj 14.4.1923	Egypt 23.9.1914; 5th Bn E LANCS attached 2nd Bn SWB 28.5.1915; WO339/79989. Two offrs with same name
BEARDSHAW, Reginald Dudley	Born Barnes London 1883, Educated King's College London, From Sgt Kings Royal Rifle Corps, T/2Lt SWB 3.4.1915, Lt 23.10.1915	Son of Herbert & Kate Emily Beardshaw; Husband of Elizabeth A (née Whittingham) Beardshaw of Dunraven Street, Aberkenfig; Served Gallipoli 24.9.1915-8.1.1916; France 15.3.1916-21.10.1916 (Died of wounds); Buried Bulls Road Cemetery, Flers; WO339/38492
BEHRENS, Robert Philip	Born Chorlton, Lancashire 4.12.1893, Educated Winchester School & Royal Military College Sandhurst, 2Lt SWB 5.2.1913, Lt 12.9.1914	Son of George Benjamin Behrens JP & Helen Elizabeth Behrens (née Davies), Vron Yw, Denbigh; Served Tsingtao; Gallipoli with 2nd Bn SWB 25.4.1915 (Severely wounded at De Tott's Battery); Died and buried at Sea; Commemorated Helles Memorial; Commemorative brass tablet St Teyrnog Church, Llandrynog, Clwyd; Commemorated Llansawel War Memorial & Llanwrda War Memorial; See De Ruvigny entry

Name	Service Details	Additional Detail
BERGER, Samuel Henry	Born Aldeby Norfolk 6.9.1886, 2Lt (SR) SWB 26.10.1914, RC 17.3.1917	Son of Samuel Sharp Steigen Berger & Emma Berger (née Wheen); Married: Hilda Lambert Milford (died Thorverton 25.12.1935), St James's Westminster 21.3.1912; Served Gallipoli with 2nd Bn SWB 10.5.1915-20.6.1915 (Sick); Died Baring Crescent, Exeter 15.7.1935; WO339/28772
BICKLEY, John Frederick	Born 1893, T/Lt 14th Bn Cheshire Regt 1.4.1915	14th Bn Cheshire Regt; Served Gallipoli with 2nd Bn SWB 29.6.1915-1.8.1915; To War Office; Resided: Roseville, Guildford Road, Fairfield, Sydney NSW (1920); Died 20.6.1965; Buried Macquarie Park Cemetery, North Ryde, Sydney NSW WO339/26716
BIRKETT, Gerald Halsey DSO	Born Richmond Surrey 17.1.1883, Educated Haileybury, 2Lt West Yorkshire Militia 21.3.1901, To South Wales Borderers, 2Lt 4.7.1903, Lt 21.4.1906, Capt 9.6.1913, Maj 4.12.1917, Lt-Col 9.12.1929, Retd 9.12.1933	Son of R H Birkett; Served in China with 2 SWB; Gallipoli 25.4.1915 (Wounded); Adjutant 2nd Bn South Wales Borderers 5.2.1912-4.2.1915, Commanded 2nd Bn South Wales Borderers 9.12.1929-9.10.1933; DSO LG 3.6.1918; MID LG 30.5.1916, 11.12.1917 & 20.5.1918; First Secretary of Army Rugby Union; Died 7.1.1961 (See SWB Journal 59); Medals in Collection
BLAKE, Arthur Joseph MC	Educated Stonyhurst College, Lt RAMC 14.8.1914, T/Capt 15.8.1915	Battalion Medical Officer; Served Gallipoli 25.4.1915-8.1.1916; 87th Fd Amb 22.9.1916; MC Citation LG 22.9.1916 (9271); MC bar LG 4.2.1918 (1601); Bar Citation LG 5.7.1918 (7891)
BLAKE, Francis Seymour	Born 1878, From Orderly Room Sergeant 15th Bn County of London Regt #398, Lt King's Liverpool Regt 15.2.1915, T/Capt 29.12.1915	Son of Alfred John & Mary Blake; Married Florence Whitehead at St Augustine's Lewisham 12.8.1906; Resided: 11 Avondale Road, Mottingham Kent; Served Gallipoli with 15th Bn King's Liverpool 11.8.1915-21.8.1915 (Wounded) & 2 SWB 9.12.1915-8.1.1916; France 15.3.1915-1.7.1916 (Killed in action); Commemorated Thiepval Memorial; WO339/23476
BODLEY, Owen Colin	Born Exeter 1884, T/Lt 9th Bn South Wales Borderers 30.11.1914, To South Wales Borderers 30.11.1914, T/Capt, RC (Ill Health) as Lt 5.1.1919	Served Gallipoli with 2nd Bn SWB 24.9.1915-8.1.1916; France 15.3.1916-6.4.1916 (Wounded - Auchinvillar); 1st Bn South Wales Borderers 11.9.1916; Occupation: Mechanical Engineer; Resided: 4 Magdalen Road, Exeter (1911) & Hopewell House, Bothenhampton, Bridport, Dorset (1949) ; Died Bridport 10.9.1949; Defence Medal; Medals sold DNW 13.12.2012
BOLTON, Geoffrey George Hargreaves CBE MC DL	Born 5.8.1894, Educated Clifton College, 2Lt 1/5 E Lancs 10.10.1914, Lt 1.6.1916, A/Capt 3.8.1917, Capt 18.4.1918, T/Lt-Col, To 5th (DF) Bn East Lancashire Regt 9.4.1921, RC 23.4.1921, Re-joined, bt Col 16.2.1925, RC 29.4.1939	Son of Henry Hargreaves Bolton JP (Colliery Owner) & Florence E (née Allen) Bolton of Heightside, Newchurch in Rossendale; Married (1) Ethel Robinson (d 1942) 1919 (2) Margaret (Daisy) Robinson 1943; Adjutant 1/5 East Lancashire Regt 24.11.1915; Served Gallipoli 1/5th E Lancs attached 2nd Bn SWB 27.5.1915 & Palestine &France; MC LG 3.4.1916; MID x 3, 10.5.1915; Commanded 5th East Lancashire Regt TA 1920-28; MBE (Civ) LG 24.6.1946 (3126); CBE (Civ) LG 11.6.1960 (3982); KStJ LG 20.6.1969 (6457); Managing Director Hargreaves Collieries, Accrington (1932); Chairman North-Western Division National Coal Board (1951); DL (Lancashire) LG 8.11.1935 (7050); High Sheriff (Lancashire) 1962; Resided; Quarry Hill, Accrington, Lancashire; Died Chatburn Clitheroe 19.3.1983

Name	Service Details	Additional Detail
BRADLY, John Frank	Born London 18.11.1888, Educated Haileybury, 2Lt (M) South Wales Borderers 1.10.1906, 2Lt (SR) 1.8.1908, Enlisted #12662 Canadian Expeditionary Force 18.9.1914, Lt (SR) South Wales Borderers 29.1.1915	Son of Frank & Sarah Grace (née Gribbin) Bradly, Bexhill-on-Sea, Sussex; Twin brother of Capt George Frank Bradly SWB, R Warwickshire Regt & RFC; Served before WW1 in 4th Bn SWB (M) & 3rd (Reserve) Bn SWB; Emigrated to Lumsden, Saskatchewan, Canada (farmer); Served 2nd Bn SWB Gallipoli 10.5.1915-28.6.1915 (Wounded); Died Malta 2.7.1915; Buried Pieta Military Cemetery Malta; Commemorated in Lumsden; WO339/31755
BRISCOE, Francis Edward DSO	Lt, T/Capt 8.8.1915, T/Maj 7.6.1917	Served 15th Bn Yorkshire Regt Gallipoli 29.7.1915; attached 2nd Bn SWB Gallipoli 10.10.1915-29.10.1915; To 6th Bn Yorkshire Regt; DSO LG 1.1.1918 (18); MID 11.12.1917 (13232); WO339/19876
BUDD, Wrinch Joseph Charles	Born Chapham 23.9.1877, Educated United Westminster Schools, T/Lt 9th Bn South Wales Borderers 27.2.1915	Son of Ebenezer Budd & Mary Maria (née Bristow) Budd, 84 Melrose Avenue, Norbury; Served with Queen's Westminsters 1894-1900; Served on active service ABW with City of London Imperial Volunteers (Mounted Infantry) (awarded QSA); Employed by Shanghai Municipal Council Electricity Dept; Served Shanghai Volunteers 1905-1914; Served Gallipoli 2nd Bn SWB 25.5.1915-28.6.1915 (Killed in action); Commemorated Helles Memorial; WO339/23775; See De Ruvigny; (Nephew (same name) 406971 Flg Offr RAAF killed flying accident over Indonesia 6.5.1943)
BUNCE, George Owen	Born Aldershot 12.12.1883, From Sergeant South Wales Borderers #6636, 2Lt 11.2.1915	Son of William Henry Bunce & Ellen (née Ford); Husband of Clara Bunce (née Stroud), 12 Marle Hill Parade, Cheltenham; Served 2nd Bn SWB ABW and Tsingtao; Served Gallipoli 25.4.1915-9.5.1915 (Killed in action); Commemorated Helles Memorial; WO339/22629
BURRELL, Percy Edmund	Born 26.3.1882, Educated Oundle School, Enlisted No. 3 Company HAC 15.10.1906, From LSgt 2nd Bn HAC #40, 2Lt (SR) 24.2.1915	Eldest son of Edmund Risoliere Burrell & Florence Joy Burrell, Blackheath; Husband of Eileen Burrell, Queen's Park, Caterham (Remarried: Mrs H G Palmer, The Gables, Barnham, Sussex); Served Gallipoli 10.5.1915-21.8.1915 (Killed in action – Hill 70); Commemorated Helles Memorial; Medals (less 1914/15 Star) sold Christies 10.11.1992; WO339/2736
BURT, Thomas Duncannon	T/2Lt 22.1.1915, 2Lt R Scots 25.1.1915, T/Lt 1.7.1917, RC (Ill Health) as Lt 1.6.1918	14th Bn R Scots; Served Gallipoli attached 2nd Bn SWB 19.11.1915-6.1.1916; To 1/5th Bn R Scots; Awarded Silver War Badge; Resided: 31 Bread Street, Edinburgh (1921)
BYRNE, Edmund James Widdrington	Born Tooting 1880, Enlisted Inns of Court OTC 4.8.1914, Lt (SR) South Wales Borderers 23.9.1914, Capt 1.5.1915	Son of the late Hon Sir Edmund Widdrington Byrne (High Court Judge) (died 4.4.1904) & Henrietta Johnstone Byrne (née Gulland); Solicitor (1904); Served France 1st Bn SWB 17.12.1914 (Wounded); Gallipoli 2nd Bn SWB 21.8.1915- 2.10.1915 (Sick); France 15.3.1916-29.4.1916 (Killed in action); Commemorated Thiepval Memorial; WO339/19029

Name	Service Details	Additional Detail
CASS, Hugh Lancelot	Born India 1891, Educated Malvern College, From Sergeant Royal Engineers #7647 & Inns of Court OTC, 2Lt (SR) 22.1.1913, To South Wales Borderers as 2Lt (SR) 3.2.1915	Eldest son of Captain Thomas Beard Cass RFA (TF) & the late Elizabeth Maud Cass, 153 Ashley Gardens Westminster; Served France (Indian Army) & Gallipoli with 2nd Bn SWB 10.5.1915-19.6.1915 (Killed in action); Buried Twelve Tree Copse Cemetery;
CASSON, Hugh Gilbert CB CMG	Born Wold, Northamptonshire 11.1.1866, Educated Wellington College & Royal Military College Sandhurst, Lt 25.8.1886, , Capt 8.11.1892, Maj 18.6.1904, Lt-Col 29.11.1911, bt Col 3.6.1915, Col 29.11.1915, Retd as Brig-Gen 19.10.1919	Third son of the Rev George Casson, Old Court, Torquay, Devon; Adjutant 1st Bn SWB 31.7.1889-31.7.1893; Served ABW 7.4.1900-26.10.1901, Tsingtao, Gallipoli 25.4.1915-11.7.1915; Commanding Officer 2nd Bn SWB 29.11.1911-19.7.1915; GOC 157 Inf Bde 11.7.1915; CB LG 1.1.1918; CMG LG 18.2.1915 & 16.3.1915; MID LG 10.9.1901, 27.11.1901, 5.8.1915, 30.5.1916, 13.7.1916, 6.7.1917 & 16.1.1918; Order of Karageorge Star (3rd class) LG 15.2.1917; Queen's South Africa medal (clasps: Johannesburg, Cape Colony, Orange Free State, South Africa 1901); Resided: Glympton Rectory, Woodstock, Oxfordshire (1926); Died Tyn-y-Coed, Arthog 5.2.1951
CHAMBERLAIN, William John	Born St Pancras 1.9.1880, From 3rd Vol Bn Royal Fusiliers, Enlisted South Wales Borderers #6185 21.6.1899, LCpl 20.1.1900, Cpl 5.7.1902, LSgt 10.9.1902, Sgt 23.3.1906, CSgt 22.5.1910, Company Sergeant Major 1.12.1913, 2Lt 11.2.1915, Lt 16.9.1915, To Labour Corps as A/Capt 20.10.1917, Retd 7.7.1919, Retd from Reserve 1.9.1930	Son of William Chamberlain of 12 Crossland Road, Chalk Farm, London; Married (1) Mary Winifred Powell at Brecon 23.8.1905 (2) Susanna C M Chamberlain in Gatooma, Rhodesia (now Kadoma, Zimbabwe) 22.7.1967; Served ABW (QSA 3 clasps, KSA 2 clasps) with 2nd Bn SWB & Tsingtao (Company Sergeant Major B Company 2nd Bn SWB); Gallipoli 25.4.1915-27.4.1915 (Wounded); France 16.12.1916-21.12.1916 (Sick); To UK from No 5 Infantry Base Depot (Rouen); Attached Chinese Labour Corps 20.10.1917-23.12.1918; Died Zimbabwe 8.9.1972; WO339/22631
COCHRANE, Ivor Edwin Morgan	Born Ynyshir Glamorgan 1896, Educated Wellington College & Royal Military College Sandhurst, 2Lt SWB 12.5.1915, T/Lt 23.10.1915, T/Capt 14.1.1917, RC 5.10.1921, Re-joined ?	(MIC incorrectly shows Edward not Edwin); Son of Dr Charles Edward & Mary Margaret Cochrane; Married Dorothy Glanville Cochrane; Served Gallipoli 30.8.1915-21.9.1915 (Wounded); Served 4th Garrison Bn Royal Welsh Fusiliers 16.8.1916; Served Salonkia with 7th/8th Bn SWB as OC C Company 24.11.1918-16.12.1918; To India with 2nd Bn SWB 21.10.1919; Resided: 22 Cromer Road, Weston-super-Mare; Died 19.7.1940 (see SWB Journal 18); Buried St Paul's Churchyard, Kewstoke (CWGC headstone)
CONNERY, Arthur William Field MC	Born Ashton under Lyne 1887, 2Lt Manchester Regt TF 14.10.1914, To Machine Gun Corps 8.3.1916, T/Lt 6.7.1916, To Railway Operating Training Centre Royal Engineers (Traffic Officer) 29.11.1918, T/Capt 16.11.1919, To 9th Manchester Regt as Lt 15.10.1920, RC as Capt 28.2.1925	Son of Lt-Col Michael Henry Connery MC (died 25.4.1921), 1/9th Bn (The Aston Territorials) Manchester Regt of Willow Bank, Henrietta Street, Ashton under Lyne; Occupation pre-WW1: Clerk, Great Central Railway Co; MC LG 30.1.1920 (1219); Married Gladys F Bowtell at Hendon 1917; Served 1/9th Manchester Regt Egypt from 13.4.1915; MGC; attached 2nd Bn SWB 27.5.1915-29.5.1915; Served South Russia 1920; To Argentina 16.11.1922; Died Buenos Aires 15.10.1934

Name	Service Details	Additional Detail
COOKE, Edmund Samuel Winter	Born Korumburra, Victoria 18.2.1895, Enlisted 1.12.1914, From Pte Australian Imperial Force (Army Veterinary Corps) #63, T/2Lt SWB 26.7.1915, 2Lt 4.5.1916, Lt 26.10.1917, To hp 18.1.1919, Retd 10.3.1920, Re-enlisted Australian Army #V371870 19.3.1942	Son of Herbert Pybus Cooke & Agnes Jane Cooke (née Orme) of Ardvaree, Young, New South Wales; Married Grace F Nicolson, Corowa NSW 1929; MC LG 4.2.1918 (1603); MC Citation LG 5.7.1918 (7901); Embarked at Sydney aboard HMAT Ajana A31 19.12.1914; Served Gallipoli Australia Imperial Force, 2nd Bn SWB 24.9.1915-8.1.1916; France 15.3.1916-20.6.1917 (Sick) & 7.10.1917-21.11.1917 (Wounded); Died Corowa NSW 13.1.1945
CREANEY, Harold John	Born Collingwood, Victoria 30.10.1887, From Staff Sergeant Major (Instructor) 6th Bn Australian IF #27, 2Lt Gen List 9.4.1915, To South Wales Borderers 9.4.1915, T/Lt 23.10.1915, A/Capt 1.5.1917, Re-joined Australian Army, Lt-Col, RC 31.10.1947	Son of John Henry Creaney & Sarah Jones; Married Ruby Grace White; Served 6th Bn Australian Imperial Force Egypt 4.12.1914 ; Served Gallipoli with 2nd Bn SWB 3.8.1915-21.8.1915 (Wounded); France 27.3.1916-22.8.1916 (Wounded); Served 51st Bn Cheshire Regt; Resided: 15 Carr Street, Geelong East, Victoria 30.9.1920; Died Sydney 25.8.1965; WO339/3108
DAVIES, Benjamin Jones BA	Born 1886, Educated Llandovery College & St David's College, Lampeter, From Cambridge University OTC, 2Lt (SR) 17.7.1912, To Public Schools Bn Royal Fusiliers, To South Wales Borderers 1.5.1915, Lt 1.9.1915, T/Capt 7.10.1915	Son of Griffiths & Catherine Margaret Davies, The Lodge, Llandyssul, Cardiganshire; Served Gallipoli 30.8.1915-22.11.1915 (Sick); France 9.2.1916-19.10.1916 (Wounded) & 13.4.1917-19.5.1917 (Killed in action); Commemorated Arras Memorial & Llandyssul War Memorial; WO339/13 or WO339/426
DAVIS, Hyman Andrade	Born Eastbourne 12.1879, Lt 3rd Bn Duke of Wellington's Regt (M) 24.8.1900, To 2nd Dragoon Guards as 2Lt 12.10.1901, RC 14.2.1903, Re-joined, T/Capt Northumberland Fusiliers 14.12.1914, RC (Ill Health) 6.3.1919	Sone of James H & Esther Josephine Davis; Married Helen Elizabeth Davis 1914; 15th Bn Northumberland Fusiliers; Served ABW; Bankrupt debts of £11,108) 1904; Served Gallipoli with 2nd Bn SWB 3.8.1915-6.10.1915 (Sick); Resided: Hyde Park Mansions, Marylebone; Died Westminster Hospital 6.1.1950
DUTTON, Charles Frederick MC DFC	Born Cardiff 1894, T/2Lt SWB 7.4.1915, T/ Lt 1.7.1915, Capt, RC 19.2.1919	Son of George Frederick & Alice Maud Dutton; MC (Citation) LG 22.9.1916 (9273); MC bar LG 15.2.1919 (2367); DFC LG 8.2.1919; Served Gallipoli 24.9.1915-8.1.1916; France 15.3.1916-8.7.1916 (Sick) & 29.4.1918-17.2.1919; Resided: 14 Cyncoed Road, Penylan, Cardiff; WO339/40231
EDWARDS, Thomas James	T/2Lt SWB 23.10.1914, T/Lt 18.4.1915, Lt 28.10.1915, To Training Reserve Bn 1.4.1917, To SWB 2.7.1917, Dismissed Service by Court Martial 8.7.1918	Served Gallipoli with 2nd Bn SWB 24.9.1915-8.1.1916; France 15.3.1916-20.5.1916 (Medically unfit); WO339/28903

Name	Service Details	Additional Detail
ELGEE, Hugh Francis	Born Otterbourne Hampshire 18.2.1880, From Royal Military College Sandhurst, 2Lt SWB 11.2.1899, Lt 16.10.1901, Capt 4.1.1908	Or ELGIE; Son of the Rev Walter Francis & Mrs Catherine (née Hammond) Elgee, Attached to Egyptian Army from 1.6.1908; Served Gallipoli with 2nd Bn SWB 30.6.1915-6.7.1915 (Killed in action); Buried Twelve Tree Copse Cemetery; Commemorated Brass Plaque St Matthew's Church Otterbourne
ELLIS, Archibald Horace Joseph	Born London 19.3.1882, Educated Harrow School Royal Military College Sandhurst, 2Lt 11.8.1900, Lt 26.8.1903, Capt 26.9.1909, Maj 1.9.1915, Retd 12.10.1918	Son of G H Ellis; Married Kathleen; Served ABW with 2nd Bn SWB 16.12.1901-19.12.1900 (invalided) & 28.5.1902-6.10.1903 (QSA only 4 clasps); Served Tsingtao; Gallipoli with 2nd Bn SWB 25.4.1915-9.6.1915 (Sick) & 8.7.1915-6.9.1915 (Sick); France with 6th Bn SWB as 2 i/c & CO 28.1.1917-7.6.1919; Resided: 59 Hyde Park Mansions, London SW1; Died London 26.9.1964
EVANS, Humphrey Pennefather	Born Benares India 1896, T/2Lt SWB 19.4.1915, T/Lt 23.10.1915	Son of Granville Pennefather Evans & Grace Woodburn (née Hennessy) Evans; Served Ceylon Tea Planters Corps; Served Gallipoli 2nd Bn SWB 16.7.1915-21.8.1915 (Wounded) & 26.9.1915-8.1.1916; France 15.3.1916-1.7.1916 (Killed in action); Commemorated Thiepval Memorial & Pirbright Parish War Memorial; WO339/55995
FFRENCH, Kyrle OBE MC BA JP DL	Born Hound Hampshire 17.3.1879, Educated Marlborough College & Pembroke College Cambridge, Lt (SR) 3rd Bn SWB 10.11.1914, Capt (SR) 1.5.1915, Capt 4.7.1916, bt Maj 3.6.1919, bt Lt-Col 28.6.1924, Lt-Col 1.5.1930, Retd from Reserve 17.3.1934	Or William Kyrle Percy FFRENCH; Son of the Rev William Stephen Ffrench, Rector of St Peter's Winchester & Ella Eugenia (née Chatfield) Ffrench; Married Lettice Evelyn Smith-Bosanquet at St Alban's Abbey 31.7.1912; Schoolmaster, Uppingham School, The Muir Central College Allahabad & City of London School; OBE (Civ) LG 3.1.1945 (122); MC LG 2.5.1916 (4428); MID LG 5.11.1915 (10997), 5.5.1916 (4518) & 5.7.1919; Served Gallipoli with 2nd Bn SWB 10.5.1915-20.8.1915 (Sick); Served War Office & later Staff Officer 55th (West Lancs) Division TA; Secretary TA Association (Brecknock, Herefordshire & Radnor); DL (Herefordshire) LG 20.12.1938 (8076); Resided: Greystone House, Winforton, Hereford (1938); Died 22.9.1952 (See SWB Journal 42); Buried St Bartholomew's Churchyard, Much Marcle, Herefordshire; Medals sold DNW 12.12.2012
FOWLER, Hugh Griffith Coke DSO	Born Brecon 12.1.1882, Educated Tonbridge School & Royal Military College Sandhurst, 2Lt SWB 11.5.1901, Lt 12.4.1905, To Reserve 12.3.1906, Capt (SR) 1.2.1913, Maj 8.1.1916, Retd 28.4.1920	Youngest son of John Bacon & Anna Jane (née Miers) Fowler of Slwch Villa, Brecon; Married Muriel Powys Aveline Maybery at Priory Church, Brecon 23.7.1912; Served ABW with 2nd Bn SWB, Served Tsingtao with 2nd Bn SWB; France with 1st Bn SWB 8.12.1914-21.12.1914 (Wounded – Festubert), Gallipoli with 2nd Bn SWB 15.5.1915-5.7.1915 (Sick), France with 1st Bn SWB Commanded 23.10.1917-21.12.1917 & Russia 1.11.1918-9.1919; DSO LG 25.8.1915 (Gallipoli); MID LG 22.6.1915, 25.8.1915 & 4.1.1917; Resided: Nythfa, Brecon; Died Brecon 7.2.1947 (See SWB Journal 31)

Name	Service Details	Additional Detail
FRODSHAM, Legh Duncan Mill	Born Streatham 1873, Enlisted as Pte #TS/3589 Army Service Corps (Remount Service) 23.10.1914, T/Lt 14th Bn Nottingham & Derbyshire Regt 8.2.1915, T/Capt 29.4.1916, RC as Capt 26.3.1920	Son of John Mill & Thérèse Jane Elizabeth Frodsham; Lloyd's underwriter, bankrupt 1907; Served ABW with Middlesex Yeomanry; Served 14th Bn & 53rd (YS) Bn Nottinghamshire & Derbyshire Regt (Foresters); Served France with Army Service Corps 22.10.1914; joined 2nd Bn SWB Gallipoli 1.7.1915; Resided Bardowie, Queen's Road Weybridge, Surrey (1911); Died Lewes 9.11.1939; WO339/23597
GELDARD, Stephen Humphrey MC	Born Birmingham 2.8.1896, 2Lt (SR) SWB 10.10.1914, Lt 10.1.1916, To Machine Gun Corps as A/Capt 20.7.1917, RC as Capt 1.4.1920	Or GELDERD; Younger son of Christopher & Janet Stuart Geldard; MC LG 4.6.1917 (5479); Served Gallipoli with 2nd Bn SWB 10.5.1915-11.6.1915 (Wounded); Resided: 35 Cole Park Road, Twickenham; Unmarried; Died 11.3.1940; WO339/28776
GIBBS, Richard Rodney	Born Shepparton ,Victoria 5.9.1892, Educated Brighton Grammar School, Victoria; From Sgt D Company 7th Bn Australian Imperial Force #408 (enlisted 17.8.1914), T/2Lt SWB 19.4.1915, T/Lt 23.10.1915, To Gen List 14.12.1916, RC as Lt 19.8.1919	Son of William Charles & Sarah Elizabeth (née Shelton) Gibbs; Married Joyce Anne Orme in Victoria 1920; Bank Clerk, Commercial Bank, Shepparton, Victoria; Served Egypt with AIF 6.12.1914; Served Gallipoli with 2nd Bn SWB 3.8.1915-14.8.1915 (Wounded) & 26.9.1915-8.1.1916 (Sick); Served West African Frontier Force in Sudan; Died Barwon Heads, Victoria 21.3.1976; WO339/3115
GLAZEBROOK, Francis Henry	Born Windermere 2.10.1893, 2Lt SWB 9.11.1914, To RWF 25.10.1916, T/Lt 1.7.1917, RC as Lt 5.7.1919, Re-joined 6th (DF) Bn RWF, RC 5.7.1921	Son of James Francis Walmisley Glazebrook (Captain, Merchant Navy) & Leila Mary (née Geddes) Glazebrook; Married Margery Frances Hugh-Jones at Marylebone 1929; Gallipoli 26.8.1915; Resided: 1 Ash Grove, Wrexham Road, Chester; Died Anglesey 6.1967; WO339/323
GOING, John DSO	Born Birdhill, Co Limerick 13.3.1866, Lt 4th Bn Gloucester (M) 6.3.1886, 2Lt South Wales Borderers 16.11.1887, Lt 31.7.1889, Capt 18.11.1895, Maj 11.12.1905, Lt-Col 29.11.1915, To hp 29.11.1919, Retd 10.6.1920	Son of John & Eliza (née Mayne) Going; Married Ethel Mary Bridger; DSO LG 8.11.1915; MID LG 9.11.1915 (10997); Served Burma 1887-89; Served Tsingtao, Gallipoli with 2nd Bn SWB 25.4.1915-8.5.1915 (Wounded); Commanding Officer 2nd Bn SWB 26.7.1915-26.9.1915 & 16.6.1916-16.11.1916; Died 6.5.1949 (see SWB Journal 36)
GREENWAY, Thomas Cattell DSO	Born Newbold Pacey 6.11.1876, 2Lt (M) SWB 27.11.1895, Lt (M) 2.12.1896, 2Lt SWB 1.12.1897, Lt 10.1.1900, Capt 19.6.1907, Maj 1.9.1915, bt Lt-Col 1.1.1919, Lt-Col 19.12.1925, Retd 19.12.1929	Son of George Cattell & Agnes Greenway of Ashorne Hill, Newbold Pacey, Warwickshire; Served Tsingtao, Gallipoli with 2nd Bn SWB 25.4.1915-4.6.1915 (Wounded); DSO LG 2.5.1916 (4428); MID LG 5.8.1915 & 5.5.1916; Commanded 2nd Bn SWB 19.12.1925-9.12.1929; Died?
GRIFFITH, Herbert Charles Marshall	Born Bedminster 5.10.1894, 2Lt SWB 17.3.1915, Lt 11.10.1915, RC 17.9.1921	Or GRIFFITHS; Son of the Rev Charles Herbert & Edith Anne (née Sergeant) Griffith; Married Beryl Jeannette Fortescue Horne at Paddington 1928; Served Gallipoli with 2nd Bn SWB 10.5.1915-22.7.1915 (Sick); Resided: 18 Mount Pleasant, Tunbridge Wells; Died Tonbridge 17.2.1958; WO339/36143

Name	Service Details	Additional Detail
HABERSHON, Cyril Bernard	Born Marylebone 1.5.1887, Educated Charterhouse School & Royal Military College Sandhurst, 2Lt SWB 29.8.1906, Lt 4.1.1908, Capt 9.12.1914, bt Maj 3.6.1918, Retd 3.6.1922	Son of Dr S Herbert Habershon of Upper Wimpole Street London; Married Clare Constance Jones Williams at Brecon 1921; Served Tsingtao; Gallipoli with 2nd Bn SWB 25.4.1915-17.6.1915 (Sick) & 25.6.1915-28.6.1915 (Wounded), France 1.4.1916-3.11.1916; Adjutant 2nd Bn SWB 1.8.1916-1.11.1916; Order of White Eagle (5th class) (Serbia) LG 10.9.1918 (10646); Resided: Hesterworth, Aston-on-Clun, Craven Arms (1941); Died Clun 10.10.1953 (See SWB Journal 44)
HALL, John Edward Kenyon	Born London 16.5.1878, Educated Eton College & Trinity College Oxford, 2Lt (SR) SWB 17.2.1915	Third son of Edward Kirkpatrick Hall JP DL, barrister; & Marion Louisa (née Webb) Hall of Kevin, Nairn; Occupation: Barrister; Served Gallipoli with 2nd Bn SWB 24.8.1915-18.9.1915 (Wounded); Died of wounds 22.9.1915; Buried at sea; unmarried; Commemorated Helles Memorial; See De Ruvigny entry; WO339/35822
HEAL, Charles Henry	Enlisted SWB #5006, From Company Sergeant Major C Company 2nd Bn SWB, 2Lt 11.2.1915 See depot description book	Married Alice Mary Heal at Calbourne 18.2.1906 (resided 132 Albany Road, Camberwell & New Close, Thorley, Yarmouth, Isle of Wight); Awarded LS&GC Medal AO99/April 1914; Served Tsingtao, Gallipoli with 2nd Bn SWB 25.4.1915-9.5.1915 (Died of wounds); Buried Twelve Tree Copse Cemetery; WO339/22640
HILL, F A	Thomas Henry; A R, Thomas, Frederick, William?	15th Bn Liverpool Regt; Served Gallipoli with 2nd Bn SWB 11.8.1915-21.8.1915 (Wounded)
INGLIS, Harold John DSO MC	Born 21.6.1885, 2Lt (SR) SWB 18.11.1914, Lt 1.9.1915, Capt 27.11.1915, To Machine Gun Corps 11.7.1918, To Tank Corps, A/Maj 23.8.1918, RC as Maj 1.4.1920, Re-joined, Lt (Gen List) 25.5.1940 Born Canada???	Son of the Rev Charles George & Edith Caroline (née Buckworth) Inglis of Nova Scotia; Married Elsie Tower at Fareham 1923; DSO (Citation) 20.10.1916 (10171); MC (Citation) LG 6.9.1915 (8842); MC action involved his brother Lt R C Inglis (qv); Served Gallipoli 10.5.1915-10.6.1915 (Wounded); France with 1st Bn SWB (Wounded 18.3.1917); Resided: Llansantffraed House, Bwlch, Brecknockshire; Died Bwlch 7.2.1967
INGLIS, Rupert Charles	Born 3.2.1884, Lt (SR) 19.12.1914 Born Canada???	Son of the Rev Charles George & Edith Caroline (née Buckworth) Inglis of Nova Scotia; Served Gallipoli with 2nd Bn SWB 10.5.1915-29.6.1915 (Died of wounds at sea); Commemorated Helles Memorial; Medals in Museum Collection; WO339/31381

Name	Service Details	Additional Detail
JOHNSON, Dudley Graham VC CB DSO MC	Born Bourton-on-the Water 13.2.1884, Educated Bradfield College, 2Lt 4th Bn Wiltshire Regt 4.3.1901, To South Wales Borderers as 2Lt 4.7.1903, Lt 2.3.1907, Capt 11.3.1914, Maj 4.12.1917, bt Lt-Col 29.12.1923, To North Staffordshire Regt 14.4.1925, Col 29.12.1927, Brig 1.7.1933, Maj-Gen 25.12.1937, Retd 27.1.1944	Son of Capt William Johnson & Rosina (née Arnott) Johnson; Married Majorie Ailsa Grisewood at Daylesford, Gloucestershire 5.6.1912; Colonel, Monmouthshire Regiment TA 26.2.1941; Colonel, South Wales Borderers 30.6.1944-31.12.1949; VC LG 6.1.1919; CB LG 6.6.1939 (3854); DSO LG 16.3.1915; DSO Bar 11.1.1919; MC LG 1.1.1918; MID LG 13.11.1914, 30.5.1916, 8.7.1919 & 20.12.1940; Adjutant 2nd Bn SWB 5.2.1909-2.9.1913; Served St Helena during ABW; Tsingtao; Gallipoli 25.4.1915 (Wounded); Commanded 2nd Bn Royal Sussex 25.3.1918-28.5.1918 (Wounded) & 5.9.1918; Commanded 2nd Battalion North Staffordshire Regt 12.4.1928;ADC to King 10.9.1936-6.1.1938; Commanded 12th (Secunderabad) Infantry Brigade 1.7.1933-20.1.1936; Commanded 4th Division 7.1.1938-24.6.1940 (present at Dunkirk); Commanded Aldershot Command 25.6.1940-123.1941; Died Church Crookham 21.12.1975 (See RRW Journal 14); Buried Christ Churchyard, Church Crookham, Hampshire; Medals in Museum Collection
JONES, Brindley Royle Skidmore	2Lt (SR) 10.3.1915, Lt 28.12.1916, To RFC, To RAF 1.4.1918, RC 1.4.1920	Served Gallipoli with 2nd Bn SWB 24.8.1915-21.9.1915 (Sick); WO339/38512
JONES, Edwards Whitmore	Born Abermule 10.1.1869, Educated Winchester College, 2Lt (M) 2.4.1889, 2Lt Leicester Regt 18.2.1891, To SWB as 2Lt 18.2.1891, Lt 1.9.1892, Capt 8.4.1897, Maj 7.7.1909, Lt-Col 9.6.1917, Retd 6.12.1919	Son of Richard Edward Jones JP DL & Catherine (née Buckley-Williames) Jones of Cefn Bryntalach Hall, Abermule, Montgomeryshire; (His younger brother Brig-Gen Lumley Owen Williames Jones DSO died of influenza 14.9.1918); Served 4th Bn SWB Militia, & in ABW with 2nd Bn SWB (invalided) 1.6.1900; Adjutant 4th (M) Bn SWB 1.8.1902-31.7.1905; Served Tsingtao; Gallipoli 26.7.1915-6.10.1915 (Sick); Mesopotamia with 4th Bn SWB 1.8.1917; Commanded 4th Bn SWB 27.8.1918; Resided: Manor House, Bodicote, Banbury (1922); Wilton House, Lansdowne Road Cheltenham (1947); Died 4.1.1947; WO339/71842
JORDAN, John (Jack)	Born Merthyr 29.11.1870, Enlisted Brecon #2414 into South Wales Borderers 10.7.1888, To Army Reserve 31.3.1895, Re-Joined 11.3.1898, Corporal 9.6.1899, Orderly Room Corporal 9.10.1899, Sergeant 18.1.1900, Colour Sergeant 23.1.1903, Discharged 31.3.1910, Re-Joined as Colour Sergeant 1.9.1914, Quartermaster-Sergeant, T/Lt 20.10.1914	Son of Joseph & Elizabeth Jordan of Pentrebach; Merthyr; Husband of Maria Pricilla Jordan; Occupation: Engine Driver; Served as Orderly Room Sergeant with 3rd Bn SWB (M) in ABW 14.2.1900-24.3.1902; LS&GC Medal AO8/1.1.1910; Served Gallipoli 2nd Bn SWB 25.5.1915-19.6.1915 (Died of wounds); Buried Lancashire Landing Cemetery; Commemorated St Sannan's Church, Bedwellty; WO339/13136

Name	Service Details	Additional Detail
KARRAN, John Bowler	Born 1892, T/2Lt 13.11.1914	Or KARRON or KARREN; Son of George Christian Karran, Master Mariner, & Matilda May (née Wolfe) Karran, of Sea Mount Castletown, Isle of Man; Served Gallipoli with 2nd Bn SWB 24.9.1915-8.1.1916; France 15.3.1916-1.7.1916 (Killed in action); Buried Y Ravine Cemetery Beaumont Hamel; WO339/895
KERR, Daniel	Born Ireland 1892, 2Lt 14th Bn Cheshire Regt 9.12.1914	Son of the late Samuel Joseph & Margaret (Maggie) (née McVicker) Kerr; Served Gallipoli attached 2nd Bn SWB 25.5.1915-6.7.1915 (Killed in action); Commemorated Helles Memorial; WO339/2170
KNOWLES, Joseph Albert OBE MC	2Lt 14th Bn Cheshire Regt 18.12.1914, T/Lt 1.10.1915, T/Capt 19.1.1917, To Gen List 11.7.1918, RC (Ill health) 15.3.1919, Capt Rydal School JOTC 31.1.1928, RC 1.4.1935, To Carnarvon ACF, RC 16.1.1945	MC LG 13.2.1917 (1541); OBE (Civ) LG 31.12.1960 (8900); Served Gallipoli attached 2nd Bn SWB 29.6.1915-21.8.1915 (Wounded); Served 11th Bn Cheshire Regt; Awarded Silver War Badge; Resided: Glen Darroch, Brooklands Road, Higher Crumpsall, Manchester; Financial Advisor, Methodist Education Committee
LAMAN, Ernest Kirkland MBE MC	Born 1876, Enlisted SWB #3800, From Sergeant-Major, Lt & QM SWB 2.1.1914, Capt QM 1.7.1917, Maj 3.1.1929, Retd 4.10.1930	Married Edyth Sybil Laman; MC LG 1.1.1918; MBE LG 12.12.1919; Served Tsingtao; Gallipoli with 2nd Bn SWB 25.4.1915-8.5.1915 (Wounded) & 14.5.1915-8.1.1916; LS&GC Medal 1.1.1910; Resided: Tytherley, Wellwood Drive, Dinas Powis; Died Cardiff 30.4.1961 (See SWB Journal 60)
LEWIS-JONES, Bertram Ivor	Born Llyswen 1897, Educated Glencolne School & Trinity College Aberdeen, 2Lt (SR) SWB 15.8.1914	Only son of Lewis Willam Hugh Jones, Solicitor, & the late Dora L Jones of Tymawr, Llyswen, Brecon; Served Gallipoli with 2nd Bn SWB 10.5.1915-18.6.1915 (Killed in action); Buried Twelve Tree Copse Cemetery; WO339/25522
LLEWELLIN, Thomas Caradoc Trevor JP DL	Born Bude 10.11.1895, From Royal Military College Sandhurst, 2Lt SWB 16.12.1914, Lt 10.5.1915, Capt 12.4.1921, Retd 4.4.1935, Re-joined, Capt Brecknock Bn SWB (TA) 1.6.1939, bt Maj (TA) 1.9.1939, Retd 4.4.1945, To Brecknockshire ACF as Lt 1.4.1950, RC 30.9.1953	Son of Thomas Johnes & Anne Elizabeth (née Heath) Llewellin; Married Faith Glyn de Winton at Brecon 1925; Served Gallipoli 10.5.1915-8.1.1916 (joined 2nd Bn SWB 9.12.1915); France 15.3.1916-6.4.1916 (Wounded); To Machine Gun Corps 25.11.1916; Resided Glynderi, Talybont-on-Usk (1938); DL (Brecknockshire) LG 3.11.1959 (6942); Died 24.4.1980 (see RRW Journal 23); Medals in museum collection
MacGREGOR, Cortlandt Richard	Born Orange County, Florida USA 7.2.1894, From Royal Military College Sandhurst, 2Lt SWB 15.2.1913, Lt 17.9.1914	Eldest son of Cortlandt George & Margaret Josephine (née Picton Turbervill) MacGregor, Llantrisant House, Llantrisant; Served Tsingtao; Gallipoli 25.4.1915-3.5.1915 (Killed in action); Commemorated Helles Memorial; (His only brother 2Lt Kenneth Cortlandt MacGregor, 2nd Bn KOSB, killed in action Ypres 26.2.1915)

Name	Service Details	Additional Detail
MARGESSON, Edward Cuninghame	Born Worthing 13.12.1871, Educated Wellington College & Royal Military College Sandhurst, 2Lt SWB 5.12.1891, Lt 13.5.1893, Capt 6.3.1898, Maj 4.2.1911	Son of Lt-Col William George and Lucy Matilda (née Beaumont) Margesson of Findon Place, Sussex; Married Marian Rowsell (née Cunningham) at Chelsea 8.10.1912; Served Niger campaign (1897) and Ashanti (1900); MID LG 11.6.1897 & 4.12.1900; Adjutant 2nd Bn SWB 13.5.1893-10.10.1894, Served Tsingtao; Gallipoli with 2nd Bn SWB 25.4.1915 (Killed in action); Commemorated Helles Memorial & St John the Baptist Church, Findon, Sussex; See Bond of Sacrifice Vol 2 pages 337/8
MASON, William Miles	T/2Lt SWB 30.10.1914, T/Lt 28.4.1915, Capt 9.7.1917, RC 18.11.1919	Served Gallipoli with 2nd Bn SWB 24.9.1915-8.1.1916; France 15.3.1916-1.7.1916 (Wounded); Served 53rd (Young Soldier) Bn SWB; WO339/104623
MAYGER, Frank James Lanham MC	Born Burton on Trent, Staffordshire 1892, Enlisted Pte F Company 1st Bn Australian Infantry #1046 14.9.1914, T/2Lt SWB 19.4.1915, 2Lt 4.1.1916, Lt 14.7.1917, Capt 20.7.1917, Retd 18.12.1918	Son of James Lanham Mayger & Lucy Emma (née Spittle) Mayger, of Trenton, Llandudno; Pre-War Occupation: Motor Engineer Sydney, NSW); MC LG 22.9.1916 (9278); MC Bar LG 26.9.1917 (9971); MC Bar (Citation) LG 8.1.1918 (575); MID LG 23.5.1918; Served Gallipoli 10.10.1915-8.1.1916; France 15.3.1916-3.7.1916 (Sick) & 21.6.1917-21.11.1917 (Wounded- Cambrai); Received MC Bar from Governor of Singapore at Tanglin Barracks 21.5.1919; Awarded Silver War Badge; Director, Scotia Lubricating Oil Co, Singapore; WO339/3136
McLAREN, Robert John	Lt 14th Bn Cheshire 29.1.1915, T/Capt 16.3.1915

Earlier service in West York Regt? | Husband of Mrs R J Mclaren, Westleigh, Brook Road, Blundellsands; 16th Bn Cheshire Regt; Served Gallipoli with 2nd Bn SWB 16.6.1915-8.1.1915 & France 15.3.1916-1.7.1916 (Missing in action); Buried Hawthorn Ridge, Cemetery No 2; WO339/18404 |
| McSHANE, Vincent | Born Felling on Tyne 1894, Educated St Cuthbert's Grammar School, Newcastle upon Tyne; 2Lt 15.10.1914, To 15th Bn Northumberland Fusiliers as T/Lt 29.12.1914 | Son of James McShane & Mary Anne, 19 Oban Terrace, Felling on Tyne; (His elder brother was Lt John Chesterton McShane RE died of wounds 28.7.1916; another brother Father James H McShane served as an Army Chaplain); 15th Bn Northumberland Fusiliers; Served Gallipoli attached 2nd Bn SWB 3.8.1915-21.8.1915 (Killed in action); Commemorated Helles Memorial; Unmarried; WO339/25648 |
| MEIN, Douglas Warford | Born St Kilda, Victoria 1878, Educated Melbourne Grammar School, 2Lt (SR) SWB 6.3.1915, T/Lt 28.12.1916, RC as Capt 1.4.1920 | Son of Dr George Augustus Mein & Jane Hetherington (née Gibsone) Mein; Married Lily Mein Dalzell in Queensland 1909; Served Gallipoli with 2nd Bn SWB 24.9.1915-8.1.1916; Bn Machine Gun Officer 26.10.1915; To Machine Gun Corps 13.2.1916; Resided: Mayfair, Marne Street, South Yarra, Victoria; Died South Yarra 16.11.1923; WO339/43154 |

Name	Service Details	Additional Detail
MORGAN, Morgan Cyril CBE MC psc	Born Cilycwm, Llandovery 1891, 2Lt (SR) SWB 11.6.1910, 2Lt 24.5.1913, Lt 27.9.1914, Capt 3.12.1915, Maj 3.6.1919, Lt-Col 1.7.1935, Retd 16.2.1937, Re-joined, A/Brig 9.12.1940, T/Brig 7.6.1941	Son of David & Mary Elizabeth (née Davies) Morgan; Married Gertrude Constance Mary Greey; (His eldest brother was Major Sir David Hughes-Morgan 1st Bart SWB); Served Tsingtao; Gallipoli with 2nd Bn SWB 25.4.1915-7.7.1915; Staff Capt 87th Inf Bde 7.7.1915; CBE LG 1.1.1944 (10); MC LG 8.11.1915; MID LG 5.11.1917, 15.5.1917, 11.12.1917 & 5.6.1919; Order of the Crown (5th class) (Italy) LG 29.11.1918; Croix de Guerre (France); AAQMG, 2nd Division; Deputy Director Walfare Services, War Office 1940-45; Secretary of City of London TA Association; Died Millbank Military Hospital 16.8.1960 (See SWB Journal 59)
MUMFORD, Clarence MC	Born, From Company Sergeant Major Army Service Corps (5th Motor Ambulance Convoy) #MI/7610; T/2Lt SWB 5.1.1915, Lt 1.9.1915, Capt 16.6.1916, RC 9.10.1919	MC LG 25.11.1916; MC Bar LG 4.2.1918 (1601); MC Bar (Citation) LG 5.7.1918; Served France with ASC 4.11.1914; Served with 2nd Bn SWB Gallipoli 16.7.1915-21.8.1915 (Wounded); France with 6th Bn SWB 2.6.1916; France 2nd Bn SWB 26.8.1917-21.11.1917 (Wounded); Awarded Silver War Badge; Died 25.10.1938 (See SWB Journal 13); WO339/19325
NEVILE, Hugh George BA	Born London 17.11.1878, Educated Oratory Edgbaston & Trinity College Cambridge, 2Lt (SR) SWB 2.10.1914, Lt 1.5.1915	2nd Son of Ralph Henry Christopher Nevile & Mildred Frances (née Scott-Murray) Nevile of Wellingore Hall, Lincoln; Served Tsingtao; Gallipoli with 2nd Bn SWB 25.4.1915-30.4.1915 (Wounded) & 25.7.1915-21.8.1915 (Missing); Commemorated Helles Memorial; Unmarried; WO339/23891
NICHOLAS, Charles Henry DFC AFC DL	Born Chelmsford 28.12.1894, Educated Berkhamsted School, 2Lt (SR) SWB 15.8.1914, Lt 1.10.1915, To Royal Flying Corps, T/Maj, To Royal Air Force 1.4.1918 as Sqn Ldr, Wg Cdr 1.7.1929, Gp Capt 26.11.1935, Air Cdr 1.1.1940, Retd 12.11.1944	Son of John Henry & Fanny Nicholas; Married Marian Field at Huddersfield 1921; Served Gallipoli with 2nd Bn SWB 10.5.1915-28.6.1915 (Wounded); RAeC Aviator's Certificate 2277 at Catterick dated 14.1.1916; Croix de Guerre (France) LG 7.2.1919 (2050); DFC (Citation) LG 28.10.1921 (8496) for Iraq; AFC LG 3.6.1919 (7034) for Egypt; Order of the Nile (4th class) LG 18.11.1919 (14002); DL (Durham) LG 17.2.1956 (994); Resided: 19 Snackgate Lane, Heighington, Darlington; Died Darlington 8.8.1966
OKELL, George Harold	Born Ashton under Lyne 8.4.1878, 2Lt 9th Bn Manchester Regt TF 17.6.1910, Lt (TF) 28.9.1910, Capt (TF) 10.10.1913, RC as Capt 15.1.1919	Or O'KELL, GH; Son of Henry & Mary Ann (née Woolmer) Okell of Aston under Lyne; Married (1) Ann Tonge at Hurst Lancashire 27.6.1906 & (2) Agnes Walton at Aston under Lyne 28.1.1913; Occupation: Solicitor in Sheffield (1906); Served Egypt 21.9.1914 & Gallipoli attached 2nd Bn SWB 27.5.1915-29.5.1915; Resided: 64 Bingham Park Road Sheffield; Died Sheffield 2.6.1947; WO374/51243
PAGE, William Frank CMG	Born 1894, Educated Clifton College, T/2Lt 29.8.1914, T/Lt 2.2.1915, RC 1.4.1920	CMG LG 13.6.1946 (2761); Served with 2nd Bn SWB Gallipoli 14.9.1915-21.12.1915 (Wounded); France 28.4.1917-11.4.1918 (Prisoner); Repatriated 25.12.1918; Colonial Adminstrator Tanganyika; Died Guernsey 2.1980; Medals sold DNW 25.2.1998; WO339/11926

Name	Service Details	Additional Detail
PALMER, Roland Gaskell	Born Sydney NSW 5.8.1876, Educated Loretto College & Royal Military College Sandhurst, 2Lt SWB 20.2.1897, Lt 17.8.1898, To Northumberland Fusiliers as Capt 7.5.1902, back as Capt 18.12.1907	First name also shown as 'Rowland'; Son of the late Robert Palmer & Emily Palmer of 38 Park Mansions, Knightsbridge; Married Olive Reed Carr in 1907; Served ABW (QSA 6 clasps & KSA 2 clasps) commanded Mounted Infantry Section SWB and in WW1 Tsingtao & Gallipoli with 2nd Bn SWB 25.4.1915 (Killed in action); MID LG 10.9.1901; Adjutant 2nd London RVC – later 6th Bn City of London Regt TF 1909 – later 5th Bn Royal West Surrey Regt TF; Commemorated Helles Memorial
PARRY-DAVIES, David Christopher	Born 1899, Educated St David's College, Lampeter, T/2Lt SWB 29.10.1914, T/Capt 23.12.1915	Son of the Rev David Rhys & Elizabeth Parry-Davies, The Rectory, Puncheston, Pembrokeshire; Served Gallipoli with 2nd Bn SWB 24.9.1915-8.1.1916; France 15.3.1916-29.4.1916 (Wounded); Died of wounds No 4 Casualty Clearing Station 10.5.1916; Buried Beauval Communal Cemetery (CWGC roll incorrectly shows 6th Bn); Commemorated Puncheston Parish War Memorial & Tenby War Memorial; WO339/13
PATTERSON, Charles Cox	Born Twickenham 8.7.1876, Educated Clifton College, Served Calcutta Horse, enlisted King Edward's Horse 8.1914, 2Lt 14th Bn Cheshire Regt 6.12.1914, T/Capt 14.12.1914	Third son of the late Charles & Helen (née Malcolm) Patterson of 36 Howitt Road, Belsize Park; Served Gallipoli with 2nd Bn SWB 10.6.1915-19.6.1915 (Wounded); Joined 1st Bn Cheshire Regt 12.1915; Killed in Action with 1st Bn Cheshire Regt 21.10.1916; Commemorated Loos Memorial; Unmarried; See de Ruvigny entry
PATERSON, Ronald Anderson	Born Islington 4.12.1893, Enlisted Pte Ceylon Planters Rifles #2013, 2Lt SWB 19.4.1915, T/Lt 23.10.1915, To Gen List 1.3.1918,	Or PATTERSON; Son of Eliza Ballantyne; Married Francis Emily Stearn at Royston 1918; Served with Ceylon Planters Rifles Egypt 17.11.1914; Served with 2nd Bn SWB Gallipoli 16.7.1915-12.9.1915 (Sick); To duty to PW Camp; Died Bishop Stortford 1983; WO339/3066
PETRE, Roderic Loraine CB DSO MC	Born 28.11.1887, Educated Downside & Royal Military College Sandhurst, 2Lt SWB 22.2.1908, Lt 22.12.1910, Capt 24.12.1915, bt Maj 3.6.1918, Maj 12.4.1928, bt Lt-Col 1.1.1929, To Dorsetshire Regt 13.6.1932, T/Brig 9.6.1935, Maj-Gen 26.6.1938, A/Lt-Gen 21.4.1944, Retd 27.11.1944	Son of Francis Loraine & Maude Ellen Petre of Farnham Royal, Buckinghamshire ; Married Katherine Sophia Bryans at Brompton Oratory 12.7.1922; CB LG 11.7.1940 (4244); DSO LG 25.8.1917 (8874); MC LG 2.2.1916 (1337); MID LG 23.9.1914, 28.1.1916 (1197), 30.5.1916, 13.7.1916 (6943), 15.8.1917 (8329), 27.8.1918 (9985), 21.2.1919 & 12.1.1920; Served Tsingtao; Gallipoli as Staff Captain 87th Inf Bde, Mesopotamia & Afghanistan 1919; Adjutant 28.5.1920-21.2.1923; Commanded 2nd Bn Dorsetshire Regt 1932-35; Commanded 12th Division BEF 1940; Died 21.7.1971
PHILPOTT, Francis Other MC	Born Foden Montgomeryshire 1889, Educated The Elms, Colwall, 2Lt (SR) SWB 15.12.1908, RC 27.9.1913, Re-Joined, T/Lt 25.2.1915, T/Capt 1.1.1916, RC 1.9.1921	Or PHILLPOTT; Son of the Rev Francis Octavius & Harriet Jane (née Bury) Philpott; Married Marion Edythe Phillips (widow née Ardagh) at Little Marcle, Ledbury 29.6.1919; MC LG 7.2.1918 (1802); Served with 2nd Bn SWB Gallipoli 29.6.1915-21.8.1915 (Wounded) & Mesopotamia with 4th Bn SWB; Resided: Oakhaven, Mapledrakes Road, Ewhurst; Died Hereford 10.9.1964; Buried St Peter & St Paul Churchyard Ewhurst Surrey

Name	Service Details	Additional Detail
RAWLE, William	Born 5.10.1887, 2Lt Gen List TF 22.7.1907, 2Lt SWB 5.10.1910, Lt 1.2.1913, Capt 28.4.1915, To Grenadier Gds 28.4.1915, RC (Ill Health) 5.3.1918	Served Tsingtao; Gallipoli with 2nd Bn SWB 25.4.1915-4.6.1915 (Wounded)
RICE, Frederick Fairfax (Fred)	T/2Lt SWB 2.3.1915	Served with 2nd Bn SWB Gallipoli 30.8.1915-1.1.1916 (Sick); France 10.4.1916-1.7.1916 (Killed in action); Buried Y Ravine Cemetery Beaumont-Hamel; Rosalie, The Green Colwall, Herefordshire; WO339/38556
ROBERTS, Alexander Hargreaves	Born Burnley 1868, 2Lt 2nd Volunteer Bn East Lancashire Regt 9.1.1904, Lt (V) 3.12.1904, Capt (V) 13.9.1905, To 5th Bn East Lancashire Regt TF as Capt 1.4.1908, T/Maj 8.11.1915, Maj 14.2.1917, Retd TF 23.7.1921	Son of Henry & Emma Jane Roberts; Married Ellen Taylor at All Souls, Langham, Westminster 6.7.1898; Pre-war Occupation: Manager, Manchester & County Bank, Burnley Road, Padiham; MID LG 13.7.1916 (6949); Served Egypt 1/5th Bn East Lancashire Regt TF; Served Gallipoli attached 2nd Bn SWB 28.5.1915; Awarded Silver War Badge (refused); Resided: Winscombe, Basford Park, Stoke on Trent (1922)
ROBERTS, Joseph Charles	Born, 2Lt SWB 17.2.1915, Lt 9.10.1915, To hp 28.8.1919, RC 7.10.1919 – Railways??	Served with 2nd Bn SWB Gallipoli 10.5.1915-5.7.1915 (Wounded); WO339/3673
ROBERTSON, George Arthur Norris	T/Capt SWB 10.3.1915,	Or ROBINSON; Adjutant 2nd Bn SWB 14.7.1917; Served Gallipoli with 2nd Bn SWB 14.9.1915-29.11.1915 (Sick); France 11.8.1916-28.11.1916 (Sick) & 8.6.1917-16.8.1917 (Killed in action - Langemarck); Buried Artillery Wood, Boezings; Medals sold DNW 12.12.2012; WO339/24013
ROSS, Willie	Born Bradford 16.10.1879, Enlisted #6082 South Wales Borderers 16.1.1899, LCpl 13.12.1899, Cpl 20.3.1901, Sgt 4.9.1902, CSgt 10.11/1907, CSM 1.12.1913, From Company Sergeant Major D Company 2nd Bn SWB, 2Lt 11.2.1915, Lt 1.9.1915, A/Capt	Son of William & Ann Ross of Broad Lane Bramley Yorkshire; Married Mary Caroline Victoria Hooton (died 1961), daughter of former 1-24/1771 Sergeant Major Samuel Hooton at St Mary's Brecon 4.9.1907; Served ABW (QSA 3 clasps, KSA 2 clasps); Served Tsingtao & Gallipoli with 2nd Bn SWB 25.4.1915-9.5.1915 (Wounded); France 26.4.1916-16.8.1917 (Died of wounds whilst Commanding D Company 2nd Bn SWB at Langemarck); Instructor Divisional School 22.4.1916-2.8.1916; Buried Artillery Wood Cemetery, Belgium; Commemorated Havard Chapel, Brecon Cathedral & Brecon War Memorial; WO339/22645
RUNDLE, Cubitt Noel	Born Calcutta 25.12.1895, Educated Victoria College Jersey & Royal Military College Sandhurst, 2Lt SWB 23.12.1914	Eldest son of Lt-Col Cubitt Sindell Rundle IMS (RAMC) & Emilie (née Stalkartt) Rundle, Waverley Terrace, St Heliers, Jersey; Served attached to 1/5th Bn Royal Scots TF (from 29.5.1915) Gallipoli 10.5.1915-19.6.1915 (Killed in action); Buried Twelve Tree Copse Cemetery; Commemorated St Saviour's Jersey Parish Memorial & the family memorial in St Saviour's Churchyard; Unmarried; WO339/3566

Name	Service Details	Additional Detail
RUSHTON, Frank Victor	Born Accrington 9.5.1887, 2Lt 2nd Volunteer Bn East Lancashire Regt 20.2.1908, To 5th Bn East Lancashire Regt TF 1.4.1908, Capt (TF) 9.7.1914, T/Maj, Maj 5.11.1920, Rejoined, Lt (A/Maj) RAPC 21.9.1939	Or RUSTON; Son of Richard & Elizabeth Rushton of Grindleton; Married Laurie Fannie Lovejoy at Ormskirk 12.1916; Served with 5th Bn East Lancashire Regt Egypt 9.1914; Gallipoli attached 2nd Bn SWB 27.5.1915; MID 13.7.1916 (6949); Resided: Stonelea, Grindleton, Critheroe, Lancs (1921); Died 20.12.1939; Buried Fulford Cemetery, Yorkshire (CWGC headstone)
SAUL, John Thomas		Cyclist Bn; Arrived 18.7.1915; To Cyclist Corps 25.7.1915
SILK, Norman Galbraith	Born Rushbrooke, Queenstown, Co Cork 30.4.1895, Educated Cheltenham College & Royal Military College Sandhurst, 2Lt 25.2.1914, Lt 15.11.1914	Only son of Rear Adm (Fleet Paymaster) Ernest Edwin Silk CBE (1862-1940) & Mrs Isabel Maud (née Wilford) Silk of Exmore, Henleaze Road, Westbury-on-Trym, Glouestershire; Served France with 1st Bn SWB 12.8.1914-31.10.1914 (Wounded - Gheluvelt); Gallipoli with 2nd Bn SWB 25.4.1915-22.5.1915 (Sick) & 2.6.1915-9.6.1915 (Killed in action); Buried Twelve Tree Copse Cemetery
SOMERVILLE, Desmond Henry Sykes CBE MC psc	Born Marylebone 6.8.1889, 2Lt SWB 18.9.1909, Lt 1.1.1912, Capt 24.4.1915, Maj 9.12.1929, Lt-Col 1.6.1937, Col 4.5.1939, Brig 7.1.1941, Retd 4.8.1945	Also Desmond Harry Sykes SOMERVILLE; Son of Aylmer Coghill & Emmeline Sophia (née Sykes) Somerville; Married Moira Burke Roche at London 6.3.1918; CBE LG 1.1.1946 (18); MC LG 2.5.1916 (4428); MC Bar (Citation) LG 5.7.1918; MID LG 5.5.1916 & 13.7.1916; Served Tsingtao; Gallipoli with 2nd Bn SWB 25.4.1915-30.4.1915 (Wounded), 25.6.1915-11.8.1915 (Sick) & 25.8.1915-8.1916; Adjutant 2nd Bn SWB 6.9.1915 & 1.1.1916-5.2.1917; Prisoner of War; Commanded 2nd Bn SWB 1.1.1937-4.5.1939; Resided: Drishane, Castletownsend, Skibbereen, Co Cork; Died 18.3.1976 (See RRW Journal 14); Buried St Barrahane's Churchyard, Castletownsend
SPARTALI, Michael BSc AMICE	Born London 22.7.1881, Educated Haileybury College & University of Glasgow, 2Lt (SR) SWB 22.2.1915	Son of Demetrius Michael & Virgina (née Ralli) Spartali, Greek Consul General to UK (1866-1882); Pre-war Occupation: Chief Surveyor, Nigerian Railways; (His brother 2Lt Cyril Spartali, 8th Bn Berkshire Regt killed in action 13.10.1915); Served Gallipoli with 2nd Bn SWB 10.5.1915-11.6.1915 (Killed in action); Commemorated Helles Memorial; Unmarried; WO339/2103
STANBOROUGH, Walter Thomas	Born Devonport 4.1873, Enlisted SWB at Brecon #4187 19.5.1893, From Quartermaster-Sergeant, 2Lt SWB 11.2.1915	(MIC index shows Walter J Stanbrough); Son of Thomas & Maria Shirley (née Bishop) Stanborough; LS&GC Medal AO72/1.7.1911; Served with Mounted Infantry ABW (QSA 3 clasps, KSA 2 clasps) wounded 13.7.1900; Served Tsingtao & Gallipoli with 2nd Bn SWB 25.4.1915-9.5.1915 (Died of wounds); Commemorated Helles Memorial; Unmarried; WO339/22647
STRINGER, Albert Edward BSc (Ned)	Born Audenshaw 18.1.1878, Educated Manchester Victoria University, 2Lt 9th Bn Manchester Regiment 2.9.1914	Son of Edward Stringer JP (died 3.6.1900) & Ann (née Wych) Stringer, Trafalgar Square, Ashton under Lyne; Pre-war Occupation: Deputy Headmaster, Municipal Secondary School, Ashton under Lyne; Served Gallipoli with 1/9th Manchester Regt TF (Ashton Territorials) attached 2nd Bn SWB 27.5.1915-29.5.1915; Killed in action with 1/9th Manchester Regt 7.6.1915; Commemorated Helles Memorial; Unmarried

Name	Service Details	Additional Detail
TIPPETTS, Cecil Malpas	Born Islington 10.6.1883, From 2Lt Oxford University OTC 22.5.1905, Lt SWB 7.9.1907, Capt 12.9.1914, To Machine Gun Corps 6.3.1916, bt Maj 11.11.1919, Maj 24.3.1924, Retd 4.3.1933	Son of James Berriman & Mary Ann (née Clark) Tippetts; Married Lilian Tippetts; Served Tsingtao & Gallipoli with 2nd Bn SWB 25.4.1915 (Wounded); Served Archangel Russia 1919; MID LG 22.5.1917 (5032) & 5.6.1919; Resided: Green Banks, Dolywern, Pontfadog, Denbighshire; Died Wrexham 1972
TRAGETT, James Clement Barrington	2Lt 3rd Bn Hampshire Regt (M) 26.5.1900, Lt (M) 9.6.1902, RC 24.1.1903, Re-joined, Lt (SR) SWB 23.9.1914, Capt 1.10.1915, RC 1.4.1920	Served Gallipoli 16.7.1915-21.8.1915 (Wounded); France 17.11.1917-3.12.1917 (Prisoner); Repatriated 30.4.1918; Resided: Roche Arms Cottage, Clungunford, Aston on Clun, Shropshire; Died London 7.11.1925; WO339/20676
TURNER, Percy Herbert	2Lt (SR) SWB 3.4.1915	MID LG 9.11.1915 (10997); Served with 2nd Bn SWB Gallipoli 10.5.1915-6.7.1915 (Killed in action); Buried Twelve Tree Copse Cemetery; WO339/2742
WADE, John Mayall	Born 1895, Educated Ashton Grammar School, 2Lt 1/9th Bn Manchester Regt 2.9.1914	Only son of Lt-Col Doctor Herbert Wade TD (who commanded 1/9th Bn at Gallipoli & was himself wounded 22.5.1915) & Ada (née Neal) Wade, 40 Park Range, Victoria Park, Manchester; Served 1/9th Manchester Regt Egypt 9.1914, & Gallipoli attached 2nd Bn SWB 27.5.1915-29.5.1915; Died 19.6.1915; Commemorated Helles Memorial; Unmarried
WADAMS, Harry Kenneth	Born Evesham 1893, From Tpr Queen's Own Worcestershire Hussars, 2Lt Gen List 10.10.1915, To South Wales Borderers at T/2Lt 10.10.1915, To Royal Army Ordnance Corps as T/2Lt 12.11.1916, T/Lt 12.2.1917, A/Maj 22.2.1919, RC as Capt 13.2.1920	Son of Edward Harry & Rhoda (née Storer) Wadams of Bengeworth, Evesham; Married Dorothy Edith Wadams; Pre-war Occupation: Clerk, Evesham District Council; Served Gallipoli 2n Bn SWB 17.11.1915-17.12.1915 (Sick); Egypt 3.1.1916 (Sick); Died Evesham Hospital 18.3.1941; WO339/22192
WALKER, Robert Konoma Beaumont MC	Born 7.6.1887, 2Lt SWB 5.10.1906, Lt 23.6.1910, Capt 1.11.1914, Maj 6.12.1927, Retd 28.2.1934

See Army List for appts | Served in Sudan 1910 with Egyptian Army, in China with 2nd Bn SWB & Gallipoli 25.4.1915-9.7.1915 (Sick) & 15.8.1915-21.8.1915 (Wounded); Attached Egyptian Army; MC LG 2.5.1916 (4428); MID LG 5.11.1915, 5.5.1916 & 25.11.1916; Khedive's Sudan Medal 1911 (clasps Darfur 1916, Fasher & Aliab Dinka); Died 11.5.1948 (see SWB Journal 34) |
| WARD, Thomas Rawdon Rattray | Born Caine Wiltshire 6.7.1861, From Royal Military College Sandhurst, Lt Prince of Wales's Own (West Yorkshire) Regt 22.10.1881, Capt 2.12.1889, Maj 23.6.1900, Lt-Col 7.3.1906, Retd 7.3.1910, Re-joined, Col | Son of Col Michael Foster Ward (late 90th LI) and Helen Christina Ward (née Clark-Rattray); Instructor Sandhurst 11.5.1895; Served ABW??; Commanding Officer Prince of Wales's Own 1906-1910; Denbighshire Yeomanry???; Commanding Officer 2 SWB 11.7.1915-26.7.1915; Commanding Officer 1st Bn Royal Dublin Fusiliers 25.7.1915-30.8.1915; Died Slough 13.9.1933 |

Name	Service Details	Additional Detail
WILLIAMS, Aubrey Ellis CBE DSO MC psc	Born Pontypool 19.5.1888, Educated Monmouth School & Royal Military College Sandhurst, 2Lt 9.10.1907, Lt 9.6.1909, Capt 22.10.1914, bt Maj 1.1.1918, Maj 9.12.1925, bt Lt-Col 1.1.1930, Lt-Col 1.6.1934, Brig 18.8.1938, Maj-Gen 10.5.1940, Retd 1.4.1941	Son of Lt-Col David Ellis Williams VD JP (Monmouthshire Volunteer Artillery) & Laura (née Butler) Williams of Griffithstown; Married Sybil Essex in Bombay 11.2.1922; Commanded 1st Bn South Wales Borderers 1.6.1934; Served with 2nd Bn SWB Tsingtao; Gallipoli 25.4.1915-28.6.1915 (Wounded) & 29.6.1915-8.1.1916; Adjutant 2nd Bn SWB 4.2.1915-19.9.1915; Commanding Officer 2nd Bn SWB 26.9.1915-11.1.1916; Bde Maj 157th Inf Bde 8.1.1916; Commanded 160th Infantry Bde 18.2.1939-10.5.1940; GOC 38th Infantry Division 11.5.1940-28.10.1940; CBE LG 1.1.1944 (10); DSO LG 15.2.1919 (2365) & 30.7.1919 (9383) (Citation), DSO BAR LG 16.8.1938 (5286) (Waziristan); MC LG 2.2.1916; MID LG 5.11.1915, 28.1.1916, 28.1.1916 (1200), 13.7.1916, 16.1.1918 & 5.7.1919; Resided: Blackbridge House, Blackbridge Road, Freshwater IOW; Died 25.3.1977 (see RRW Journal 16); Ashes intered All Saints Freshwater
YOUNG, John Douglas MC	Born 2.1889, From Corporal, 2Lt Royal Bucks Hussars 4.11.1914, Lt 2.1.1916, Capt 15.11.1917, To Manchine Gun Corps 3.4.1918, A/Maj 24.5.1918, To Royal Bucks Hussars 27.2.1918, RC as Maj 19.8.1922	Buckinghamshire Yeomanry (Royal Bucks Hussars); Arrived Egypt 21.4.1915; MC LG 2.2.1916 (1328), MC (Citation) LG 5.7.1918 (7936); MID LG 28.1.1916 (1197); Served Gallipoli (attached 2nd Bn SWB), Egypt, Palestine & France; Land Steward Middleton Stoney; Died France 21.4.1928; Buried All Saints Churchyard, Middleton Stoney, Oxfordshire

Abbreviation	Description
(M)	Militia Commission
(SR)	Special Reserve Commission
(TF)	Territorial Commission
(V)	Volunteer Commission
A/	Acting Rank
ABW	Anglo-Boer War 1899-1902
Bart	Baronet
Bt	Brevet Rank
DL	Deputy Lieutenant of the County
Gov	Governor
Hp	Half-Pay
JP	Justice of the Peace
Kt	Knight
L/	Local Rank
RC	Resigned/Relinquished Commission
SR	Special Reserve
T/	Temporary Rank
TA	Territorial Army
TF	Territorial Force

Appendix II

Officers and Soldiers of the 2nd Bn South Wales Borderers who were killed, or died of their wounds, during the Gallipoli campaign

Name	First Names	Number	Rank	Date of Death	Buried or Commemorated	Comment
Abbot	Charles Henry	10657	LCpl	26/04/1915	Helles Memorial	
Adams	Frank	6045	Pte	17/06/1915	Cairo	
Adams	Len	24712	Pte	21/08/1915	Helles Memorial	
Adams	William	13208	Pte	05/08/1915	Twelve Trees Cemetery	
Allen	Harry	10166	Cpl	28/06/1915	Helles Memorial	
Allen	William Thomas	16067	Pte	14/05/1915	Helles Memorial	
Andrews	Albert Thomas	10667	Pte	08/05/1915	Helles Memorial	
Andrews	Fred	10880	LCpl	08/05/1915	Helles Memorial	
Andrews	Sam	15440	Pte	29/08/1915	Alexandria	
Antill	Alfred Mansfield	18889	Pte	28/06/1915	Twelve Trees Cemetery	
Aries	William	10128	Pte	22/08/1915	Helles Memorial	
Armstrong	Sep	13573	Pte	28/06/1915	Helles Memorial	
Ashworth	Stuart	24710	Pte	13/08/1915	Helles Memorial	At sea, HMT Royal Edward
Aspinall	Robert	24257	Pte	13/08/1915	Helles Memorial	At sea, HMT Royal Edward
Atkinson	Alf	14130	Pte	19/06/1915	Helles Memorial	
Bailey	John	24601	Pte	13/08/1915	Helles Memorial	At sea, HMT Royal Edward
Ball	Charles	9747	Cpl	26/04/1915	Helles Memorial	
Barnes	Tom	10750	Pte	06/06/1915	Helles Memorial	
Barrett	William Dave	1399/	Pte	08/05/1915	Helles Memorial	
Bartram	Geo	24715	Pte	21/08/1915	Helles Memorial	
Beck	Edwin James	11657	Pte	13/08/1915	Helles Memorial	At sea, HMT Royal Edward
Behrens	Robert Philip		Lt	20/04/1915	Helles Memorial	
Bennett	Francis Stanley	15510	Pte	28/06/1915	Helles Memorial	
Bennett	Stephen	8927	Pte	13/08/1915	Helles Memorial	At sea, HMT Royal Edward

Name	First Names	Number	Rank	Date of Death	Buried or Commemorated	Comment
Beresford	Charles	15174	Pte	21/08/1915	Helles Memorial	
Bird	Ernest Owen	10003	Cpl	19/06/1915	Twelve Trees Cemetery	
Blakeman	Albert	35026	Cpl	13/08/1915	Helles Memorial	At sea, HMT Royal Edward
Blundell	John Thomas	9531	Cpl	05/06/1915	Helles Memorial	
Bonner	Geo	10065	Pte	02/05/1915	Haidar Pasha Cemetery	
Boucher	John	10464	Pte	28/04/1915	Helles Memorial	
Boxall	Geo	24635	Pte	17/09/1915	Alexandria	
Bracey	Arthur	10740	Pte	28/04/1915	Helles Memorial	
Bradley	John Franck		Lt	02/07/1915	Malta	
Brindle	Nathaniel	24615	Pte	28/12/1915	Lancashire Landing Cemetery	
Briscoe	Windham	13483	Pte	14/05/1915	Helles Memorial	
Broom	Henry Edward	9481	Pte	21/08/1915	Helles Memorial	
Brown	Ernest	15589	LCpl	25/07/1915	Helles Memorial	
Brown	James	9609	LCpl	09/05/1915	Helles Memorial	
Brown	Launcelot Wake	10160	LCpl	02/05/1915	Helles Memorial	
Buck	John	11200	Pte	06/07/1915	Helles Memorial	
Buckley	Joe	24693	Pte	06/08/1915	Helles Memorial	
Budd	Wrinch Joseph		Lt	28/06/1915	Helles Memorial	
Bunce	George		2Lt	09/05/1915	Helles Memorial	
Burgess	Thomas George	14874	Pte	07/06/1915	Twelve Trees Cemetery	
Burrell	Percy Edmund		2Lt	21/08/1915	Helles Memorial	
Butt	Charles	8726	Pte	26/04/1915	Helles Memorial	
Caddick	Len	11767	LCpl	06/07/1915	Helles Memorial	
Cain	Tom	15402	Pte	19/06/1915	Twelve Trees Cemetery	
Campbell	David	15068	Pte	21/08/1915	Helles Memorial	
Campion	William	9660	Pte	08/05/1915	Helles Memorial	
Carey	Charles Patrick	9164	Pte	26/04/1915	Helles Memorial	
Carroll	John	14074	Pte	25/04/1915	Helles Memorial	
Carty	Dan	14034	Pte	10/05/1915	Helles Memorial	
Cass	Hugh Lancelot		2Lt	19/06/1915	Twelve Trees Cemetery	
Castleman	Edward John	9177	LCpl	05/06/1915	Helles Memorial	
Challis	Thomas	19120	Pte	06/07/1915	Pink Farm Cemetery	
Chaston	Fred	5258	CSM	22/08/1915	Helles Memorial	
Cheeseman	Howard George	10441	Sgt	28/06/1915	Helles Memorial	
Chignell	Albert	10159	Pte	25/05/1915	Helles Memorial	
Chilcott	Simon	13740	Pte	28/06/1915	Helles Memorial	
Claffey	Joe	6755	Pte	28/10/1915	Netley, England	
Clarke	Henry	15465	Pte	19/06/1915	Twelve Trees Cemetery	

Name	First Names	Number	Rank	Date of Death	Buried or Commemorated	Comment
Clarke	William Tutton	10243	Pte	08/05/1915	Helles Memorial	
Clements	Alf	13833	Pte	24/11/1915	Skew Bridge Cemetery	
Clements	John	9253	Sgt	07/07/1915	Lancashire Landing Cemetery	
Cleverley	Fred	10136	LCpl	21/08/1915	Helles Memorial	
Cockayne	Henry E.	9893	LCpl	11/06/1915	Helles Memorial	
Coils	Cornelius	24733	Pte	13/08/1915	Helles Memorial	At sea, HMT Royal Edward
Coles	Thomas	15352	Pte	19/06/1915	Helles Memorial	
Connor	James	10831	LCpl	21/08/1915	Helles Memorial	
Conway	Arthur	9288	Pte	25/04/1915	Helles Memorial	
Cook	Fred	10356	Pte	08/05/1915	Helles Memorial	
Cooper	Joe Henry	24571	LCpl	13/08/1915	Helles Memorial	At sea, HMT Royal Edward
Coward	George Percy	11224	LCpl	20/09/1915	Helles Memorial	
Cox	Martin	10230	Pte	29/06/1915	Lancashire Landing Cemetery	
Cran	William Ernest	9627	Pte	07/06/1915	Helles Memorial	
Crean	James	13628	Pte	11/06/1915	Twelve Trees Cemetery	
Critcher	Albert	18870	Pte	21/12/1915	Twelve Trees Cemetery	
Crossley	Harry	24606	Pte	13/08/1915	Helles Memorial	At sea, HMT Royal Edward
Cullen	Archibald Patrick	18627	Pte	21/08/1915	Helles Memorial	
Cunningham	Frank	24732	Pte	13/08/1915	Helles Memorial	At sea, HMT Royal Edward
Cunningham	John	13161	Pte	18/06/1915	Twelve Trees Cemetery	
Cunningham	Owen	13515	Pte	08/05/1915	Helles Memorial	
Cussick	William	9557	Pte	02/05/1915	Helles Memorial	
Daniels	Henry	14265	Pte	13/08/1915	Helles Memorial	At sea, HMT Royal Edward
Davies	Albert William	10574	LCpl	29/06/1915	Twelve Trees Cemetery	
Davies	David John	10304	Pte	21/08/1915	Helles Memorial	
Davies	Frederick James	10674	Pte	13/09/1915	Alexandria	
Davies	John	11966	Pte	06/07/1915	Twelve Trees Cemetery	
Davies	John	18596	Pte	21/08/1915	Helles Memorial	
Davies	John Rees	10111	LCpl	08/05/1915	Helles Memorial	
Davies	Stanley	9777	Pte	10/05/1915	Alexandria	
Davies	Wyndham James	14899	Pte	21/08/1915	Helles Memorial	
Davis	Horace Charles	10617	Pte	08/05/1915	Helles Memorial	
Day	Francis	10330	Pte	11/06/1915	Twelve Trees Cemetery	
Denning	Joe	24740	Pte	20/09/1915	Helles Memorial	
Dewsbury	Ernest	6139	LCpl	19/06/1915	Twelve Trees Cemetery	

Name	First Names	Number	Rank	Date of Death	Buried or Commemorated	Comment
Dixon	George	7492	Pte	21/08/1915	Helles Memorial	
Dowsell	Reginald	19588	Pte	16/10/1915	Malta	
Dye	Sidney Charles	24583	Pte	01/01/1916	Helles Memorial	
Edge	William	24624	Pte	21/08/1915	Helles Memorial	
Elgee	Hugh Francis		Capt	06/07/1915	Twelve Trees Cemetery	
Evans	Ben. Charles	24994	Pte	21/08/1915	Helles Memorial	
Evans	Evan	11378	Pte	21/08/1915	Helles Memorial	
Evans	Harry	10558	Pte	03/05/1915	Helles Memorial	
Evans	John Allen	9844	Cpl	19/09/1915	Hill 10 Cemetery	
Evans	Percy Samuel	22534	Pte	02/11/1915	Lancashire Landing Cemetery	
Evans	Phillip	24938	Pte	13/08/1915	Helles Memorial	At sea, HMT Royal Edward
Farmer	William. Thomas	24939	Pte	13/08/1915	Helles Memorial	At sea, HMT Royal Edward
Farr	Walter	24944	Pte	13/08/1915	Helles Memorial	At sea, HMT Royal Edward
Farrell	Eugene	18516	Pte	08/05/1915	Helles Memorial	
Fisher	Charles	8143	Pte	28/04/1915	Helles Memorial	
Fitzgerald	Edw.	10501	Pte	06/06/1915	Helles Memorial	
Foley	Charles	10634	LCpl	26/04/1915	Helles Memorial	
Ford	Francis John	10629	Pte	28/06/1915	Helles Memorial	
Forster	James	19430	Pte	21/08/1915	Helles Memorial	
Francis	Idwal	9516	Pte	22/05/1915	Alexandria	
Francis	Richard Mark	10786	Pte	28/06/1915	Helles Memorial	
Fury	Michael	10458	LCpl	11/07/1915	Helles Memorial	
Gall	Isaac	11720	Cpl	21/08/1915	Helles Memorial	
Gant	William	9286	Pte	26/04/1915	Helles Memorial	
Geoghegan	John	9979	Pte	06/07/1915	Alexandria	
George	Lionel	13679	Pte	30/07/1915	Alexandria	
Gibbs	Ernest	24754	Pte	13/08/1915	Helles Memorial	At sea, HMT Royal Edward
Gibbs	William	9182	Pte	06/08/1915	Twelve Trees Cemetery	
Giddings	Arthur William	10445	LCpl	26/04/1915	Helles Memorial	
Gilby	George William	7242	CSM	28/06/1915	Twelve Trees Cemetery	
Goddard	Walter	13340	Pte	03/07/1915	Malta	
Golding	Fred	24570	Pte	13/08/1915	Helles Memorial	At sea, HMT Royal Edward
Goldstone	William. Thomas	8812	Pte	28/06/1915	Twelve Trees Cemetery	
Goodenough	Albert Jesse	10462	Pte	25/04/1915	Helles Memorial	
Goodier	John William	14790	Pte	11/06/1915	Helles Memorial	
Gooding	Thomas John	12502	LCpl	21/08/1915	Helles Memorial	

Name	First Names	Number	Rank	Date of Death	Buried or Commemorated	Comment
Goulston	Henry	9723	Pte	23/05/1915	Helles Memorial	
Green	Absalom	9004	Pte	28/06/1915	Helles Memorial	
Green	John Thomas	10442	Pte	28/04/1915	Helles Memorial	
Griffiths	Alfred James	24953	Pte	13/08/1915	Helles Memorial	At sea, HMT Royal Edward
Griffiths	Henry	10642	Pte	26/04/1915	Helles Memorial	
Griffiths	Henry	14993	Pte		Twelve Trees Cemetery	See Jones, Henry
Griffiths	Tom	8344	Pte	21/08/1915	Helles Memorial	
Groves	Richard Arthur	24605	Pte	08/11/1915	Helles Memorial	
Hadley	Thomas Charles	12232	Sgt	04/09/1915	Azmak Cemetery	
Hales	Albert Edward	13153	Pte	13/08/1915	Helles Memorial	At sea, HMT Royal Edward
Hall	John Edward Kenyon		2Lt	22/09/1915	Helles Memorial	At sea
Hall	Maurice	8183	Pte	29/06/1915	Twelve Trees Cemetery	
Hanson	Henry	24837	Pte	28/08/1915	Helles Memorial	
Hardiman	Walter William	24762	Pte	13/08/1915	Helles Memorial	At sea, HMT Royal Edward
Hardy	Cecil	19593	Pte	16/11/1915	Alexandria	
Harries	Willie	10789	Pte	13/08/1915	Helles Memorial	At sea, HMT Royal Edward
Harris	Arthur	19599	Pte	21/09/1915	Azmak Cemetery	
Harris	John Herbert	18911	Pte	12/08/1915	Helles Memorial	
Harris	W	19644	Pte	04/12/1915	Skew Bridge Cemetery	
Harrison	Theopholus George	14610	Pte	11/11/1915	Alexandria	
Hart	Nelson	10313	Pte	25/04/1915	Helles Memorial	
Hart	William	19596	Pte	13/08/1915	Helles Memorial	At sea, HMT Royal Edward
Hassall	Joe	10621	LCpl	29/06/1915	Lancashire Landing Cemetery	
Hayes	Harry	11088	Pte	13/08/1915	Helles Memorial	At sea, HMT Royal Edward
Hayes	Pat	19555	Pte	25/09/1915	Malta	
Hayward	Alf	13427	Pte	28/05/1915	Helles Memorial	
Heal	Charles Henry		2Lt	09/05/1915	Twelve Trees Cemetery	
Herbert	Tom	9709	Pte	21/08/1915	Helles Memorial	
Hester	Geo.Joseph	10892	Pte	15/05/1915	Helles Memorial	
Hewson	Tom	6954	Pte	08/01/1916	Malta	
Hickman	William	24562	Pte	13/08/1915	Helles Memorial	At sea, HMT Royal Edward
Higham	Alf	24759	Pte	21/08/1915	Helles Memorial	

Name	First Names	Number	Rank	Date of Death	Buried or Commemorated	Comment
Hill	Frank	19181	Pte	06/07/1915	Helles Memorial	
Hitchings	John Lewis	14960	Pte	22/09/1915	Azmak Cemetery	
Hodge	Sidney Jabez	10143	Pte	15/05/1915	Helles Memorial	
Hodgkinson	William.	24764	Pte	13/08/1915	Helles Memorial	At sea, HMT Royal Edward
Hogg	Henry	9983	Pte	16/04/1915	Helles Memorial	
Hood	Charles	19603	Pte	13/08/1915	Helles Memorial	At sea, HMT Royal Edward
Hook	Fred	8679	LCpl	02/05/1915	Helles Memorial	
Hooker	Tom	9527	Pte	02/05/1915	Helles Memorial	
Hopkins	John	14873	Pte	21/08/1915	Helles Memorial	
Howard	John	10027	Pte	28/05/1915	Helles Memorial	
Howe	Reg.	10072	Pte	28/06/1915	Helles Memorial	
Howell	James	15459	LCpl	24/08/1915	Helles Memorial	
Hughes.	Geo	13952	Pte	21/08/1915	Helles Memorial	
Hughes.	John Hugh	19797	Pte	13/08/1915	Helles Memorial	At sea, HMT Royal Edward
Hughes.	Tom	18748	Pte	13/08/1915	Helles Memorial	At sea, HMT Royal Edward
Hughes.	William	10554	Pte	05/07/1915	Malta	
Hughes.	William	15121	Pte	28/05/1915	Helles Memorial	
Hunt	Richard Henry	9725	Pte	21/06/1915	Helles Memorial	
Hunter	William.	24529	Pte	13/08/1915	Helles Memorial	At sea, HMT Royal Edward
Hurley	James	19989	Pte	03/11/1915	Skew Bridge Cemetery	
Hurley	John	10967	Pte	13/08/1915	Helles Memorial	At sea, HMT Royal Edward
Hyatt	Edward	19362	Pte	06/09/1915	Helles Memorial	
Ingham	Geo. Edward	18747	Pte	06/07/1915	Helles Memorial	
Inglis	Rupert Charles		Lt	29/06/1915	Helles Memorial	At sea
Isaac	Thomas	6450	Sgt	19/08/1915	Green Hill Cemetery	
Jackson	Thomas James	18440	Pte	10/06/1915	Twelve Trees Cemetery	
James	George Herbert	6823	Sgt	28/05/1915	Helles Memorial	
James	Jarvis	13324	Pte	26/04/1915	Helles Memorial	
James	Noah	13768	LCpl	27/06/1915	Twelve Trees Cemetery	
James	Robert	18433	Pte	25/04/1915	Helles Memorial	
James	Thom	13951	Pte	03/07/1915	Helles Memorial	
James	William Robert	18927	Pte	13/08/1915	Helles Memorial	At sea, HMT Royal Edward
Jaycock	Edward Alfred	15561	Pte	21/12/1915	Pink Farm Cemetery	
Jenkins	Llewellyn	13380	Pte	21/11/1915	Skew Bridge Cemetery	
Jennings	John R	10303	Cpl	31/05/1915	Pink Farm Cemetery	

Name	First Names	Number	Rank	Date of Death	Buried or Commemorated	Comment
Jeremiah	William	11099	Pte	19/06/1915	Helles Memorial	
Jinks	William James	10668	Pte	08/05/1915	Helles Memorial	
John	Daniel	9737	Pte	08/09/1915	Gibraltar	
Johnson	Harry	19591	Pte	28/06/1915	Helles Memorial	
Johnson	Thomas Francis	19177	Pte	07/10/1915	Alexandria	
Jones	Alfred William	9999	Sgt	28/06/1915	Twelve Trees Cemetery	
Jones	Charles	10580	LCpl	29/06/1915	Mudros	
Jones	David	11911	Pte	10/10/1915	Alexandria	
Jones	David William	15151	Pte	29/06/1915	Pink Farm Cemetery	
Jones	Evan	18825	Pte	19/06/1915	Twelve Trees Cemetery	
Jones	Garfield	11085	Pte	05/07/1915	Alexandria	
Jones	George Thomas	10508	Pte	28/04/1915	Helles Memorial	
Jones	Harry	13518	Pte	29/06/1915	Helles Memorial	
Jones	Henry	14993	Pte	05/07/1915	Twelve Trees Cemetery	Served as Griffiths, H
Jones	Henry	18862	Pte	20/06/1915	Mudros	
Jones	Henry	24957	Pte	25/09/1915	Helles Memorial	
Jones	Herbert	10182	Cpl	08/05/1915	Helles Memorial	
Jones	Lewis	14081	Pte	22/08/1915	Helles Memorial	
Jones	Thomas Charles	13454	Pte	19/06/1915	Helles Memorial	
Jones	Thomas Robert	15346	Pte	01/07/1915	Helles Memorial	
Jones	William	9450	LCpl	05/07/1915	Mudros	
Jones	William Henry	9811	Pte	28/06/1915	Twelve Trees Cemetery	
Jones	William	11130	Pte	21/08/1915	Helles Memorial	
Jones	William Isaac	10171	LCpl	28/04/1915	Helles Memorial	
Jones	William Henry	13624	Pte	22/08/1915	Hill 10 Cemetery	
Jones	Wyndham	10542	Pte	12/06/1915	Helles Memorial	
Jordan	John (Jack)		Lt	19/06/1915	Lancashire Landing Cemetery	
Joshua	Oswald	11769	Pte	29/08/1915	Alexandria	
Kay	Tom	19572	Pte	13/08/1915	Helles Memorial	At sea, HMT Royal Edward
Keefe	Ellis John	9866	Pte	08/05/1915	Helles Memorial	
Keefe	William George	9424	Pte	26/04/1915	Helles Memorial	
Keeling	Sam	10338	Pte	21/08/1915	Helles Memorial	
Keirle	Albert	10589	Pte	15/05/1915	Alexandria	
Kerr	Daniel		Lt	06/07/1915	Helles Memorial	Cheshire Regiment
Kibble	Reuben	25055	Pte	21/08/1915	Helles Memorial	
King	Walter	10859	Pte	02/05/1915	Helles Memorial	
Kirby	Edward	24704	Pte	21/08/1915	Helles Memorial	

Name	First Names	Number	Rank	Date of Death	Buried or Commemorated	Comment
Knapp	Alfred	14442	Pte	26/04/1915	Helles Memorial	
Knope	John	24577	Pte	26/09/1915	Lancashire Landing Cemetery	
Knowles	Geo Thomas	11261	Pte	11/06/1915	Helles Memorial	
Knowles	John	24511	Pte	13/08/1915	Helles Memorial	At sea, HMT Royal Edward
Knowlson	William	10961	Pte	18/08/1915	Malta	
Lavender	Daniel	13751	Pte	06/07/1915	Twelve Trees Cemetery	
Lavender	Thomas	10992	Sgt	07/01/1916	Helles Memorial	
Lawrence	William Joseph	14634	Pte	28/04/1915	Helles Memorial	
Leach	Harold	7309	Sgt	06/05/1915	Helles Memorial	
Lee	Anthony	13816	Pte	06/12/1915	Skew Bridge Cemetery	
Lee	Wilfred	19184	Pte	13/08/1915	Helles Memorial	At sea, HMT Royal Edward
Lester	Henry Francis	24576	Pte	26/12/1915	Alexandria	
Lewis	Alfred Henry	9677	Pte	30/06/1915	Pink Farm Cemetery	
Lewis	Edward	11802	Pte	13/08/1915	Helles Memorial	At sea, HMT Royal Edward
Lewis	Gwilym	8024	Pte	28/06/1915	Helles Memorial	
Lewis	Henry	14890	Pte	21/08/1915	Helles Memorial	
Lewis	Thom	10640	Pte	25/04/1915	Helles Memorial	
Lewis-Jones	Bertram Ivor		2Lt	18/06/1915	Twelve Trees Cemetery	
Leyshon	Charles	6888	Pte	26/04/1915	Helles Memorial	
Liddicoat	Glynn	24687	Pte	19/09/1915	Azmak Cemetery	
Lloyd	John	14961	Pte	19/06/1915	Helles Memorial	
Lofthouse	William	9675	Pte	19/06/1915	Pink Farm Cemetery	
MacGregor	Cortlandt Richard		Lt	03/05/1915	Helles Memorial	
Mandall	John	9035	Cpl	25/12/1915	Helles Memorial	
Manns	Frank	10450	Pte	26/04/1915	Helles Memorial	
Margesson	Edward Cuninghame		Maj	25/04/1915	Helles Memorial	
Marshall	Arnold	7879	Pte	28/06/1915	Helles Memorial	
Marshall	John	8924	Pte	21/08/1915	Helles Memorial	
Martin	Austin	14897	Pte	16/06/1915	Pink Farm Cemetery	
Martin	Ben. C.	24842	Pte	21/08/1915	Helles Memorial	
Maskell	Ernest	24521	Pte	21/08/1915	Helles Memorial	
Mason	James	8125	LCpl	28/05/1915	Helles Memorial	
Mason	William Henry	10078	Pte	11/05/1915	Helles Memorial	At sea
Matthews	Edwin J.	6201	Pte	28/06/1915	Helles Memorial	
McCarthy	John	17760	Pte	15/07/1915	Rhymney, Wales	
McCarthy	William.	10537	Pte	08/05/1915	Helles Memorial	

Name	First Names	Number	Rank	Date of Death	Buried or Commemorated	Comment
McGrath	William Herman Henry	11949	CQMS	30/08/1915	Helles Memorial	
McPhillips	Geo	13666	Pte	28/06/1915	Helles Memorial	
McShane	Vincent		Lt	21/08/1915	Helles Memorial	Northumberland Fusiliers
Mead	Rueben	13240	Pte	16/09/1915	Azmak Cemetery	
Mellors	Harry	19125	Pte	06/07/1915	Helles Memorial	
Mesquitta	Percy	10299	LCpl	08/05/1915	Helles Memorial	
Millard	Clifford	13677	Pte	24/07/1915	Pink Farm Cemetery	
Millichamp	Alfred	6475	CSM	08/05/1915	Helles Memorial	
Mills	William	19429	Pte	13/08/1915	Helles Memorial	At sea, HMT Royal Edward
Millward DCM	Tom	9600	Pte	08/05/1915	Helles Memorial	
Molineaux	Tom	15613	Pte	13/08/1915	Helles Memorial	At sea, HMT Royal Edward
Moneypenny	Charles	18858	Pte	17/09/1915	London	Nunhead Cemetery
Morgan	Charles	10675	Pte	24/05/1915	Alexandria	
Morgan	David	18724	LCpl	20/06/1915	Lancashire Landing Cemetery	
Morgan	Richard	10435	Pte	13/08/1915	Helles Memorial	At sea, HMT Royal Edward
Morris	Charles	10170	Pte	21/08/1915	Helles Memorial	
Morris	Frank	15604	Pte	21/08/1915	Hill 10 Cemetery	
Morris	William	13805	Pte	08/05/1915	Helles Memorial	
Moss	Edward	19630	Pte	13/08/1915	Helles Memorial	At sea, HMT Royal Edward
Munns	Ernest Alfred	13426	Pte	21/08/1915	Helles Memorial	
Murphy	John	9448	Pte	19/06/1915	Twelve Trees Cemetery	
Murray	Sam	24600	Pte	13/08/1915	Helles Memorial	At sea, HMT Royal Edward
Napper	Llewellyn	9809	Pte	14/05/1915	Helles Memorial	
Neville	Hugh George		Lt	21/08/1915	Helles Memorial	
Nightingale	Fred	19611	Pte	13/08/1915	Helles Memorial	At sea, HMT Royal Edward
Noonan	Tom	24947	Pte	13/08/1915	Helles Memorial	At sea, HMT Royal Edward
Norris	Claude	10087	LCpl	08/05/1915	Helles Memorial	
Nunn	Frederick Walter	10179	Sgt	13/08/1915	Helles Memorial	At sea, HMT Royal Edward;
O'Brien	David	10780	Pte	08/05/1915	Helles Memorial	
O'Brien	Pat	9235	Cpl	07/05/1915	Helles Memorial	
O'Connell	Terence	10725	Pte	25/04/1915	Helles Memorial	

Name	First Names	Number	Rank	Date of Death	Buried or Commemorated	Comment
O'Kelley	Robert	13552	Pte	24/08/1915	Mudros	
Olsen	Patrick	13775	Pte	28/06/1915	Helles Memorial	
Palmer	David	10910	Pte	13/08/1915	Twelve Trees Cemetery	
Palmer	Roland Gaskell		Capt	25/04/1915	Helles Memorial	
Palmer	William John	11327	Pte	16/08/1915	Helles Memorial	
Park	John	18607	Pte	15/06/1915	Helles Memorial	
Parker	Alfred	24634	Pte	13/08/1915	Helles Memorial	At sea, HMT Royal Edward
Parker	Daniel	14152	Pte	28/04/1915	Helles Memorial	
Parson	Lewis Samuel	10167	Pte	21/08/1915	Helles Memorial	
Partridge	James	10527	Pte	28/06/1915	Helles Memorial	
Payne	Henry	9699	Pte	28/04/1915	Helles Memorial	
Pearce	Edward	13388	LCpl	20/06/1915	Lancashire Landing Cemetery	
Pearce	Edward	25007	Pte	13/08/1915	Helles Memorial	At sea, HMT Royal Edward
Pearson	Richard	18741	Pte	28/04/1915	Helles Memorial	
Peattie	Andrew	24870	Pte	29/12/1915	Lancashire Landing	
Phillips	Albert	10079	Sgt	26/04/1915	Helles Memorial	
Phillips	Sam	13576	Pte	16/09/1915	Hill 10 Cemetery	
Phillips	William	13557	Pte	28/06/1915	Helles Memorial	
Pike	Henry	13156	Pte	21/08/1915	Helles Memorial	
Plummer	William	15648	Pte	14/05/1915	Helles Memorial	
Porter	Harold	9608	Cpl	12/05/1915	Helles Memorial	At sea
Pounds	Charles Powell	9478	Pte	16/09/1915	Azmak Cemetery	
Powell	Albert	14771	Pte	22/08/1915	Helles Memorial	
Powell	Geo	13548	Pte	08/05/1915	Helles Memorial	
Price	Edward Sydney	10670	Pte	06/07/1915	Twelve Trees Cemetery	
Price	Isaac	6946	Pte	28/06/1915	Port Said	
Price	William. Henry	9816	Pte	25/04/1915	Helles Memorial	
Pritchard	Sam	25033	Pte	02/09/1915	Alexandria	
Pritchard	William	11097	Pte	11/06/1915	Twelve Trees Cemetery	
Prosser	James	15499	Pte	19/06/1915	Twelve Trees Cemetery	
Pugh	John	13695	Pte	28/06/1915	Twelve Trees Cemetery	
Purnell	John	8796	Pte	10/10/1915	Bedwellty, Wales	
Ralph	Sam	13993	Pte	25/11/1915	Helles Memorial	
Reed	William Albert	11431	Pte	21/08/1915	Helles Memorial	
Rees	Philip Alfred	13954	Pte	28/06/1915	Helles Memorial	
Rees	William	13745	Pte	08/05/1915	Helles Memorial	
Reeves	Tom	15729	Pte	14/05/1915	Helles Memorial	
Reveley	Charles	10317	Pte	26/04/1915	Helles Memorial	

Name	First Names	Number	Rank	Date of Death	Buried or Commemorated	Comment
Reynolds	George Edward	18034	Pte	26/04/1915	Helles Memorial	
Richards	Tom	10284	Cpl	21/08/1915	Helles Memorial	
Richardson	Arthur	10060	Pte	02/05/1915	Helles Memorial	
Richmond	Arthur	24618	Pte	13/08/1915	Helles Memorial	At sea, HMT Royal Edward
Ridgway	John	24703	Pte	14/08/1915	Twelve Trees Cemetery	
Riley	Pat	24919	Pte	13/08/1915	Helles Memorial	At sea, HMT Royal Edward
Roberts	James	10422	LCpl	29/04/1915	Helles Memorial	
Robinson	James	9131	LCpl	02/05/1915	Helles Memorial	
Rogers	Edward	14163	Cpl	12/06/1915	Twelve Trees Cemetery	
Rogers	William	8636	Sgt	12/06/1915	Helles Memorial	
Rolph	Walter	15184	Pte	28/06/1915	Helles Memorial	
Rowlands	Edward	14043	Pte	09/05/1915	Helles Memorial	
Rudd	John	18548	Pte	19/06/1915	Helles Memorial	
Rudd	William	19642	Pte	04/12/1915	Helles Memorial	
Rundle	Cubitt Noel		2Lt	19/06/1915	Twelve Trees Cemetery	
Rutter	Thomas Henry	24675	Pte	09/09/1915	Azmak Cemetery	
Salmon	Percy John	19194	Pte	12/10/1915	Malta	
Salter	Harry	10112	Pte	13/08/1915	Helles Memorial	At sea, HMT Royal Edward
Saunderson	William	9798	Pte	17/05/1915	Lancashire Landing Cemetery	
Savigair	Charles	14666	Pte	08/05/1915	Helles Memorial	
Sawyer	Charles Benjamin	9567	Sgt	21/08/1915	Green Hill Cemetery	
Scullard	Henry	24867	Pte	21/12/1915	Twelve Trees Cemetery	
Seel	William	25506	Pte	13/08/1915	Helles Memorial	At sea, HMT Royal Edward
Sewell	Harry	7000	Pte	29/04/1915	Helles Memorial	
Shakesheff	George	6866	Pte	19/06/1915	Helles Memorial	
Sharp	Albert	10919	Pte	28/06/1915	Twelve Trees Cemetery	
Shearn	Geo	15263	Pte	22/08/1915	Helles Memorial	
Sheppard	Geo.	10344	Pte	14/05/1915	Helles Memorial	
Shore	John	10343	Pte	03/05/1915	Helles Memorial	At sea
Sibley	Sam	9633	Pte	20/05/1915	Alexandria	
Silk	Geo	9170	Pte	02/05/1915	Helles Memorial	
Silk	Norman Galbraith		Lt	09/06/1915	Twelve Trees Cemetery	
Simmonds	Thomas Joseph	9477	Pte	01/07/1915	Twelve Trees Cemetery	
Simpson	Geo	19095	Pte	13/08/1915	Helles Memorial	At sea, HMT Royal Edward
Sloman	Ainsley	24533	Pte	21/08/1915	Helles Memorial	

Name	First Names	Number	Rank	Date of Death	Buried or Commemorated	Comment
Smith	Albert	8174	Pte	13/08/1915	Helles Memorial	At sea, HMT Royal Edward
Smith	Geo	9274	Pte	28/04/1915	Helles Memorial	
Smith	James	10531	Pte	28/06/1915	Twelve Trees Cemetery	
Smith	Len	11646	Pte	29/06/1915	Twelve Trees Cemetery	
Smith	Richard	10755	Pte	29/06/1915	Helles Memorial	
Smith	Sydney William	24520	LCpl	13/08/1915	Helles Memorial	At sea, HMT Royal Edward
Smith	Tom	9767	Pte	02/05/1915	Helles Memorial	
Smith	William Harvey	10417	Pte	25/04/1915	Helles Memorial	
Smyth	Pat	10296	Pte	29/06/1915	Helles Memorial	
Spartali	Michael		2Lt	15/06/1915	Helles Memorial	
Sprawson	Albert	24809	Pte	13/08/1915	Helles Memorial	At sea, HMT Royal Edward
Stanborough	Walter Thomas		2Lt	13/05/1915	Helles Memorial	
Stickler	Herbert	7006	Pte	15/06/1915	Twelve Trees Cemetery	
Straney	William George	10229	LCpl	28/06/1915	Helles Memorial	
Stringer	Albert Edward		2Lt	07/06/1915	Helles Memorial	Manchester Regiment
Sturgess	Ivan Arthur	9912	LCpl	11/06/1915	Twelve Trees Cemetery	
Sullivan	John	18704	LCpl	07/09/1915	Malta	
Sweet	John	14011	Pte	04/07/1915	Helles Memorial	
Taylor	Herbert	10856	Pte	06/07/1915	Helles Memorial	
Terrill	Arthur	10172	LCpl	08/05/1915	Helles Memorial	
Thomas	Caleb	10401	Pte	08/05/1915	Helles Memorial	
Thomas	David Glasbrook	18454	Pte	05/07/1915	Helles Memorial	
Thomas	Edward	13207	Pte	24/12/1915	Mudros	
Thomas	Edward	15469	Pte	06/07/1915	Helles Memorial	
Thomas	Geo	10336	Pte	02/05/1915	Helles Memorial	
Thomas	George	19901	LCpl	26/12/1915	Twelve Trees Cemetery	
Thomas	Hadyn	11373	Pte	18/06/1915	Twelve Trees Cemetery	
Thomas	Levi	8226	Pte	25/04/1915	Helles Memorial	
Thomas	Rees	13744	Pte	19/06/1915	Twelve Trees Cemetery	
Thomson	Walter	10326	Cpl	21/08/1915	Helles Memorial	
Thurman	Reg.	24623	Pte	21/08/1915	Helles Memorial	
Tickle	Harry	24538	Pte	13/08/1915	Helles Memorial	At sea, HMT Royal Edward
Toole	William	14750	Pte	21/08/1915	Helles Memorial	
Toothill	John Henry	18525	Pte	28/06/1915	Helles Memorial	
Tudor	Harrison	9921	Cpl	28/06/1915	Helles Memorial	
Turner	Percy Herbert		2Lt	06/07/1915	Twelve Trees Cemetery	Cheshire Regiment

Name	First Names	Number	Rank	Date of Death	Buried or Commemorated	Comment
Turner	William	18620	Pte	28/06/1915	Helles Memorial	
Vann	Geo	13244	Sgt	28/06/1915	Helles Memorial	
Vinall	Alfred	9899	Pte	25/04/1915	Helles Memorial	
Vincent	Harold	25040	Pte	21/08/1915	Helles Memorial	
Vizard	Richard	10628	Pte	25/04/1915	Helles Memorial	
Walker	Reg	9922	Pte	07/07/1915	Helles Memorial	
Walton	George	9345	LCpl	26/04/1915	Helles Memorial	
Ward DCM	John James	10423	Sgt	28/06/1915	Twelve Trees Cemetery	
Ware	Sidney	8015	Pte	13/08/1915	Helles Memorial	At sea, HMT Royal Edward
Warren	Geo	24825	Pte	02/12/1915	Skew Bridge Cemetery	
Waters	Charles	10080	Pte	25/04/1915	Helles Memorial	
Watkins	Oliver George	25052	Pte	18/08/1915	Hill 10 Cemetery	
Watts	Percy	11827	Pte	25/07/1915	Pink Farm Cemetery	
Weaver	John James	24834	Pte	15/09/1915	Helles Memorial	
Weaver	William	15229	Pte	19/06/1915	Helles Memorial	
Weech	Sam	14007	Pte	13/08/1915	Helles Memorial	At sea, HMT Royal Edward
Wells	Geo.	8744	Pte	28/04/1915	Helles Memorial	
Welsh	Michael	11122	Pte	01/07/1915	Helles Memorial	
West DCM	James	9952	Pte	20/05/1915	Helles Memorial	
Weston	Henry	13356	Pte	03/05/1915	Helles Memorial	
Wheeler	John Arthur	18566	Pte	06/07/1915	Twelve Trees Cemetery	
Whittaker	William	14050	Pte	26/06/1915	Alexandria	
Whyle	James	9267	Pte	24/07/1915	Helles Memorial	
Wilkey	Edward	13757	Pte	12/09/1915	Hill 10 Cemetery	
Williams	Charles Henry	19128	Pte	13/08/1915	Helles Memorial	At sea, HMT Royal Edward
Williams	Edward	18577	Pte	21/08/1915	Helles Memorial	
Williams	Evan John	11548	Sgt	04/07/1915	Malta	
Williams	Frank	10059	Pte	08/05/1915	Helles Memorial	
Williams	Frank	11608	Pte	16/08/1915	Helles Memorial	
Williams	Fred	9766	Pte	26/04/1915	Helles Memorial	
Williams	Joe	18469	Pte	28/06/1915	Helles Memorial	
Williams	Joe	19911	Pte	18/09/1915	Azmak Cemetery	
Williams	John	25035	Pte	21/08/1915	Helles Memorial	
Williams	John Owen	10873	Pte	08/05/1915	Helles Memorial	
Williams	Luther	25029	Pte	21/08/1915	Helles Memorial	
Williams	Thomas	11748	Pte	26/08/1915	Helles Memorial	
Williams	Wallace	10566	LCpl	26/04/1915	Helles Memorial	
Willmott	Joe	19397	Pte	24/09/1915	Alexandria	

Name	First Names	Number	Rank	Date of Death	Buried or Commemorated	Comment
Wilson	Albert	14788	Pte	28/06/1915	Helles Memorial	
Wilson	Arthur	13432	Pte	21/08/1915	Helles Memorial	
Wilson	Joe	24656	Pte	19/09/1915	Azmak Cemetery	
Wood	Albert Samuel	10824	Cpl	28/12/1915	Lancashire Landing Cemetery	
Woodford	Fred	18875	Pte	21/08/1915	Helles Memorial	
Woods	John	10354	Pte	26/04/1915	Helles Memorial	
Woods DCM	Tom	9813	LCpl	21/08/1915	Helles Memorial	
Woolley	Edward Henry	10103	Pte	12/12/1915	Alexandria	

Appendix III

Officers of the 4th Bn South Wales Borderers who served at Gallipoli
11 July 1915–8 January 1916
(including SWB officers on the staff of HQ 40 Bde)

Name	Service Details	Additional Detail
ADDAMS-WILLIAMS, Donald Arthur (Arthur)	Born Llangibby 28.4.1896, Educated Marborough College, 2Lt 18.11.1914	Son of the Rev Herbert Addams-Williams, Rector of Llangibby, Monmouthshire & Grace Addams-Williams (née Lysaght); Killed in action 13.8.1915; Buried 7th Field Ambulance Cemetery; WO339/1527; See du Ruvigny
AUSTIN, Thomas Carnelly MacDonald	Born Leytonstone 27.8.1891, Educated City of London School & Oriel College, Oxford, 2Lt 22.8.1914, T/Lt 1.2.1915, T/Capt 11.12.1915	Son of the Rev George Beesley Austin & Mrs Elen Austin, 7 Mowbray Road, Upper Norwood; MID LG 28.1.1916 (1200); Killed second attempt to relieve Kut 9.4.1916; Buried Amara War Cemetery; WO339/11325
BACON, Roger Sewell MBE Kt	Born 22.1.1895, Educated Rugby School & Balliol College, Oxford, 2Lt 8th Bn Cheshire 22.8.1914, T/Capt 1.1.1917, Rejoined as Lt 15.1.1940, T/Maj	Eldest Son of Sewell Bacon; Married Catherine Grace Connolly 1946; Served Gallipoli; MBE (Mil) LG 1.1.1943 (11); Chief Justice, Gibraltar 23.3.1946; Justice of Appeal, East African Court of Appeal 13.10.1955; Knighthood LG 12.6.1958 (3512); Died London 17.2.1962
BELL, Aveling Francis	Born Surbiton 2.5.1895, Educated Wellington College, 2Lt 17.10.1914	Son of the late Francis James Bell & Mrs Lilla Francis Bell, Chillington, Lovelace Gardens, Surbiton; Killed in action 12.8.1915; Commemorated Helles Memorial; WO339/25805
BERESFORD, Marcus John Barré de la Poer DSO	Born Ashbrook, Co Londonderry 10.4.1868, Educated Cheltenham College, From Militia, 2Lt 6.7.1889, Lt 18.11.1891, Capt 1.4.1897, Maj 29.11.1907, Retd 7.9.1909, Re-joined 30.8.1914, T/Lt-Col 7.11.1915, Retd as Lt-Col 9.4.1919	DSO LG 3.6.1916; MID LG 13.7.1916 (6948); Served ABW attached 8th Mounted Infantry; Adjutant 2nd Bn SWB 1.8.1902-31.7.1905; Married Alma (née Methven); Second-in Command 4th Bn SWB; Landed Gallipoli 15.7.1915; Commanded 4th Bn SWB 7.11.1915-17.5.1917; Served ABW 3.2.1900-31.5.1902; Killed in air raid 26.7.1944 (See SWB Journal 26); Resided: Learmount Castle, Co Londonderry; WO339/106961

Name	Service Details	Additional Detail
BICKFORD-SMITH, William Nugent Venning MC	Born 14.5.1892, 2Lt 22.12.1914, T/Lt 1.2.1915, T/Capt 10.8.1915, RC as Maj 1.9.1921	Son of Roandue Albert Henry & Caroline Louisa Marianne (née Skinner) Bickford-Smith of Trevarno, Helstone, Cornwall; MC LG 7.2.1918 (1801); Adjutant 4th Bn SWB 23.5.1916; Died 3.9.1975; WO339/20850
BIRCH, Frederick William	Born ???, Educated Royal Military College Sandhurst (Queen's India Cadet), 2Lt Durham LI 11.2.1888, To Indian Army as Lt 21.9.1888, Capt, Maj 30th Punjabis 11.2.1906, Retd 22.3.1911, Re-joined, Maj South Wales Borderers 18.9.1914	Son of the late Harry Holwell Birch & Sarah Henrietta Birch; Husband of Mrs Mary Dorothea Birch of 25 Florence Park, Redland, Bristol; Father of Frederick William Alexander Birch; Served Samana & Hazara (1891); Tirah (1887-88) with 30th Punjabis; Killed in action 17.4.1916; Commemorated Basra Memorial
BLAXLAND, John Bruce BA	Born Bebington, Cheshire 11.5.1891, Educated Hereford Cathedral School, Birmingham University & Selwyn College Cambridge, 2Lt 9.9.1914, T/Lt 1.2.1915, T/Capt 1.5.1915	Son of the Rev Bruce Blaxland MA (Vicar of the Abbey Shrewsbury) & Mrs Constance Gordon (née Rae) Blaxland of Lilleshall, Shropshire; Unmarried; Gallipoli 15.7.1915 (wounded 10.1915); Re-joined battalion late 1916; Assumed Command of Bn 16.1.1917; Killed in action before the Kut 24.1.1917; Buried Amara War Cemetery; Commemorated Hereford Cathedral; See Du Ruvigny; WO339/20848
BUCHANAN, Angus VC MC MA	Born Coleford 11.8.1894, Educated Monmouth School & Jesus College Oxford, 2Lt SWB 27.11.1914, T/28.6.1915, T/Capt 21.12.1915, RC 2.9.1917	Son of Dr Peter Buchanan VD JP & Hannah Allen (née Williams) Buchanan; Unmarried; Wounded 6.8.1915; Re-joined with draft 7.12.1915; VC LG 26.9.1916; MC LG 3.6.1916; Order of St Vladimir (4th class) LG 15.5.1917; MID LG 6.3.1916, 13.7.1916 (6948), 24.8.1916, 17.10.1916 & 15.5.1917; Wounded 5.4.1916, 24.9.1916 & (severely) 13.2.1917; Died Coleford 1.3.1944; Buried Coleford Cemetery; Memorial tablet St John's Church Coleford; WO339/2467
BURY, Eric Pryse	Born 18.2.1893, 2Lt SWB 1.9.1914, T/Lt 28.6.1915, T/Capt 16.1.1917, Attached Indian Army as T/Maj 20.6.1920, RC 3.9.1920, To Clifton College JOTC, RC as Capt 18.5.1925	Second son of Charles Bury (Solicitor) & Aimee Gwynneth (née Pryse) Bury, Merlin Haven, Wotton under Edge, Gloucester; Served Gallipoli theatre 4th Bn SWB 28.6.1916; Served Welsh Regt 10.2.1916; Served France 1st Bn SWB 15.1.1917-28.3.1917 (sick); India General Service Medal (clasp Afghanistan NWF 1919); DAAG Kahat Karran Force 20.6.1919-15.9.1919; Schoolmaster Clifton College Bristol; Resided: 20 Canynge Square, Bristol; Died 1978; Buried St Mary, Wotton under Edge, Gloucestershire

Name	Service Details	Additional Detail
CAHUSAC, Arthur Nigel OBE MC	Born 1.12.1889, From Royal Military College Sandhurst, 2Lt 6.11.1909, Lt 10.4.1912, Capt 28.4.1915, To hp 30.10.1917, Retd (Ill Health) 20.11.1922	OBE (Civ) LG 1.1.1941 (13); Served Tsingtao 2nd Bn SWB; With draft to 4th Bn SWB Gallipoli 1.12.1915; Adjutant 4th Bn SWB 28.12.1915-25.5.1916; Wounded 9.4.1916; MC LG 22.12.1916 (12556); MID LG 19.10.1916; Married Christian Leckie Orr Ewing 1918; Chief Secretary St John's Ambulance Association 1918-1953; Died 14.11.1955; Medals sold Astons 23.4.2009
CALDWELL, Robert Nixon CMG MC	Born 16.8.1888, Educated Fiji & Melbourne Grammar School, T/Lt 22.3.1915, T/Capt 1.4.1916, T/Maj 7.6.1918, RC 13.11.1920	Third son of Charles William Caldwell, Suva, Fiji; Married Leila Hope Duncan 1920; MC LG 3.6.1918; MID LG 13.7.1916 (6948) & 14.12.1917 (13234); CMG LG 1.1.1947 (5) for services to Fiji; Served 4th Bn SWB (wounded 9.4.1916) and 5th Bn SWB 3.7.1917-15.1.1918; Held many Executive Positions in Fiji; Died 4.1.1967; WO339/25688
COOPER, Leonard Grosse	Born Abergavenny 15.6.1892, Educated Llandovery College & Jesus College, Oxford, 2Lt 29.8.1914	Youngest son of Walter Percy Cooper, Ambleside, Abergavenny, Managing Director of Seargeant Bros Ltd; To Lemnos 15.7.1915; Landed ANZAC cove 4.8.1915 with C Company 4th Bn SWB; Killed in action 9.8.1915: Thought to have been buried in temporary Cemetery near 39th Field Ambulance; Commemorated Helles Memorial; See Du Ruvigny; WO339/11887
DURAND, Alan Edmond	2Lt 6.5.1915, T/Lt 1.7.1917, To Manchester Regt 8.5.1918, RC 1.9.1921, Re-joined, Lt RAPC 8.3.1941, Lt/Paymaster 8.9.1942	MID LG 13.7.1916 (6948); Served Gallipoli 4th Bn SWB (wounded 5.4.1916)
EVERETT, Ronald Tylor MBE	Born Lewisham 1882, Enlisted City of London Yeomanry 1.3.1912; From Cpl 2nd County of London Yeomanry (Westminster Dragoons) #1526, 2Lt 11.9.1915, T/Lt 8.9.1916, T/Capt 21.11.1916, RC as Capt 19.4.1919	Son of Robert John & Emily (née Malzy) Everett; MBE (Mil) LG 1.1.1919; Occupation: Stockbroker's clerk; Served Egypt 5.11.1914; Served Gallipoli & Mesopotamia (Wounded Falahiya 5.4.1916) re-joined 31.7.1916; Military Governor of Kifri; Resided: 50 Parliament Hill, Hampstead Heath, London NW3 (1923); Medals sold DNW 31.3.2010; Died Huntingdon 1951; WO339/44587
FAIRWEATHER, Joseph	T/Lt 5.11.1914, T/Capt 28.1.1915, Maj	Younger son of Joseph Fairweather (Sculptor) of Dundee & Jane (née McIntyre); Joseph's elder brother was Colonel James McIntyre Fairweather DSO (killed in action German East Africa 18.2.1917); Wounded Gallipoli 9.8.1915; Re-joined 4th Bn 30.9.1916; Killed in action before the Kut 15.1.1917; Commemorated Amara War Cemetery; WO339/12898

Name	Service Details	Additional Detail
FARROW, Jack	2Lt 1.9.1914, T/Lt 1.2.1915, T/Capt 10.8.1915, Lt 1.1.1916	MID LG 28.1.1916 (1200) & LG 13.7.1916 (6948); Wounded 9.8.1915; Killed in action 9.4.1916; Commemorated Amara War Cemetery; WO339/11972
FLEMING, George William MA MB ChB	Born Port Glasgow 19.5.1888, T/Lt RAMC 7.12.1914, T/Capt 7.12.1915, RC 7.12.1917, Re-joined 26.11.1919, Retd 16.5.1924, Re-joined 2.9.1939, bt Maj 4.3.1941, To Reserve 4.10.1945	Regimental Medical Officer 4th Bn SWB; Wounded Gallipoli 4th Bn SWB 9.8.1915; Served France 3.1918-4.1918 (invalided), Germany 1919-20, Mesopotamia 1920-23; Served BEF 1939-40, MEF 1940-42; Died 5.3.1962
GILLESPIE, Franklin Macauley	Born Colchester 19.8.1872, Educated Dover College & Royal Military College Sandhurst, 2Lt 25.7.1891, Lt 22.2.1893, Capt 6.3.1898, Maj 26.9.1909, Lt-Col 19.8.1914	2nd Son of Lt-Col Franklin Gillespie RAMC & Harriet Eliza Phillis (née Freeth) of Heath Hollow, Camberley; Married Agnes Rose Pryce-Jones daughter Sir Pryce Pryce-Jones of Dolerw, Newtown 27.7.1905; Two sons served with SWB in WW2; MID LG 2.1.1900 & 28.1.1916 (1200); Served West African Frontier Force 14.11.1896-5.4.1897 & 14.11.1896-5.4.1897; Served ABW 21.7.1901- 1.5.1902; Adjutant 5th Vol Bn SWB 18.4.1903-14.7.1908; Commanded Regimental Depot (Brecon) 2.1914-8.1914; Commanding Officer 4th Bn SWB 19.8.1914-9.8.1915; Killed in action 9.8.1915; Thought to have been buried in temporary Cemetery near 39th Field Ambulance; Commemorated Helles Memorial; Commemorated Newtown War Memorial; Medals in Regimental Collection
GOULD, Ralph Bohn	Born 1890, 2Lt 12.5.1915	Son of A K Gould & Mrs A M Gould, 25 Kingshall Road, Beckenham, Kent; Served Gallipoli 7.10.1915; Died of wounds 20.12.1916; Buried Amara War Cemetery; WO339/41312
GRASDORFF, Reginald William Henry	Born Wandsworth 4.11.1896, 2Lt (SR) 6.2.1915, T/Lt 1.7.1917, To RFC, To RAF 1.4.1918, RC 1.4.1920	Served Gallipoli from 27.5.1915; Professional Actor; Change surname to PURDELL LG 16.6.1944; Resided: 15 Poulett Gardens, Cross Deep, Twickenham (1944); Died London 22.4.1953; WO339/2739
HAMMOND, Thomas Edwin FRCS	Born Penrhiwfer 5.8.1888, Educated Cheltenham College & St Bartholomew Hospital, Lt 7.2.1915, A/Capt, A/Maj	Son of the late Edwin Hammond (Manager Cambrian Colleries) & Mrs Jane (née Jenkins) Hammond, of Newport Road, Cardiff; Served as Civilian (Red Cross) in France 7.10.1914-27.1.1915; Served Gallipoli as Regimental Medical Officer 4th Bn SWB; Wounded on evacuation 8.1.1916; MID LG 13.7.1916 (6951); Surgeon, Alderhay Orthopaedic Military Hospital Liverpool; Newport Military Hospital; Assistant Surgeon Cardiff Royal Infirmary 1924; Urologist, Welsh National School of Medicine; Died Northampton 25.3.1943; Unmarried; Buried Cefn Merthyr

Name	Service Details	Additional Detail
HEMINGWAY, Stewart	2Lt 12.12.1914, Lt	Son of William & Maria Hemingway of Kilmeaque, Co Kildare; Served ABW with South African Constabulary (QSA, KSA); Transport Officer 4th Bn SWB; Served Gallipoli theatre from 15.7.1915; Hemingway's body was recovered by Capt Buchanan who was later awarded the VC for his gallant actions; Died of wounds 6.4.1916; Commemorated Basra Memorial; WO339/21035
HILLMAM-MILLER, James	Born 1875, Educated Christ Hospital, T/Lt SWB 30.11.1914	Son of T C Millar of 48 Woodville Gardens Ealing; Married Phoebe Moncrieff Maclachan at St Mary's West Kensington 18.4.1899 (divorced 6.12.1909); Member of the Stock Exchange London 1904; Served C Company 4th Bn SWB Gallipoli theatre 15.7.1915; Died of wounds 10.8.1915; Buried at sea; Commemorated Helles Memorial; WO339/2874
HOOPER, Arthur William MBE MC	Born ????, From LSgt South Wales Borderers #9814, 2Lt 25.9.1914, T/Lt 22.6.1915, T/Capt 15.8.1918, Capt 9.4.1921, To Indian Army as Capt/QM 25.9.1929, Maj, Retd 8.4.1945	Served Gallipoli theatre 15.5.1915; Wounded 9.8.1915; MC (Citation) LG 11.1.1919 (625); LG MBE 1.1.1945 (15) WW2
HUGHES, David	2Lt 18.12.1914, To MGC 24.10.1916, T/Capt, RC as Capt 2.12.1920	WO339/3916
JENKINS, Tudor Morgan	2Lt 1.9.1914, T/Lt 5.1.1916, To Reserve as Capt 21.7.1920, RC as Capt 10.3.1926	Served D Company 4th Bn SWB Gallipoli theatre from 15.7.1915; Prisoner of war 30.4.1917-1.1.1919; Resided: 22 Manor Road, Manselton, Swansea; WO339/11982
JONES, Roderick Idrisyn CB CBE DL (Taffy)	Born Welshpool 4.10.1895, Educated Cardiff High School & Manchester University, From Spr Royal Engineers, 2Lt South Wales Borderers 6.5.1915, T/Lt 6.8.1917, To 88th Carnatic Infantry (Indian Army) 25.8.1918, Capt 3.2.1920, To Indian Army (Supply &Transport Corps) Maj 3.2.1934, Lt-Col 8.5.1941, A/Brig 18.4.1943, Col 8.5.1944, Maj-Gen 19.5.1948, Retd 19.5.1948	Younger son of the Rev John Idrisyn Jones; Married Mollie Audrey MacGregor 1927; Served Gallipoli theatre 18.10.1915 & Mespotamia with 4th Bn SWB; CB 1947; CBE LG 6.6.1946 (2729); OBE LG 16.2.1943 (858); MID (Iraq, Syria & Persia) LG 3.2.1944 (828); Served in Iraq, Syria, Persia, Libya & Burma; Honorary Colonel (AER) Royal Army Service Corps 3.5.1955; Civil Defence Gloucestershire 1951-61; DL (Gloucestershire) LG 15.1.1963 (507); Resided: Gun House, Gunhouse Lane Bowbridge, Stroud; Died Stroud 10.7.1970
JONES, Thomas Gordon	From Pte RAMC #1426, 2Lt 12.9.1915, T/Capt 27.1.1916, To Gen List 3.3.1917, RC (Ill Health) 22.11.1919	Served Egypt 23.9.1914-12.9.1915 with RAMC; Gallipoli & Mesopotamia with 4th Bn SWB (wounded 5.4.1916); Resided: 5 Faulkner Road, Newport; WO374/38502

Name	Service Details	Additional Detail
KEIGHLEY, Frederick Walter MC (Eric)	From Cpl Canterbury Mounted Rifles 7/355, 2Lt 31.8.1915, T/Lt 18.9.1916, To Indian Army 22.11.1917, Capt 31.8.1919, Lt (RNVR)	Son of Frederick Walter William Keighley of Leamington Spa; Married Ursula Anna Mary Evelyn Wood at the Chapel Royal St Peter's ad Vincula, HM Tower of London 24.2.1936; Landed Gallipoli with ANZAC; joined 4th Bn SWB 25.8.1915; MC LG 22.12.1916 (12556); MID LG 19.10.1916 (10051); Resided: Hill Cottage, Slinfold, Horsham; Died Slinfold 4.9.1947
KITCHIN, Charles Edward DSO	Born 27.4.1877, Educated Bradfield College & Royal Military College Sandhurst, 2Lt 8.9.1897, Lt 23.11.1898, Capt 19.6.1907, To Reserve 1.9.1912, Re-joined 7.9.1914, Maj 30.9.1915, T/Lt-Col 27.10.1916, bt Lt-Col 3.6.1918, Lt-Col 30.4.1919, To Reserve as Lt-Col 30.11.1919	DSO LG 3.6.1916; Order of St Anne (3rd class) LG 15.5.1917 (4726); MID LG 28.1.1916 (1200) & LG 13.7.1916 (6948); Adjutant 4th Bn SWB; Commanded 4th Bn SWB 28.12.1915-16.1.1917 & 3.5.1917-27.9.1918; Wounded 16.1.1917; Died Tonbridge Kent 25.6.1948 (See SWB Journal 34)
LUCAS, Clifton Malet	Born Sydney, New South Wales 13.10.1885, (previous service with Punjabi Rifles), Enlisted Pte 7th Canadia Infantry Battalion #16968 at Valcartier Quebec 18.9.1914, 2Lt SWB 10.12.1914, T/Lt 1.4.1916	Son of Colonel H C E Lucas of The Hermitage, Teignmouth; Occupation: Land Surveyor; Served Gallipoli with C Company 4th Bn SWB (wounded 6.8.1915); Killed attached 15th Bn Welsh (Mametz Wood) 10.7.1916; Commemorated Thiepval Memorial; WO339/3721
MacMULLEN, John Francis (Mac)	2Lt 13.11.1914, T/Lt 3.10.1916, To Army Service Corps 3.10.1916, A/Capt 4.5.1918, Capt 9.12.1919	Gallipoli 6.10.1915; Wounded on evacuation 7.1.1916; Resided: Knapp House, Devon; Died in road accident Devon 16.9.1945
MELLISH, John George	Born 1897, Educated Ilminster Grammar School & West Buckland School, 2Lt 5th Bn Wiltshire 11.6.1915	Son of the Rev John B Mellish & Fannie A Mellish of Ilminster; Served Gallipoli 4th Bn SWB & Mesopotamia with 5th Wiltshire Regt; Seriously wounded relief of Kut 4.1916; Killed in action 10.3.1917; Commemorated Basra Memorial & St Mary's Church Ilminster; Medals sold DNW 27.6.2005; WO339/3431
MELLSOP, John Arthur OBE	Born Chatham 19.12.1877, Educated Duke of York's School, Enlisted SWB 12.1891, From QMS South Wales Borderers #3876, Lt QM 25.8.1914, Capt 25.8.1917, Maj 25.8.1929, To hp (Ill Health) 1.11.1930	Son of 2-24/1613 Pte John Arthur Mellsop C Company 2-24th (carved the 24th Memorial at Rorke's Drift); Served QM 4th Bn SWB in Gallipoli & Mesopotamia and in India as QM 2nd Bn SWB (1919-1929); OBE LG 3.3.1919 (2994); LS&GC 1.1.1910; MID LG 19.10.1916 (10051) & 30.4.1919 (5446); Resided: Craig y Nos, Addiscombe Close, Kenton, Middlesex; Died 15.2.1931
MILLER, James Hillman	- See James Hillman-Miller	

Name	Service Details	Additional Detail
MUNDY, Pierrepont Rodney Miller DSO OBE MC	Born 16.7.1891, 2Lt (SR) 4.3.1911, Lt (SR) 18.4.1913, Capt 21.6.1915, To 6th Bn KAR, L/Maj 6.9.1929, Maj 13.6.1932, Lt-Col 8.9.1938, A/Col 5.10.1941, Retd 19.12.1948	Son of Admiral Godfrey Harry Brudges Mundy CB DSO MVO (1860-1928) & Rose (née Mundy) Mundy; Served Gallipoli 4th Bn SWB 15.7.1915 (commanded D Company), France 1st Bn SWB 28.3.1916-3.5.1916 (sick) & Salonica 7th Bn SWB 24.7.1918; DSO LG 1.2.1919, DSO Bar LG 21.10.1941; OBE LG 6.3.1935; MC LG 2.2.1916; MID LG 28.1.1916 (1200), 30.1.1919 & 8.7.1943; Croix de Guerre (French); ADC to Gov-Gen New Zealand 1920; Died 3.2.1983 (See RRW Journal 28)
NAPIER, Joseph William Lennox 4th BART OBE of Merrion Square, Dublin	Born 1.8.1895, Educated Rugby & Jesus College Cambridge, 2Lt 16.2.1915, T/Lt 25.2.1916, RC 3.9.1920, To Royal Artillery 1st Home Counties Brigade (TA) as Lt 20.3.1920, RC, Re-Joined, Lt RA 6.9.1939, Capt, Maj, T/Lt-Col	Son of Sir William Lennox Napier (qv); Married Isabelle Muriel Surtees 12.2.1931; Served Gallipoli D Company 4th Bn SWB 15.7.1915 & Mesopotamia (wounded before the Kut); Prisoner of war held by Turks 30.4.1917-16.12.1918; OBE LG 19.10.1944 (4783); Died 13.10.1986
NAPIER, William Lennox 3rd BART of Merrion Square, Dublin	Born Chambly Montreal 12.10.1867, Educated Uppingham & Jesus College Cambridge, Lt Sussex Artillery Volunteers 13.11.1886, Capt (V) 6.7.1889, RC 29.11.1890, To 5th Vol Bn SWB as Capt (V) 1.4.1897, Maj (V) 18.10.1902, To 7th Bn RWF TF as Maj 1.4.1908, Lt-Col (TF) 1.7.1908, RC 17.1.1910, To 4th Bn SWB as T/Maj 24.9.1914	Elder son of Sir Joseph Napier 2nd Bart, & Maria Octavia (née Mortimer) Napier; Married Lady Mabel Edith Geraldine Napier (née Forster) at Hinxton Cambridge 5.8.1890; Served 1st Sussex Artillery Volunteers, 5th Vol Bn SWB, 7th Bn RWF TF & 4th (Service) Bn SWB; Killed in action 13.8.1915; Buried 7th Field Ambulance Cemetery, Gallipoli; See De Ruvigny's entry; WO339/21833
OWEN, Geoffrey Mickleburgh	Born Machen 1895, 2Lt 30.11.1914, T/Lt 7.4.1916, T/Capt 24.7.1918, RC 20.11.1920	Served Gallipoli with 4th Bn SWB 28.6.1915 (joined Bn 31.7.1915) & Mesopotamia; Resided: Fir Grove, Ottery St Mary, Devon; WO339/3641
PHILLIPS, Owen Sherwood	Born Bredicot Worcestershire 21.7.1892, Educated Worcester Royal Grammar School & Keble College Oxford, 2Lt 26.8.1914	Only son of John Prinniger Phillips & Kate (née Sherwood) Phillips of Bredicot, Spetchley, Worcestershire; Served B Company, 4th Bn SWB; Killed in action 21.8.1915; WO339/11634
PURDELL, Reginald William Henry	- See GRASDORFF, Reginald William Henry	
ROGERS, Hender Molesworth MC	Born Sancreed, Cornwall 4.4.1883, Educated Oxford University, 2Lt KSLI (SR) 16.5.1915, Lt 1.7.1917, T/Capt 24.10.1918, RC as Capt 1.4.1920	Served Gallipoli with 4th Bn SWB from 1.12.1915, present at evacuation; MC LG 3.6.1919 (6833); Deputy Assistant Provost Marshal 24.10.1918-30.11.1919; Resided: Ferriby, Penzance, Cornwall

Name	Service Details	Additional Detail
STAPLES, Edward George	2Lt 31.8.1914, T/Lt 28.6.1915, T/Capt 27.10.1916, RC 13.9.1919	Served Gallipoli with C Company, 4th Bn SWB 15.7.1915; Wounded 9.8.1915; re-joined 6.10.1915; Re-Joined 30.9.1916; Prisoner of war held by Turks 30.4.1917-16.12.1918; Resided after WW1: Kampla, Uganda; Published a number of books in 1930s on the Nature of Uganda; WO339/12682
STOCKWOOD, Iltyd Henry MA LLB	Born Porthcawl 29.7.1892, Educated Bradfield College, Cambridge University, 2Lt 26.8.1914, T/Lt 28.6.1915, T/Capt 25.5.1916, To Tank Corps 25.5.1916, To RAF 15.6.1918, Hon Capt (Observer) 13.9.1918, RC 5.8.1920, Re-joined, Capt 7th (DF) Bn Welch Regt 9.4.1921, RC 16.7.1921, Capt 6th Bn WELCH TA 1.1.1922, RC 17.1.1923, Re-joined, A/Maj SWB 15.4.1940, Maj (WS) 18.6.1942, T/Lt-Col 18.6.1942, RC as Lt-Col 30.6.1947	Son of Samuel Henry Stockwood & Alice Emma (née Taylor) Stockwood; Served Gallipoli with 4th Bn SWB 15.7.1915 and France & Belgium with Tank Corps; Served 6th Bn SWB in WW2; Solicitor, Messrs Stockwood and Williams, Bridgend; Died 6.8.1970 (See RRW Journal 3)
TESSIER, Norman York	Born Portsmouth 1882, T/Lt 16.9.1914, RC 4.3.1919	Son of Arthur Charles & Margaret Maud Tessier; Married Cora Winifred Bishop at Steyning 9.1923; Served Gallipoli with A Company, 4th Bn SWB 15.7.1915; Occupation: Dental Surgeon; Resided: 37 Fourth Avenue, Hove, Sussex; Died Hove 28.3.1956; WO339/12526
THOMAS, Hopkin Morgan	Born 1877, From CSgt SWB, 2Lt SWB 25.9.1914, Lt 26.2.1915, T/Capt 15.8.1918, Capt 15.2.1921, Retd 2.7.1921 Army Cyclist Corps??	Served Gallipoli with 4th Bn SWB from 10.1915; Resided: 41 Preston Avenue, Newport 1923; Died whilst boarding a tramcar in Bristol 17.3.1938 (see SWB Journal 13); WO339/10997
USHER, Cyril George MC	Born Clifton, Bristol 22.4.1892, 2Lt 1.9.1914, T/Lt 12.2.1915, T/Capt 24.7.1918, RC 17.7.1920, Re-joined, Lt Gen List 6.4.1941, Maj (WS), RC (Ill Health) as Lt-Col 28.10.1946	MC LG 16.8.1917 (8385); MC Bar LG 25.8.1917 (8854); Married Dorothy Margaret Worsford at St George's Hanover Square 1923; Served Gallipoli with 4th Bn SWB 1.9.1915; Adjutant 4th Bn SWB; Assistant Resident Commissioner, Kismayu, Jubaland 12.12.1923 & Mombasa 20.8.1925; Magistrate, Mombasa 8.5.1928; Died Katrine Bibby Hospital Mombasa 13.6.1968
WILLIAMS, Ivor Phillips	Born Shrewsbury 1894, From Pte Shropshire Yeomanry, 2Lt King's Shropshire LI,	Son of John & Hannah Williams of Oakfield, Shrewsbury; 3rd Bn KSLI attached 4th Bn SWB Gallipoli 10.1915; Killed in action 7.1.1916; Commemorated Helles Memorial; WO339/48355
WILLIAMS, John	2Lt Brecknocks Bn SWB 26.10.1914, Lt 1.6.1916	MID LG 13.7.1916 (6948); Atkinson WW1 history refers '2Lt JP Williams'; London Gazette lists 'Williams, 2nd J., Brecknockshire Bn'; WO374/74912-23

Name	Service Details	Additional Detail
YATES, Hubert Peel DSO	Born 6.10.1874, From Militia, 2Lt 9.12.1896, Lt 25.6.1898, Capt 19.6.1907, Maj 1.9.1915, Bt Lt-Col 3.6.1916, Lt-Col 8.3.1923, Retd 5.12.1925	DSO LG 23.11.1916 (11400); Order of St Anne (3rd class) LG 15.5.1917 (4726); MID 19.7.1916 (6947),13.7.1918 & 19.10.1918; Married Gertrude Letitia Molyneux Sarel at Frimley 11.10.1905; Adjutant 4th Bn SWB; Served Gallipoli 15.7.1915; Commanded 6th King's Own 28.10.1915- 9.4.1916 (wounded); Commanded 2nd Bn South Wales Borderers 22.2.1923-19.12.1925; Died Cambridge 15.8.1949

SWB Officers on the staff of HQ 40 Infantry Brigade at Gallipoli

Name	Service Details	Additional Detail
GODWIN-AUSTEN, Alfred Reade, Sir KCSI CB OBE MC psc 40 Brigade Staff Captain	Born Frensham 17.4.1889, Educated St Lawrence College, Ramsgate & Royal Military College Sandhurst, 2Lt South Wales Borderers 6.11.1909, Lt 5.1.1912, T/Capt 4th Bn SWB 22.10.1914, Capt 28.4.1915, bt Maj 3.6.1917, Maj 28.2.1930, bt Lt Col 1.7.1929, To DCLI as Lt Col 15.3.1936, Colonel 14.10.1937, Brigadier 14.9.1938, Maj-Gen 23.8.1939, A/Lt-Gen 18.9.1941, Lt-Gen 29.3.1946, General 1.5.1946, Retd 6.3.1947	Son of Lt-Col Alfred Godwin Godwin-Austen (late 24th & 89th Foot) & Sara Matilda (née Orred) Godwin-Austen; KCSI LG 18.6.1946 (3071); CB (Somaliland) LG 30.5.1941(3091); OBE LG 3.6.1919; MC 2.6.1916 (5570); MID LG 13.7.1916, 15.8.1917, 5.6.1919, (Palestine) 15.9.1939, 26.7.1940, 11.2.1941; & 15.12.1942; Served Gallipoli 6.1915-12.1915, Egypt 12.1915-2.1916, Mesopotamia 2.1916-31.10.1918; Staff Capt 40th Infantry Brigade, 1.1.1915-20.11.1915; CO 2nd Bn Duke of Cornwall's Light Infantry, 15.3.1936-14.10.1937; Comd (Brig), 14th Infantry Brigade GOC, XIII Corps, North Africa, 1941-42; Colonel 2nd Bn Monmouthshire Regt 11.12.1948-20.3.1963, Colonel South Wales Borderers 1.1.1950-16.4.1954; Died Maidenhead Hospital 20.3.1963 (See SWB Journal 64); Memorial Plaque, Brecon Cathedral

Name	Service Details	Additional Detail
MORGAN-OWEN, Llewellyn Isaac Gethin CB CMG CBE DSO psc 40th Brigade Bde Major	Born Bronwylfa, Rhyl 31.3.1879, Educated Shrewsbury School, Trinity College Dublin & Staff College Camberley (1913-14), 2Lt 4th Bn RWF Militia 8.5.1899, 2Lt 20.1.1900, Lt 22.3.1902, Capt 9.6.1909, Maj 1.9.1915, bt Lt-Col 3.6.1917, Col 3.6.1921, Maj-Gen 21.4.1933, Retd 30.3.1938, Re-employed during WW2	Son of Timothy Morgan-Owen MA JP & Emma (née Maddox) Morgan-Owen of Llwynderw, Llandinam, Caesws, Montgomeryshire; Married Ethel Berry Walford at Holy Trinity, Abergavenny 22.9.1910; Gallipoli, Mesopotamia, Germany and Waziristan; CB LG 4.6.1934 (3558); CMG LG 26.8.1918; CBE LG 19.12.1922; DSO LG 2.2.1916; Brigade Major 40th Infantry Brigade 17.9.1914-11.1.1916; Commanded 52nd Bn South Wales Borderers 5.2.1919-5.10.1919; Assistant Commander 160 (South Wales) Brigade TA 3.1.1929-30.4.1931; Commander 9th Infantry Brigade 1.5.1931-20.7.1933; Colonel, South Wales Borderers 30.6.1931-30.6.1944; Died Maidenhead Hospital 14.11.1960 (See SWB Journal 59); Buried Brookwood Cemetery, Surrey; Memorial Plaque Brecon Cathedral
TRAVERS, Jonas Hamilton du Boulay CB CMG JP DL 40th Brigade Comd	Born Sandgate 8.11.1861, Educated Westward Ho! College, Haileybury College & Royal Military College Sandhurst, 2Lt 108th Foot 22.1.1881, To South Wales Borderers, Lt 1.7.1881, Capt 25.2.1889, Maj 29.11.1899, Lt-Col 29.11.1907, bt Col 10.4.1908, T/Brig-Gen 24.8.1914, Retd as Brig-Gen 1.4.1919	Son of Colonel Richard Henry Travers (late 10th, 24th & 48th Foot) & Caroline Mary Houssemayne (née du Boulay) Travers; Gallipoli (6.1915-16.11.1915), Egypt & Palestine; CB LG 1916; CMG LG 1.1.1918 (3); MID LG 10.9.1901, 29.7.1902, 6.1.1916, 28.1.1916, 25.9.1916 & 12.1.1918; Adjt 3rd Vol Bn SWB 2.9.1891-1.2.1896; Commanded 2nd Bn South Wales Borderers 29.11.1907-29.11.1911; Commander South Wales Infantry Brigade 16.4.1912-15.5.1914; Commander 40th Brigade 5.9.1914-17.10.1915; GOC 159 Infantry Brigade 15.3.1916-18.12.1917; Died Criccieth 19.3.1933 (see SWB Journal 4)

Appendix IV

Officers and Soldiers of the 4th Bn South Wales Borderers who were killed, or died of their wounds, during the Gallipoli campaign

Name	First Names	Number	Rank	Date of Death	Buried or Commemorated	Comment
Addams-Williams	Donald		2Lt	13/08/1915	7th Field Ambulance Cemetery	
Alder	Philip	12501	Sgt	22/08/1915	Alexandria	Died of wounds
Aldridge	George	12735	Pte	09/08/1915	Helles Memorial	
Anthony	William	12838	Pte	06/08/1915	NZ No2 Cemetery	
Badham	William John	12661	Sgt	07/01/1916	Helles Memorial	
Ballinger	Thomas	12616	Pte	23/07/1915	Helles Memorial	
Barwell	John	12764	Pte	09/08/1915	Helles Memorial	
Beadle	Charles	12782	LCpl	09/08/1915	Helles Memorial	
Bell	Aveling		2Lt	12/08/1915	Helles Memorial	
Bellis	Harry	19815	Pte	21/08/1915	Helles Memorial	ex Cheshire Regt
Bennett	Albert George	12456	Pte	11/08/1915	Azmak Cemetery	
Bennett	Frederick	8535	Sgt	09/08/1915	Hill 60 Cemetery	
Bentley	Frank	13350	Cpl	09/08/1915	Helles Memorial	
Bevan	Frederick James	12608	Pte	11/08/1915	7th Field Ambulance Cemetery	
Boulton	Frank	15037	Pte	13/08/1915	Helles Memorial	
Bridge	Joseph	8003	Sgt	09/08/1915	Hill 60 Cemetery	
Broad	Ernest	12520	Pte	12/08/1915	Helles Memorial	
Brown	Charles	19794	Pte	17/08/1915	Helles Memorial	At sea, ex Cheshire Regt
Bush	William Augustus Walter	13390	WO2 CSM	25/09/1915	Helles Memorial	At sea
Butler	John	14283	LCpl	12/08/1915	Helles Memorial	
Cartlidge	Charles	12772	Pte	06/08/1915	Helles Memorial	
Caughlin	John	13931	Cpl	08/08/1915	Helles Memorial	
Chadwick	Charles Edward	19813	Pte	24/08/1915	Embarkation Pier Cemetery	ex Cheshire Regt
Coles	Thomas H	14259	LCpl	20/08/1915	7th Field Ambulance Cemetery	

Name	First Names	Number	Rank	Date of Death	Buried or Commemorated	Comment
Cooper	Isaac	12994	Pte	11/08/1915	Helles Memorial	
Cooper	Leonard		2Lt	09/08/1915	Helles Memorial	
Cooper	Thomas	12629	Pte	10/08/1915	7th Field Ambulance Cemetery	
Crocker	George	12886	Pte	20/08/1915	Lemnos	Died of wounds
Davies	Arthur Vernon	12480	LCpl	21/08/1915	Helles Memorial	At sea
Davies	John	12295	Cpl	11/08/1915	Helles Memorial	At sea
Davies	Joshua	12309	Pte	07/08/1915	Helles Memorial	
Davies	Robert	14142	Pte	13/08/1915	Hill 60 Cemetery	
Davies	William Llewelyn	12792	Pte	10/08/1915	Helles Memorial	At sea
Donovan	Patrick	12263	Sgt	11/08/1915	Azmak Cemetery	
Downing	Thomas	19510	Pte	19/12/1915	Lala Baba Cemetery	
Driscoll	Dennis	14227	Pte	07/08/1915	Helles Memorial	
Driscoll	Humphrey	12449	LCpl	09/08/1915	Helles Memorial	
Dutton	James	19497	Pte	07/01/1916	Helles Memorial	ex Cheshire Regt
Dyke	John	19482	Pte	19/12/1915	Green Hill Cemetery	
Edmunds	William	12374	Pte	11/08/1915	Helles Memorial	
Edwards	Ben	13077	Pte	18/12/1915	Alexandria	Died of wounds
Edwards	David	13186	Pte	12/08/1915	7th Field Ambulance Cemetery	
Edwards	Thomas	12776	Pte	10/08/1915	No.2 Cemetery	
Edwards	William John	12731	Pte	09/08/1915	Helles Memorial	
Ellis	William Henry	12942	Pte	07/08/1915	Helles Memorial	
Errington	Thomas	19833	Pte	03/09/1915	Malta	Died of wounds; ex Cheshire Regt
Evans	George	13004	Pte	09/08/1915	Hill 60 Cemetery	
Evans	Glyndwr	12952	Pte	09/08/1915	Helles Memorial	
Evans	John Henry	12671	LCpl	07/01/1916	Helles Memorial	
Fidler	Thomas	14043	LCpl	05/11/1915	Paignton, England	Died of wounds
Fitzgerald	William	13271	Pte	09/08/1915	Helles Memorial	
Ford	Charles Henry	12839	Pte	12/08/1915	Helles Memorial	
Fox	John Edward	12768	Pte	12/08/1915	7th Field Ambulance Cemetery	
Franklin	Richard	13076	Pte	18/08/1915	Lemnos	Died of wounds
Garratt	John William	19823	Pte	12/08/1915	Helles Memorial	ex Cheshire Regt
Gibbs	Frederick Henry	13202	Pte	09/08/1915	Helles Memorial	
Gill	Stanley	24671	Pte	07/01/1916	Helles Memorial	ex RAMC
Gillespie	Franklin		Lt-Col	09/08/1915	Helles Memorial	
Gooderidge	John James	12898	Pte	09/08/1915	Hill 60 Cemetery	
Gorman	Thomas Henry	12536	Pte	21/08/1915	7th Field Ambulance Cemetery	
Green	George	12504	Pte	07/08/1915	Helles Memorial	
Greville	Arthur Rees	12945	Cpl	11/09/1915	Malta	Died of wounds

Name	First Names	Number	Rank	Date of Death	Buried or Commemorated	Comment
Halford	George	13852	WO1 RSM	12/08/1915	Alexandria	Died of wounds
Hayes	Herbert Charles	12823	Pte	07/08/1915	Helles Memorial	
Hayes	Ivor Wesley Harcourt	13258	Pte	07/08/1915	Helles Memorial	
Hemmings	George	12507	LCpl	24/08/1915	Alexandria	Died of wounds
Hennerley	William	19832	Pte	05/10/1915	Alexandria	Died of wounds
Hennessey	Christopher	12231	LCpl	11/08/1915	Azmak Cemetery	
Henstock	Fred	19839	Pte	10/08/1915	Helles Memorial	ex Cheshire Regt
Hill	Bert	13264	Pte	07/08/1915	Azmak Cemetery	
Hillman-Miller	James		Lt	10/08/1915	Helles Memorial	
Hines	William	12837	LCpl	09/08/1915	Hill 60 Cemetery	
Howells	James	13265	Pte	17/08/1915	7th Field Ambulance Cemetery	
Hughes	Ephraim	12505	Pte	09/08/1915	Helles Memorial	
Hughes	John	24996	Pte	07/08/1915	Helles Memorial	ex Lancers
Humphreys	Arthur	12644	Pte	09/08/1915	Helles Memorial	
James	Rowland	12548	Pte	15/12/1915	Malta	Died of wounds
James	Thomas	12383	Ptc	12/08/1915	Helles Memorial	
John	Thomas	12498	LCpl	3rd Jan 1916	Helles Memorial	
Johnson	James	12754	Pte	13/08/1915	Alexandria	Died of wounds
Jones	David	12970	Pte	22/08/1915	Green Hill Cemetery	
Jones	George	13306	LCpl	08/08/1915	Helles Memorial	
Jones	James	13445	WO2 CSM	09/08/1915	Hill 60 Cemetery	
Jones	John	13067	Pte	12/08/1915	Helles Memorial	
Jones	John Richard	14231	LCpl	09/08/1915	Helles Memorial	
Jones	John Thomas	12234	Pte	12/08/1915	Helles Memorial	
Jones	Kenneth	13058	Pte	09/08/1915	Hill 60 Cemetery	
Jones	Richard Walter	12690	Sgt	21/03/1916	Alexandria	
Jones	Samuel	13327	Pte	13/08/1915	Helles Memorial	At sea
Jones	William	13166	Pte	11/08/1915	7th Field Ambulance Cemetery	
Jones	William Henry	12539	Cpl	09/08/1915	Helles Memorial	
Jones	William Llewellyn	12996	Pte	10/08/1915	Helles Memorial	
Jukes	Eli	14232	Pte	22/08/1915	Helles Memorial	
Kelly	John	12906	Pte	10/08/1915	Embarkation Pier Cemetery	
Kelly	Michael	12789	Pte	09/08/1915	Helles Memorial	
Kempson	Thomas	13896	Pte	18/08/1915	Helles Memorial	At sea
Kenny	John	13293	Pte	29/10/1915	Green Hill Cemetery	
Kerton	Tom	13279	Pte	11/08/1915	Helles Memorial	

Name	First Names	Number	Rank	Date of Death	Buried or Commemorated	Comment
Knight	George	12727	Pte	12/08/1915	7th Field Ambulance Cemetery	
Kynaston	Thomas	12969	Sgt	22/08/1915	Helles Memorial	
Lawrence	John	13052	Pte	12/08/1915	Helles Memorial	
Lear	Phillip	12936	Pte	07/08/1915	Helles Memorial	
Lear	Windsor	12287	Pte	11/08/1915	Azmak Cemetery	
Lester	John	19863	Pte	07/01/1916	Helles Memorial	
Lewis	Arthur	12543	Pte	07/01/1916	Helles Memorial	
Lewis	Thomas	13879	Pte	13/08/1915	Helles Memorial	
Lineham	William Edward	13140	Pte	24/08/1915	Alexandria	Died of wounds
Litson	George Walter	13934	Pte	09/08/1915	Helles Memorial	
Lloyd	Henry	13143	Cpl	22/08/1915	Helles Memorial	At sea
Lloyd	Richard Tyson	12290	Pte	11/08/1915	Helles Memorial	
Marland	William	19817	Pte	12/08/1915	Helles Memorial	ex Cheshire Regt
Martin	Arthur	13276	Pte	21/08/1915	7th Field Ambulance Cemetery	
Mathias	Henry George	12397	Pte	11/08/1915	Azmak Cemetery	
McCarthy	Bartholomew	13958	Pte	14/05/1916	Merthyr Tydfil, Wales	Died of wounds
McCarthy	David	12828	Pte	07/08/1915	Helles Memorial	
McCarthy	William	12359	LCpl	12/08/1915	Helles Memorial	
Morgan	Arthur	24993	Pte	10/08/1915	7th Field Ambulance Cemetery	ex Hussar
Morgan	Edward Thomas	12856	Pte	12/08/1915	7th Field Ambulance Cemetery	
Morgan	Frederick	18603	Pte	15/11/1915	Hill 10 Cemetery	
Morgan	Joseph	13001	LCpl	09/08/1915	Helles Memorial	
Morgan	Thomas George	12989	Pte	18/08/1915	Malta	Died of wounds
Morris	Harry Weston	12229	Pte	04/04/1916	Alexandria	Died of wounds
Moss	Arthur Henry	12496	LCpl	11/01/1916	Lemnos	Died of wounds
Moynihan	Denis	13119	Pte	7th Oct 1915	Green Hill Cemetery	
Napier	Sir William		Maj	13/08/1915	7th Field Ambulance Cemetery	
Neild	Arthur	19822	Pte	14/09/1915	Helles Memorial	At sea, ex Cheshire Regt
Nisbeck	Edwin	12721	Pte	08/01/1916	Helles Memorial	
O'Brien	William	12659	Pte	17/07/1915	Lancashire Landing Cemetery	
Osmond	Harold Edward	12833	Pte	03/11/1915	Malta	Died of wounds
O'Sullivan	Michael	12360	Pte	13/08/1915	Azmak Cemetery	
Owen	John	12720	Pte	09/08/1915	Helles Memorial	
Palmer	Arthur	12940	Pte	07/08/1915	Helles Memorial	
Peat	John George	14116	LCpl	07/08/1915	Helles Memorial	
Phillips	Owen		2Lt	21/08/1915	7th Field Ambulance Cemetery	

Name	First Names	Number	Rank	Date of Death	Buried or Commemorated	Comment
Pleace	James	13129	Pte	26/11/1915	Alexandria	Died of wounds
Potter	William	12799	LCpl	10/08/1915	Helles Memorial	
Powell	Edgar	12224	Pte	07/08/1915	Helles Memorial	
Powell	Oliver	12316	Pte	09/08/1915	Azmak Cemetery	
Price	Joseph	13957	Pte	07/08/1915	NZ No2 Cemetery	
Price	Thomas	13125	Pte	07/01/1916	Helles Memorial	
Price	William Powell	13036	LCpl	12/08/1915	7th Field Ambulance Cemetery	
Pritchard	Alfred	18783	Pte	25/12/1915	Malta	Died of wounds
Probert	Meredith	13622	Pte	27/01/1916	Ebbw Vale, Wales	Died of wounds. Served as Wilcox
Reynolds	Edward	13127	Pte	09/08/1915	Hill 60 Cemetery	
Reynolds	Herbert	12664	Pte	11/08/1915	Lemnos	Died of wounds
Richards	Frank	12742	Pte	09/08/1915	Hill 60 Cemetery	
Richards	Frederick	13027	Cpl	07/08/1915	Helles Memorial	
Roberts	Harold Freeman	13132	Pte	17/08/1915	Helles Memorial	
Rudd	Thomas	11292	LCpl	08/01/1916	Helles Memorial	
Rudge	Anthony	12983	Cpl	09/08/1915	7th Field Ambulance Cemetery	
Rule	Benjamin	19837	Pte	25/07/1915	Helles Memorial	ex Cheshire Regt
Saunders	James	14180	Pte	09/08/1915	7th Field Ambulance Cemetery	
Saunders	Philip Montague	12818	LCpl	07/08/1915	7th Field Ambulance Cemetery	
Saunders	William M.	14415	Pte	27/09/1915	Malta	Died of wounds
Savage	William H	12563	Sgt	21/08/1915	Helles Memorial	
Shanly	James	13215	Pte	27/09/1915	Alexandria	Died of wounds
Slee	Frederick	24564	Pte	07/08/1915	Helles Memorial	ex RHA
Smith	James Frederick	12866	LCpl	09/08/1915	Azmak Cemetery	
Smithers	Henry	13138	Pte	09/08/1915	Helles Memorial	
Spencer	Charles	13302	Cpl	09/08/1915	Helles Memorial	
Stinchcombe	Alfred	12426	Pte	10/08/1915	Azmak Cemetery	
Taylor	Frederick J	12559	Pte	07/08/1915	Helles Memorial	
Thomas	David William	12777	Pte	12/08/1915	Helles Memorial	
Thomas	Ellis	12751	Pte	15/08/1915	Helles Memorial	
Thomas	Frederick Charles	12588	Pte	13/08/1915	Helles Memorial	At sea
Thomas	John Henry	24959	Pte	11/08/1915	Azmak Cemetery	ex Dragoon
Thomas	William	13289	Sgt	09/08/1915	Helles Memorial	
Tillings	Alfred	12472	Pte	17/10/1915	Malta	Died of wounds
Tinklin	Harry John	12849	Pte	09/08/1915	7th Field Ambulance Cemetery	
Tovey	Gustus	12439	Pte	13/08/1915	Azmak Cemetery	
Treston	Morgan Henry	12372	Pte	22/08/1915	Helles Memorial	
Tuson	Ernest	12848	Pte	22/09/1915	Azmak Cemetery	

Name	First Names	Number	Rank	Date of Death	Buried or Commemorated	Comment
Tyler	Albert Henry	12817	LCpl	13/08/1915	Helles Memorial	
Venables	Alfred James	12673	LCpl	09/08/1915	Helles Memorial	
Watkins	Edward	13206	Pte	24/08/1915	Helles Memorial	At sea
Watkins	Herbert	12473	Pte	09/08/1915	Azmak Cemetery	
Watkins	William Henry	12944	Pte	22/08/1915	Helles Memorial	
Werrett	Austin Tudor	12627	LCpl	13/08/1915	Helles Memorial	
Whitfield	James	19781	Pte	11/08/1915	Azmak Cemetery	ex Cheshire Regt
Whittey	Walter	19845	Pte	18/08/1915	Helles Memorial	ex Cheshire Regt
Wilcox	Meredith	13622	Pte			See Probert, Meredith
Williams	Albert John	25022	Pte	07/08/1915	Helles Memorial	ex Hussar
Williams	Fred	12560	Pte	02/09/1915	Lemnos	Died of wounds
Williams	George	12995	Pte	23/07/1915	Helles Memorial	
Williams	Ivor Phillips		2Lt	07/01/1916	Helles Memorial	KSLI
Williams	James	14074	Pte	13/08/1915	Helles Memorial	
Williams	Richard Robert	19808	Pte	12/08/1915	Helles Memorial	ex Cheshire Regt
Williams	Sidney	12475	Pte	09/08/1915	Azmak Cemetery	
Williams	Tom James	13016	Pte	10/08/1915	7th Field Ambulance Cemetery	
Williams	William	12652	Pte	09/08/1915	Helles Memorial	
Willis	Tom	12425	Sgt	23/09/1915	Azmak Cemetery	
Wyatt	George Albert	12984	Pte	11/08/1915	7th Field Ambulance Cemetery	
Yates	James Edwin	12630	Pte	09/08/1915	Helles Memorial	

Postscript

The Man in the Arena

President Theodore Roosevelt of the United States of America, lecturing at the Sorbonne in Paris in 1910, said the following words which encapsulate the endeavours of the South Wales Borderers at Gallipoli:

It is not the critic who counts; not the man who points out how the strong man stumbles, or where the doer of deeds could have done them better. The credit belongs to the man who is actually in the arena, whose face is marred by dust and sweat and blood; who strives valiantly; who errs, who comes short again and again, because there is no effort without error and shortcoming; but who does actually strive to do the deeds; who knows great enthusiasms, the great devotions; who spends himself in a worthy cause; who at the best knows in the end the triumph of high achievement, and who at the worst, if he fails, at least fails while daring greatly, so that his place shall never be with those cold and timid souls who neither know victory nor defeat.

* * *

May light eternal shine upon them and may they rest in peace.

Select Bibliography

Unpublished Sources

Diaries held by the Royal Welsh Museum Brecon:

Battalion War Diaries:
    2nd Bn South Wales Borderers War Diary 1915 – BRCRM: d.1949.8
    War Record of the 4th Bn South Wales Borderers 1915 – BRCRM: 1948-16-i
    1/4th Bn the Welch Regiment War Diary – CARWR: 1394-3-i
    1/5th Bn the Welch Regiment War Diary – CARWR: 1394-1
    8th Bn the Welch Regiment War Diary – CARWR: 1394-10

Personal Diaries:
    Lieutenant Colonel F M Gillespie – BRCRM: 2012-49
    Lieutenant Colonel CE Kitchin – BRCRM: r.1948.16.2
    Lieutenant (QM) EK Laman – BRCRM: 2013.176
    Sergeant SD Bean – BRCRM: d.1948.8.6

Diaries held by the National Archives Kew:
    Major MJB de la P Beresford.
    Lieutenant Hugh Neville TNA: WO 339/23891

Published Sources

Aspinall-Oglander, Brig Gen C.F. *Official History of the Great War – Gallipoli Vols 1 and 2.* (William Heinemann, London, 1931)

Atkinson, Capt C.T., *The History of the South Wales Borderers 1914 – 1918* (The Medici Society, London, 1931)

Best, Geoffrey, *Churchill – A Study in Greatness* (Hambledon and London, London, 2001)

Brereton, John, *A History of the Royal Regiment of Wales (24th/41st Foot) 1689-1989* (RHQ RRW, Cardiff, 1989)

Broadbent, Harvey *Gallipoli – The Fatal Shore* (Penguin Group Australia, Sydney, 2005)

Carlyon, L.A., *Gallipoli* (Doubleday Australia, Sydney, 2001)

Chambers, Stephen, *Anzac - Sari Bair* (Pen and Sword, Barnsley, 2014)

Chambers, Stephen, *Gallipoli – Gully Ravine* (Leo Cooper, Barnsley, 2003)

Chambers, Stephen, *Suvla – August Offensive* (Pen and Sword, Barnsley, 2011)

Chasseaud Peter & Doyle Peter, *Grasping Gallipoli* (Spellmount, Staplehurst, 2005)

Coates,Tim, *The Dardanelles Commission Parts 1 and 2* (The London Stationery Office, London, 2000)

Corbett, Sir John, *History of the Great War – Naval Operations Vol 2* (Longmans Green and Co., London, 1921)

Creighton, the Reverend O., *With the 29th Division in Gallipoli* (Longmans Green and Co., London, 1916)

Fewster, Kevin, *Bean's Gallipoli* (Allen and Unwin Australia, Sydney, 2007)

Gilbert, Sir Martin, *The Straits of War – Gallipoli Remembered* (Sutton Publishing, Stroud, 2000)

Gillam, Maj J.G. DSO, *Gallipoli Diary* (George Allen and Unwin, London, 1918)

Gillon, Capt Stair, *The Story of the 29th Division* (Thomas Nelson and Sons, London, 1925)

Godwin-Austen, A.R., *The Staff and the Staff College* (Constable and Co., London, 1927)

Hamilton, General Sir Ian, *Gallipoli Diary*, 2 volumes (Edward Arnold, London, 1920)

Hickey, Michael, *Gallipoli* (John Murray, London, 1995)

James, Robert Rhodes, *Gallipoli* (The Macmillan Company, New York, 1965)

Lee, John, *A Soldier's Life – Gen Sir Ian Hamilton 1853-1947* (Macmillan, London, 2000)

Liddle, Peter, *Men of Gallipoli – The Dardanelles and Gallipoli Experience August 1914 to January 1916* (Penguin Books, Harmondsworth, 1976)

Liddell Hart, Basil, *Lawrence of Arabia* (Halcyon House, New York, 1937)

Mackenzie, Compton, *Gallipoli Memories* (Cassell and Co., London, 1929)

Moorehead, Alan, *Gallipoli* (Hamish Hamilton, London, 1956)

Myatt, Frederick, *The British Infantry 1660 – 1945* (Blandford Press,, Blandford, 1983)

Prior, Robin, *Gallipoli – The End of the Myth* (Yale University Press, London, 2009)

Steel, Nigel & Hart, Peter *Defeat at Gallipoli* (Macmillan, London, 1994)

Travers, Tim, *Gallipoli 1915* (Tempus, Stroud, 2004)

Van der Vat, Dan, *The Dardanelles Disaster* (Duckworth Overlook, London, 2009)

Ward, Dudley, *Regimental Records of the Royal Welch Fusiliers (23rd Foot) Vol 4 – 1915 to 1918* (RHQ RWF, Wrexham, 1995 reprint)

Index

Index of People

Bean, Sergeant Sidney 69–70, 72, 99–100, 102, 115

Beresford, Major Marcus John 134, 139, 158

Birdwood, General Sir William 83, 131, 201, 212

Birkett, Captain Gerald Halsey 76, 81, 114, 140

Blake, Lieutenant Francis Seymour 57, 70, 97, 101, 120, 145, 150, 174, 200, 221–222, 229–230

Brand, Captain J.C. 188, 209, 252

Byrne, Captain Edmund James Widdrington 175, 196, 203, 221, 254

Carden, Vice Admiral Sir Sackville 35, 37–38, 61

Casson, Lieutenant Colonel Hugh Gilbert 57, 63–64, 69, 82, 86–87, 96, 101, 107, 115, 117, 120, 131, 140, 187, 196, 217, 253–254, 272

Churchill, Winston 31, 34–38, 42, 54, 270–271, 279

Cox, General Herbert 104, 109, 160, 166, 180

Davies, Major General 196

de Lisle, Major General Beauvoir 107, 124, 168, 190, 238, 248, 252

Fowler, Captain Hugh 102–103, 117–120, 151, 280

Gillespie, Lieutenant Colonel Franklin Macauley 138–139, 142, 146, 153, 159, 162, 271, 280

Godley, General Sir Alex 83, 177, 192–193

Going, Major John 87, 96–97, 101–103, 109–110, 117–119, 133, 167, 172–173, 187, 273

Greenway, Captain Thomas Cattell 87, 90, 96, 109–110

Hamilton, General Sir Ian 37–40, 54–56, 59, 61–63, 66, 76–77, 80, 83–85, 95, 106, 111–112, 116, 121, 131, 144, 147–148, 153, 159, 168–169, 182, 184, 195–196, 201, 207, 224, 238–239, 258, 261, 270

Hunter-Weston, Major General Aylmer 62, 66, 80, 83, 85, 91, 98, 107

Kitchener, Lord Horatio 34–39, 55, 61, 63, 112, 134, 138, 143–144, 161, 174, 184, 186, 191, 201, 205–206, 212, 224, 226, 258, 270

Kitchin, Captain Charles Edward 134, 136, 140, 155, 159–160, 165, 170–171, 178–180, 195, 210–211, 223, 225, 236, 243–244, 272, 280

Laman, Captain Ernest Kirkland 48–52, 273–274, 276, 291

Liman von Sanders, General Otto 40, 56, 76, 85, 91, 106

Margesson, Major Edward Cuninghame 64, 67, 70, 72–73, 76, 199

Mellsop, Lieutenant John Arthur 133–134, 138, 141, 145, 151, 153, 160, 177, 181, 206

Monro, General Sir Charles Carmichael 206–207, 224, 254

Morgan, Lieutenant Colonel M. 93, 119–120, 243, 266

Mundy, Captain Pierrepont Rodney Miller 136, 140, 153, 158, 162

Napier, Major General Lennox Alexander Hawkins 162–163, 279

Napier, Major Sir William Lennox 135–138, 161, 163, 181, 280, 319, 326

Napier, Lieutenant Joseph William 136, 162, 319

Nevile, Second Lieutenant Hugh 72, 87, 133, 174

Palmer, Captain Roland Gaskell 77–78, 88, 106

Paterson, Captain Charles 118, 131, 253

Robertson, Captain George Arthur Norris 190, 222, 227

Shaw, General 135, 159, 182, 203, 236

Silk, Lieutenant Norman Galbraith 87, 114, 185, 257

Somerville, Captain Desmond 69–71, 74, 87, 124–125, 140, 186, 191, 275

Stopford, General Sir Frederick 144, 168, 261, 270

Tragett, Lieutenant James Clement Barrington 131, 133, 174

Walker, Captain Robert Konoma Beaumont 98, 100, 109, 117, 120, 125, 151, 172, 174, 254

Williams, Captain Aubrey Ellis 45, 103, 110, 119–120, 122–123, 132, 135, 140, 151, 160, 172–173, 186, 190–191, 218, 221, 253–254, 268, 273

Index of Places

Achi Baba 55, 62, 69, 85–87, 95, 106, 112, 145, 199, 201, 228–231

Africa 32, 37, 44, 46–47, 57, 63, 136, 264

Aldershot 44, 46–47, 50, 264

Alexandria 39, 54, 57–60, 95, 101–102, 114, 133, 136, 139–140, 151, 175, 182, 236, 252–253, 258, 262, 265, 268

Ari Burnu 62, 66, 76

Asia 33, 142, 204, 213, 242

Avonmouth 57, 135–136, 175, 258, 264

Baghdad 33, 143, 271

Belgium 33–34, 277, 279

Brecon 43–44, 50, 72, 134, 191, 223, 254, 257, 265–266, 268, 271–273, 275–276, 279, 312, 328

Bulair 55, 62, 76, 112, 145

Bulgaria 34, 184, 191, 197, 199, 204

Cairo 102, 175, 254

Cape Helles 55–56, 62, 66, 69, 72, 74, 76–78, 102, 112, 121, 131, 148–149, 168, 195–196, 202, 204–206, 209–211, 220–221, 226–227, 230, 233, 236, 245, 250, 258, 260, 280

Chailak Dere 147, 153, 181, 264

China 36, 47, 52, 57, 63–64, 272

Chocolate Hill 148, 154, 166, 168, 174, 180, 187, 194–195, 197, 229–230

Chunuk 76, 112, 144, 149, 154–155, 158, 192, 216, 264–265

Constantinople 33–35, 37, 39, 54–56, 105, 112, 145, 214

Damakjelik Bair 147, 153–156, 181–182, 192

Dardanelles 31, 33–39, 48, 55–57, 62–64, 66, 69–70, 76, 111–112, 114, 135, 138–139, 142, 212, 224, 234, 238–239, 270, 279

De Tott's Battery 63–64, 68, 72, 199

Egypt 34, 37, 39–40, 46, 54, 57, 105, 124, 139, 175, 271, 275

Eski Line 114, 150, 198–199, 208, 214, 229, 246–247, 250

Far East 32, 34, 36, 47

France 31–34, 36, 38, 42, 48, 54, 63, 102, 121, 191, 197, 202, 212, 243, 254–255, 263, 272, 277, 279

Gaba Tepe 56, 62, 66, 76, 84, 146

Gallipoli 31, 34–41, 48, 50, 52, 54–56, 59–63, 67, 72–73, 84, 89–90, 106, 111, 121, 132–134, 136, 138, 140–142, 148, 154, 162–163, 175, 184, 186, 201, 204–206, 209, 212, 216–217, 220, 222, 224–225, 227, 233, 235, 238, 252, 255–256, 258, 260, 262, 264, 267–272, 275, 277–281, 329

Gibraltar 42, 44, 46–47, 50, 57, 137–138

Greece 34, 184, 191, 197, 204

Gulf of Saros 55–56, 62, 66

Gully Beach 62, 93, 99, 101–105, 108–110, 113–114, 116, 119, 121, 125, 129, 132, 139, 141–142, 150–151, 230, 252

Gully Ravine [Zighin Dere] 86-87, 97, 99, 103, 109, 112-113, 116, 120-123, 133, 142, 150, 196, 243, 249, 252, 258

Helles 55–56, 62, 66, 69, 72, 74, 76–79, 102, 112, 114, 121, 131, 139, 142, 144–146, 148–149, 168, 176, 195–196, 202, 204–206, 208–211, 216, 220–221, 226–227, 230, 233, 236, 242, 244–245, 250, 252, 258, 260, 271, 279–280

Hill 10 148, 166–168, 176

Hill 236 67, 81–82, 86

Hill 60 148, 157, 167–168, 177, 180–182, 206

Hill 70 [Scimitar Hill] 148, 168-169, 174, 195

Hong Kong 47, 130–131

Imbros 116, 129–130, 175, 189–191, 195–196, 198, 201–202, 212, 215, 235, 248, 251–252, 260

India 32, 43, 46–47, 50, 53, 59, 273, 275

Ireland 41–42, 46, 48, 138, 256–257, 275

Kabak Kuyu 160, 177, 193

Kent 41, 50, 209, 257, 272

Kilid Bahr Plateau 55, 62, 112

Krithia 75, 85–87, 89, 91, 95–99, 101–103, 106–107, 110, 112–113, 121, 124, 139, 146, 196, 201, 203, 213, 215, 218, 230, 232, 236–237, 239–241, 246–247, 250–251

Kum Kale 55–56, 62, 64, 66, 73, 76, 85–86, 114, 230, 250

Lala Baba 191–193, 233–235, 260, 268

Lemnos 59–61, 64, 66, 76, 106, 129–132, 138, 142, 145, 175, 217, 236, 242, 252, 258, 260, 262, 264–265, 269

Malta 57, 60, 124–125, 138, 182, 264, 275

Mesopotamia 143, 163, 222, 255, 260, 262, 270–271

Morto Bay 56, 62, 64–70, 72, 81, 85–86

Mudros 60, 64, 132, 136, 138–140, 142, 144, 182, 190, 221–222, 230, 235–236, 247, 252–254, 264, 268

the Nek 148, 258, 260, 280

New Zealand 37–38, 54, 83, 95, 97–98, 147, 158, 166, 180–181, 264, 275, 277

North Wales 257–258, 261, 263

Parsons Road 199, 201, 208, 229

Pink Farm 133, 196, 221, 227

Portsmouth 46, 262, 275

Romanos 198–199, 203, 227

Russia 31–34, 191, 270

S Beach 63, 67–68, 70–72, 81–82, 84–86, 102, 272, 275

Salonika 184, 204–205, 212, 270

Sari Bair 55–56, 62, 111, 146–148, 154–155, 165, 168, 177, 181, 184, 258, 265, 268, 278

Sedd el Bahr 34, 62, 73, 79, 81, 85, 258

Serbia 32–33, 199, 201, 233

South Africa 32, 37, 44, 46–47, 57, 63, 136, 264

South Wales 43, 186, 254

Suez 34, 253–254, 277

Suvla 55, 144–151, 154–155, 161, 164, 166–169, 171–172, 175, 177–180, 182–186, 188–193, 195–200, 204, 206, 220–222, 226, 233, 235–238, 242–243, 246, 248, 251, 255, 258, 260–262, 265–270, 275, 279–280

Tekke Tepe 148, 168, 260

Tientsin 36, 47, 52

Troy 62, 79, 142

Turkey 31–36, 39, 41, 54–56, 89, 113, 116–118, 121, 258, 262, 279

V Beach 62–63, 79–80, 82, 85, 102, 129, 139, 166, 229–230, 247, 258

Wales 41, 50

X Beach 62, 78, 81, 86, 90–91, 94, 96–97, 103, 121, 197, 203, 209, 219

Y Beach 62–64, 66, 76–78, 80, 82, 86–88, 90, 97, 103–104
Y Ravine 122–124, 142–143, 150–151

Index of Military Formations & Units
Corps:
Australian and New Zealand Army Corps (ANZAC) 54, 56, 61–62, 64, 66, 76–77, 82–84, 93, 95, 111–112, 130–131, 144–148, 150–154, 158, 168, 177, 182, 187, 192, 194, 202, 204, 220, 226, 233, 236–237, 252, 258, 262, 264, 275, 277–278, 280
IX Corps 144, 149, 168, 175, 178, 180, 192

Divisions:
Royal Naval Division 36–37, 54, 59, 62–63, 66, 76, 78, 87, 196, 199, 204, 219, 229, 231–232, 237, 248
13th Division 135, 139, 142–143, 155, 162, 181, 191–192, 194, 207, 243, 248–249
29th Division 36–37, 39, 47–48, 54, 62–64, 66, 77–78, 80, 82–83, 85, 92–93, 95, 98, 101–102, 108, 111, 123–124, 139, 144, 148, 168, 175, 185–187, 194–195, 204, 206, 220, 238–240, 258, 272
52nd Division 112, 122, 131, 196–199, 202–204, 209, 220, 222, 231–232, 237, 272
53rd (Welsh) Division 258, 261, 264
Brigades:
Indian Brigade 99, 103–104, 108–109, 116, 122–123, 160, 177
New Zealand Brigade 83, 95, 97–98
40th Brigade 112, 134–135, 147, 159, 181, 192, 194, 207, 234, 236, 242, 258, 260, 264
86th Brigade 59, 87, 91–92, 95, 121–123, 132, 168–169, 176, 184, 186–187, 233, 236–237, 267
87th Brigade 36, 47, 78, 86–87, 90, 92, 95–98, 107–109, 122, 168–169, 172–174, 195–196, 203, 219, 250
88th Brigade 87, 92, 95–97, 104, 107–109, 122, 125, 148, 174, 187–188, 237, 246
156th Brigade 121–122, 200, 213

157th Brigade 131, 217, 219, 227, 231–232, 237, 253–254, 272–273
158th Brigade 166–167, 258, 260, 266

Regiments (including constituent battalions):
Border Regiment 36, 78, 86–87, 91–96, 109, 113–114, 121–123, 143, 167, 169, 172–174, 176, 184, 187–189, 199–202, 208–209, 214–215, 219–220, 229, 231–232, 239, 241, 247, 251
Dublin Fusiliers 62, 79, 108, 114, 116, 124, 139, 141–142, 237–238
Essex Regiment 78, 96, 148, 230
Gurkhas 95, 99, 107–109, 122–124, 146, 155, 158, 160, 166, 177, 180–181
Hampshire Regiment 79, 85, 129
King's Own Scottish Borderers 62, 64, 76–78, 86–87, 90–91, 95–99, 109, 119–123, 132, 143, 150, 167, 169, 172, 174–175, 184, 196, 198–199, 203–204, 209, 214–215, 218–219, 227, 231, 238, 240, 246, 254, 275
Lancashire Fusiliers 62, 78, 91, 95–96, 99, 102, 105, 109, 121–123, 258, 263
Royal Inniskilling Fusiliers 36, 78, 85–88, 90–92, 95–98, 103–104, 109, 116–117, 119, 121–124, 143, 150, 169, 172–174, 189, 197, 203, 209, 218–219, 240–241, 246
Royal Marine Light Infantry 37, 54, 62, 64, 72, 77, 81, 94–95, 263
Royal Regiment of Wales 41, 72, 223, 256, 263
Royal Welsh Fusiliers 41, 53, 134–138, 140, 167, 226, 234, 256–259, 260–263, 266, 268–269, 279–280, 298, 312, 322, 328
8th Royal Welsh Fusiliers 226, 258, 260, 268–269
14th Sikhs 95, 108–109, 124, 128
1st South Wales Borderers 36, 53, 163, 223, 253, 272–273, 275
2nd South Wales Borderers 36, 46, 48, 60, 62–64, 66, 69, 71–72, 77–78, 82, 84–87, 90–92, 95–98, 100–101, 107, 110, 113–114, 116–118, 121–122, 128–129, 131–134, 142, 144–145, 148, 150–151, 167–169, 172–173, 176–177, 183–184, 188, 190, 202–204, 208, 213–214, 217, 219–220, 227, 229, 239, 241–243, 246, 249–250, 252–253, 272–273, 275

4th South Wales Borderers 111–112, 133–134, 138, 141, 145, 147, 151, 153, 156–157, 159, 161, 170, 177, 180, 192–193, 220, 225, 242–243, 258, 260, 264, 267–268, 271

4th Welsh Regiment 184, 187, 264, 266

5th Welsh Regiment 261, 264–266, 268

5th Wiltshire Regiment 134, 141, 147, 153, 155, 158, 234

Worcestershire Regiment 148–149, 160, 187

Other branches:

Royal Army Medical Corps 57, 70, 97, 159, 173

Royal Engineers 48, 50, 59, 114, 143, 169, 187, 202, 204, 219, 229, 234

Royal Navy 32, 34–36, 50, 56, 61, 69, 77, 87, 106, 212, 263

Ships:

Alaunia 59–60, 64–65, 94, 97, 101, 217

Cornwallis 64–68, 73, 81–82, 108

Dublin 42, 46–47, 62, 77, 79, 102, 108, 114, 116, 124, 138–139, 141–142, 237–238

London 37–39, 44, 48, 59, 76, 160, 168–169, 184, 205, 251, 257, 262, 264, 270, 279

Queen Elizabeth 37, 60–61, 73, 77, 82–84

River Clyde 62, 67–68, 79–80, 82, 102

Swiftsure 78, 104, 108

Triumph 61, 64, 105–106, 280, 329

Index of General & Miscellaneous Terms

Aircraft 104, 146, 182, 187, 197, 200, 202, 207-208, 218, 227, 235, 246–247, 267

Artillery 36, 39, 56, 58, 62–64, 66, 76, 84, 87–88, 90–92, 95, 100, 106, 110–111, 114, 116–117, 119, 122, 125, 143–144, 149–150, 163, 168–169, 172, 174–175, 185, 194, 202, 205, 209, 213–215, 217–218, 223, 232–233, 236–237, 239–241, 243, 267, 272

'Asiatic Annie' 114, 232, 249, 251

'Black Marias' 121, 145, 230–231, 240, 248

Boer War 32, 37–38, 43, 47, 63, 136, 213, 258, 264

Bomb throwers 107, 114, 208

Cardwell reforms 42, 44–45, 58, 257, 263

Colours 43, 45–47, 50, 53, 59, 257, 263, 269, 272, 275, 279

Crimean War 55, 256–257, 263

Dardanelles Committee 111–112, 212, 224

Dysentery 116, 129, 142, 146, 167, 169, 175, 182, 185–186, 190–191, 196, 207, 226, 253, 268, 272, 279

Helles Memorial 72, 79, 114, 176, 216, 271, 280

Military Cross 50, 71, 114, 222, 273, 275

Napoleonic Wars 48, 256, 263

Sickness 42, 116, 189, 194–195, 197–198, 226, 266, 268, 279

Snipers 65, 70, 72, 76, 81, 93–94, 96, 110, 113, 125, 131, 139–140, 160, 162, 166–167, 195, 207, 239–240, 258, 265

Submarines 57, 105–106, 136–138, 191, 235, 253

Victoria Cross 38, 44-46, 89, 102, 117, 160, 213, 257–258, 263–264, 271–273, 280

War Council 34, 36, 39, 201

War Office 37, 133, 161, 224